'No one is better qualified to wri[...] music than an ex-organist of the [...] tradition, Andrew Gant has rese[...] bringing a wonderfully lively ac[...] the written page.' Peter Phillips

'The time is right for a new overall picture of English church music, particularly one taking into account the excellent new repertoire that has appeared over the last thirty or so years. Andrew Gant has provided a comprehensive and thoughtful survey that is also eminently readable.' James Bowman

'You might be forgiven for thinking a book on this scholarly topic might be a dry read. However, I am captivated by Andrew Gant's warmth and evident joy, whilst conveying an extraordinarily thorough treatment of English church music's history.' Roxanna Panufnik

'As a former director of choirs at the Chapel Royal and The Guards' Chapel, Gant has false relations and diminished fourths, not to mention hockets, coming out of his professional fingertips. He also has an infectious desire to make sure that we, the congregation, derive as much pleasure from them as he does … this is a story of church music that celebrates the sheer pleasure of raising a joyful sound to the Lord.' Kathryn Hughes, *Guardian*

'Making sense of English church music's relationship to the turbulent history of English Christianity is hard enough, but Andrew Gant manages to combine this with a lively survey of the music itself. Forbidding technical terms are described in a deft way that makes us curious to hear the music … as for the current state of English church music, Gant is refreshingly optimistic' Ivan Hewett, *Daily Telegraph*

'*O Sing unto the Lord* is an illuminating and entertaining history [...], stretching back well over a millennium. Drawing on his own extensive experience as choirmaster at the Chapel Royal, Andrew Gant cov[...]n, without recourse [...]

ANDREW GANT is the author of *Christmas Carols: A History of our Favourite Christmas Carols, from Village Green to Church Choir* (Profile, 2014). He is a composer, choirmaster, university lecturer and writer. He has directed the choirs of The Guards' Chapel, Worcester College Oxford, and Her Majesty's Chapel Royal. He lectures in music at St Peter's College, Oxford.

O SING UNTO THE LORD

A History of English Church Music

ANDREW GANT

P

PROFILE BOOKS

This paperback edition published in 2016

First published in Great Britain in 2015 by
PROFILE BOOKS LTD
3 Holford Yard
Bevin Way
London WC1X 9HD
www.profilebooks.com

1 3 5 7 9 10 8 6 4 2

Typeset in Caslon by MacGuru Ltd

Printed and bound in Great Britain by
CPI Group (UK) Ltd, Croydon CR0 4YY

A CIP catalogue record for this book is available from the British Library.

ISBN 978 1 78125 248 2
eISBN 978 1 78283 050 4

Contents

For Kathy

'Since singing is so good a thing
I wish all men would learn to sing.'

William Byrd

PREFACE

A FREEZING SATURDAY IN February. A packed football ground in England. The match is tense. The ref gives a free kick. The crowd stamps and jeers and shouts, a song swells and stirs from the stands:

> … you're too fat, you're too fat,
> You're too fat to re-fe-reeeeee!
> You're too fat to referee!

The tune is a hymn. The words are not. How do these fans know this tune? Are they all church-goers? Do they sing in male-voice choirs? Are they all secretly Welsh? Probably not. But they do know 'Cwm Rhondda'.

Church music turns up in some surprising places. Its tunes, the sound of voices singing together, those familiar words: these things reach deeper into our shared folk memory than any other kind of music. It is an older and more continuous tradition than the symphony, the opera or the pop song. It is more fundamentally English than any of these. It is the music we learned first, around the school piano and at end-of-term concerts. It's the only kind of music we all do (almost everybody has sung a Christmas carol or a hymn at some time), and we reach for its familiar associations at important shared moments of our lives – weddings, funerals, rugby matches – whether or not we believe the words, or understand them, or have ever given them a moment's thought.

English church music exists in two different overlapping traditions: art music, for trained professionals; and a species of folk music – tunes, basically – for everyone.

And, in its many and various guises, it remains enduringly, perhaps surprisingly, popular. The music of Eric Whitacre and Karl Jenkins tops the classical charts, unheard of for new work. Discs of early choral music sell throughout the world, including in those countries where the indigenous tradition could hardly be more alien. BBC Radio 3's *Choral Evensong* is the longest-running continuous radio series ever, and is still going strong. A recording of Thomas Tallis's *Spem in alium* achieves huge sales (partly through being used in the film *Fifty Shades of Grey* to accompany a close encounter of the steamy kind. Nobody knows for certain the kind of event for which Tallis wrote the piece, but presumably it wasn't that).

In one of its other guises, church music charts the contours of English history. Religious movements, which have done so much to shape our national character, are represented in music, from the ornate mysteries of the Latin Mass to the fripperies of the Restoration anthem, from stern Puritan hymns and confident Victorian bombast to the more fractured, complex world-view of the twentieth century. Great political events leave their mark in music: a battle or a plot swaps a couple of monarchs around, and the Almighty is hymned for His wisdom in engaging the right management here on earth. On a day-to-day level, the practice of church music holds a mirror up to society: who heard it, and who didn't; who was allowed to make it, and who wasn't; who taught it, and how; who paid for it, and why.

And English church music exists in such a variety of forms, ushering into the light the people who knelt to hear it in so many places: the scholar in his college, the nobleman at household prayers, the recusant in her country house and the Digger in the field, the choirboy in his cassock, and the peasant in the parish with his serpent and his viol. Their music allows us to hear them talking to each other and to their God, as no written text can. No art form gets closer to their soul, because they knew when they made it that their soul depended on the honesty and integrity of this particular form of art.

This history makes no attempt to be exhaustive; rather it seeks to identify certain themes and threads and allows one or two careers to represent a theme and one or two works to represent a career. Motifs and ideas recur through the ages like a favourite twist of melody – how 'art' music differs from 'parish' music and why; the debate between those who think fancy music gets in the way of the words and those who just like singing; the church as employer and patron; how genius works. Central to the story of church music are its people – the choir-boy, the parish clerk, the publisher; its texts – the eternal resonance of the book of psalms; its social function – choirs as a way to meet your girlfriend or count your peasants; and its ideas – the Reformation, the Enlightenment, education. Some questions keep on turning up in every generation: should you let secular forms like folk-songs, dance rhythms and instruments into church? Does English music like, or need, foreigners? To what extent has our tradition has been able to embrace those of other creeds and none (even Richard Dawkins, self-appointed high priest of public atheism, finds beauty here[1]). And a little light theology: who gets to sing to the English God? A priest? A chorister? Or can you do it yourself? These arguments have rumbled through the centuries – and still do.

The phrase 'English church music' needs a little unpicking too. Which church? Who counts as 'English'? And quite a lot of 'church' music was never meant to be sung in church at all. So, for the purposes of this history, the phrase is taken to mean the music of Christian denominations in England, occasionally visiting other shores where the tradition has notable antecedents or offshoots. 'Church music' means music used in an act of worship, whether that act takes place in a church or not. Thus the Masses of William Byrd (emphatically music for worship but illegal in an actual church) are included, while Handel's sacred oratorios (created for a paying audience in a theatre) are not.

So this is a history not just of the music itself, but of the people who made it. It is an attempt to track public events and official doctrine, and the soundtrack that goes with them. It is the story of the part that church music has played in ordinary lives, and the way it reflects those lives back to us. It's the biography of a tradition. A book about people, and a story of England.

I

In the Beginning

Hymnum canamus gloriae

Bede

AND DID THOSE FEET, in ancient time, walk upon England's mountains green?

Probably not. But the story that Jesus Christ came to these islands with his uncle, Joseph of Arimathea, in search of a cheap source of tin, proved enduringly popular. Shakespeare and Blake both mention it. It may even hover somewhere behind the versions of the folk-song 'I saw three ships', in which the singer sits 'under a sycamore tree' watching the Saviour sail up the English Channel. There are no sycamores in Bethlehem.

There was plenty of music in early worship. The psalms are full of it. 'Praise him in the sound of the trumpet: praise him upon the lute and harp', commands Psalm 150 in the 1549 Book of Common Prayer translation. This is the music Jesus himself, and maybe even Moses, would have known. There was singing too. Liturgy, or formal worship, was chanted. The disciples sang what the King James Bible calls 'an hymn' at the Last Supper.[1] Every generation has, to some extent, used sacred music in this kind of intimate, domestic context.

Evidence about the actual music of the earliest churches has to be gleaned from hints and accounts. One such hint lies in the way sacred texts were written down. Professor Diarmaid MacCulloch notes that 'the contrast between Judaism, the religion of the scroll, and Christianity, the religion of the book, would have been evident in their liturgies when the codex of scripture was used as a performed chanted text'.[2] Copies of the Greek gospels from around 200 pick out the sacred name of Jesus in a special kind of abbreviation, which may imply a particular way of singing. What this music sounded like remains a matter of the purest speculation. But having to imagine it surely serves to make it sound richer and more compelling. It's like the old idea that the pictures are better on the radio. Heard melodies are sweet, but those unheard are sweeter.

We can get another hint from working backwards from what has survived. There is a church in Aleppo which, MacCulloch says, 'is likely to represent a living tradition from the oldest known musical perform-ance in Christian history'.[3] Its musicians are the descendants of a worshipping community from Edessa, now in Turkey, which created a unique repertory of hymns and chant from around the turn of the third century and was forced across the border into Syria in the 1920s. If the tradition does finally fall victim to the latest outbreak of appall-ing violence in the region, it would not be the first time church music has been the casual, incidental victim of a wider tragedy.

Recordings of this music can be heard online. To modern ears, it sounds like nothing so much as the chanting of Eastern Orthodox churches, or even of the muezzins of Islam. This is because it pre-dates the great schism of Christianity into its Western and Eastern branches in 1054. The musical fallout of this divide was that the Western part embraced Latin chant and the pipe organ while the East did not. In its earliest centuries, the music of the Christian world may perhaps have sounded more 'eastern' than 'western'. One of the intriguing results of approaching music from the other end, as it were, is that it can make music which we normally consider early, even primitive, sound amaz-ingly sophisticated and modern. Ninth- and tenth-century plainsong sounds smoothly learned and refined after listening to the music of Edessa, like walking through the airy spaces of a great Gothic cathedral after banging your head in a catacomb or on the ceiling of a cell in a Celtic beehive, somewhere off the coast of Ireland.

Celtic Christians were a determined breed. One of their saints, Ia, apparently sailed from Ireland to Cornwall on a leaf. They built their characteristic beehive-shaped stone huts in places like Skellig Michael, a rocky island overlooking the Irish Atlantic coast, in around the sixth century, within a couple of hundred years of the Roman Emperor Constantine's conversion and adoption of Christianity as the official religion of his empire in the early fourth century. The music of these men and women – Ninian, Patrick, Columba, Brendan and Bride – was Celtic chant, a body of single-lined songs, with texts in Latin. Nothing survives of this repertoire, but the wealth of religious artefacts and objects from the period makes it clear that this was a sophisticated worshipping community which valued beauty in worship and had the skills to create it. Among their relics are bells, the earliest surviving instruments of church music, used for the swearing of oaths as well as playing. Pioneering, too, was their use of religious communities, for both men and women (separately), their remote outposts the antecedents of the monasteries and nunneries whose walls would later bear witness to so much of the history of English church music.

Among the first church musicians in these islands were fourth-century Irish monks, their names long since lost to us, bellowing bad Latin into the wind with a West Scots accent, clutching a Celtic cross and huddling in their stone Atlantic eyries. These places are among the most evocative in Christianity, closer in spirit to the menhirs and mounds of Brittany than to the smooth, modern comforts brought over by the Normans.

During the sixth and seventh centuries, the peoples who became known as the Anglo-Saxons encountered Christianity from two directions: from Celts like Columba and Aidan in Iona and Lindisfarne to the north; and, to the south, from a certain gentleman arrived from Rome, St Augustine.

In 664 the Synod of Whitby set out to reconcile the two approaches. It was mostly concerned with working out how to find a date for Easter (and is thus responsible for plumping for one confusing formula rather than the other, which has messed up the school holidays once a year from that day to this), but its lasting legacy for music was in establishing the idea that the rules of the liturgy were those laid down in Rome. Music had a superstructure against which it could flourish like the green bay-tree for the next 900 years. The fruit which it brought forth in due season was the continuing growth of plainsong.

Plainsong gives us our very first written-down musical notes, which probably date from around the ninth century. Before that, the style and colour of musical worship can best be imagined from other surviving artefacts. *Christ* is a long poem written in the ninth century by a shadowy figure who signed himself 'Cynewulf' and it deals with key themes and events in the Christian narrative, including Advent, the Nativity and the Ascension, freely mixing already well-established liturgical texts like the great 'O' Antiphons with the voices of Mary and Joseph to create a solemn, almost impressionistic, epic drama. Christ has replaced Arthur as the hero-figure of myth and legend. It is good to imagine these words sung around a great fire in a dark hall, perhaps to the accompaniment of some kind of harp. Like the disciples, the Angles and the Saxons didn't just sing sacred music in church.

Among more obviously liturgical texts of the period, The Book of Kells of *c*.800 and the Lindisfarne Gospels of *c*.700 are artefacts of lavish beauty. The worshipping communities which took so much care over these works of liturgical art would surely have poured as much skill and devotion into how they were used. The Alfred Jewel of the late ninth century is the gold head of an aestel, or pointer, one of seven sent by King Alfred to each of his bishops, along with a copy of Pope Gregory's book Pastoral Care, telling them 'I command, in God's name, that no man take the staff from the book, nor the book from the church'.[4] Ceremonial pointers of this kind remain in use in other traditions, for example Judaism. Perhaps we can be forgiven for picturing Alfred's bishops also using them to sing from another book sent over from Rome by Gregory – the Latin psalms.

WHY DO PEOPLE SING in church at all? Liturgy is a form of theatre: speech, delivered according to certain rules in order to heighten and enhance the response of the listener. Often this is to substantial crowds in large buildings, or in the open air. The earliest preachers, men of the road like St Paul, would have experimented with finding the particular pitch and resonance of their own voice which worked best, settling on or around a single pitch – singing, in effect. Think of a parade-ground sergeant major, or Martin Luther King in a town square – their voices have a rise and fall which can easily be notated in music. Ralph Vaughan Williams described the phenomenon in a letter to an academic anthropologist with an interest in speech and music, Dr Charles Myers:

> I am glad you think that song (at all events) came through excited speech. I once heard a Gaelic preacher ... and when he got excited he recited on a fixed succession of notes:

Now this ... is the starting point for many British Folksongs.[5]

And the starting point, too, for plainsong, and for the same reasons. Looked at from this perspective, English church music is almost a naturally occurring phenomenon, the melodious flowering of 'excited speech'. It is built on the rise and fall of the language in the same way that its ancient churches emerge out of the stone and grass and air of its pleasant pastures and mountains green.

When Augustine arrived from Rome in 597 (coincidentally, the same year Columba died, 600 miles to the north), a process began of consolidating Christianity in the British archipelago into something disciplined and based on Rome. Musically, this meant Gregorian plainsong, and the process was to take more than half a millennium, culminating in the complex, forbidding glories of the Sarum Rite, or Use of Sarum, in the eleventh century.

Plainsong is a codified collection of monodic (that is, single-lined) tunes, each associated with a particular text. The music is based on a series of scales known as modes, which were given Greek names (Phrygian, Dorian, Mixolydian, etc.) in acknowledgement of the fact that this was partly an attempt to recreate the lost music of classical antiquity.[6] The very earliest musical notation has noteheads known as 'neumes' but no stave lines, and thus indicates when the melody moves up or down, but not by how much or the precise pitches or intervals. This form of notation is probably a kind of memory aid, shorthand for a tune which the singer already knew and was singing from memory. When staves did begin to be used, they had four lines. Rhythm is not indicated: the flow of the music comes from the Latin words. Some schools of plainsong have a variety of elaborate squiggles and marks above and below the musical line, which presumably indicate some kind of interpretative instruction, but their exact meaning continues to elude even the most patient modern scholars and performers. Clefs give relative, but not absolute, pitch, telling the singer where the tones and semitones of the particular mode fit on the four lines of the stave, but not the actual starting note, which was given out by a cantor or chorus-leader.

Like folk music, the same musical characteristics seem to spring up independently in monodic chant in different places. What differed was the precise liturgical application of music to words, which in turn affected the structure of the music rather than its actual sound: if a particular prayer is repeated in the Celtic rite, this will create a 'refrain' in its music which may not be present in another liturgy.

There is something elemental about plainsong. It is almost as if it is a naturally occurring phenomenon, which is why its music has been successfully incorporated – uninjured – into later compositions of all possible styles by composers of all possible kinds, and used in all manner of different contexts. Search the web today and you will find recordings of plainsong made by modern monks, marketed as a kind of spiritual sedative in response to New Age ideas or research into the production of alpha-waves in the brain. How different from the home life of St Benedict and his followers.

THIS WAS THE MUSICAL WORLD which Augustine inhabited when he picked his way across the sand and shingle of the Isle of Thanet one grey Kentish dawn, no doubt wondering, like Caesar before him, why anyone would leave the Mediterranean sunshine for this.

He found fertile ground. The historian Bede wrote up Augustine's peregrinations in the engaging Latin of his *Historia ecclesiastica gentis Anglorum (The Ecclesiastical History of the English People)*, completed in 731. Bede brought his cast of nobles, natives, clergy and soldiers brilliantly to life. Occasionally they break into song. Book II of the *Ecclesiastical History* thrills its readers with tales of Picts and storms and drownings and beheadings, then introduces us to a rather calmer character called James, a deacon of York: '... who, because he was such an expert in singing in church, brought peace once again to the province and increased the numbers of the faithful, and also, as a master of the church, many singers after the customs of Rome and Canterbury began to exist'.[7] For James, church music was part of the training and daily practice of the educated, middle-ranking priest.

Bede described an exchange of questions and answers between Augustine and Pope Gregory I, who sent him to England. Bede cast the exchange as an entertaining master–pupil dialogue in the Socratic manner, and we learn about the instructions for the ordering of Christian life in Britain which Gregory has given his envoy. Regular liturgy, with music, was part of it.

By Bede's own time, a century after Augustine arrived, the musical component of monastic life was well established. In around 679–80, Benedict Biscop, abbot of Wearmouth and Jarrow, made his fourth visit to Rome. One of his particular requests to the Pope was for the services of an experienced choirmaster, and he returned with a man called John, formerly chief cantor of St Peter's and abbot of the monastery of St Martin. John set about teaching the monks of Wearmouth how to sing in the Roman manner. Much of his teaching was preserved in the monastery library, where he became known as John the Archchanter.[8]

Bede was born on land belonging to the Wearmouth monastery. In 680, at the age of seven, he was entrusted to the care of Biscop, the abbot. His duties certainly included singing. In 685, plague reduced the musical strength of the monastery to Bede – by now around thirteen years old – and his teacher Ceolfrith. For a week the two of them struggled through the daily psalms, their voices a ragged octave apart, but couldn't manage the antiphons which went with them. After a week, Ceolfrith could 'bear it no longer', and he and his young protégé 'with no little labour' built up the regular cycle of chanted services with a group of new colleagues. The music of Wearmouth, so nearly stilled by the plague, continued on its daily round.[9]

Over the next few centuries, the British churches held a series of meetings at which they regularised their practice in all sorts of areas, including music. The second Council of Clovesho of 747 decreed 'That all the most sacred Festivals of Our Lord ... in the method of chanting, shall be celebrated in one and the same way, namely, according to the sample which we have received in writing from the Roman Church. And also, throughout the course of the whole year, the festivals of the Saints are to be kept on one and the same day, with their proper psalmody and chant, according to the Martyrology of the same Roman Church.' Another canon of this Council described the round of daily services or 'hours', at which the monks 'must not dare to sing or read anything not sanctioned by the general use, but only that which ... the usage of the Roman Church allows'.[10]

Several key pillars of the musical superstructure are in place here: the monastic setting; the liturgy repeating in daily, weekly and annual cycles of greater and lesser elaboration; authority from Rome, brought back to these islands by men like Biscop, on regular trips south. This architecture would continue to support and nurture English church music and echo to some of its most creative glories until Henry VIII brought it petulantly to the ground.

The next stage was the growth and further standardisation of monasticism, albeit with occasionally variable levels of worldliness and standards of devotion and observance. The most numerous, widespread and influential monastics were the Benedictines. Benedictines are not an order with a central authority: each house of men or women is an autonomous community whose members have chosen to live by the 'Rule' of St Benedict.

Benedict probably composed his 'Rule' around the mid-sixth century, and it achieved widespread use across Europe in a common form from around the seventh to the ninth century. It makes detailed provision for the ordering of services, treating the several Latin verbs for 'to say' and 'to sing' as interchangeable and synonymous.[11] For example, chapter nine is entitled 'How many psalms to be said [dicentur] at the night office'. An opening response ('Domine labia mea aperies' – 'O Lord open thou my lips') is said three times ('tertio dicendum'), then psalms are read, 'or else chanted' ('aut certe decantandum'). Then follows the 'ambrosianum' (the Ambrosian hymn, or Te Deum laudamus), more psalms, then readings, each with a response either spoken ('dicantur') or sung ('cantantur'). Then six more psalms 'cum Alleluia canendi': to be sung with Alleluia. Gospel reading, prayer ('Quirie eleison': 'Lord, have mercy'), and so ends the Vigilae nocturnae.[12] This pattern of a fixed, daily order of service, with the responses and canticles staying the same each day, the psalms and readings slotted in according to a cycle, is instantly familiar to the church musician today.

The vast, ruined walls of Whitby and Glastonbury still resonate with the sheer power which these institutions exercised over their tiny, isolated communities. Local churches, where they existed at all, were plain, fortress-like buildings of wood or stone, like St-Peter-on-the-Wall on its flat Essex coast at Bradwell-on-Sea or St Andrew, Greensted-juxta-Ongar, a few miles inland. Few windows allowed any light to lighten the earthy soul of the peasant within. He could hear mass, but he couldn't sing it. Church music was still the preserve of the tonsured initiate.

Monasteries and their music achieved a hugely dominant position in English life in the centuries before their sudden, final degradation, but were still not without their setbacks. The turn of the first millennium was a period of 'fightings within and fears without', of violent squabbles between the tribes and kingdoms of England, and of raids and rumours of raids from Danes and Vikings to the north and Normans to the south.

THE VIKINGS BROUGHT ALMOST nothing of their Old Norse religion with them, although their ceremonies had used some music.[13] A much later writer, the twelfth-century Giraldus, suggests that the Vikings introduced two-part polyphony, and in particular the distinctive fondness for harmonising in thirds, but this is at best highly

speculative, and seems in any event to be part of Giraldus's rather tendentious habit of arguing the primacy of all things Welsh, including
music.[14] The Vikings' main (negative) contribution to the development
of musical life was in attacking and disrupting English monasteries on their raids across the North Sea, requiring a series of revivals
under King Edgar and his bishops in the tenth century. The *Regularis
Concordia* of *c*.970 places music in the context of Benedictine Reform,
for example in the Easter liturgical drama Quem quaeritis: 'When,
therefore, he that is seated shall see these three draw nigh, wandering about as it were and seeking something, he shall begin to sing
softly and sweetly, Whom seek ye?... At the command the three shall
turn to the choir saying Alleluia.'[15] This text features in the celebrated
Winchester Troper (of which more in the next chapter), an intriguing
example of the ritual elaboration of the liturgy, with music, below the
rood-screen, alongside the ancient ceremonies of the boy bishop and
the feast of fools.

The Vikings' most lasting contribution was their magnificent
churches, for example St Magnus's Cathedral, Orkney, whose acoustic
properties are still much prized (by local composer Sir Peter Maxwell
Davies, among others) a thousand years after it was built.

The next set of uninvited guests, the Normans, came from a similar
Rome-centred religious and musical environment to that of their
unwilling hosts. They continued and consolidated the dominance of
religious orders, particularly the Benedictines, further codifying and
elaborating the liturgy and its music, and bringing with them the influence of the principal monastic houses of France.

They weren't always welcome. The historian Henry Mayr-Harting
describes the reception given to one Norman monk when he was
appointed to a vacant English abbacy: 'the monks of Glastonbury ...
detected the attitude of a conqueror in Thurstan of Caen, though there
the casus belli was the style of chant, the monks wanting to keep their
old chants as against those which Thurstan wanted to foist on them
... In a fit of uncontrollable anger, Thurstan set his knights onto the
monks. Three of them were killed and many more injured in their own
church where they tried to take refuge.'[16] This horrific incident was not

the only time in this story that church music provided the spark that ignited factional violence.

Gregorian plainsong (named after Augustine's patron, Pope Gregory I) reached its highest and most elaborate form in the abstruse complexities of the Use of Sarum. A 'Use' is a liturgical scheme or system, which specifies the number of services per day, the texts for each service, the number of feast days per year, the quantity of music. There were various 'uses' developed in various centres – York, Lincoln, Bangor, Hereford – which held sway in their locality, but all were derived and elaborated from the Roman rite, and all were broadly similar. It was the Use of Sarum, neatly written down within easy reach of important monastic and population centres in the south of England, which achieved the widest reach and most lasting influence.

When William the Conqueror landed at Pevensey in 1066, he brought his nephew, a nobleman called Osmund, with him. Osmund was an able administrator, and William appointed him to a series of important positions. In 1078, he became Bishop of Salisbury (or Sarum) and subsequently wrote a Breviary and Missal, as well as other liturgical books, to be used in his brand-new cathedral inside its defensive wall on top of the windy old hill fort.

He did his job well. His 'Use' built on the practice of English Benedictines and others, sensibly allowing for the incorporation of local customs as well as those of his Norman countrymen, all of it drawn from a common ancestry in Rome. It was widely used in the south of England (including at Westminster) and in Scotland, Wales and Ireland. The founding (or refounding) and reform of monasteries in the Norman period allowed the Use to become established as the musical and textual source-book of formal English church music through to the Reformation, and a profound influence on Protestant liturgy and music thereafter. It is, therefore, worth taking the time to look at some of its principal features.

The services into which music was fitted fall into two main types: the cycle of seven services, repeated at the same times each day, known as the daily Office; and the mass. Texts sung in the Office include canticles, psalms, responsories, prayers, and (from the eleventh century) four beautiful hymns to the Virgin Mary, much used by later polyphonic composers. Texts sung at the mass fall into two groups: the 'ordinary', that is, the parts sung at every mass (Kyrie, Gloria, Credo, Sanctus, Benedictus, Agnus Dei); and the 'propers', texts which change according to the season or saint under scrutiny (Introit, Offertory, Communion, etc.) All of it, of course, is in Latin. These groups of texts formed the basis of pretty much all English church music from that day on, often carrying their melodies, or the memories of their melodies, with them.

The tunes vary in complexity according to the type of text and its position in the liturgy. The simplest melodies are those for multi-versed texts like psalms, with just a little flourish at the end of a single pitch or reciting note. 'Responsorial' singing alternates between a soloist and a body of singers, 'antiphonal' between one group and another. Sometimes a text is repeated between each verse as a refrain. Ornamental texts like Alleluias get elaborate melodies, without reciting notes and with lengthy melismas. Texts sung often, like the ordinary of the mass and the Magnificat, have several musical settings of varying length and complexity. Hymn-like songs include the thirteenth-century *Pange lingua*, with its regular, six-lined, strophic shape, elegant tune and straightforward metre – nice and easy to remember. The liturgical shape of all these texts (psalm-chants, strophic hymns with metrical texts, texts with internal repetitions and refrains, call and response, freely composed, expressive anthems with emotional highs and lows built into the melody) was carried forward by composers into the polyphonic period, through the Reformation and beyond.

This is the earliest music where we can confidently say we know what the melody sounds like, and it has survived in use to the present day. Choirs (and congregations) still sing the gorgeous, fluid, expressive melodies of *Salve regina* and *Ave Maria*. Scroll through the stations on the radio in your hire car in France or Italy and you will come across the sound of nuns warbling these tunes with devotion and vibrato. Sing 'The Lord be with you: and also with you' during parish communion, and you are singing Sarum plainsong, albeit refracted through the changes of language and performance style of the last thousand years and more. Plainsong is like Lego: based on the smallest and most universally applicable shapes, it is infinitely expandable and adaptable, as serviceable to the nun singing herself to sleep in her cell as to a cathedral full of worshippers on Christmas Day.

The Roman Church loves feasts. Sarum fits the musical and liturgical system of daily services into the larger grid of the church year, with its pattern of seasonal events such as Easter and Christmas, and many saints' days. Feasts are either simple or double, with three, nine or twelve psalms, texts read and sung at various places in the building, with a strict liturgical choreography of coloured cassock, hand gestures, kneeling, sitting, bowing (head, shoulders, waist, genuflection or total prostration), and lots of looking things up in your Breviary and Missal. There are copes and candles, thurifers and crucifers, dozens of deacons and plenty of priests. Go to Westminster Cathedral in London today, and you will get some flavour of all this elaboration by watching the nervous neophyte among the tenors, desperately trying to follow the squiggly logic of neumes and quelismas from a book balanced in one hand, then find the psalm in another book, then back to the first for the Gloria Patri (unless it's a saint's day when it's on a different page), all the time trying not to drop the lot while processing up a flight of steep steps and not tripping over his cassock.

This is complex stuff. The level of detail seems to grow organically, by itself, each generation mastering the arcana of the last, then adding some new ones, like a family with a restricted gene pool magnifying its peculiarities with each shuffling of the DNA. This is not for the man below the rood-screen, who can listen, but not take part. He wouldn't expect to. He's not even going to notice for another five hundred years or so, never mind want to do anything about it. He would no more expect to understand and participate than he would expect his donkey to do so.

There were objectors from the very beginning. Complexity obscures the words, worldly beauty the spiritual content, so they said. Calvin, Cranmer and Cromwell did not invent this particular gripe. As early as 1140, Peter the Venerable, Abbot of Cluny, accused one of his critics of heresy, no less, for claiming that 'God laughs at ecclesiastical chants because he loves only the holy will, and is not to be summoned by high-pitched voices, or caressed by well-turned tunes'. Peter was proud of his monastery's music. Visitors described their sung liturgy as 'a corner of heaven'. To the monks, it was part of the *vita angelica* – the angelic life – and they had just two hours a day free from their singing. Both abbot and critic had a point.

The same arguments turned up in England. Aelred, Abbot of Rievaulx, wrote a chapter headed 'The vain pleasure of the ears': 'Sound should not be given precedence over meaning, but sound with meaning should generally be allowed to stimulate greater attachment. Therefore the sound should be so moderate, so marked by gravity that it does not captivate the whole spirit to amusement in itself, but leaves the greater part to the meaning.' He goes on to compare elaborate singing to 'the neighing of horses', demonstrating 'manly strength set aside, it is constricted to the shrillness of a woman's voice'.[17]

Around the tenth century, as Gregorian plainsong entered its glory years, musicians started experimenting with adding musical lines to the basic plainsong tune, radically altering its function, expanding its artistic reach and ushering in the polyphonic style which was to dominate English church music until the seventeenth century and give it some of its greatest glories. So far, church musicians had been priests and monastics. Chanting was a heightened way of reading the liturgy, and as such it was performed by men and women in orders of various kinds. Greater musical elaboration had already led to some of them being given specific, designated musical responsibilities, with special skills and training. The rise of multi-voiced music, with its even greater requirement for professional expertise, continued this logical process. Singing in church was no longer the preserve of the ordained or the tonsured. Individuals could be prized chiefly for their skill in singing.

The choir was born.

2

Music for a New Millennium

Ðær is engla song, ëadigra blis;
(There is angels' song, heavenly bliss)

Cynewulf, from *Christ*, part III

MUSICALLY, THE NEXT STAGE was to add a second voice to the first: two voices, singing different notes, at the same time. This was a radical step, with implications beyond the purely musical.

For much of its later history, English church music has been an all-male pursuit. In the beginning, this was not the case. Musical monasticism applied to both men and women. Plainchant was as much a part of the daily life of the nunnery as of the monastery: one of the beauties of single-lined music is that it can be sung at any pitch convenient to a particular group of singers. There were also 'double' monasteries, where men and women lived in separate buildings (or separate floors of the same building) within a single community, coming together to sing the daily Office and mass in the abbey church or minster. These 'double' monasteries died out almost entirely in the years leading up to the Norman Conquest, under the combined assault of ecclesiastical rule changes, Viking raids and scandal: 'living together gives occasion for incontinence',[1] as the twentieth Canon of the Second Council of Nicaea put it rather prudishly in 787.

Long into the era of polyphony, men and women had their own distinct repertoires. The nuns of Barking and Syon Abbeys, for example, were criticised by the Cistercian general chapter for singing three-part polyphony from the late thirteenth century.[2] Music which needed high and low voices at the same time presented a particular problem. The solution was to train up the youngest members of the male half of the monastic estate to sing alongside their adult colleagues: choirboys.

Boys and young men had always sung in monasteries – as novices, neophytes and trainee monks (Bede was not untypical in joining his monastery at age seven) – but so far they had simply sung the same single-lined music as the grown-ups, dropping an octave when their voices broke. Polyphonic music required a whole different set of skills, which would reach astonishing levels of virtuosity and sophistication by the time of the Reformation.

The process began with one or more singers adding notes a fourth or a fifth above the main plainsong tune. There were strict rules, codified and developed in a number of European treatises from the ninth century on, like the widely circulated *Musica enchiriadis* of the ninth century, the earliest surviving attempt to codify the rules for creating polyphonic music. Singers mastered the principle and then were able to add an upper part 'ex improviso', or at sight. The practice formed an important element of musical education, and improvising according to set rules around a given plainsong was to form part of the professional musician's training up to the Reformation and beyond. The added part is the *vox organalis*, and the two voices combined are known as *organum*. *Discantus* is 'note-against-note', less florid than *organum* per se or *organum purum*. By the early eleventh century, theorists allowed some variation on the strict rules, enabling new, rich-sounding intervals to emerge and giving some freedom to the performer about which possible variant to employ.

This music, especially the early *organum* style, sounds plain and ascetic to our ears, accustomed as they are to modern inventions like the triad: voice-parts move in eerie parallel, or one part sticks largely on a single tone, like a drone. It sounds like something from another planet. But the sound of two voices singing different notes must have been revelatory to the late first-millennium church musician – like the turning on of a light, or seeing something in colour for the first time, or the inhabitants of Plato's cave, used to reality experienced only as flickering shadows on a wall, suddenly turning and seeing the world in all its definition and possibility.

So our young pre-Norman singer in his monastery, watched over by some musically highly literate monk, was no longer just learning by rote a large body of pre-existing single-lined chants. He was mastering the art of adding an increasingly florid new tune to the plainsong being sung by his chum standing next to him, discovering how and when he could add little changes and flourishes, beautifying the liturgy, making pretty harmonies, enjoying himself and colouring in the curves and corners of the familiar old tune with something much more fun to sing, and much more sonorous and sensuous to listen to.

ONE OF THE EARLIEST and finest collections of English church music vividly evokes the range and ambition of the style, while leaving accurate reconstruction tantalisingly out of reach. The two manuscripts known as the Winchester Troper date from the mid to late tenth century and are associated with the Old Minster at Winchester, and in particular with a monk called Wulfstan, who was, according to his own account, a 'child oblate' when the body of St Swithun was moved to the New Minster in 971. He is later described in the Minster records as 'Cantor. Sacerdos' – cantor, priest.[3]

There are many hundreds of texts in the two volumes: Alleluias, Sequences, Graduals, Introits, sections of the ordinary of the mass, 'tropes' (additional texts added to a pre-existing text), and others. The tropers contain only the *vox organalis* or added melody, not the original plainsong itself. One singer sings the chant from a different book or from memory; another adds the second voice part from the troper.

The pages are handsome and mysterious. Initial letters line up down the left-hand margin in gorgeous greens, reds and purples: 'A' for Alleluia, 'K' for Kyrie, 'X' for Xriste. The handwriting is impeccable, the Latin instantly readable, much neater than much of the crabbed handwriting of 500 years later, or indeed than the scrawled mixture of Anglo-French and Latin at the beginning of the books. Above every line of text is a series of musical markings. Some look remarkably like modern quavers and semiquavers, some are little curves and squiggles, some dots and dashes. In the more elaborate sections, the musical notation scurries off by itself, taking off at 45 degrees to the words and out beyond the end of the line of text.

Working out how this music might conceivably go requires looking at the plainsong it is designed to fit, applying contemporary theoretical rules for adding the second part, and trying to make sense of the ups and downs of the surviving notation. Scholars have arrived at different conclusions, and a definitive realisation is, alas, probably impossible. As before, this notation is probably more a memory aid giving the rough outline of a melody the singer already knows, than a precise indication of every note. What is clear, however, is the explosion of creativity which the concept of multi-voiced music released, the care, skill and devotion which went into the creation of this music and these books, and the sophistication of the men and boys who composed and sang it. Its effect must have been impressive indeed.

LITURGY IS LIKE THEATRE. It was a short step for certain liturgical narratives to evolve into mini-plays. Liturgical drama focused on the more obviously theatrical parts of the Christian story, like Christmas and Easter, with their opportunities for handing out the roles of shepherds and angels, Marys and gardeners. A perennial favourite was the Quem quaeritis, the discovery of the empty tomb on Easter Day. This is the text from the Winchester Troper:

Quem quaeritis in sepulcro O Cristicole?
Jesum Nazarenum crucifixum O celicole.
Non est hic, surrexit sicut dixerat.

Whom seek ye in the tomb, followers of Christ?
Jesus of Nazareth who was crucified, Celestial ones.
He is not here, he is risen, as he foretold.

The women are sent out into the world to tell the good news. The dramatis personae are listed in red and purple, and the 'acting' was probably one step up from a dramatic recitation to music, the players moving around chancel and choir in a stylised re-creation of the story. There is some evidence that Bishop Ethelfrith built organs at Winchester. One or two organ notes, on a kind of drone (or *organum*) can be a very effective way of recreating this early chant.[4]

There is a distinction between drama in church, which remained in Latin, and the imported vernacular European kind, which took on its English accent in the following centuries as it moved into the market square. Spoken text was in English, Anglo-French or a regional dialect. Performance was outside, during the day, using either stylised staging like a wooden scaffold to represent heaven or a hill, a doorway for a house, a tree for a forest; or a train of carts and waggons, each decked out for a particular scene in the show – the Garden of Eden, the Kingdom of Heaven, the Castle of Perseverance – which could be moved about as part of the performance and trundled off to the next venue when it was over. Subject matter was usually a Bible story: Adam and Eve, the Holy Innocents, the Passion and Resurrection; or occasionally an allegory or morality play. Music was used to comment on the action more often than to advance the narrative, and usually took the form of a liturgical text, sung in Latin, borrowed along with its music from the choir stalls. Musical instruments also featured. The audience stood or sat around among the performers, who may have been members of a town guild and were effectively semi-professional actors. Singers were simply members of the company, or, for the more elaborate or illustrative music like the angels singing 'Gloria in excelsis' from atop their wooden scaffold on Christmas Day, the men and boys of the local cathedral or abbey. Actors – always male – wore the clothes of their own time, not an imagined re-creation of biblical dress.

The links to the world of Elizabethan theatre are clear. The twelfth-century *Play of Adam (Le Jeu d'Adam)* is in Anglo-French. Stage directions are in Latin: paradise is a high place ('constituatus paradisus loco eminentori') surrounded by flowers and fruits to make it seem as delightful as possible ('ut amoenissimus locus videatur'). Nine Latin texts are sung by a Chorus, surrounding the devotional and theological themes of the action with music: 'In principio creavit Deus celum et terram', the play begins, 'In the beginning God created the heaven and the earth'. The choir responds 'formavit igitur Dominus' – 'so God made [man]'.[5] Music accompanies each appearance of God (wearing a bishop's stole), and casts a mantle of deep seriousness around the all-too-human vulnerabilities and failings of Adam (who wears a red tunic).

There are later plays in a variety of languages and dialects from Cornwall, East Anglia, cathedral cities like Norwich, York and Chester, and most other parts of England. The entire Christian world-view is encompassed in groups of plays like the celebrated Mystery cycles from York and Chester. Music illustrates the action: the Candlemass Day Play has the stage direction: 'here shal Symeon bere Iesu in his armys, goyng a procession rounde aboute the tempill; and al this wyle the virgynis synge nunc dimittis'.[6]

Towards the end of the tradition in the first half of the sixteenth century the texts sung with the drama began to include devotional songs and original compositions as well as liturgical items. The music was occasionally in two and three parts – and the words in English. There is one surviving example of two-part Latin songs in a fifteenth-century York play, and one example dating from 1534 of songs with English texts and up to three voice-parts, including the famous 'Lully, lulla, thou little tiny child/O sisters, too', known to us (geographically erroneously) as the 'Coventry Carol'. Shakespeare may well have seen these plays as a boy, and may have acted in them at school, too, with didactic, moralising songs illustrating rhetorical points, the ancestor of the consort song, the theatre song and the verse anthem.

Like so much else, the tradition of religious plays with music petered out in the upheavals of the sixteenth and seventeenth centuries, but we catch its echo today, as we perch precariously on a plastic chair in a draughty gym, grinning through the annual Nativity play, as the action pauses for a moment to accommodate a quick blast of 'Away in a Manger' on the school piano, with all the dear children lined up on their wooden stage like their medieval forebears – eight Virgin Marys, four Kings and a couple of stroppy-looking sheep beating each other up in the back row.

IN THE MIDDLE OF WINTER 1165–6 Henry II presided in person over the trial of a group of heretics in Oxford. His judgement was ruthless. The accused, both men and women, were branded on the forehead and chin and 'driven from the city with ringing blows into the intolerable cold', chanting 'Blessed are they which are persecuted for righteousness' sake' and 'Blessed are ye when men shall revile ye'. But 'nobody showed the slightest mercy towards them, and they died in misery'.[7] An isolated incident, but a sad precursor of things to come. Church music turns up in some unpleasant places.

This account of the musical performance by the condemned that chilly Oxford day was written thirty years later, and 200 miles away, in Yorkshire, by the chronicler William of Newburgh.[8] Writers like William give vivid local colour to our ideas of how church music was used around the twelfth century, but caveat lector applies: they often describe events which they did not, and could not, have witnessed; they are usually promulgating a particular interpretation; and, like Shakespeare, they use the language and practices of their own time even when talking about events long past, or even entirely fictional. For example, Geoffrey of Monmouth tells us that, at his coronation, King Arthur 'was attended with a concert of music of all kinds, making wonderful melody', and that there were 'so many organs and so many voices' that the soldiers couldn't decide which to listen to first.[9] The methodical William of Newburgh didn't think much of the more creative Geoffrey of Monmouth, commenting that 'whatever this man published of Arthur and of Merlin are mendacious fictions', and thought Bede much the more reliable historian, which is certainly right.

Walter Map, a contemporary of William's, preferred rattling off a good ghost story to anything as dull as telling us about church music, though he does have a bizarre account of a group of heretics who, instead of singing hymns as they should, sit in darkness and silence in the temple, grinding their teeth as a huge black cat descends at the end of an enormous rope.[10] Matthew Paris, a Benedictine monk, is the best of these chroniclers. His lavish histories are full of delicious evocations of the 'voces cantantium dulcissimas' and the 'voces psallentium

Two extracts from the 'Worcester fragments' (late thirteenth, early fourteenth century), showing texted and textless lines being passed between the voices, some (fairly restrained) 'hocketing' in example a, and the repeating bass known as a pes *(or 'footprint') in example b.*

et dicentium in sublime' which surrounded his daily life as a monk in the magnificent Abbey at St Alban's.[11]

These men allow us to hear what it was actually like listening to church music in the England of the twelfth and thirteenth centuries, alongside a lot of really good history, some less good history, and some great folklore – such as the first written tales of vampires and the story of two young children, discovered living wild in the forests of East Anglia, who had turned bright green from eating nothing but beans. In these books the serious and the sacred sit alongside the fabulous and the fantastic, grinning at each other, like the Green Man and the local saint embalmed in stone over the church door.

Meanwhile, back in the safety of the choir stalls, our clever choristers were beginning to relish the intellectual and musical opportunities opened up by the development of polyphony, adding not just one but two additional voice parts to a plainsong tune. Students would learn how to stand over one of their weighty volumes of plainsong – the Missal, the Psalter or the Breviary – one or more of them singing the melody perhaps from memory, another improvising a part pitched above the main tune, and yet another adding a third melody below. As before, there were rules, which had to be learned. Get it right, and they would make magical new sounds – three-part chords. It was a kind of real-time musical crossword puzzle, just the kind of thing to appeal to the educated medieval mind; this was an era which loved its theory, its treatises and its teaching manuals.

The earliest written-down three-part polyphony, like the beautiful twelfth-century European Codex Calixtinus, doesn't indicate rhythm. The codification of rhythm was an important step. Each note of the plainsong now had a fixed length related to an underlying pulse: one, two, three units on a given note. Tunes became organised into rhythmic patterns, which were then repeated according to a set procedure, so that the rhythm, as well as the scale, was organised according to a 'mode' or pre-defined pattern. By the fourteenth century this had evolved into the technique known as 'isorhythm' (where a tenor goes through the same pitches twice or more, and the same rhythms appear in the upper parts over the same pitches of the tenor). Dark Ages these were not.

These developments added a thrilling new freedom. Musical forms included the *conductus*, a kind of sacred song, and the *rondellus*, a form of round, in which a single melody is passed either between two upper voices over a repeating figure underneath, or between all three, with one or more of the voices vocalising, without words, at any given time so that the text is always heard. The Welshman Giraldus described the effect in 1194: 'as many voices as you can see heads', making 'one consonant polyphonic song'.[12] The Benedictine Walter Odington (also known as Walter of Evesham Abbey), gave more detail in around 1300. He described the technique known as 'voice-exchange', (two voices alternating one melody between them). Text can be manipulated between voice-parts too, by having different texts in each voice-part, or one or more lines with no text at all. One of Odington's examples has three melodies. Only one of them has text. If three singers start together, each beginning with a different tune, the music fits together as a round, with the words always present in one of the parts. It's a wonderful effect.

A third element which can be handed between voice-parts is silence. 'Hocket' is a linear technique whereby a single melody is shared between (usually) two voices, one singing while the other rests. Hockets on their own (rather than as a technique within *organum* or motets), began to appear around the end of the fourteenth century, by which time the art of notation allowed rests of precise rhythmic duration to be written down.[13] The result is music bursting with joyful, syncopated life. Many writers have posited an etymological link between the words 'hocket' and 'hiccup', which is disputed by the more serious-minded, naturally, but certainly makes sense if you try to sing it. It sounds like jazz, and for good reason: the 'scat' style of Ella Fitzgerald and Cab Calloway is really the same idea, a textless vocalisation on the tune of a song. Needless to say it annoyed the Pope.

It is a feature of this story that we often find out most about a particular musical practice when someone complained about it. If the authorities didn't like something, they described at considerable length exactly what it was they wanted to stop. Pope John XXII's complaint, therefore, is worth looking at in some detail as a vivid, if tendentious, account of high-art sacred music in the 1320s.

Some disciples of the new school, much engaged with the way they divide musical time into measured divisions, put in new kinds of notes which singers of the old ways do not know; church music is sung to semibreves and minims [in this context, fast notes] and to these little plucked notes. They chop the melody up with their hocketing, oil it with their descant, and even sometimes stuff it with even more upper parts, the 'triplis' and the 'motetis', which are actually taken from popular songs. So they ignore the basis of their music in the melodies of the antiphoner and the gradual, and forget the foundation they build on. They no longer even know the chant, because they can't hear it, buried under the multitude of their notes, so that the demure risings and fallings of the modest plainsong, which is how we can tell which tune we are listening to, are completely obscured. Thus their voices run about all over the place and won't be quiet, their ear is drunk with melody rather than soothed, and they copy in their gestures what they sing from their mouths. So that the required end of devotion is abandoned, and a wanton lasciviousness is encouraged.[14]

If there is one theme that runs through the whole of this history, it is probably clerical authorities trying to stop the music getting too much attention. This is in part the old story of not wanting music to obscure the words. But it's also about power and control. A fourteenth-century pope can use almost exactly the same language to describe the evils of music as the twelfth-century abbot of a monastery and a sixteenth-century English Puritan. Some medieval writers expressed themselves with an admirable lack of squeamishness about sexual impropriety in monastic houses, and music took its share of responsibility. Florid upper voice-parts represented the illicit intertwining of bodies. Even certain scales, harmonies and intervals were thought to be inherently suspect, an idea which had been around for a long time: in the mid-twelfth century, John of Salisbury complained about 'such melodies as lead to the abyss of lust and corruption'. One modern scholar has neatly characterised this association between certain sounds and loose morals as 'the lascivious career of B flat'.[15] It's the favoured argument of the reactionary throughout the ages, the slippery slope. Surely, though, church music by itself never led anyone into lasciviousness. The Pope's complaint had curiously little impact. It is possible that the passage about music was added to his Bull some time after it was first issued. Whatever its provenance, Pope John XXII's invective gives a good flavour of the kind of arguments swirling around music in the medieval period and beyond, and their limited effect on actual musical practice.

Another important debate (which has not entirely gone away) was around who church music is for. At the end of the thirteenth century, the theorist Johannes de Grocheio said that the motet was 'not intended for the vulgar who do not understand its finer points and derive no pleasure from hearing it: it is meant for educated people and those who look for refinement in art[16]' (though, as always, care must be taken with the slippery art of translating not just from another language but from another age: the medievalist Christopher Page believes that the Latin words *vulgaribus* and *literati* in this passage mean laity and clerics, not just the uneducated and the educated[17]). Like much else, the thirteenth- and early fourteenth-century motet was mainly a European, specifically a Northern French, creature, but there was a notable English branch of the family, with its distinctive fingerprints in both music and notation. There is no single substantial English source to compare with the several which survive in France, but there are single items, fragments and scraps of individual pieces, many with connections to the cathedral city of Worcester. Over one hundred pieces can be resurrected.[18] The main sacred forms are all here: tropes, sequences, Alleluias, and many songs to the Virgin Mary. Most are in three parts, some in two, a few in four. Almost all are in Latin, a handful in expressive English ('Jesu Cristes milde moder stud beheld hire sone'), some in both. All divide the basic pulse into groups of three shorter rhythmic units. Motets are structured according to complex rhythmic patterns, including the 'isomelic', which uses repetition of phrases within and between parts, and the 'periodic', which matches phrases of similar length. As in other periods of experimentation and change, composers had to invent new kinds of notation as they went along, all discussed at length in learned Latin theses from across Europe, providing much raw meat for later scholars to gnaw on.

Many of the compositions are based around a plainsong in the tenor: the word 'tenor', indeed, comes from the Latin *tenere*, 'to hold', meaning the part which 'holds' the plainsong. Later, this line became known as the *cantus firmus*, or 'fixed song', around which polyphonic lines were draped. The second and third musical lines do not necessarily use the same words as the plainsong, or even the same language.

Another type has a repeating bass figure, often of just a few notes, known as a *pes* or 'footprint', sometimes itself taken from a snatch of a well-known popular song or dance. This 'swung' bass is one of the most characteristic and evocative sounds of medieval polyphony, probably most familiar to us today from a secular piece, 'Summer is icumen in'. This idea of a short phrase strolling along in the bass, with variations played out over the top, composers playing around with irregular phrase-lengths and deliberately getting the two elements of their piece out of synch with each other, gets lodged in the English musical mind and turns up again in the music of Henry Purcell ('The Lord is Great' in *O Sing unto the Lord*) and Benjamin Britten ('There is no Rose' from *A Ceremony of Carols*, where it is allied with a medieval poem to the Virgin in English and Latin), like a twist of DNA which shows its face every few hundred years.

Much care was lavished on the words. Many of these pieces were addressed to a particular saint, often a locally venerated celebrity like Augustine of Canterbury. Where the two upper voices have different texts, the sheer sound of the words is caressed and manipulated to set up echoes and resonances between them:

Ave magnifica Maria
Ave mirifica Maria
Salve salvifica deigera Maria
Ave mundifica puerpera Maria.

Other pieces use assonance and alliteration between different texts in different voices sung simultaneously: 'Domine coelestis/Dona coeli factor/Docebit ...' In another piece, two poems about Thomas Becket and places in Kent are put together: 'Thomas gemma Cantuariae/ Thomas cesus in Doveria'. The abbey at Reading, similarly, had music for St James, whose severed hand was their chief relic and attraction.[19]

This was also perhaps the first sacred music which was recognisably English, with thirds, sixths, and even the occasional four-part 'major' chord to end, producing an amazingly modern sound. The *pes* motets can easily be imagined sung in some outdoor celebration or procession in some chilly English cathedral town, or while digging in the monastery garden.

There's a reason why this music can sound a bit secular. Exactly the same musical style was used for songs about summer (' … is icumen in') and singing (*Sub Arturo plebs*, and the French song *Musicorum colegio*, which names the seven chums who sang together in a chapel in France, including 'J. Anglici', or 'Joe the Englishman'). Sometimes the sacred and secular shared not only the same musical style but the same music. Richard Ledrede, Bishop of Ossory, handed his Franciscan colleagues a book of sixty Latin hymns, known as the *Red Book of Ossory*, between about 1320 and 1360. Some of them have the *incipit*, or opening phrase, of a secular Latin song marked alongside. This gives the reader the tune for each poem. Ledrede's clerical brethren, however, are left in no doubt which text they are to sing:

> Note: Listen, reader, the Bishop of Ossory has made these songs for the vicars, priests and clergy of the Cathedral church, for singing on the major feast days and days of penance, so that their throats and their holy prayers to God should not be defiled by theatrical, turpid and secular songs; and, since they are the singers, to provide them with notes which they already know, to use according to the dictates of what is required.[20]

Today's choirs should make more use of the motets of the twelfth to mid-fourteenth centuries. The penitential pieces, and in particular the songs to the Virgin, relish the expressive imagery of the poetry. The *pes* motets are exhilaratingly cheerful, the upper voices pattering out a rhyming Latin text while the bass swaggers along underneath. Some of the pieces take extravagant delight in the voice-exchange technique of chucking the words back and forth between the different voices, the textless voice hocketing away happily with odd little rhythms and rests and syncopated short notes on the off beats: just the sort of thing which so irritated Pope John XXII.

The aesthetics of the thirteenth- and fourteenth-century motet are subtle and fluid. Some theorists compare it to a stained-glass window: the florid, expressive upper voices built on the supporting superstructure of the chant, in much the same way that coloured glass floats above the firmness of the cathedral wall; in one sense forming part of the same structure, in another providing an efflorescence and illumination above and beyond its structural function. It's a useful image (though challenged, of course, by some scholars[21]). The English motet never achieved the same (perhaps slightly self-regarding) sophistication of its cross-Channel *confrère*, but it is a lot of fun.

So far, English church music had been mainly a provincial branch of European practice: Gregorian chant from Rome, *Ars Nova* from Paris. By the early fourteenth century English sacred music sounded exactly that – English. It may be significant that the first composers whose names are actually ascribed to particular, identifiable compositions are Frenchmen of the late twelfth and early thirteenth century, while the first named English composers appear much later, men like Leonel Power and Roy Henry who feature in the Old Hall manuscript of around 1420, and John Dunstaple a few decades later. On the other hand, it may not: ascription is a chancy business, often done not by the composer himself but by other people writing about the music long after it was written. Much of our information about the early Parisian composers, for example, comes from a scribe, probably himself an Englishman, working in Paris in the 1270s and '80s, more than half a century after the composers he describes, who is known to us as 'Anonymous IV' (which makes him sound like something from the CIA). The survival of manuscripts, too, is largely a matter of luck. What is clear, however, is that there was regular traffic of people, ideas and music between England and Europe and that English church musicians broadly followed European practice in the thousand years or so after the arrival of St Augustine.

Like all written authorities, the other St Augustine (of Hippo, not Canterbury), can be raided to support a particular point of view. In the late fourteenth century, the English religious reformer John Wycliffe quoted Augustine to articulate once again the running theme that enjoying the music too much was bad: 'As oft as the song delighteth me more than that which is sungen, so oft I acknowledge I trespass grievously.'[22] Wycliffe's life and thought prefigured many of the themes of the Protestant Reformations of 150 years later. For music, this meant translating the psalms into English, for singing. Music is only bad when it gets in the way of the words. The Prologue to an even earlier translation than Wycliffe's, made in the first half of the fourteenth century by Richard Rolle, makes this explicit:

> Grete haboundance of gastly [ghostly, or spiritual] comfort and ioy in god comes in the hertes of thaim at says or synges devotly the psalms ... This scripture is cald boke of ympnes [hymns] of crist. Ympne is lovynge of god with sange. Til an ympne falls thre thyngs. lovynge of god. ioynge of hert or thoght. affectuouse thynkynge of goddis luf. Sange is a gret gladnes of thought.[23]

He notes that the name given to the book of psalms, the 'psalter', is derived from the name of a musical instrument, the 'psaltery'.

These early proto-Protestants pre-echoed some of the sadder aspects of the Reformation too. They fell out with each other. Rolle didn't approve of what he called 'yvel men of lollardry', a name given to the followers of Wycliffe: Wycliffe himself was posthumously burned. But a prefatory poem to Rolle's work puts a critical finger on what these men were trying to do, and on why the psalms in translation run through the history of English church music like a chain of gold: 'his englysching ryt aftur the latyn taketh cours And makes it compendious, short gode and profetabul to mannys soule'.[24] Cranmer himself couldn't have put it better.

This is the world of Chaucer's pilgrims. All musical life is here:[25] Chaucer's young Squire sings and plays his flute all day long; the well-fed Friar 'hadde a murye note, Wel koude he synge, and pleyen on a rote'; the Pardoner, with his fake relics of pigs' bones, has mastered all the arts necessary to make the 'parson and the people his apes', including music:

Wel koude he rede a lessoun or a storie
But alderbest he song an offertorie ...

The rather more devout (if a little maidenly) Clerk 'made a-nyghtes melodie, So swetely that all the chambre rong; And angelus ad virginem he song'. The Prioress is an educated woman: 'Ful weel she soong the service dyvyne, Entuned in hir nose ful semely'. She introduces us to a little boy, just seven years old, who hears *Alma Redemptoris* (one of the hymns to the Virgin Mary), and nags an older classmate to translate it for him,

... thanne sange it wel and boldely,
Fro word to word accordynge with the note...
This litel child, as he cam to and fro,
Ful murily than wolde he synge and crie...
He kan nat stynte of syngyng by the weye.

Chaucer's Summoner has a mother sing Te Deum in the streets to her dead child, 'withouten noyse or claterynge of belles'; his Merchant interrupts a lovers' tryst when 'evensong rong, and that they moste aryse'; the Miller tells us that 'the belle of laudes gan to rynge, And freres in the chauncel gonne synge'.

A slightly earlier writer, the wonderful William Langland, casts the allegorical Sloth as a priest who 'bigan Benedicite with a boke' (belch), 'kan neyther solve ne synge' (can't sing, can't do sol-fa), and 'kan noght parfitly my Paternoster as the preest it syngeth' (can't sing the Our Father as a priest should).

These are real people: fictional, of course, but drawn from life. For the first time, we can hear this music out of the mouths of the people Chaucer and Langland met and heard and knew in the daily bustle and stink of the streets and courts and chambers of fourteenth-century London. Chaucer heard choirs singing polyphony too. Surely he is describing the sound here, in *The Parliament of Fowls*:

On every bow the bryddes herde I synge,
With voys of aungel in here armonye;

Or here, in *The Book of the Duchess*, with its detailed reference to the 'solemn service' and to voices singing high and low (which may also mean loud and soft), just as the theorists and composers of the Worcester fragments had taught them to do:

> With smale foules a gret hep
> That had affrayed me out of my slep,
> Thorgh noyse and swetness of her song.
> And, as me mette, they sate among
> Upon my chambre roof wythoute,
> Upon the tyles, overal aboute,
> And songen, everch in hys wyse,
> The moste solempne servise
> By noote, that ever man, y trowe,
> Had herd; for some of hem song lowe,
> Som high, and al of oon acord.
> To telle shortly, att oo word.
> Was never herd so swete a steven,
> But hyt had be a thyng of heven,

This is a first-hand account of the actual sound of the polyphony of the Worcester fragments, or the Old Hall music, or perhaps something in between. Go to a pub in Southwark today and you may well hear singing, but it probably won't be church music. But Chaucer's pilgrims thought nothing of breaking into song as they trudged along the muddy lanes of Deptford and Rotherhithe, urging on their donkeys and mules, leaving the tower of St Mary Overie behind them and stamping through the puddles towards St Alfege's and the distant village of Greenwich across the fields. For them the pilgrimage itself was an act of worship, the open road as good a place to sing praise as the shrine of St Thomas at Canterbury or the various churches, chantries, pubs and monasteries where they would stop along the way.

This kind of music required an education. All these singers, birds, boys and belching friars had to learn how to do it. They would have had to be members of, or have studied at, or be employed by, one of the main types of organisation which supported choirs and choral singing: cathedrals, monastic or secular; large collegiate-style parish churches; aristocratic households with private chapels; the country's ancient places of education; or monasteries. Between the Conquest and the Reformation nearly half of England's cathedrals were home to communities of monks, mostly Benedictines, while the other half were run by priests who were not monks, in what were known as 'secular' foundations. Both types of community maintained choirs of men and boys to sing the daily Office and mass, and to offer up musical worship in defence of the souls of their patrons, their founders and the people who paid for the roof.

Some large parish churches, usually in prosperous market towns, maintained 'colleges' of clergy, and had all the trappings and accoutrements of a mini-cathedral: cloisters, outbuildings and farms. St Mary Ottery in Devon is like a scale model of Exeter Cathedral, with its squat, square towers, the fourteenth-century clock charting the movements of the stars, the Lady chapel and gallery in Beer stone, white as paper, the ambulatory with a list of incumbents written up on a board, beginning 700 years ago with the evocative words 'Roger the Chaplain', and the fan-vault in the Dorset aisle, its pencil-thin tracery pointing the way to heaven for the rich merchant who paid for it, the confident seventeenth-century governor who lies on his tomb with his little dog by his feet. Outside there is a pretty row of houses, like a cathedral close, where Coleridge was born; and the footprint of the cloister in the grass, unworried now by the attentions of Henry VIII.

Rich men built themselves big houses, and the richest and (perhaps less importantly) most devout created private chapels within their architectural prodigies. In the medieval house, like Broughton House in Oxfordshire, the chapel is a small, dark room up a steep staircase, with a squint for the owner to look down on the worship from the warmth of his private apartments. By the late Tudor period, the household chapel had taken on the roomy glamour of that at the Vyne in Hampshire. Music would be provided by trained professionals, retained by the noble family, who were about halfway up the domestic pecking order, and perhaps by a houseboy or two with nice voices. Other household chapels had galleries where the nobility could sit and listen (or nod off), or from where music could echo around the gorgeously decorated spaces below. The greatest nobles, like the Percy family at Alnwick Castle and Cardinal Wolsey at Hampton Court, treated themselves to fully fledged choral foundations at home, with a paid-up staff of boys and singing-men to give glory to their lords on earth and in heaven.

But by far the most important private household chapel was the monarch's own. Much sacred music was made in rooms and chambers, for entertainment and personal devotion: a number of sixteenth- and early seventeenth-century pieces exist in 'sacred' sources, for use in church, and 'secular' versions for use at home. Often the musical forces involved, and sometimes the music itself, is different according to intended circumstances of use. Country-house worship, and its music, has a particular resonance in the history of Catholicism in Tudor and Stuart England.

Devout and scholarly nobles and clergy put time and money into endowing places of education, with chapels and music. William of Wykeham, the Bishop of Winchester, stipulated ten chaplains, three clerks and sixteen choristers when he founded the College of St Mary (soon known as New College), Oxford, in 1379. Their duties were substantial: the seven canonical 'hours' and seven masses daily, and, for the choristers, making the fellows' beds. In return the choristers (local charity boys) were fed (on leavings, if this proved sufficient), and were taught Latin and grammar. King's Hall in Cambridge (now part of Trinity College) existed partly to continue the education of choristers from the monarch's private chapel when their voices broke. All colleges of this type had chapels, with musicians charged with helping the soul of the founder on its way. Some still do. One college, Eton, earned a notable name in the history of English church music at the turn of the sixteenth century.

All these types of institutions that supported church music survived the Reformation (with certain adjustments), except one: monasteries. Our Prioress would not have learnt to sing the service 'ful weel' after 1536.

Among other places supporting church music of various kinds were a few large parish churches in major cities. Some maintained paid choirs, for example St Mary-at-Hill in Billingsgate, which gave Thomas Tallis his first job in London. In the country, the estate church blurred the distinction between parish and noble household. The local nobleman would appoint the priest, collect the tithe, oversee (perhaps through the good offices of some well-meaning female relative) whatever embryonic schooling the village children received (which might have supplied him with a choirboy or two to add an octave to the Office and sing carols at Christmas), and furnish the building with whatever resources, musical and otherwise, suited his taste. At the Reformation, government commissioners attempting to seize church property were often told they couldn't have it, since it belonged not to the church but to the nobleman whose family put it there in the first place. The church at the bottom of his drive, and its music, was essentially an extension of his household.

Chantries were central to the vitality of liturgical music-making one level below the wealthy choral establishments, and the place where most people might encounter church music in their daily lives. Here, a single priest or monk, or a small group, was paid to sing mass, every day, to honour the local saint and earn credits in the afterlife for the person who built it and left the money to pay him.[26] He was a professional worshipper. It was his job.

An anonymous ballad (later set to music by Benjamin Britten) puts the chantry priest and his music in the context of daily life:

> As it fell on one holy day,
> As many be in the year,
> When young men and maids together did go,
> Their matins and mass to hear.
>
> Little Musgrave came to the church door,
> The priest was at private Mass,
> But he had more mind of the fair women
> Than he had of Our Lady's grace.[27]

The very ordinariness of this opening, the stuff of a thousand popular verses, shows just how conventional this little scene is. It's a feast day, one of many in the church year. Men and maids go together, social considerations prominent, as always, among reasons for going to church. They do not say or sing the service, or attend it, they 'hear' it. This day, as usual, it's matins and mass. Music is plainsong, perhaps with little Musgrave and a couple of local choirboys adding some decorous harmony to the bits they know. Musgrave is late: by the time he arrives the priest is 'at private Mass' of the Virgin, whose 'holy day' it is. Tomorrow's mass may be of the Saviour, the souls of the dead or the local saint: Ethelburgha, Sidwell or Frideswide, whose colours hang over the altar in the brand-new side aisle of his big, light, parish church, familiars closer in spirit to the household gods of the Romans than to the unborn abstractions of Calvin and Luther.

We can meet little Musgrave and his contemporaries through their music. Listen to one of the jazzier Worcester fragments and you can see why singers loved it and the Pope didn't. Yes, it's musically rewarding and great fun. And, yes, you can't hear a single word. Those who, like Wycliffe and Augustine, were more interested in 'that which is sungen' than in 'the song'[28] can be forgiven for believing that this music was more about worldly enjoyment than holy writ: the singer, not the song.

Technically, it was a period of advance and consolidation. Composition was formerly a process of assembling the polyphonic lines of a composition one at a time: take a complete plainsong; then add an upper part to the whole; then, perhaps, a lower part as well. Now, you have to conceive the whole thing together. It's like the difference between the medieval house-builder, adding on an extra room or storey when he needed it so that the house seems to tumble upwards and outwards almost at random, and the confident Renaissance prodigy, imagined all at once in a sunburst of creativity in glass and stone by a proud Elizabethan architect, hungry for reputation, and his rich client, nervously awaiting both his monarch and his bill – Hatfield Old Palace to Hatfield House.

The next hundred years would bring plenty of turmoil in the public realm. But for church music, it was a period of relative stability and considerable achievement. The fifteenth would be a big century.

3

The Fifteenth Century:
Possibilities and Promise

Deo gracias Anglia redde pro victoria.
(give thanks to God for the victory of England)
From the 15th-century 'Agincourt carol'

THE FIFTEENTH CENTURY BOASTS two significant collections of sacred music – one from each end of the century – with perhaps our first big composer in between. No other century shows such an explosion in the range and technical ambition of its sacred art music. There is some discussion about the phases of this developing style, particularly in regard to the musical influences which flowed both ways across the English Channel, and as usual our understanding depends heavily on what has chanced to survive and where, both of the music itself and the writings of contemporaries who were interested in it. What is certain, however, is that this was a period of relative musical and liturgical stability, and that musicians used it to consolidate and advance a distinctive, mature, confident and genuinely English style, much admired in France. By the turn of the sixteenth century, English church music was a thing of substance, with some notable and accomplished composers on its books.

The Old Hall manuscript dates from about 1420.[1] It takes its name from the village of Old Hall Green in Hertfordshire, where it somehow got itself squirrelled away safely in a school until after the Reformation. Like all large collections (1483 pieces), it represents compositional activity over a period of years, perhaps the two decades or so before it was assembled. The distinctively English accent can be discerned developing and growing through this music, in particular an interest in knotty canons and contrapuntal devices. The continuing interchange of musical ideas with the Continent can also be inferred from the inclusion of distinctively French types like isorhythmic compositions. Unlike major sources before and after, most of the pieces are settings of sections of the ordinary of the mass. The layout was also evolving: about half the items put all the voice-parts on the same large page, one above the other, so all the singers could read from one copy, implying a fairly small group. Occasionally a single named voice-part is split into two musical lines, a device known as 'gimell', used to striking effect by the next generation. There is a wedding motet by Thomas Byttering for Henry V's marriage to the French Dauphine, Catherine of Valois, in June 1420 (the one tenderly satirised by Shakespeare for her inability to speak English and Henry's clumsy attempts to woo her in French), and music by the King himself, written under the pseudonym 'Roy Henry' (a bilingual pun on 'Henri Roi').

Henry V is the first in a long list of English monarchs whose personal fingerprints show up in their sacred music. Not only was he a composer, and the object of suitably sycophantic musical offerings on notable occasions like his wedding, he also began the habit of kings taking their choirs on journeys abroad as part of their retinue.

Church music became part of courtly display, partly to show off the artistic and intellectual superiority of the court, and partly to invoke divine approbation for the actions of the Almighty's divinely appointed representative here on earth. Important events like treaties, marriage contracts and the seeing-off of an enemy were celebrated in the monarch's chapel with music. Foreign expeditions would include a body of priests and musicians to sing the daily liturgy. For Henry V, this meant taking the men and boys of the Chapel Royal with him to France, where they sang mass in the open air before the battle of Agincourt.

Little boys singing on a battlefield presents a curious image today.

A mass movement from the 'Old Hall' manuscript (late fourteenth, early fifteenth century). Most of the other music in the collection is on a larger scale than this perfect little miniature.

But this sort of foray always involved a vast caravan of hangers-on, a travelling circus, in some ways as much for show as for actual fighting. Boys were part of the cast. Shakespeare has boys at his Agincourt, commanded by their King to 'Let there be sung *Non nobis* and *Te Deum*'.[2] Their originals were the choristers of the King's own chapel. Their musical descendants are the pipers and drummer-boys pattering out the rhythms of millions of miles of military marches across the centuries, like Vincent Bosse, the little barefoot Frenchman, eagerly feasting on Petya Rostov's vodka and mutton to keep out the cold of Pokrovskoye at the end of *War and Peace*.[3]

The music of Old Hall is tough meat. To today's chorister and congregation, its cerebral canons, complex rhythmic patterns and lack of obvious tonality can make it sound more like the work of a twenty-first-century modernist than part of the sound-world of the Renaissance. The music we sometimes call 'early', the music of William Byrd,

Thomas Tallis and John Taverner, is actually later than we think, comfortingly modern, approachable and familiar. Brave choirs can make a distinctive choral Eucharist, especially for lower voices, by selecting carefully from among the many items in Old Hall, some of which are very short.

Church musicians of all sorts and conditions still received their basic training by learning how to add, first, a part above, then another below, a plainsong. There were rules: the upper part finds a harmony note above the tune; the lower finds a sort of simplified fundamental bass, and both close onto certain permitted consonant intervals at the end of a phrase. Once you knew the rules, you could improvise three-part harmony at sight (what one modern scholar has called 'a sort of medieval jam session'), all reading from the basic plainsong. Manuscripts exist where someone has marked the permitted harmony notes above the plainsong with little dots, no doubt as an aide-memoire to a perhaps unresponsive pupil, so that next time he could get the upper part right without having it written down.

The technique is called 'faburden', and it produces some highly distinctive and characteristic sounds, familiar to the English church musician over several centuries. Parallel harmonies move with the rise and fall of the plainsong, in particular the chains of first-inversion triads, where the upper part is a fourth above the chant, the lower a third below. These sounds are central to the development of English sacred choral music at all levels: the sweet consonances and chains of 6/3 chords created by faburden become the calling-card of English sacred composition through the fifteenth century and beyond. They are present in carols like 'There is no Rose', and in art music like the opening bars of Tallis's *Lamentations*.

In both name and musical content, faburden is closely related to but distinct from its French cousin, *fauxbourdon*. The word is of uncertain etymology: in medieval English 'burden' is the lowest voice of two or three, and may be related to the later use of the word to mean the refrain of a song. Across the Channel, the *bourdon* part of the word has been related to a staff or stick, particularly that of St James, and thus to an organ pipe or wind instrument like a shawm.

Later writers also noted similarities to the words for 'bee' and 'mule' (hence *fauxbourdon* = 'mule's larynx', or 'bagpipe', with its drone bass – ingenious, but certainly not mentioned at the time). *Fauxbourdon*, meaning 'false bass', seems to be a back-formation by later etymologists. The English composite 'faburden' appeared around the turn of the fifteenth century.

As an educational method, faburden was influential and long-lasting. It gave musicians an instinct for harmony and part-singing, and remained in regular use in teaching right through all the polyphonic advances of the Renaissance: Thomas Morley gratefully described its benefits as late as the end of the sixteenth century. Professional musicians were expected to have it: in 1432 the collegiate church at Hemingbrough, Yorkshire, needed a vicar-choral, who would be required, according to the job description, 'to synge a tribull til faburdun'.[4] It also provided a method of making music when only three or four reasonably competent musicians were gathered together, and especially when they didn't have access to expensive part books. Rich foundations could do grand polyphony, remote parishes and chantries had matins and mass chanted by a priest and a clerk, and places whose musical resources lie somewhere in between – a curate, a choirboy and couple of monks – could ornament their liturgy by improvising in faburden from a single copy of the Gradual or antiphoner. The ordinary singers sang the plainchant, the musically trained clerks the faburden (until, that is, the tune goes wrong: the clerks at Faversham in 1506 were told to 'set the choir' on the right pitch, then sing the added parts, until 'where plain song faileth one of them shall leave faburden and keep the plain song unto the time the choir be set again'[5]).

Today's choir has lost the idea that music can be created by the singer, on the spot. To us, music arrives, on paper, already complete and unalterable, from a composer who is probably not present and probably dead. But aurally literate singers, including children, can still do this. Get one of them to sing a song they all know (anything will do), another to add a simple descant by finding the next harmony note above the tune, a third to add a bass by following the harmony and supplying the missing note of the chord, and they will be doing something their medieval forebears did every day. It won't work perfectly, but with a bit of experimentation some of the tune will be coloured in with illuminating harmony. Your choir will be doing something it didn't know it had forgotten how to do.

ONE OF THE ISSUES IN considering the career of John Dunstaple is how to spell his name. We used to call him Dunstable, like the town he probably came from. Modern scholars prefer Dunstaple. His contemporaries used both. Musically, Dunstaple bridges the gap between Old Hall and the Eton Choirbook at the end of the century. He lived from *c.*1390–1453. He has no pieces in the Old Hall collection, though his slightly older contemporary, Leonel Power, with whom he shares some notable musical characteristics, is Old Hall's most represented composer. There is one work by Dunstaple listed in the contents of the Eton book, a testament to his standing a full half-century after his death, though sadly the music has not survived.

Little is known about Dunstaple, but there is enough to testify to his influence, his learning, his status and his importance. He was prized for his skills not just in music but in astronomy and mathematics too (subjects closely allied with music in academic thinking of the time), and enjoyed the generous patronage of several members of the Plantagenet family and court. His music has turned up all over Europe (indeed, more so than in England) and contemporaries made a point of acknowledging the reach of English musical developments. In around 1440 the French poet Martin le Franc wrote praising Burgundian composers for having adopted the English way of writing, in imitation of Dunstaple:

> For they have found a new practice, a way of making sweet
> consonance, in music high and low, in different shades, and rests
> and pauses, and have taken on the English manner, following the
> example of Dunstable. By this method their joyous, noble song is
> made deliciously pleasing.[6]

The Flemish writer on music, Johannes Tinctoris, said a little later, 'in this age the capabilities of our music increased so miraculously that it would seem to be a new art. Of this new art, as I might in fact call it, the English, among whom Dunstable stood out as the greatest, are held to be the source and origin.'[7]

Dunstaple continued and consolidated the process of musical cross-pollination across the Channel, absorbing Northern European ideas like the polytextual motet into his own work, while reflecting more English developments like the increasing use of the sweet-sounding 'imperfect' consonances and the 'major' mode back into continental thinking. He and Leonel Power were also among the first to apply the *cantus firmus* technique to entire mass settings, presenting the plainsong throughout in 'long' notes in the tenor, the words of the ordinary fitted to it, free polyphony composed around it in the other parts. Le Franc neatly lists the features which stand out to him as being distinctively *Angloise*, elements familiar to us already from Worcester and Chaucer: the *frisque concordance*, a fresh, or sweet, use of pleasing harmony; lines both *haulte* and *basse* used to embellish the plainsong; *fainte*, perhaps 'feint', or hints of imitation between voice-parts; *pause*, or silences punctuating the line.

The music of Dunstaple survives into the collection assembled some fifty years after his death for the choir at Eton. Like Wykeham's colleges in Oxford and Winchester, Eton had singing boys on the statutes as part of its foundation. The choirboy is such a central character in this story that it is worth making his acquaintance now.

Several early statutes of choral foundations refer to 'poor boys'. Poor, maybe, but certainly not stupid. Choirmasters recruited them where they could, for their good ear, nice voice and quick intellect – then as now. Grander choirs took boys from more modest ones. Choirmasters' indentures tell us they learned 'Prykenote', that is 'mensural' or 'measured' music which is 'pricked' onto paper, or written down, and 'ffaburdon deschaunte et counter', which are improvised. Sight-singing was crucial: it meant not just reading what is written in front of you, but learning how to add lines to plainsong. Inventories of the earliest choir schools tell us what else was on the curriculum: Whittington's Grammar, Aesop's Fables, Ovid's Metamorphoses. A schoolbook compiled by John Stanbridge, who was headmaster of Magdalen College

School, Oxford, from 1488, has the boys learning Latin in the form of useful, everyday phrases:

Qua voces cantat? What part syngest thou?
Guttur meum est raucus. My throate is hoarse.[8]

Boys at places like Magdalen had domestic duties as well as musical, making beds and waiting at table. They were looked after, too. Records at the best-regulated places include regular requests for payment for lute strings, firewood, shoe leather (winter and summer) and coats, and loaves and ale for breakfast. Some choirs could afford an early proto-type of that notable species, the choir-school matron. Others made the choirmaster deal not just with the music, but also with finding the boys somewhere to live (sometimes with him and his family), getting them places at college or in some upmarket household when their voices broke, nursing them when they were sick and burying them when they died. In return, boys got away from what might be a provincial or poor background into a stimulating educational environment, a relatively well-off organisation and the daily company of like-minded musicians, boys and adults. They learned music to a high level: most, if not all, of the country's leading Renaissance and Baroque composers began life as choirboys, and many were actively composing while still singing treble. This was a thorough, daily, practical immersion in musical theory and practice – learning with and from your friends. As well as music, singing in a choir taught discipline, concentration, comradeship and teamwork. Senior choristers got special privileges – walking on the grass in the cloister or carrying the cross – which their younger col-leagues could aspire to. Some things have changed over the centuries, others not at all.

Grander parish churches ran to something approaching this degree of musical magnificence. St Mary-at-Hill in London 'payd for a pricked song Booke for the chirch' in 1485 (and in 1532 'paid for ij quayres of papur Rial to mende the pryiksong boke xiiij d',[9] which suggests it had plenty of use).

The Eton Choirbook[10] was assembled in the first years of the six-teenth century. Like the Old Hall collection of a century earlier, it represents the high end of musical art during the three decades or so before the pieces were collected and transcribed. Sixty-four of the original ninety-three pieces survive. As with Old Hall, phases of musical style can be discerned: the earlier pieces make much play of textural contrast between sections for full choir and passages for reduced voices; a second phase features *cantus firmus* motets, pushing the older technique of polyphonic lines woven around a plainsong to its limit of length and inventiveness, and beginning to employ that characteristic trick, the 'false relation'; the third tranche moves away from reliance on plainsong and into the more recognisably modern sound-world which led to Tallis and Taverner, with entirely free composition in all parts, nascent imitation, and a greater reliance on a tonal centre growing out of the old plainsong modes.

All but a few of the pieces enthusiastically extol the virtues of the Virgin Mary, often in highly flavoured language, the musical argument draped around the elaborately drawn-out words at considerable length. Voice ranges are extreme. Most of the pieces have four, five or six voice-parts. There is one eight-part piece and one nine-part. One splendid canon, Wylkynson's setting of the Credo, *Jesus autem transiens*, generates thirteen voice-parts at the same time. The increase in range, technique and emotional reach compared with the three-voice mass settings of Old Hall is exponential, the equivalent of the shift from Haydn's orchestra in 1800 to Richard Strauss's in 1900. The music is massive, long, complex and decorative: King's College Chapel in sound.

By this date, all the composers are named, including John Browne, William Cornysh, Robert Fayrfax, Robert Wyilkyinson, Richard Davy and Walter Lambe. Like all large collections, the contents list demonstrates whose reputation is still high from the previous generation: the name of Dunstaple is listed, a full half-century after his death. The era of 'Anon.' and of having to guess the identity of a composer from odd, disconnected bits of evidence is largely (though not entirely) gone. This, together with increasing amounts of biographical information, begins to give us a picture of the lives of these musicians. Like Power and Dunstaple, almost all enjoyed aristocratic patronage, including from the monarch and his family.

Most of the composers were members of the King's own household chapel. They enjoyed high status, getting degrees and doctorates from Oxford and Cambridge, for which they composed submission pieces in a suitably academic style. They occupied high-profile situations. Cornysh, for example, led the Chapel Royal at the gorgeous and elaborate music-making at the Field of the Cloth of Gold in 1520. This was sacred music as international diplomacy, which in this case meant showing off to the French, a hundred years to the day after Thomas Byttering's motet was used for exactly the same purpose at Henry V's wedding celebrations. Men like Cornysh and his contemporary Robert Fayrfax were kept busy in music-making of all kinds at court and were handsomely rewarded for it, often in the form of lordships of manors and prebendal stalls; sinecures with income but no duties. Their works were copied by skilled scribes in handsome volumes, their names displayed with honour. There were gifts and dinners, and even, a little later, pensions for their wives when they died. This pattern of high-level patronage and individual reputation formed the basic employment model for the professional English church musician up until the eighteenth century.

The first phase of the Eton Choirbook collection is represented by pieces like Gilbert Banester's *O Maria et Elizabetha*. The distinctive voice of John Browne appears in the second tranche. The final phase of music, from around the turn of the sixteenth century, is the most brilliant, represented by pieces like Fayrfax's athletic Magnificat and *Gaude Virgo* by Cornysh. Robert Wylkynson's second, nine-voice setting of *Salve regina, Mater misericordiae* (one of fifteen settings of this text in the collection) was copied in later, and is the latest piece included.

One of the great joys of the recent history of church music has been how scholarship and performance practice has allowed much wonderful music to emerge from the historical shadows. John Browne is one of England's finest composers. His haunting *Stabat mater* matches extraordinary harmonic and rhythmic imagination to the plangency of the text. Subtle, fluid changes of texture over long, expressive spans are contrasted with the short, harsh, hammering-in of the nails at 'Crucifige'. Where Browne is mystical, Cornysh provides the brilliance, a pairing comparable to Gibbons and Weelkes in temperament. Fayrfax, more cerebral in character, and Nicholas Ludford (slightly younger and not represented in the Eton book) deserve to be considered in the same company.[11]

The Eton collection shows us, too, just how good the choirs were. Education and daily performance at the Chapel Royal and other similarly well-endowed choral establishments were thoroughly professionalised. Browne's *Stabat iuxta* is in six parts, four tenor and two bass. This was written for no ordinary choir.

For these choirs and their composers, the main musical forms remained broadly consistent in the century and a half before the Reformation, a period of relative musical and liturgical stability which allowed composers to keep doing the same things better and on a larger scale, rather than having to invent entirely new approaches every few years as their descendants would be required to do.

The principal musical forms were the mass, the Magnificat and the antiphon. To later composers, a mass is just a mass, the text always the same, suitable for singing at any celebration through the year. In the fifteenth century, each celebration had a particular theme or object, reflected in musical settings. The most common was the Lady Mass, with music based on one or other of the plainsong tunes associated with the Blessed Virgin, for performance on one of the (many) feast days linked to Mary. Writing a complete Mass 'de Sancta Maria' was a common requirement for the awarding of a university degree. Masses were also dedicated to Jesus Christ, a selection of saints or the souls of the dead.

The Magnificat became the composer's text of choice from the many included in the daily cycle of monastic offices, or 'hours'. Although the routine of nine daily services was complex and demanding, it was never the case that all the services required equally elaborate music. Provision for music varied according to the time of day and, particularly, whether it was a feast day, and, if so, how important. Morning and evening became the musical focus, with moments of musical fellowship before and after the daily chores of running a monastic house. Certainly more music exists for matins, vespers and compline than for the other daily offices. Thus, when Cranmer executed what looks at first like the radical discontinuity of rolling the eight 'hours' into two new English services in the mid-sixteenth century, he was perhaps, at least as far as the music is concerned, as much regularising an existing trend as tearing up the rule book and starting again. At ground level, sudden changes are perhaps not always as sudden as they look.

The antiphon is a devotional text addressed to a particular object of veneration, again most often the Virgin Mary. Other musical forms derived from their position in the liturgy include the Respond, Alleluia, hymns, canticles and psalm verses (all in Latin, of course).

Plainsong was at the heart of composition for choir. In the days of the Worcester fragments, a short phrase might be hewn from plainsong and repeated, without alteration. By the days of Eton, this had evolved into an entire plainsong tune being sung in long, slow notes in one part, usually the tenor, with florid counterpoint woven around it in the other parts. The plainsong, and the technique, are known as *cantus firmus*. Next, composers would pass the plainsong between voice-parts, then borrow parts of the melody and fashion their own tunes out of its distinctive rise and fall, which they would pass between voice-parts in a technique known as 'imitation'. The opening plainsong-based phrase would flow seamlessly into freely composed music. Initially, imitation was a way of decorating the opening of a piece; in the High Renaissance it became a fully integrated feature of musical construction. Finally, composers moved away from plainsong melodies as a basis for their own invention and composed their own tune to each bit of the text. Imitative passages alternated with more block-like, homophonic textures to assemble a large-scale structure, full of variety and contrast. The music was an architectural response to the mood and flow of the words, rather than a way of letting the listener actually hear them.

The choir itself had also taken on a distinctively English flavour. Voice ranges became more extreme. In one sense, sacred choral music grew outwards from the plainsong, adding a part above, then beneath, then more. In England, the voice-parts just kept going, putting the musical spotlight onto two highly distinctive voice types which do not feature so prominently in the music of other countries: the low bass and the high treble. As with purely musical tricks like the 'English' cadence, we can only speculate as to why this particular sonority caught on here. Perhaps composers were writing initially for individual singers with remarkable voices and found they liked the sound, as happened two centuries later with Henry Purcell and his 'stupendious bass', John Gostling. Perhaps it was just the natural instinct to expand the reach and colour of their sound-world. Whatever its origins, the sound of these extreme voice types, often used together in distant duet, is one of the most memorable features of the high-art church music of the late medieval period.

Fayrfax and Cornysh were among the best composers of the generation which saw in the new half-millennium. They brought the high medieval style to its apogee. They also represent the first example of a notable feature of this story, that of composers coming in pairs, their working lives proceeding in parallel and overlapping. This phenomenon provides a fascinating opportunity to examine the same musical world through two different pairs of eyes and ears.

William Cornysh was active in music at court from around 1493. Robert Fayrfax joined the Chapel Royal in 1497. Cornysh was involved in the music at the wedding of Arthur, Prince of Wales, and Catherine of Aragon in 1501. In the same year, Fayrfax took his MusB at Cambridge and his DMus three years later (formally awarded in 1511), earning him the usual style of 'Mr Dr Fayrfax'. Both were at the funeral of Henry VII and coronation of Henry VIII in 1509, Fayrfax by now at the top of the seniority list. Cornysh succeeded him as Master of the Children of the Chapel Royal in 1511 and led them on a propaganda trip to France in 1513. Both men were in France again for the musical junketings at the Field of the Cloth of Gold in 1520. Fayrfax died in 1521; Cornysh in 1523.

Their Latin music shows the heady mixture of a mature inherited tradition with the excitement of experimentation, from Fayrfax's rather old-fashioned interest in number patterns and symmetry to Cornysh's modern, flamboyant, wide-ranging writing in his Magnificat. Fayrfax had the truly creative musician's gift of approaching each piece in a slightly different way, pushing at boundaries and reinventing style as he went: one mass setting presents an entire plainsong tune as a *cantus firmus*; another derives a nine-note ostinato from its plainsong and then presents this in all sorts of inversions and retrogrades, while another has no *cantus firmus* at all. Both men also wrote songs for domestic performance and entertainment, including some with a passing devotional tinge to the words.

They were true Renaissance men – poets, scholars, courtiers and academics; to them the intellectual knots of a puzzle canon or a new-coined bit of imitation were inseparable from the expressive intent of music and words. They were men of the world, too, with good jobs, top pay, and plenty of opportunities for extra income for things like 'setting of a Carrall upon Xmas day', or for 'a boke of Antemys',[12] or providing lute strings and lodgings for the King's choirboys. They were hard-working professionals, performing daily in the King's chapel and dealing with the business end of running a prestigious choir. At the same time they had to negotiate the perilous waters of their times, like everyone else: Cornysh spent time in prison for an unknown offence, during which he indulged in the traditional occupation of a gentleman in such conditions – writing poetry. In it, he calls himself 'Nysshewhete', a pun on his name, where 'corn' has become 'wheat', and the two syllables of the name are transposed.

The music of Fayrfax, in particular, was copied and used for many decades after his death: as for Dunstaple before him, this was a clear sign of his reputation and importance in an age which, often as much for practical as for aesthetic reasons, tended to value the new in its music over the old. Today, Fayrfax and Cornysh have their rightful place in scholarly editions and in the repertoire of specialist ensembles. Occasionally, one or two of their pieces finds its way back to where it was originally intended to live – in choral worship. They deserve it. A few of these pieces, like Cornysh's little *Ave Maria* and Fayrfax's Magnificat 'regale' (for the King), will frighten neither choir nor clergy. Music didn't begin at the Reformation. More than one modern collection calling itself 'Tudor' church music ignores the first two Tudor monarchs, largely or entirely, while including the music of composers like Orlando Gibbons and Thomas Tomkins, who weren't Tudor at all. The first phase of Tudor church music contains some of the best stuff; and certainly among the most distinctive. Nudging our repertoire backwards a little bit will enrich it considerably, as well as shedding light on our appreciation of and approach to the music that came next, the work of Thomas Tallis and William Byrd. An important factor in assessing the sheer range and quantity of the work of William Cornysh is that he almost certainly had the considerable advantage of being two different people. There was a William Cornysh who ran the choir at Westminster Abbey and died around 1502. One later compiler called the composer of three secular songs 'William Cornyssh Junior', though there are no other instances of this appellation. One suggestion is that the elder Cornysh composed the Latin works in Eton and elsewhere, the younger the theatrical items and secular songs for Henry VIII's court, and that they may have been father and son, though the evidence is not completely definitive. Nor are they the only family to throw this particular spanner in the historical works. The Farrant and Mundy families also contributed pluralities of composers to court and choir stall, often with the same given names, creating considerable confusion about who wrote what and held which post when, not to mention the families of foreign musicians like the Bassanos, who provided probably around forty to fifty individuals for the English royal musical service between the fifteenth and the seventeenth centuries.

THE OLD HALL AND ETON collections are visually breathtaking. No future age took such pains to make its music look good. The vivid blues, reds and golds, the gorgeous incipits with their trailing borders of flowers, the capital letters with their squat, Tudor faces staring out at us, are unfaded five and six centuries on. In Old Hall, even the stave lines are red, the notes colour-coded to identify the voice-parts in some mathematically contrived canon, the same principle of visual cues used by Osmund and the Normans to help poor, confused English monks find their way around the massive books of Sarum plainsong in the years following the Conquest.

This period saw the appearance of a distinctively English off-shoot of the main tradition, sharing some of its characteristics, but in a more approachable form, a sort of Dunstable's little brother: the fifteenth-century carol. The carol, in the sense of a seasonal piece, usually cheerful in character, had existed within both the composed and the folk traditions for as long as those traditions can be traced. By the fifteenth century, the style of the manuscripts gives some clue to the social status which this music had achieved. While the music of Eton is transcribed with the greatest artistic skill onto single folios bound together, the thirteen carols in the manuscript preserved at Trinity College, Cambridge, are on a long bit of parchment, rolled around a stick at each end.[13] This was a song-sheet, owned and used by a minstrel or town wait at a fair or revel, or perhaps, given the provenance of the source, by students at some dinner or Twelfth Night knees-up, with timbrels and dances, psalteries and lutes, bagpipes and loud cymbals. The carols are in English, with occasional words or phrases in Latin dropped in, known as 'macaronic' poetry. The carols are cast in verse-and-refrain format, in two or three parts. The music uses the parallel harmonies gleaned from its more learned brethren, but they are short, easy and characterful, the repeating refrain perhaps picked up by the listeners as they went along: 'There is no rose of such virtue, as is the rose that bare Jesu'. The solo voices elaborated the imagery in the intervening verses: 'For in that rose contained was, heaven and earth in little space. *Res Miranda*.'

There was plenty of music for the organ, too. This was a small instrument of up to forty-six notes. An organ would be placed at a particular altar for the ceremonies held there, so that a larger parish church might have two organs of different sizes, the smaller for Lady Mass at the chantry altar in the side aisle, the larger for daily use in the nave. Bigger churches had more organs – Durham Cathedral had five. The organ didn't accompany the voices. One of the singers would move to the keyboard to rattle off an increasingly elaborate voluntary at certain fixed points during the service (not after, as became the custom later). Organ music also had a specifically liturgical function. A psalm would alternate between choir and organ, singers taking the odd-numbered verses and the organist adding a frilly little improvisation on the psalm tone in place of the even-numbered verses. This added variety, gave the singers a pause for breath, and helped set and keep pitch. It also meant, of course, that half the words of any given psalm were missed out, which rather reduces the devotional point, as well as making something of a nonsense of meaning and grammar, at least in some cases. Apparently this didn't matter.

Devotional music was sung in the noble home, around the fire or with household musicians in the privy chamber on a winter's evening. A couple of large collections of domestic music from the middle part of Henry VIII's reign[14] include the occasional canon on 'Sing we to God', a macaronic Christmas piece or Passion carol, alongside lots of love songs and plenty of 'trolly-lolly-lo'. Sacred choral music in the home became much more prevalent in the Elizabethan period, partly because of the large diaspora of trained musicians who had formerly worked in monasteries and were then released into the community, looking for a job and somewhere to live.

Further down the social scale, the peasant and the porter had their almost-devotional music too: working-songs and drinking-songs calling down the aid of their favourite saint to make their drudgery divine. There are no manuscript sources for this type of music. An oral tradition, by definition, leaves no footprints. But later, when folk-songs did start to be written down, it is apparent that there was plenty of Christian imagery muddled up with the pagan and all sorts of other influences in these texts, and that they are part of an ancient and continuous tradition. This, for example, was current enough to be written down in the reign of Henry VIII:

Westron wynde, whan wilt thow blow?
The smal rain down doth raine.
Cryst, yf my love were in myn armes,
And I in my bed againe.

The holy name is invoked almost incidentally, to call down aid upon – in this case – a quick cuddle under the sheets. Nor is it surprising to hear our illiterate peasant praying and hymning his way to making hay of either kind. Religion and daily life, like religion and politics, were not different – they were aspects of the same thing. Everything you did began and ended with an invocation to Saint or Virgin: greeting your neighbours, signing off your accounts, sitting down to a meal, sneezing, feeding your animals. Worship was like sex and farming: an instinct, and a necessity. You had to learn how to do it, but you didn't have to have an opinion about it, or even think about it, still less question it. These things just are.

A shared infatuation links the texts of the Eton book with the Trinity carols and much else besides: the Virgin Mary. Mary was everywhere in pre-Reformation England. Her cult softened the stern, masculine character of Christian iconography, and poets, painters, musicians, glass-makers, sculptors in wood and stone and makers of rood-lofts lavished on her the sort of personal devotion that Moses could only dream of. Kings and choirboys would go about their daily lives under her watchful protection, singing their love songs to the vulnerable young mother of God.

As the Reformation approached, English religion was at ease with itself. This was the last moment when everyone believed the same things. Continental reformers had not yet begun to dismantle the old certainties. Musically, this meant substantial, sometimes sumptuous polyphony in well-established and well-funded organisations. Choral music was woven into the ancient plainsong fabric of the Sarum Rite: much of the rest of the liturgy was sung to plainsong by ministers and choir, and the tunes, with their atavistic associations with text and feast, were bound into the choir's music; sometimes with plainsong verses of a hymn or canticle alternating with polyphony, sometimes with the plainsong buried deep inside the polyphonic texture or hinted at in points of imitation, sometimes all of these. Parish churches would imitate the music of their cathedral or monastery according to their resources. Music formed part of the training and inheritance not just of the professional but of monks, nuns, chantry priests, parish clerks and choirboys. Their music was heard not just in the regular, ancient cycle of services in church, but in Rogationtide and saints' day processions around the parish and in theatrical spectaculars in the town square.

Minstrels and artisans had their musical devotions too. Snatches of liturgy and devotional songs were whistled and sung all the time in streets and courts and behind shuttered casements, and the shepherd in his field sang out to his saint as often and as unselfconsciously as he did to his dog: seven whole days, not one in seven. And the authorities, of course, wanted to control this as well as every other aspect of religious observance. 'Wolde God', wrote Myles Coverdale in 1538, 'that our Mynstrels had none other thyng to play upon, neither our carters and plowmen other thyng to whistle upon, save psalms, hymns, and such like godly songes ... And if women at the rockes, and spynnynge at the wheles, had none other songes to passe their tyme withal than such as Moses's sister songe before them, they shold be better occupied.'[15]

What were these people like? They were like us. Some were as sophisticated as any musicians of any age, anywhere. Some no doubt were beginning to relish the music for its own sake. Some enjoyed the status and comforts it brought them. Many felt safe in the comforting familiarity of songs they had known since before they could read. There was music, too, for the many who had never learned to read, and never would, and would probably prefer to fart their way into heaven. All believed what they sang without question.

Labels can obscure as much as they reveal. The term 'Middle Ages' sounds like a barren desert between two oases of sophistication, like the Middle West of the United States. If the word 'Renaissance' includes the making of things of beauty with enthusiasm, skill and the highest possible art, then it started the moment the Romans left: indeed, it never really stopped, apart perhaps from occasional little local unpleas-antnesses with Vikings or Cromwells. 'The Reformation', too, sounds like an event. If anything, it was more a process – or, perhaps, several events and several processes, which in some ways are still being played out. Musically, the revolutionary idea of the Reformation was that you could sing to your God yourself in church, not just listen to a trained initiate do it for you in a secret, private language which he understood and you didn't. This idea is rooted in doctrine, and creates a divide which runs from before the Reformation and forward for the rest of this history, between music written for and by the trained professional, and music meant for anybody, anytime, anywhere. To some extent, the musical divide remains to this day, between the robed choir in one parish and the music group in the next. Ask the musical historian 'what were the long-term effects of the Reformation?', and you might get the answer given by Zhou Enlai when he was asked the same question about the French Revolution: 'It's too early to tell'.[16]

So as the 1520s gave way to the 1530s, and Henry VIII was looking around for new ways to amuse himself, English church music was in good voice. Friars and choirs had learnt how to make some of the most exquisite sacred harmonies ever heard in these islands. But you didn't necessarily need a friar to sing to your God.

Chaucer would certainly have agreed with that.

4

Keeping your Head: the Approach of the Reformation, 1509–1547

To see how English would do in song.

Thomas Cranmer

IN 1528, TWO STUDENTS were led down to a dungeon beneath a chapel in Oxford and left there to die. In 1543, three men were lashed to a pyre in a field near Windsor and put to death by burning.

Such cruelty becomes depressingly familiar as the century grinds on. However, for the historian of church music these two events have something interesting in common. In each case, another man was tried along with the poor unfortunates. In each case, this lucky individual escaped punishment. In each case, this person was a musician.

When Thomas Wolsey founded Cardinal College in Oxford, one of his first employees was the most important composer of the generation immediately preceding the Reformation, John Taverner. Born around 1490, his earliest known employment was at the collegiate church at Tattershall, Lincolnshire, which had a large choir and active musical tradition. He was in Oxford by 1526, leading the costly devotions at Wolsey's new college. Two years later, in a show trial staged by the Dean and others, John Clarke, John Frith and Taverner were 'founde to be heretikes', and were 'cast into a pryson of the College where salt fysh lay, through the stinke whereof they al being infected, the saide clerke being a tender yong man … died therein'. Taverner, 'although hee was accused and suspected for hyding of Clarkes bookes vnder the boardes in his schole, yet the Cardinall for hys Musicke excused hym, saying, that he was but a Musician, and so he escaped'.[1] Lucky man.

John Marbeck came even closer to entering the house and gate of heaven rather earlier than he might have wished. He was born around 1505, making him part of the last generation to learn their art under the old, pre-Reformation dispensation, and became a singer and organist at St George's Chapel, Windsor. One mass setting and two antiphons by Marbeck survive: flamboyant, melismatic, full of contrast and word-emphasis, using *cantus firmus* and occasional imitation – the pieces are good Catholic stuff. On 16 March 1543, his house was searched and some writings of Calvin, copied by Marbeck, were seized. Two days later he was summoned before the Privy Council. The next day he was sent to prison. The charge against him was that he had described the mass, to which he had contributed with such skill and devotion just a few years earlier, as 'pollutyd difformyd sinfull and open robery of the glory of God … and that certayne and sure it is that Christ himselfe is made in this masse mens laughinge stocke'.[2] In similar circumstances to Taverner's, the Dean of St George's acted as judge, jury and executioner, along with various bishops and others whom he later described, with a touch of unintentional gallows humour, as 'good woorkers for my dispatch'.[3] They condemned Marbeck to die. But on 4 October 1543, some weeks after his co-accused had gone to the flames, a full pardon was issued to 'Johes Marbeck de nova Wyndesour in com Berks Organplayer'.

The history of these two very different men sheds some light on the business of making music in a perilous time. For a start, musicians couldn't afford to get caught with the wrong books, any more than anyone else could. However, to be condemned to die your behaviour had to stray into the territory of the treasonable or the seditious. Nobody was executed just for writing music: Taverner, after all, was 'but a Musician'. In addition, they were given some degree of protection because their musical skills were of value to the employer, both for personal pleasure and worldly status: thus Wolsey pardoned Taverner 'for his music'. This consideration for musicians became increasingly important as the sixteenth century went on, especially for composers with a Catholic background. They were also to a certain extent bound into the establishment: Marbeck owed his life to the influence of Bishop Gardiner. Later composers (again, especially Catholics) were careful to cultivate important friends.

Further insights into the lives of composers at the time can be gleaned from what these two men did next. In Taverner's case there is a scarcity of hard evidence, but he appears to have returned to Lincolnshire and joined the choir at St Botolph's, Boston, until the elaborate and expensive choral music there was discontinued in the later 1530s. He doesn't seem to have held any further musical appointments after that. Opportunities, and perhaps enthusiasm, for magnificent Catholic music were evaporating. What did you do when your life's work suddenly became the object of official disapproval and your job vanished? John Foxe tells us that 'this tauerner repented hym very much that he had made songes to popish ditties in the tyme of his blyndness',[4] and some much-repeated accounts have him actively involved in the degradation of religious houses. Neither allegation has any basis whatever in evidence, but they do illustrate some of the currents swirling around the composer at this time. It is certainly true that he personally corresponded with Thomas Cromwell about the burning in 1538 of the rood-screen (that most East Anglian of medieval glories) at St Botolph's. He seems to have had, or to have learnt, the ability to adapt his lifestyle, as much as his musical style, to changing circumstances, and to have staged like Shakespeare a graceful semi-retirement into the comfortable pursuits of a prosperous local worthy, spectacles on nose and pouch on side, away from active participation in musical life and its attendant dangers of getting on the wrong side of the doctrinal fence, ending up as an alderman honoured with a burial plot under the celebrated Boston Stump, the splendid tower of St Botolph's. He played the game.

Marbeck, unlike Taverner, was undoubtedly guilty of a deep and close involvement with reformist theological thought. As well as the text copied from the writings of 'the greate Clerke' Calvin, he had written his own concordance to the English Matthew Bible of 1537, a vast undertaking which was 'taken from me and utterly lost' at the time of his trial. He later wrote the whole thing out again, shortening it (to 900 pages) to make it more affordable. He made a celebrated musical setting of parts of the 1549 Book of Common Prayer, then devoted himself to authoring tracts with titles like *The Rippinge up of the Popes Fardell*, which leave little room for doubt where his allegiances lay. Unlike Taverner, he was unambiguous in his rejection of his earlier pursuit of 'the study of Musike and plaiyng Organs, wherin I consumed vainly the greatest part of my life'. But he kept his job at Windsor (playing organs), and his sons became pillars of the Elizabethan ecclesiastical and academic establishment.

Forces are at work here. Each composer brought his own baggage of background and belief and each accommodated himself as best he could to the latest blast of the doctrinal trumpet. This involved doing at least some of what your employer told you, even if your own musical and religious instincts were heading in a different direction. There is a touch of The Vicar of Bray (the original, incidentally, witnessed the Windsor burnings) about these men: 'And this is law, I will maintain unto my Dying Day, Sir. That whatsoever King may reign, I will be the Vicar of Bray, Sir!'

Surviving and prospering through the turbulent years of the Reformation took considerable skill at the dangerous Tudor game of human chess, and these men were good at it. Taverner and Marbeck both died peaceful and prosperous at a good age. So did those two later great standard-bearers of Catholic music, Tallis and Byrd (despite, in Byrd's case, sailing pretty close to the wind on occasion). So did William Hunnis, Protestant and musician, who became embroiled in a bizarre plot, involving the use of alchemy, to murder Mary I. You needed to know how far you could go, when to keep your head down, and what to do if you got into trouble.

You needed to be adaptable, too, musically as well as personally. But it would be a mistake to think that each phase in the Reformation was matched by a sudden and complete change of musical lifestyle – by everybody, all at the same time. This was a war, and like all wars, as well as dispatches from the musical front line, there was a great deal of low-level muddling through, getting on with it, adapting, getting by. The musical big boys invented new kinds of music in response to changing conditions, but, perhaps to a surprising degree, they carried elements of their pre-Reformation training and practice with them into the music of the reformed church, and indeed back again. This became particularly noticeable during the periods of religious restriction under Edward VI and Elizabeth I. At ground level, as well, things changed, but things stayed the same too: you might sing less, on fewer occasions, with fewer musicians, but you still sang, and some of your services and their music remained recognisable: scaled down, sung less often, with some of the words and the language changed, but still there.

Like most human activity, worship and its music are largely governed by habit. This Reformation was an insurrection by the government against its own people, a war waged by Injunction, Ordinance and Visitation, with the added complication that the government kept changing sides. It is perhaps not surprising that each change was followed by a certain amount of confusion and delay – waiting for the latest Injunction, trying to work out what it meant, and watching its uneven progress around different parts of the country, with their diverse regional characteristics and traditions. The Tudor musician, ever the pragmatist, did his best to carry on being true to his inheritance and beliefs, while at the same time not getting into trouble, at least until the next change came along.

With the Reformation, English church music hit puberty. Before this, you didn't have to think about whether you accepted the authority of the Pope, or if the Virgin Mary answered your prayers: Mum and Dad were always right. Afterwards, there was a period of rapid experimentation, and a series of associations with partners of wildly varying character, none of which – perhaps fortunately – lasted very long. Eventually, church music settled into a more stable, long-term relationship with the new orthodoxy that grew from the Elizabethan settlement. Something had been lost too. There was a coherence, a prelapsarian innocence, about late medieval English religion. But there were also a lot of nursery stories, childish things, which needed to go. Change was necessary.

Music was never a principal component of the intellectual case for reform in England. Rather, it was affected when the structures which supported it, both physical and intellectual, started to be dismantled. Government commissioners did not ride into town demanding the end of sacred music: rather, they required the end of idolatry to the saints and they wanted the money which paid for the local monastery and its choir. The music disappeared along with these things. Music was collateral damage, as art often is in war. Broadly speaking, the forces of the Reformation made their mark on English church music in three main ways: changes to the liturgy and rules for the use of music; the loss of existing books and manuscripts; and the destruction of choirs and worshipping communities.

In the last years of Henry VIII's reign, despite the widespread appearance of English primers and the placing of an English Bible in every church, the musical liturgy was still that of the Roman church. Musically, there was calm before the storm. But the winds were gathering force and, once again, the ripples on the musical surface give us an insight into the currents which were beginning to rage and swell beneath.

For the professional composer writing for a professional choir, the main musical forms were those which had been pre-eminent for the last century and a half: the mass, in its various types; the Magnificat; and the antiphon, with a wide range of other types of choral composition available, as befitted the mature, ancient, complex musical liturgy. Musical style was elaborate and architectural, a syllable extended in eternal melisma, punctuated with rests, a plainsong melody often anchoring the music in 'long' notes in an inner part. There was rarely any real attempt to deliver the actual text with anything approaching clarity or directness. The choral antiphon would be addressed to Mary above all others. The evening hymn in her honour, '*Salve regina*', or one of the other great texts, had long been part of daily life in monastery, college and church, and was sometimes even sung around the streets to call down a blessing on your neighbour's door. When composers brought them indoors, they were slotted, like other polyphonic items, into the appropriate place in the liturgy, where their music emerged organically out of the plainchant of the Sarum Rite.

Intimations of a simpler style appear throughout the pre-Reformation period, but must be approached with care. In 1519, after a visit to Cambridge, Erasmus articulated the reformers' usual objections to the Catholic style: 'Modern church music is so constructed that the congregation cannot hear one distinct word. The choristers themselves do not understand what they are singing, yet according to priests and monks it constitutes the whole of religion.'[5] In 1519 Wolsey said that monasteries should be places 'where no lascivious melody seduces the ear of the bystander, nor worldly praise and favour sought through the division of notes ... [and] the split or broken song commonly called "Pricksong" in English ...', preferring 'modest and plain song'.[6]

As well as a possible indication of a potential move towards a new musical style, this could be just another example of the sort of criticism that had been bubbling along for centuries, of 'lascivious' (that word again) melodies divided into lots of notes. Or maybe Wolsey was just trying to assert central control over a powerful sector in society, and music, not for the last time, was a convenient whipping boy. Perhaps he was just trying to make sure the best choir around was his own, which certainly got him into trouble with the King a few years later.

Among other possible indicators of a shift in style was a particular kind of mass composition, which was smaller in scale and more modest in demand. These were based on a striking variety of musical themes and compositional principles. There were the *Western Wind* masses of Taverner, Christopher Tye and John Sheppard, based on a popular song; plainsong masses by Taverner and Sheppard; pieces based on the older principles of pre-worked mathematical plans, like Nicholas Ludford's three-part setting; masses 'Upon the Square', a kind of mathematical *cantus firmus*, by William Whitbroke and others (found in the Gyffard Part Books, probably copied out in the 1550s); pieces incorporating snatches of polyphony borrowed from elsewhere in an early form of 'parody' technique, such as Taverner's *In nomine* mass; and some with no external musical material incorporated at all.

Perhaps most striking of all, versions of Latin Mass settings appeared with the words translated into English and shoe-horned uncomfortably onto the original vocal line. Parts of two of Taverner's masses were arranged in this way.

Whether Taverner contributed or not to an upswell of musical reform, either deliberately by simplifying his own style or unwittingly in having his music adapted to English words, Marbeck certainly did. Leaving the Catholic style far behind, he wrote an approachable little carol in three parts, in English, *A Virgin and Mother*, which formed a neat stylistic halfway house between his earlier polyphonic Latin music and the total simplification of his music for the Book of Common Prayer of 1549 – the composer as professional, and as pragmatist.

Assessing these smaller-scale works as evidence of a concerted move towards a simpler style is not entirely straightforward. There are relatively few of them, and there is a big caveat about dates: in a period of rapid change and dodgy survival rates among manuscripts it is often difficult to be sure if a particular source belongs definitively to a particular phase of liturgical and political reform and, therefore, how accurately it reflects the forces at work on the composer at the time. Motivation is difficult to assess as well. It is possible that composers wrote in a simpler style just because they wanted to (these were artists who were perfectly capable of looking at their art in new ways as they went along, and of talking to each other about it), or for practical reasons: the longer pieces were for big occasions with large choirs, and the shorter pieces weren't.

It is certainly possible to identify a trend towards a more direct style of composition in the mid to later part of Henry VIII's reign. However, it is conjecture to infer that this trend was a response by composers to an increasing general interest in reformist ideas. Big changes to the liturgy only kicked in after Henry's death.

Alongside this slimmed-down music for the old rite is music for the new English service books. Thomas Wriothesley, Lord Chancellor, noted the singing of an English Te Deum by a group 'called by Papists the new sect'.[7] One manuscript, probably 'pricked' for a London church of middling musical magnificence, sets canticle texts from the

English primers of 1535, 1539 and 1545. The caveat about dating music applies again, but the fact that there is music to each successive translation implies that the music was composed at the same time as the various versions of the words, i.e. during the last decade-and-a-bit of Henry VIII's reign. Myles Coverdale published his *Goostly Psalmes* in English, with single-lined music based heavily on existing melodies from Lutheran, Sarum and other sources, but although this early foray into vernacular psalm-singing was an attempt at perhaps the most important development of all, it was a false start: politics intervened, and Coverdale's book fell from favour, along with its patron and promoter, Thomas Cromwell.

A little further afield, it was rumoured that an English version of the mass was being held in villages north of London. The Litany, a sequence of prayers for singing in procession, was certainly translated in 1544. Wriothesley noted the impact of this change: on 24 September 1545 there was a solemn sermon at St Paul's, 'the bishoppe of London in procession, his pontificalibus singing Te Deum'. On 18 October, just three and a half weeks later, 'Paules quire song the procession in English by the Kinges injunction, which shall be song in everie parish church throughout Englande everie Soundaie and festival daie and non other.'[8] Henry VIII gave his reasons in a letter to Cranmer: the people 'have come very slackly to the Procession' because 'they understood no part of such prayers or suffrages, as were used to being sung and said'.[9] So Cranmer obediently had the Litany sung in English, to the same tunes to which it was formerly sung in Latin. The trick was to hang onto melodies which people already knew – or at least their flavour – but put the words in their own language. A simple idea, but revolutionary in effect, it led directly to the work of Marbeck and thence to every English parish and prayer book from that day to this. Cranmer put it better than anyone (as usual) in his famous letter to Henry VIII, and it is worth quoting in full:

> It may please Your Majesty to be advertised that, according to Your
> Highness' commandment, sent unto me by Your Grace's secretary,
> Mr. Pagett, I have translated into the English tongue, so well
> as I could in so short time, certain processions to be used upon

festival days if after due correction and amendment of the same Your Highness shall think it so convenient. In which translation, forasmuch as many of the processions in the Latin were but barren, as me seemed, and little fruitful, I was constrained to use more than the liberty of a translator: for in some processions I have altered divers words; in some I have added part; in some taken part away; some I have left out whole, either for because the matter appeared to me to be little to purpose, or because the days be not with us festival days; and some processions I have added whole because I thought I had a better matter for the purpose than was the procession in Latin.

The judgment whereof I refer wholly unto Your Majesty, and after Your Highness hath corrected it, if Your Grace command some devout and solemn note to be made thereunto (as it is to the procession which Your Majesty hath already set forth in English) I trust it will much excitate and stir the hearts of all men unto devotion and godliness.

But in my opinion, the song that should be made thereunto would not be full of notes, but, as near as may be, for every syllable a note, so that it may be sung distinctly and devoutly as be in the matins and evensong Venite, the hymns, Te Deum, Benedictus, Magnificat, Nunc Dimittis, and all the psalms and versicles; and in the mass Gloria in excelsis, Gloria Patri, the Credo, the Preface, the Pater Noster, and some of the Sanctus and Agnus. As concerning the Salve festa dies, the Latin note, as I think, is sober and distinct enough, wherefore I have travailed to make the verses in English and have put the Latin note unto the same.

Nevertheless, they that be cunning in singing can make a much more solemn note thereto. I made them only for a proof, to see how English would do in song. But because mine English verses lack the grace and facility that I wish they had, Your Majesty may cause some other to make them again that can do the same in more pleasant English and phrase. As for the sentence, I suppose it will serve well enough.

Thus Almighty God preserve Your Majesty in long and prosperous health and felicity!

From Bekisbourne, the 7th of October
Your Grace's most bounden chaplain and beadsman,

T. Cantuarien
To the King's most excellent Majesty[10]

Here is yet another tilt at that clerical straw-man, the 'song … full of notes'. Here, too, is an interesting early promotion of 'matins and evensong' as the main musical meals of the day once Cranmer has put English church music on a diet.

But change doesn't often go in a straight line. Henry VIII was a complex and contradictory figure. In many ways, he was a conservative. Alongside his various reasons for demanding changes of governance and doctrine in the church (power, money and sex, mostly), he insisted on keeping the old liturgies of the Sarum Rite. The last part of his reign can be read as something of a reactionary period.

Even while English bibles and primers were appearing everywhere by official decree, Henry continued to stage public celebrations of the 'Masse of the Holy Ghoste, with Te Deum', to mark notable public events like military victories or to suck up to some desirable foreign royal. Such events continued right through to the end of his reign, and indeed beyond: when he died, choirs sang him to his rest in the Requiem Mass, with Dirges, in the traditional, time-honoured Catholic way. This was church music as political theatre, with royal authority appropriating all the trappings of the old papal dispensation, music included.

Cranmer's late attempts at further reform got nowhere. He tried, in the last couple of years of Henry's reign, to push through more changes with musical import, including monthly rather than weekly cycles of psalm-singing, and two main services each day rather than eight. But even though this was all part of a Latin Breviary, not the fully reformed English prayer book where these ideas eventually saw the light of day, he failed to get them through. Perhaps by this stage the King was more concerned with the state of his leg than the state of his church. Change occurs in stop-start phases as well as by crossing lines in the sand.

Certainly, the Injunctions imposed on the music at Rochester Cathedral in 1543 have a distinctly old-fashioned feel to them: '… the master of the choristers shall be at Mattins, Mass, and Evensong in all double feasts and ix lessons, and shall himself keep the organs at the same feasts ... And he to cause the choristers to sing an anthem after every Compline in every work-day. And ... to have the organs played in Commemoration ... the priests, clerks and choristers, with the master of the choristers, shall sing every even and day of feasts duplex, minus duplex, maius ac duplex et principalis duplex. And every holy-day in the year an anthem in pricksong ... on work-days the choristers shall sing the Lady mass in pricksong with the organs ...'[11] This was exactly the sort of stuff the reformers wanted rid of. No sign here of Cranmer's move towards simplification.

Away from the centre, church music around the country reveals a similar pattern of some movement towards reform in the second half of the 1530s, followed by a period of official reaction as the authorities struggled to control the genie they had unwittingly uncorked. Unsurprisingly, at ground level there was the usual mixture of conformity, confusion, disobedience, disagreement and delay. The 1530s saw the appearance of a great many English primers, or service books. Typically, the King tried to standardise the 'almost innumerable soorts'[12] of books, and the music that went with them, into one, the *King's Primer* of 1545. Leading up to this, each phase of reform included its musical action and reaction.

In 1536 an Act abolished many of the cherished old feast days, much marked in music. Priests now had to 'teatch their parishiones the "Pater Noster", "Avee" and "Creede" ... in our maternall English tonge'. An Order of 1537 told the vicars-choral of Ripon to stop spending so much time in the pub. The rather more hard-line 1538 Injunctions kicked the old saints out of the Litany altogether, because the people 'had no time to sing the good suffrages'.[13] The Ave bell, rung to buy time off purgatory, was silenced too, another banished voice of the familiar old musical order. A 1541 Proclamation made vivid record of the musical element of the colourful old folk ceremonies of the boy bishop and the Lords of misrule: '... children be strangely decked and apparelled to counterfeit priests, bishops and women, and so be led with songs and dances from house to house ... and boys do sing mass and preach in the pulpit'.[14] Here was another link between the old liturgical drama and the new choirboy plays. Here, too, was another example of the best description coming from the person who is trying to put a stop to it, in this case Cranmer: these superstitious frivolities are to be 'left and clearly extinguished'.

Next, Bishop Stephen Gardiner's Act of 1543 'for the Advancement of the True Religion' took aim at music with a religious content outside church, particularly 'printed ballads, rhymes, etc.', whereby 'malicious minds' intend 'subtilly and craftily to instruct His Highness' people, and specially the youth of this his realm, untruly. For reformation whereof, His Majesty considereth it most requisite to purge his realm of all such books, ballads, rhymes, and songs, as be pestiferous and noisome'.[15] (Interestingly, Gardiner made some specific exceptions, including the works of Chaucer, which can get pretty pestiferous at times and aren't always entirely suitable for the edification of youth, at least not about the things which Bishop Gardiner, the Mary Whitehouse of the 1540s, had in mind.)

Reactions to the new measures were mixed. The Vicar of Rye responded to the 1536 abolition of saints' days by ignoring it and simply carrying on celebrating them as he always had, 'with solemn singing, procession and decking of the church'.[16] Conversely, some reform-minded parsons took their parishes beyond even legal requirements and refused to sing the Litany at all, in any language. Others stuck to their reactionary guns and carried on with their Latin, like the parson of Ripple, who told his people, 'I am commanded to show you the paternoster in English: you may do as you will in learning of it, but it is against my opinion,' adding rather expressively, 'I liken the paternoster in English to the hard shell of a nut and the paternoster in Latin to the sweet kernel.'[17] Some parishes had differences of opinion within the same congregation, their neighbourly disputes about doctrine and practice sounding pretty much like any other family row.

Between the extremes there was creative compromise. Many of the primers took the halfway road favoured by Cranmer and later by Marbeck in keeping the shape, meaning and liturgical function of a particular text but simply rendering it in an English version, redirected towards an approved object of veneration. *Salve regina* became *Hail, Holy*

King. By keeping some of the rhythm of the words, the translators were presumably encouraging people by implication to sing it to the same tune as before, or a variant of it. Things change, but things stay the same.

The 1545 primer was an attempt to consolidate all the various forces of reform and reaction acting on the liturgy and its music into one common position. It contained a prayer by Erasmus, who, a quarter of a century earlier, had so elegantly articulated the principal problem with the old church music (you can't hear the words). Erasmus used an appropriately musical metaphor for the church of 1545, where there is 'no agreement of opinions, but as it were in a misordered quire, euery man singeth, a contrary note'.[18] This is not a bad description of the mixed messages reaching the English church musician of the 1540s, at all levels of society. Worse was to come.

IT IS OFTEN DIFFICULT to assess the provenance and importance of the manuscripts we have. It is even more difficult with the ones we don't have. One thing is certain: there are lots of them. Manuscripts can vanish for a number of reasons. First, if authorities like Bishop Gardiner didn't want you to have something, then it was better not to have it. Second, there was simply no point keeping music you weren't allowed to sing. Third (as always), practicalities: paper was valuable, and could be re-used for something else. Fourth, it was a long time ago, and many have just got lost. One parish had its books eaten by rats during an outbreak of plague. Others were raided by illumination-hunters in the nineteenth century.

To survive, then, a manuscript needed to pass through the hands of the opportunistic, the thrifty or the bloody-minded. It definitely needed a good slice of luck. Even long before the Reformation, some manuscripts came down to us through the prudent efforts of some conscientious medieval recycler. One of the Worcester fragments was found stuffed into an organ pipe to cure a cypher. Three Kyries by Dunstaple were cut in half and used as flyleaves for a printed book and music by Dunstaple and others was used to form the binding of a psalter. An anonymous mass setting was used by a lawyer's clerk in Coventry to hold a handful of legal records together.

Who the music belonged to matters as well. The Tudor age is lit-
tered with the corpses of wealthy and cultured men who fell out of
favour, and when they did, their libraries as much as their lands and
titles were up for grabs. If they happened to end up somewhere reasonably safe, like a university, or in some sufficiently remote castle where
the family liked music, such as Arundel in Sussex, then a book of music
might find itself tucked away discreetly on a shelf or in a chest, or possibly under the floorboards, and just stay there.

Other books survived as a result of people's disobedience. Many
who were ordered to hand in or destroy or degrade their liturgical books
simply didn't. In 1539 Myles Coverdale found a great many unaltered
'popish books'[19] in the nest of sylvan popery between Newbury and
Henley-on-Thames (which includes Stonor Park, host to many later
country-house Catholics from Edmund Campion to Graham Greene).
Some people followed the letter but not the spirit of the new rules.
Ordered to obliterate the Pope and saints from their books of music,
they conformed by scoring the faintest possible diagonal line across the
page, leaving text and music perfectly legible, or by gumming a little
bit of paper gently over the offending name so that it could be (and
indeed was) simply taken off again when the old ways came back, as
they surely would (and indeed did).[20]

The parish church of St Helen's, Ranworth, near Norwich, still
plays proud host to its jaw-droppingly beautiful antiphonal of about
1440–80. The Mass of the Nativity is written out to elaborate Sarum
plainsong, with all the tropes and graduals and other texts proper to the
feast. The child Jesus appears in a sunburst inside the illuminated initial
letter. Notes, staves, haloes and flowers appear in gorgeous greens and
reds and blues, half a millennium after they were made.[21] The pages
dedicated to St Thomas Becket have faint pen-lines running across
them, corner to corner, top to bottom, made under the watchful eye of
some commissioner sent from London, who was trying, as others had
tried before, to get rid of Becket once and for all. The crossings-out
are as effectual as the day they were put there – not at all. Somebody
made this book. Among the great many musically trained individuals
who lost their careers at the Reformation were scribes and copyists,

patiently practising their penmanship in monastery or workshop, collecting and mixing their precious pigments, perched on a high stool, peering at parchment – artists and artisans, eternally anonymous.

Mostly, survival of a piece of music is just luck. Who knows how the Old Hall manuscript ended up in a school in Hertfordshire? Who knows why some of the Eton music survived and some didn't? These handsome volumes make it only too painfully apparent what has been lost. Like the lowering walls of some destroyed monastery looming Ozymandias-like over its muddy English field, the sheer scale and beauty of the fragments we have reveal just how impressive the tradition of sacred art-music really was at the beginning of the sixteenth century, and just how chancy the business of survival has been in the years since. Hungry Etonians of the 1540s may not have actually used the *cantoris discantus* part of Fayrfax's *Stabat mater* to wrap chips in, but they would have done so if they had the chance.

Even as the music itself was disappearing, the organisations which supported its performance were being systematically dismantled too. Religion and education, like religion and everything else, were inextricably connected. Many priests, and assorted other pillars and buttresses of the administrative classes, first mastered the music of their daily mass as children in their local monastic house or collegiate church.

Not everyone enjoyed the experience. Thomas Tusser was a choirboy at the collegiate chapel at Wallingford Castle in the late 1520s and records 'what bare robes, what stale bread, what college fare, what penny ale' were offered to the 'wretched boys', smarting from their 'pinched noses'. But music set him up for life. He had a good voice, and was 'impressed' into the choir of St Paul's Cathedral where he was taught by John Redford, whom he admired greatly. Redford got him a place at King's College, Cambridge, when his voice broke, and then music provided his entrée to life at court:

> Since being once at Cambridge taught
> At court ten years I made assaie,
> No Musicke then was left unsought,
> Such care I had to serve that waie.[22]

Then it was bucolic retirement into the life of a prosperous Elizabethan landowner, where 'my music since hath been the plough', and the writing of a long poem on 'Good Husbandry' with advice on, among other things, 'Howe to cure the wrigling of ye tayle in a sheepe', 'What is to be done with measeled hogs', and 'How to fastene loose teeth in a bullocke'. He found time to record with some relish the Christmas festivities on his demesne, the 'banket [banquet], the rich with the poore', the 'many Carols' in which he no doubt added a well-fed tenor or bass to tunes learnt as a boy, and the 'football playing, at which they are very dexterous in Norfolk'.[23]

For the adult musician, the closure of the monasteries meant losing your job and possibly your home too. Thomas Tallis became a 'singing-man' of Waltham Abbey in Essex late in 1538. He got £20 back pay and £20 'reward' (a sort of severance package) when Waltham became the last English abbey to be dissolved on 23 March 1540. Cromwell and Henry received the annual revenues of £1,079. The sheer scale of the first wave of the Dissolution almost beggars belief: around 800 smaller houses, probably with modest musical resources, were closed in the four years from 1536, as well as the fifty or so larger institutions which could manage elaborate polyphony, with all the educational and administrative back-up which such daily musical magnificence implies.

Nor was it just monasteries where music was abolished or severely curtailed. St Stephen's, Westminster, a private 'free' chapel where Nicholas Ludford worked, closed in 1548 (the vicars-choral getting £6 13s 4d). The music at Christ Church, Oxford (formerly Cardinal College) survived the fall of Wolsey, but in reduced form, and with no role for its presiding genius, John Taverner. The physical equipment of music suffered in the general degradation too. Organs were classed alongside other unnecessary and idolatrous ornaments like banners, images and rood-screens, and met the same fate.

The market town of Evesham in Worcestershire still owns a Bible which was in use at the very moment when services in the town's Abbey were stopped. John Bicester, a monk at the Abbey, wrote an account of what happened directly onto the pages of the Bible, in the margins and around the text, in his own hand:

And the yere of our Lorde 1539 the monastery of Evesham was suppressed by King Henry VIII, the XXXI yeare of his raygne the XXX day of Januer at evensong tyme, the Convent being in the quere, at thys verse 'Deposuet potentes', and wold not suffer them to make an ende. Phillypp Ballard beying Abbott at that tyme and XXXV relygius men at that day alive in the seyde monastery.[24]

This is the only first-hand, eyewitness account of the actual moment of Dissolution. Nothing could illustrate more vividly the effect that this planned, systematised destruction had on music: the singing was stopped, forcibly, not just in the middle of the service but in the middle of the Magnificat, in the middle of the verse. 'Deposuit potentes', they sang, 'He hath put down the mighty.' Henry's troops wouldn't even allow them to finish the verse: 'and hath exalted the humble and meek'.

The dismantling of Evesham Abbey shows the extent to which this reformation and dissolution were not about religion, but about power. This huge church, once as imposing as the cathedrals of Norwich or Salisbury, so central to its community that it needed not one but two parish churches clustered like moons around its walls, has simply vanished. Bits of it have turned up in the High Street, stuck onto houses and shop-fronts – like a carrot on the face of a snowman. The enterprising owners spotted a nice corbel or a fancy lintel coming down from the Abbey walls and just helped themselves. But, like other chapters in this story, what looks like unalloyed bad news turns out to have another side. English church music did not roll over and die, as the traditions in some other European countries were to do, even under an attack of this ferocity. Its heart beat too strongly for that. English institutions adapt, compromise, fudge and carry on, rather than snap and break, which is why many of them endure to this day. English church music reinvented itself, and so did its people.

Some monastically trained musicians ended up working for the Elizabethan nobility as 'music of the house'. At the top end of the hierarchy, Taverner and Ludford managed gracefully enough. Tallis, a younger man still in mid-career, quickly got himself a new job at Canterbury, one of several former monastic houses which refounded itself as a cathedral and kept its music going under the new rules. Pay-offs for redundant professional musicians could often be pretty generous. John Bicester, the monk who recorded the dissolution of his home and place of employment at Evesham, found himself comfortably installed as vicar of a nearby parish. Most importantly of all, by destroying or degrading so many musical opportunities around the country, the forces of Dissolution and Reformation concentrated all that history and energy into just a few choral establishments, and one in particular: the Chapel Royal. For the ambitious, able church musician, the monarch's private chapel and its choir were about to become the only game in town – and would remain so for the next three hundred years.

JOHN TAVERNER IS ONE of a number of composers in this story to do us the favour of dying at a convenient point in the narrative, thus placing his life's work neatly within a particular historical phase. Taverner died in 1545, little more than two years before Henry VIII, and is the last major composer to remain unaffected by the reforms of Edward VI. His work is full of variety and new approaches, and he pushed forward compositional techniques like imitation and freedom from being tethered to a plainsong. His musical signatures include short repeated phrases and motifs within the polyphony, almost like an ostinato, giving his music a driving, muscular quality, which is full of life. He clearly influenced the generations which followed him. He was an artist of the first rank, and a man of his times.

Nicholas Ludford (c.1485–1557) worked at the Chapel of St Stephen, Westminster. St Stephen's seven choirboys must have been thoroughly well trained to sing Ludford's spacious music in the usual pre-Reformation styles, including a mass setting with two treble parts throughout. The choir, alas, was to become another statistic in the list of musical casualties of the 1540s. No music by Ludford survives after this date.

John Redford (c.1500–47), who was also considerate enough to die in the same year as Henry VIII, is the first composer to contribute almost exclusively organ pieces to the music of the English church. Like vocal composition, his technique is to place a plainsong in measured notes in one part of the texture (usually the middle or bottom), and weave freely composed, often elaborate lines (usually two, occasionally three) around it. This style of keyboard writing didn't change much up to the works of William Byrd, Orlando Gibbons and John Bull a century later, though the level of virtuosity went up. Redford was on the music staff at St Paul's Cathedral, where he also helped nurture the early growth of an intriguing hybrid of the English choral tradition and the liturgical drama: troupes of cathedral and chapel boy choristers moonlighting outside the choir stall as fully functioning theatrical companies.

There was some sacred music-making in the home, too, at least in the best-regulated households. Two principal collections of this kind survive, known respectively as the Henry VIII manuscript and the Fayrfax book.[25] Both contain mostly secular songs and instrumental pieces, but there are devotional pieces here too, including some by both of the eponymous composers, Henry and Fayrfax, as well as Cornysh and others. This was not liturgical music, but was meant to be sung in the privy chamber and around the fire in the Great Hall, for entertainment and enlightenment; as Sheryngham's *Ah, gentle Jesu* has it, 'come to school, record well this lesson'. This informal type of domestic devotion became more popular and important as the century went on.

These, then, were some of the forces at work on the creative instincts of the musician during the early stirrings of the English Reformation, and some of the ways in which he responded. But what did he think about it? What did Tavener think about it? Who knows? After five centuries there is almost no reliable information about what went on in some of these men's lives, never mind in their heads. Besides, for a musician living under a regime that sought to control his thoughts and his music as well as his actions, the golden rule is, don't let your feelings show.

But they do show. It is remarkable, given the circumstances, the degree to which the modern listener can hear the composer's character, his sympathies, his own authentic voice, in the music. This was even more true of the next generation, who were required to contribute uncomplainingly to one extreme and then the other, accommodating their conscience where they could. The history of English church music was about to pass into the hands of the children of Henry VIII.

5

The Children of Henry VIII: Reformation and Counter-Reformation, 1547–1558

Hynder not musycke
>> Christopher Tye, Preface to The Actes of the Apostles

WHEN ADOLF HITLER CAME to power in 1933, Richard Strauss remarked 'thank God – at last a Chancellor who appreciates the arts'.[1] In 1963 Dmitri Shostakovich declared, 'I'm scared to death of them. They've been pursuing me for years ... I've been a whore. I am, and always will be, a whore.'[2] In 1575 Thomas Tallis and William Byrd told Elizabeth I that 'compared to the greatest artists you are easily their superior ... it depends entirely on what you show us of your good will whether we write any more music, or give up now'.[3] These composers all lived under regimes which valued music, and worked for rulers who appreciated it personally and provided patronage and position to its creators. Their patrons knew how to use music to promote their own ideas about themselves and their nations. Music was useful to them – but only if it was the right kind of music.

The sixteenth-century English composer was a craftsman, turning a technical hand to whatever type of church music was needed. But, like Shostakovich, he was also doing what his employer wanted: making his music, making his money, and at the same time staying safe. The craftsman and the whore battled it out for the soul of every composer, and as the century reached its mid-point the battle was heating up.

Henry VIII was succeeded by three of his children, suckled by three different mothers on three very different traditions of religion and music. Henry fathered a number of other children on his reluctant nation as well: the English church, for one, its music for another. And like his real descendants the different branches of his musical family turned out very differently from each other and struggled to get on. At length, an uneasy compromise emerged, exploited most effectively and illustrated most elegantly by the best of the Tudor composers, Thomas Tallis and William Byrd. Under the benevolent but controlling eye of their Queen, they left us (among much else) anthems in English, anthems in Latin, then anthems in English *and* Latin. Nothing could better illustrate Elizabeth I's 'middle way' in music; the perfect English compromise. No single factor had more influence on the church music of mid-sixteenth-century England than the personality of the monarch of the day.

With the accession of the Protestant boy-king Edward VI in 1547, the self-righteous zeal of the reformers was let loose. What they wanted, above all, was the Word. The Bible, in English. What they didn't want was saints, superstitions, ceremonies, and Latin. Music got it in the neck almost incidentally, partly because it got in the way of understanding, and partly because of its well-known tendency to lead directly to moral decay and loose living.

In about 1549 Thomas Becon criticised highly placed individuals who 'spend much riches in nourishing many idle singing men to bleat in their chapels'.[4] Erasmus had put it slightly more politely: 'in college or monastery it is still the same: music, nothing but music'.[5] William Turner, another Protestant reformer, declared that, in his view, 'they that sing Latin service and understand no Latin, as the most part of choristers, singing-men and soul-priests, and many body-priests also, commonly do, ... worship not God nor serve God with singing of the Scripture in Latin, and so I prove it'.[6] (Soul-priests were chantry priests who sang mass for the souls of the dead – nothing to do with James Brown in *The Blues Brothers*.)

Becon and Turner were both appointed to important positions as chaplains at the court of Edward and his Protectors, so theirs is the authentic voice of the new government. Interestingly, Turner also gives an example of something he does approve of: 'The Germans, which of late left the Pope, left also the Pope's tongue, and now sing all service and psalms in their own tongue.'[7]

It wasn't long before the music of the continental reformers was present in person as well as by example. In July 1550 the church of Austin Friars in London, the newly vacant former home of a community of Augustinians, began to host a congregation of Dutch and French Protestant refugees who sang services in their own languages. Communities of Flemish, Wallonian and Italian exiles followed. Their worship was specifically permitted and protected by order of the Privy Council, causing the usual nervousness among those who thought change was taking place too quickly. Their music was the psalm-chant: metrical, unaccompanied, requiring some trained musicians to begin the singing before the 'tota ecclesia' joined in the 'magna gravitate psalmum' in their 'lingua vulgari', so that everyone understands what was being sung: 'omnia quae canuntur intellegi',[8] as their bishop soberly instructed them.

This was not the first time psalm-singing was heard in our land. Rhymed translations for singing date back to Henry II's reign, and as well as the versions by Richard Rolle and John Wycliffe in the fourteenth century, there are notable versions by Thomas Brampton at the beginning of the fifteenth and by Sir Thomas Wyatt a century later. But this was where psalm-singing took hold. It became absolutely central to this story: the emblem of the reformers' desire to hear the words, and the only music sung in the ordinary parish church until the eighteenth century. Becon had got his way. 'Music may be used,' he sniffed, 'so it be not abused. If it be soberly exercised and reputed as an handmaid unto virtue, it is tolerable.'[9]

IN TIMES OF CHANGE, top composers have to think on their feet. Tye and Sheppard show us how it was done. Near-contemporaries, both men held notable musical appointments outside London, then gravitated to court around the same time. Both wrote fine music for each successive phase of change. They learnt the highly sophisticated art of the pre-Reformation composer, and maintained their standards through the changing demands placed on the professional church musician as a succession of monarchs performed their stately rotating dance. They didn't know, as we know now, that each wave of reform would be succeeded, superseded and swept away by another. Their music lets us see them living their musical life as it was, one cold day in Oxford, London or Donnington-cum-Marche (Tye's parish near Ely), an immediate, real-time commentary on the legal, intellectual and emotional hinterland of each stage of their lives. Each man brought his own background of music and faith to his art and his craft, and reveals them, willingly or not, to us. One reveals more sympathy for the Catholic tradition – John Sheppard; the other for the Protestant – Christopher Tye.

Sheppard was born around 1515, Tye probably up to a decade earlier. Tye received his early training and experience at King's College, Cambridge (one of a disproportionate number of East Anglians among the musical elite of the period), and in the early 1540s both composers got new jobs as choirmasters, Tye at Ely Cathedral, Sheppard at Magdalen College, Oxford. Both composed music for Henry VIII's Sarum liturgies, showing a confident mastery of the old manner and the influence of Taverner, as well as evidence of the new trend towards music on a smaller scale. Both composed masses on the same tune, 'Western Wind'. Both had become Gentlemen of the Chapel Royal by the time of Edward VI's reign (with some uncertainty about the exact circumstances of both appointments caused by lacunae in the Chapel Royal records) and slotted into the new dispensation with unhesitating professionalism. Both composers contributed perfect little English anthems, for example, Sheppard's *A New Commandment* and Tye's *Give Almes of thy Goods*, which deliver the text with crystal clarity and total lack of elaboration, exactly as Cranmer required. *Give Almes* has no melisma at all: 'to every syllable a note'.

Both Tye and Sheppard chose to set the Easter text *Christ, Rising Again*. Sheppard's setting is for men's voices, a practice which has been taken to show that the loss of the elaborate, coloratura style of singing by the boys at the Chapel Royal and elsewhere may have led to a fairly rapid breakdown of their musical contribution altogether (though there are big pieces for the boys at this time and, if the old style of singing did fail under Edward, it returned with great triumph under Mary and Sarum). Tye's sonorously scored six-voice version of *Christ, Rising* shows the tendency of both men to try discreetly to escape Cranmer's restrictions and make English sacred music sound (just a bit) more like the rich polyphony of vanished times.

This tendency to sneak something of the familiar old musical sonorities into the new liturgies became even more pronounced as both men took up the brand-new challenge of writing English service music. Not much in the genre by Tye survives, but his beautiful, restrained Nunc Dimittis applies confident, skilful handling of pretty thoroughly worked-out imitation, with melisma, to the words of the 1535 primer, one of the earliest English versions. The music sounds like condensed Palestrina. Cranmer might be forgiven for looking askance at this bending of his rules for musical effect. If so, he would have been flabbergasted by the sheer grandeur of Sheppard's settings of the evening canticles.

The First Service divides voice-parts and uses antiphonal effects between the sides of the choir. The Second Service goes much further. It's a huge piece, dividing the singers into two four-part choirs, then combining them into one eight-part texture, extending certain verses of the text with an unblushing sense of freedom which harks back to the antiphon tradition. Stylistically, it is the first 'Great' service. It's glorious. But Protestants, who wanted above all to hear the words, might have wondered on whom exactly the glory was being reflected.

This was music written for the Chapel Royal. Restrictions on what the composer could do were never as strict in the monarch's own chapel, where the congregation could be trusted and watched (another factor in the consolidation of the musical pre-eminence of the Chapel Royal after the Reformation). Even bearing in mind this relative freedom, works like Sheppard's Second Service show the surprising degree to which composers wanted and managed to carry echoes of their art with them across the dividing lines of Reformation and Counter-Reformation. They were to face change again.

As usual, the new regime was much quicker at announcing what musical practices were now forbidden than in telling people what was to replace them.

The 1547 Injunctions of Edward VI to the Church of England get straight to the point. At Canterbury, 'all sequences [the latest accretion to the mass] to be omitted', and 'henceforth all masses by note shall be sung within the choir', not 'in other places of the church'. At York, 'you shall sing or celebrate in note or song within church only one mass that is to say High Mass only and none other' and you shall 'sing your Evensong and Compline without any Responds ... You shall hereafter omit and not use the singing of any Hours, Prime, Dirges or Commendations ... You shall sing, say, use or suffer none other anthems in your churches but these.' At Windsor, 'the choristers shall daily say Mattins in English before the beginning of service in the morning; and likewise Evensong in English before the choir begin Evensong' (it implies that at this very early stage the sung service is still in Latin, which is why the choristers have the words read to them in English first). At Lincoln, 'they shall from henceforth sing or say no anthems of our Lady or other Saints, but only of our Lord, and them not in Latin'. At Winchester College 'they shall henceforth omit to sing or say *Regina caeli*, *Salve regina*, and any suchlike untrue or superstitious anthem'. At Canterbury there was to be 'no talking nor jangling be used in the quire'.[10]

Compared to the level of detail about what you couldn't sing, there were few instructions about what you could. But when the authorities did give some clues, the direction of their thinking was clear enough: 'all psalms shall be sung with such leisure and deliberation as the pronouncing of them may be perceived both by the singer and of the hearer' (still not a bad prescription for how to sing psalms); 'all graces to be said or sung at meals ... and other prayers ... shall be henceforth said or sung in English'; 'choosing out the best [of the old Latin prayers] and most sounding to Christian religion they shall turn the same into English, setting thereunto a plain and distinct note for every syllable one'[11] (another go at Cranmer's only partly successful attempt at this line of reform a couple of years before).

Everywhere, the English Litany replaced the Latin. On St

Matthew's Day, six months into the reign of Edward VI, St Paul's choir kept 'a solempne procession on their knees in English, with Te Deum', with perhaps the smell of burning papist books wafting in from Paul's Cross outside the west door to take their minds off their poor, sore knees on the cold, old flagstones.

Most remarkably, on the 'fourthe daie of November', Thomas Wriothesley attended the young king at mass at Westminster Abbey, where 'Gloria in excelsis, the Creede, Sanctus, Benedictus and the Agnus were all songen in English'.[12] Wriothesley doesn't mention the musical setting used: given the solemnity of the occasion, it must have been something like the English versions of mass movements by Taverner rather than a monodic setting in the manner of Cranmer and Marbeck. (Wriothesley also persisted in using the old Latin names for most of the movements, even when they are sung in English, one of those odd little peculiarities we still stick to.) English liturgies were sung elsewhere, too, though these were experiments, expressly designed as temporary, interim measures. Musically, the first two years of Edward's reign were a period of wait-and-see. The Tudor musician was getting used to it.

On 21 January 1549, Parliament passed into law the single most important document in the history of English church music, The Booke of the Common Prayer and Administration of the Sacramentes. This book continued the process of clarification and simplification. No longer was there to be 'more business to find out what should be read, than to read it when it was found out'.[13] Feast days went; psalms were sung in a monthly cycle; new 'Collects', or short prayers summing up the theme of a Sunday or saint's day, were provided; and the Latin canticles and hymns of the eight daily monastic 'hours' were rendered into two new English services – matins and evensong.

Naturally, some resisted change, and others pretended it wasn't happening. Bishop John Hooper complained that some priests were clinging to the old ways, 'and, that popery may not be lost, the mass priests, although they are compelled to discontinue the use of the Latin language, yet most carefully observe the same tone and manner of chanting to which they were heretofore accustomed in the papacy.'

In other words, they did what they were told by singing in English, but made it sound as much like the Latin as possible. Martin Bucer, a German Protestant reformer, made the same point: 'some turn the prescribed forms of service into mere papistical abuse, and although these are now in the vulgar tongue, the "sacrificers" recite them of set purpose so indistinctly that they cannot be understood'.[14] They obeyed the new rules, but not so as anyone would actually notice. And, what's more, they were doing it on purpose. It's the perfect exemplar of a nice clear policy being devised in London, and what happens to it by the time it reaches the ground.

The problem with this new liturgy was that, by definition, not a note of music existed for singing it. Choirs which were probably quietly congratulating themselves on having survived the Dissolution were suddenly silenced. Their entire repertoire had become obsolete, at a stroke. Importantly, in this respect the English Reformation was not like its European cousins. In Europe, reformation was an upward force, driven by the instincts of the people in opposition to the authorities. Popular movements like these brought their music with them: Luther his hymns, the Swiss their psalm tunes. In England, musicians had to invent an entirely new kind of music in response to instructions handed down to them from above by the state. Small wonder there was confusion and resistance.

And still the Injunctions kept coming. In early 1550 St George's, Windsor, was told it now needed 'only ten choristers', and that its singing-men should be recruited with 'more regard to their virtue and learning than to excellency in music'. (Couldn't they have both? Apparently not). Two years later, York was told that 'there be none other note sung or used ... saving square note plain, so that every syllable may be plainly and distinctly pronounced, and without any reports or repeatings which may induce any obscureness to the hearers' and 'that there be no more playings of the organs' and 'that the Master of the Choristers for the time being who ought to play the organs in time past ... can no more do so'. St Paul's was told to 'leave the playing of the organs at the divine service'. Highly skilled musicians were being asked to deliver the kind of stuff which any parish priest and his clerk could manage. No wonder the top talent was increasingly gravitating towards the Chapel Royal, where Sheppard and Tye were managing to get away with something altogether more interesting.

The second Book of Common Prayer of 1552 was, if anything, even less helpful to the musician. Yet against this not very sympathetic background, composers began the task of creating a genuinely English style. The Lumley Part Books are a rare and fascinating survival of Edwardian church music.[15] Texts (psalm verses and canticles) come from a variety of recent psalters, primers and prayer books. Music is in four, sometimes three parts, mostly for men's voices, and almost entirely chordal and homophonic, with some gentle and well-controlled imitation and polyphony. Only three of the twenty-nine pieces can be ascribed (on grounds of musical borrowings from other pieces): two are by Tallis, one by Tye. For the first time, composers really seem to be enjoying the vigour of the English language:

> O Lord, our Lord, how marvellous
> Is thy great name most glorious.

> Ye Rains, ye Dews, ye boisterous Winds,
> O Winter and Summer, O Fire and Heat,
> Moistures, Frosts and Cold in your kinds,
> Ye Nights, ye Days and ye Snows great,
> Lightnings and Clouds, Darkness and Light,
> O Praise the Lord both day and night.

One piece has the verses sung by two voices, the chorus answering in refrain, a very early prototype of what would become the 'verse' style. Many pass the music between the two sides of the choir in the antiphonal style borrowed from psalm-chanting, again to become a principal feature of later music. The limitations imposed on musical elaboration in Lumley seem to have focused the composers' inventiveness on the elements they are allowed to enjoy, principally a cheery, sometimes syncopated rhythmic swagger. The inventive vigour of this music, and the intrinsic interest of the early English versions of the text, should earn the Lumley collection more performances today.

Music from the 'Lumley' Part Books, probably compiled during the reign of Edward VI (1547–53), some of the very earliest liturgical music in English. The early version of the canticle text (Benedicite) has an irresistible swagger which the anonymous composer has more than matched. Eschewing elaboration didn't mean the music had to be boring.

The other principal source of Edwardian church music is the Wanley Part Books.[16] Like Lumley, the set has a book missing, the pieces are all anonymous and only a couple can be ascribed by musical cross references with other sources. Wanley contains more pieces than Lumley, including many settings of texts from the 1549 prayer book. Composers tried their hand at the new burial and wedding services, as well as music for morning and evening, anthems using the new Collects and moralising little passages from the Bible ('Walk while ye have light') and, most interestingly, the earliest music for the English communion. Composers set all the parts of the ordinary, something the few Elizabethan and Jacobean composers of communion services did not do. These are, in fact, the only complete settings of the communion in English before the modern era. Wanley is also the source of the English versions of mass movements by Taverner.

There is an experimental feel to the music of Wanley. Some of it is harmonised chant, like an Anglicised faburden, some uses the kind of short-breathed imitation favoured by Tye in his English Nunc Dimittis. Some of the music is not very good: composers hadn't quite got the hang of the slightly lumpy word-stress of some of the English texts, or of how to keep imitation going. But some of it is. Much is for men's voices, and choirs which fashion a communion service around the settings and appropriate Collects from Wanley will find themselves with something atmospheric, approachable and short.

Psalm-chanting really began to take off. Robert Crowley, a printer, published *The Psalter of Dauid newely translated into Englysh metre in such sort that it maye the more decently, and wyth more delyte of the mynde, be reade and songe of al men* in 1549,[17] the same year as the first prayer book. His music represents a remarkably assured early example of the chant style, with some of the harmonic tricks later incorporated by Tallis. Crowley laid the four voice-parts out on a single page, one above the other, like a score. Interestingly, the names he gave the parts are, in descending order, 'Contertenor', 'Tenor', 'Playne Songe', and 'Bassus', showing that in this, as in much else, the new English music was borrowing from the old Latin style, in this case harmonising a plainsong in the tenor by adding parts above and below. How the words fit the chant is not always made entirely clear. This style, like all the church music of Edward's short reign, is work in progress.

John Sheppard, Catholic and professional, wrote over thirty chant settings of metrical psalm-texts for the new liturgy. But most significant of all is a modest publication by a courtier, employed not as a musician but as a 'grome of ye Kynges Maiesties robes', Thomas Sternhold. Sternhold's introduction to his little book of psalms (just nineteen in all) shows clearly that this kind of devotional music was intended for the home, not church or chapel: 'trusting that as your grace taketh pleasure to hear them sung sometimes of me, so you will also delight not only to see and read them yourself, but also to command them to be sung to you of others.'[18] No music was included: the two metrical schemes used (common and short metre) enable Sternhold's versions to be sung to a variety of tunes which educated individuals like Sternhold and his monarch already knew. The work was taken up and expanded by another versifier, John Hopkins, a clergyman, after Sternhold's death in 1549, and the enlarged book was reprinted several times during Edward's reign. Between them, Sternhold and Hopkins had started something significant.

A brand-new musical form also made its appearance in Wanley and elsewhere: the 'ABB' anthem. The first part of the text, usually biblical, was sung to simple, restrained homophony (the 'A' section), then the voices diverge into modest polyphony ('B'), then this second passage is repeated ('B'). It's almost as if the composers knew that Cranmer was sitting in the corner of the Chapel Royal listening, so they start by giving him 'to every syllable a note', then try to slip in a demure bit of musical invention, then, when he doesn't object (or hasn't noticed), do it again. The results are exquisite. There are examples by all the leading composers, but perhaps the very best is Tallis's *If Ye Love Me*: the perfection of simplicity, the Reformation in sound.

Professional church music fared rather better than it might have after the double shock of the Dissolution and the complete rewrite of the musical and liturgical rules. By 1550 the closing down of places with choirs had mostly come to an end. Some forty remained: twenty-nine cathedrals (fifteen of them re-foundations after the dissolution of their monastic houses), and a variety of college and school chapels, large parish churches and a few private chapels. The biggest, best-funded and most musically active was the Chapel Royal. All musical innovation emanated from there from this point on.

Away from London, change, as always, proved more difficult to manage. The authorities were so busy trying to contain the competing voices of those who resisted change and those who wanted it to move faster, that they had almost nothing to say about music, which in the period before the introduction of the new Book of Common Prayer probably continued much as before. Probably the biggest change was the drying-up of the supply of musically literate men to staff the churches. No longer did the local monastery allow easy access to church music of whatever quality it could manage, nor did it instruct the next parish priest and clerk in the ancient musical inheritance of their predecessors. The town did not now gather for its weekly Jesus Mass every Friday. Chantries were abolished altogether in 1547, so the priest did not now sing mass for your grandfather or your baby that was born dead, nor did he visit the sick, comfort the dying, or teach the children of your village how to pray, read, sing and tie their shoelaces. And by doing away with these things, the government made itself a great deal of money. Music was the casual victim of these ignorant armies.

One ceremony which suffered a direct assault was the parish procession. One of the 1547 Injunctions stopped congregations beginning mass by making their ancient, solemn progress around the parish, singing and bearing the banners of their saint. The Litany now had to be sung inside, in English, while kneeling. That way the people would hear and understand what was being sung and avoid 'challenging of places in procession'[19] (after which, of course, the clergy and people of the English church have never again been remotely bothered about whether their place in a procession makes them look important). Bells were silenced, too.

Other musical activity with deep, atavistic roots in the parish community included the evening offering to the Virgin, the *Salve regina* and the Little Office. These were suppressed in the Lincoln diocese in 1548, clearly implying that a year and more into the reign of Edward VI they were still clinging on tenaciously out in the flat bits of the country.

Edward Seymour, Duke of Somerset and Lord Protector wrote personally to the Vice Chancellor of Cambridge in September 1548 to impose 'one uniform order' on services, not least because otherwise 'there might peradventure some dissension or disorder arise amongst you within the university, to the evil example of other'.[20] The Fens were not easy to reach.

As always, plenty of ordinary people simply ignored the new rules. By June 1549 the new prayer book had the force of law. Corpus Christi now ceased to be designated a public holiday. Half of all Londoners took the day off anyway, no doubt singing their illegal and idolatrous melodies around the streets just as lustily as they always had. Another lurch, forwards and backwards, centred around Somerset's arrest in October 1549, leading to a further tightening of the vice: in January 1550 parishes were ordered to surrender 'antiphoners, missals, scrayles, processionals' and 'primers in latin or English',[21] a slightly desperate acknowledgement that Latin primers were still out there. Does the scribe betray his masters' frustration by awarding a capital letter to the English primers but not the Latin? This time there were heavy fines and imprisonment for non-compliance. More music was lost, both on paper and, perhaps even more importantly, in people's minds. A church in Winchester sold off its books by weight, as waste paper. They got nine shillings for one and a half hundredweight, less than half the fine they would have received for keeping just one of them.

What parish church music needed was someone to regularise what the people already knew and what they were now required to do into something which met their needs, which they could (and would) manage, and which the authorities would approve. The ideal candidate would be thoroughly steeped in the musical inheritance of the old Sarum style, and be passionately committed to the ideals of the reformers. Cometh the hour, cometh the man. Perfectly qualified on both counts was the Windsor organist and almost-martyr, John Marbeck.

If The Booke of Common Praier was the central document of the new church, its central musical document was Marbeck's *Booke of Common Praier Noted*. Marbeck set the communion, morning and evening services, and some other liturgies from the new prayer book, to simple, single-lined music, which is either based on the familiar old

Sarum tones or closely imitates their style. Writing music which is simple, but at the same time memorable and treats its text and listeners with respect, is one of the hardest things the composer of church music has to try to do. Marbeck did it perfectly. It was the first time a trained professional composer had reached out to the man and woman in the pew. His music has survived in use to this day: because it began life as an adaptation of existing music to new circumstances, it lent itself readily to further adaptation when later ages rewrote the words in their own image. 'Dominus vobiscum', or 'The Lord be with you', is answered 'et cum spiritu tuo', or 'and with thy spirit', or 'and also with you', or some other form of words, to more or less the same tune. His is one of the very few types of music you can hear today in both your local evangelical parish and in the BCP church down the road. His book is a very English compromise, and a very English stroke of genius.

For all its eventual importance, Marbeck's book managed only one edition in Edward VI's reign. It was born into a time of uncertainty and rapid change. But by the end of the boy-king's short life, English church music was finding its way. As well as in church, devotional music was increasingly sung in the home, always with a didactic and moralising purpose: Christopher Tye's *The Actes of the Apostles*, dedicated to Edward VI, is 'to sing and also to play upon the lute, very necessary for students, to still their wits after study'.[22]

There were far fewer choirs than before, at both professional and parish level, with less music, less money, fewer singers and no organ. But they were still there. Musicians of all kinds had found a way of keeping their art going into the new order. Some very fine composers were converging on the Chapel Royal to continue the business of creating a brand-new English style. For texts, they were beautifully served by the translators and compilers of the new liturgies, less so by the earliest poets and devotional writers of the Reformation:

> And while they lokt, up steadfastly
> To heaven as he up went,
> Beholde, two men stood there them by,
> And white was their garment.

Left *Sarum plainsong, c. 1530.* Right *part of the Creed from Marbeck's* Booke of Common Praier Noted *of 1550. The principle of keeping the style and look of the music the same but simply fitting the English words to it, is clear: a simple idea, but revolutionary.*

The English church had a while to wait yet for its Herberts, its Baxters and its Donnes.

In the six brief years of Edward's reign, the English church musician was asked to cope with rapid, far-reaching and confusing change not of his own choosing. He did pretty well and it was a skill he was going to need again.

MYLES COVERDALE WAS PREACHING in Exeter Cathedral when news of the accession of Mary I reached the town. One by one, his congregation got up and walked out. Protestants feared that the gains of the last six years were about to be lost. Catholics hoped that the losses of the last six years were about to be restored. Musicians, like the rest of the population, occupied all parts of the spectrum of opinion.

Reginald Pole enunciated the new religious orthodoxy: 'the observatyon of ceremonyes, for obedience sake, wyll gyve more light than all the readynge of Scrypture can doe…'[23] So much for the 'herytykes' insistence on the Word. St Paul, it seems, was a Catholic all along. Pole goes on: 'yt semyd nothinge here amongste you to take awaye holy water, holy breade, candells, ashes, and palme …'[24], and he could have added, antiphons, polyphony, top B flats and Latin.

Composers sympathetic to the Catholic Counter-Reformation responded with a burst of creativity all the more energetic for having been repressed. Thomas Tallis turned from the crafting of English miniatures to the musical preoccupations of his earliest mature works, but with a new-found confidence in handling massive textures and long spans. The glorious, arching *Gaude gloriosa Dei mater* exemplifies the style, though as with other pieces of the period there is some uncertainty about whether it was composed late in the reign of Henry VIII or under Mary (as analysed in forensic detail by the scholar John Milsom[25]). The 'Amen' alone takes about as long to sing as the whole of his motet *If Ye Love Me*. His trademark false relation adds spice to cadences, and the Virgin Mary is back where she belongs, at the heart of music and worship.

Vox Patris caelestis by William Mundy, who was born around 1528 and is thus one of the younger of the generation of Catholic composers writing for Mary I, equals even Tallis. Mundy alternates sections for reduced voices with great chordal blocks of homophony, and triple with duple time passages, in the old pre-Reformation manner. His treble is high, his bass is low. Gimell, the technique of a single voice-part becoming two (so that the two men or boys singing the same part would diverge onto two different lines for a section of the piece before rejoining each other again), is used with confident relish. The Virgin is hymned in heaven with the frankly earthy imagery of the Song of Songs.

Mass composition was taken up again. There was plenty of interest in the old ways of doing things. Tallis's *Missa puer natus est nobis* sets the mass texts to phrases from the Christmas plainsong in the tenor, sung in various retrogrades and other mathematical patterns, with six other voice-parts freely woven around it, in a consciously archaic style. There are masses by William Whytbroke and Mundy composed 'upon

Under Mary I composers could spread their wings again with all the freedom of their earlier art. Part of Gaude gloriosa, Dei mater *by Thomas Tallis.*

a square', a technique whereby a short melodic phrase is chiselled from a plainsong and then subjected to various repetitions and variations as a *cantus firmus*. The Latin Magnificat, the third person of the holy trinity of musical forms, also came back into use, with new settings.

The source for these settings is the important Gyffard Part Books, probably copied during Mary's reign, though some of the music may be of earlier date. Unusually, Tallis's *Missa puer natus* mass can be dated with reasonable confidence. It was almost certainly written for the visit of Philip of Spain in 1554, when he married Mary in Winchester Cathedral. Like English kings, Philip considered a fully staffed chapel choir part of the baggage of the itinerant monarch. He used his choir to make his presence in London felt, as Henry Machyn, the English diarist, noted: in November a Spanish gentleman was buried at St Martin-in-the-Fields, 'with syngyng to the cherche, and the morowe-masse, boythe Spaneards and Englyssmen syngyng'; in late November the Spaniards sang mass at Westminster Abbey 'to pray to God to gyffe hym thankes of owr quen of her qwyckenyng with child'; on 2 December, at mass at St Paul's, 'both the quen's chappell and the kinges and Powlles qwer song'.[26] This was music as courtly display, and must have been as intimidating as it was impressive to the poor natives who, in Machyn's account, seem to be shoved to the musical sidelines. Not for the first time, professional church music was an unsettling place to be.

'Puer natus est', of course, means 'unto us a child is born'. Tallis's use of this plainsong, together with the coincidence that the service was held close to Christmas and the rumoured pregnancy of the Queen (wrong, as it turned out), provide convincing circumstantial evidence that the *Missa puer natus est* was composed for and sung at this three-choired celebration in December 1554. Whatever the politics, the impressive body of musicians assembled that day in the vast spaces of old St Paul's must have sounded, and looked, magnificent. Probably present among the Chapel Royal boys on that auspicious occasion was a talented lad of around thirteen called William. His elder brothers Simon and John were singing with St Paul's choir. Brother joins brother in these joint choirs again in the years to come. By a curious coincidence an adult singer in the ranks of the Chapel Royal that day had the same name as the father of the three boys, though he was himself probably not a relation: Thomas Byrd. Also present were William Mundy and, among many others, the two composers whose parallel careers have illustrated for us the approaches of the Catholic and the Protestant to times of

change – Sheppard and Tye. Both responded with admirable professionalism to yet another swing of the pendulum. One of them, naturally enough, did so with more enthusiasm than the other.

The amount of Latin church music composed by John Sheppard in
the five years of Mary's reign is impressive. He looks back to his pre-
Reformation inheritance, but with a calm, authoritative voice that is all
his own. *Verbum caro factum est* is a stately, pealing respond for Christmas, the ancient plainsong ringing out both within and between the
sonorous blocks of polyphony like the Rock of Ages. On the last chord,
the treble part suddenly divides into three. It's like a light coming on.
Perhaps his most distinctive pieces are the shorter works, especially
those for the evening offices: *In manus tuas, Domine*, and *In pace in
idipsum dormiam*. Plainsong is never far away. Having hymned himself
to sleep so beautifully, Sheppard died in late 1558. Ever the professional,
he had had no objection to signing the oath of allegiance to Elizabeth
I, though he did not live to serve her actively. He would surely have
found her approach congenial.

Christopher Tye's *The Actes of the Apostles* and subsequent holy
orders, on the other hand, imply a greater allegiance to the reformed
church. His surviving contribution to Mary's Counter-Reformation
is smaller than Sheppard's. There are more English pieces by Tye than
Latin, but the Marian music is highly distinctive. *Omnes gentes, plaudite
manibus* is vigorous, imitative, continental-sounding and modern. It
almost feels like a madrigal. There is no plainsong in sight. *Peccavimus*,
by contrast, is a soulful, large-scale Jesus antiphon in seven parts, the
words a lament for the sins of the world (and, by implication, of those
who have set English religion on the wrong path), a sure sign of the
changing times. This piece deserves its place alongside the grandest
motets of the reign. With the accession of Elizabeth, Tye, perhaps now
in his mid-fifties, decided to retire back to his native East Anglia, where
he became a not very conscientious parish priest. He died around 1571.

The music of Sheppard and Tye lets us hear two fine composers of
possibly different religious instincts responding to change, first-hand,
in real time: the early Latin Masses, the smaller *Western Wind* masses;
then English anthems, English service music, chants and songs for

domestic devotion; then Latin anthems synthesising change. Sheppard wrote (or at least left) more music which inclined towards the sounds of the old Catholic world, even when he was not supposed to. Tye attempted to realise the ideals of the Reformation in music with an English accent: his little four-part songs to his own verse paraphrase of *The Actes of the Apostles* are almost like Lutheran chorales, and a couple of them have survived in use as short anthems and hymns. Thankfully, though, his own words to these tunes have largely not survived. They are clumsy stuff. Even East Anglians deserve better than this. Evangelicals, then as now, don't always appreciate that simplicity of language does not have to equal poverty of meaning and expression.

Mary's reign produced probably the first example of a notable sub species of composition: an anthem written by three composers working together. *In exitu Israel* is by 'Sheppard', 'Munday' and 'mr birde', three Chapel Royal musicians. The composers wrote a section each, neatly marked on the manuscript. Later composers did this too, and it is a mark of the collegiality of a choir like the Chapel Royal, where people worked alongside each other on a daily basis on all aspects of music-making, including composition. This is particularly noteworthy where experienced adults are handing on their skills to the younger generation: 'mr birde' is probably the first appearance on paper of the work of William Byrd, aged probably not more than eighteen. The piece is thoroughly workmanlike: teachers and pupil doing a good job together.

Music on the ground, too, reflected changes at political, social and doctrinal levels. Parish choirs before the Reformation were probably made up of whatever mixture of chantry priests, parish clerks, paid singers, small boys and volunteers was available. Under Edward VI, chantry priests, lay clerks, organs and all the old music vanished. Under Mary, some of this came back: organs were restored, Latin service books printed and bought (or quietly retrieved from the back of the vestry cupboard), choirs encouraged once again. In 1556 Bishop Brooks instructed the Gloucester diocese 'that the churchwardens of every parish, where service was accustomed to be sung, shall exhort all such as can sing and have been accustomed to sing in the time of the schism, or before, and now withdraw themselves from the choir, to exercise themselves in singing and serving God there.'[27] But note the date. This was three years into Mary's reign, and even then, singers had clearly not taken up their old duties, at least not in Gloucester. Just as in 1547, in some respects change took hold gradually.

The authorities allowed a brief period of grace during which people were still allowed to observe at least some Protestant practices. Some were aching to start singing in Latin again, but, in the absence of an actual Act of Parliament, didn't quite dare to. Then, when Catholic doctrine was reasserted by law, some did what they were told, and some didn't. As usual, geography mattered. As early as August 1553, 'the olde service in the lattin tongue with the masse was begun and sunge in [St] Paules ... and likewise it was begun in 4 or 5 other parishes within the cittie of London, not be commaundement but of the peoples devotion'. Diarist Henry Machyn records 'goodly masse songe, in Laten', at St Nicholas, Fish Street, and St Nicholas, Bread Street, on 23 and 24 August. Similarly, by September, 'ther was veray few parishe churches in York shire but masse was song or saide in Lattin.'[28] Some had disagreements, sometimes violent, within and between parishes. Many conformed, with or without their conscience. Parson Herne of St Petroc's parish, Exeter, was a convinced Protestant in Edward's reign, but took up the Latin Mass again in December 1553. His friend Alderman Midwinter 'poynted unto him with his fynger, remembringe as it were his olde protestations that he wold never singe masse agayne; but parson herne openly yn the churche spak alowde unto hym. It is no remedye man, it is no remedy.'[29] Parishes that had got rid of their Catholic paraphernalia, including music books (rather than walling them up in a niche), had to find money for new ones. Nobles who were handed a church's valuables a few years before for safe-keeping didn't always want to give them back.

Protestants at parish level hated the reintroduction of superstitious ceremonies and their music. On Palm Sunday 1556, the vicar of Bampton, Lincolnshire, struck the base of the church door with the cross as the choir sang out 'let him enter, the King of Glory'. From the back of the crowd a parishioner, Laurence Burnaby, interrupted their singing with the cry 'What a sport have we towards. Will our vicar ronne at the quintine [i.e. jousting] with God Almightie?'[30]

But, once again, change did not always occur in straight lines. Mary might have wanted her saints back, but she didn't want all of the old superstitions. Here again, the people proved difficult to manage. On 5 December 1554, 'the which was saint Nicholas' eve, at evensong time, came a commandment that saint Nicholas should not go abroad, nor about. But, notwithstanding, there went about these St Nicholases, in divers parishes, as St Andrews Holborn, and St Nicholas Olyffe in Bredstreet'.[31] As in previous reigns, the state needed a service book to bring uniformity. The Wayland primer appeared in 1555. It said nothing about music: what, and when, you sang continued to evolve; some, but not all, of the traditional Catholic feasts were back. That totemic Catholic favourite, *Salve regina*, was still rendered in its English version – addressed to Christ, not the Virgin: 'Hail, heavenly kynge'. Catholics can compromise too (a bit).

Bishop Edmund Bonner took up the familiar task of setting out the state's requirements in strict and particular detail. As usual, music is incidental, not central. People were 'borne in hande that they had gotten God by the fote ... sometimes by readyng, playynge, singing and other like meanes'.[32] Music was one of the ways people were led astray, and one of the tools for bringing them back. It was propaganda, the public face of obedience, and a means of manipulation. It also merited a mention in a disciplinary context. Bonner asked if any good singer 'since the setting forth and renewing of the old service in the Latin tongue, absent and withdraw himself from the choir'. If so, he was to get himself back into the choir stalls at once and start singing. One choirman got told off for singing the Sursum corda in a pub.[33]

Another form of music to attract Bonner's critical attention was street music. Like Gardiner in Henry's reign, he took aim at all 'slanderous books, ballads or plays, contrary to Christian religion'.[34] And well he might. England had a mighty tradition of scurrilous words being set to well-known tunes and sold cheaply on the streets. For about a penny you could buy:

An admonition ... to Warne the Papistes:

... If that you lyke not for to have
This blessyng in a rope,

Leave of[f] you Rebels for to rave
And cursse your Dad the pope.[35]

Nothing undermined the authorities like being laughed at, and they knew it. This sort of thing would get much ruder in the next big wave of popular anti-Catholicism in the 1670s and 80s.

Some Protestant musicians felt they had no choice but to leave the country. Just as for European Protestants coming to England in Edward VI's reign, and indeed English Catholics going the other way, exile was a useful tool. William Wittingham published a collection of metrical psalms 'approved by the famous and godly learned man John Calvin'[36] in Geneva in 1556, consolidating the links between the English Puritan wing of Protestantism and the various footholds established by the Calvinists around Europe. The psalm was their musical messenger, and in due course it would become embedded in the English mainstream. Wittingham was not above a bit of conventional rudeness about his enemies ('Satan hath … most impudently abused this notable gift of singing, chiefly by the papists, his ministers … by strange language that cannot edify … [and] by hiring men to tickle the ears'). He ended up as Dean of Durham, going, like his beloved psalms, from exile to establishment as the wheel turned once more.

Like Wittingham, most musicians tried to keep out of the way of trouble. Not so William Hunnis, Gentleman of the Chapel Royal. In 1555 he was arrested and accused of being part of a conspiracy to rob the exchequer, then use the funds to travel to France, convert a foreign coin called 'ealdergylders' into gold by means of alchemy, then return to England, murder Mary and Philip and put the Protestant Princess Elizabeth on the throne. The notes of his interrogation and confessions seem to put Hunnis right at the heart of this barmy scheme, and in March 1555 he was taken to the Tower.[37] This was treason, at a time when just being an avid Protestant, as Hunnis was, was enough by itself to condemn you to the flames. Persecution was in full fury in 1555. It is, therefore, nothing short of astonishing that Hunnis escaped with his life. There seems to be no possible explanation for the quality of mercy shown to him other than that musicians were somehow afforded a degree of protection, perhaps because the monarch personally valued their services in the Chapel Royal. It was not a consideration given to poor Cranmer. When Elizabeth acceded (without the help of alchemy) Hunnis got his job back and went on to become Master of the Children at the Chapel, as well as writing devotional poetry which was often set to music by his principal colleagues, and a leading light in the world of choirboy theatricals. The life of a prominent church musician was certainly never boring.

Alone among the children of Henry VIII, Elizabeth I achieved a settlement for English church music which endured. She did so largely through her successful use of the policy of not dying. Had her reign lasted five or six years, like those of her two half-siblings, church music today would be different.

BY 1558, THE REFORMATION had touched the lives of every musician who had lived through it. None more so than Thomas Tallis. His places of work, by themselves, chart its consuming progress: early training at a priory (Dover) like any bright, musical boy; a wealthy parish church (St Mary-at-Hill) to smooth the path to London; a monastery (Waltham) just as they were ceasing to exist; a newly refounded cathedral (Canterbury); finally, the long-cherished post at the now pre-eminent Chapel Royal. He left us perfect music for every phase of change and his body of work is, perhaps, more interesting precisely because of the pressures he faced.

Always, he played the game. He joined Waltham in late 1538, right in the white heat of the Dissolution. Why? The writing must have been pretty clearly visible on the song-school wall. But Waltham was an important centre, close to London, and personally hosted Cranmer and Henry VIII in these years, as well as Anne Boleyn shortly before: there is a strong hint of an ambitious musician cultivating important friends (and leaving with two years' pay for probably little more than eighteen months' work). There is an image, popular today, of the Tudor Catholic composer weeping and wailing in solitude, bemoaning his fate in sad, self-imposed internal exile, despised and rejected by the world around him. But Tallis played a blinder. This was a man who did well out of the war.

As well as the living, the Reformation affected the dead. Perhaps no liturgy exemplifies the change from the late medieval to the early modern mind-set better than music for the departed soul. Before the Reformation, the faithful (and well-off) Christian would seek, and pay for, their own 'Dirige' (or 'Dirge') and mass, with the associated prayers known as 'Placebo', to be sung after their death with as much regularity and ceremony as they could afford. Some such endowments would go on indefinitely: a few, for example in university college chapels, still do.

Paying your way into heaven has provided a convenient target for the pot-shots of reformers and iconoclasts, in this period and since. But the liturgy of the dead also provided an ongoing cycle of prayer, securely funded, with duties and responsibilities for the church musician, from the smallest parish side aisle to the grandest cathedral. These voices now ceased. In 1549, John Fisher, a Gentleman of Henry VIII's Chapel Royal, provided in his will for 'the priests, clerks and singing men of the King's Chapel and Vestry, for singing at his dirige and mass, £4',[38] a touching instance of the collegiality of such musical foundations. It seems unlikely that his friends were able to sing him to his rest as he had asked them to do.

Ceremonies changed too. The parish procession was one of those semi-magical rituals where the religious, social and corporate life of the parish gets all muddled up together, and as a result reformers loathed it. Priest and people would carry banners of their saints, a cross, and maybe some colourful local celebrity like a cloth dragon, singing and ringing handbells as they went around the parish to a field at its edge where a cross stood by a lane. There, the priest would say 'the gospels to the corn in the field ... that it should better grow',[39] as a clearly rather shocked William Tyndale put it. The old and poor were given their dole. The young, no doubt, sneaked off to the woods. Everyone else, praying over, stopped for a beer. At Clare in Suffolk in the 1520s, 'at a tree called Perryes Crosse at thende of that streete, the vicare redde a ghospell as the uttermoste parte of their bounds. And then they had there some ale or drinkings.'[40] Or, in the mightily affronted words of one commentator, 'those uplandyshe processions and gangynges about ... be spent in ryotyng and in belychere'.[41]

Such traditions had deep roots. Reformers found it hard going digging them out. A century later, writers like George Herbert and Richard Baxter were still reporting their existence. But the English parish sounded different after 1560. Inside the church, ceremonies evolved as well. Mass became communion; compline and vespers morphed into evensong. But even in a simple thing like giving a ceremony a name, people don't manage change in as orderly a manner as we might like. John Foxe, writing in the 1570s, talks about someone attending 'evensong' in Oxford in 1520, and a Devon vicar is referring to 'Second evenyng prayer' (like the old First and Second Vespers) as late as 1571.[42]

Art music changed as well. But care must be taken in making too detailed an alignment between changes in musical style and political and other changes. Often it is impossible accurately to assign a particular English anthem, for example, to the reign of Elizabeth or of Edward, or a Latin composition to Henry or Mary, or even later. Sometimes we can only be absolutely sure that a piece wasn't written in a particular year because the composer was dead. A collection, published or in manuscript, might contain pieces written over many years, so the date of the collection (even when known) will not represent the date of composition of all its contents. This uncertainty makes ascribing too much detail of musical style to a particular period potentially hazardous. By the same token, reversing the process and dating pieces of music to a particular historical period on the grounds of style alone is also perilous. The argument quickly becomes circular: we believe pieces of this period had these qualities; this piece has these qualities; therefore this piece belongs to this period, which proves that pieces of this period had these qualities. It's a false syllogism: all cats have four legs; that animal has four legs, therefore that animal is a cat.

The really revolutionary feature that links all these changes is the sound of the church musician singing in English. It is easy to fail to appreciate just how shocking, and liberating, this change was. It was like being given the keys to the palace, previously jealously guarded by an impregnable and unreachable elite, and allowed to run through the courts and galleries by yourself, sitting on the furniture and chatting to the king. Revolutionary becomes the right word. As a result,

English church music got its own lyricists for the first time. Foremost among them was Thomas Cranmer. He was not the only one, and indeed didn't claim personal authorship of the Book of Common Prayer: the very many English versions of Bible, Psalms, primers and prayer books borrow freely from each other, and no doubt writers often worked together, as composers also sometimes did. Modern notions of individual authorship (like the modern notion of the individual) don't apply. But Cranmer was the compiler-in-chief. His voice and his choices are present in the beautiful, meticulously crafted yet simple language of the Collects and canticles of his book. He writes like an angel, but he writes as a man. Like all the best religious writers, his subject is not really God at all, it is human nature. He is writing about us. When he talks of being 'wearied by the changes and chances of this fleeting world'[43] he could be Prospero bidding farewell to his books, or Macbeth to ambition.

This story will encompass many fine composers, but there is no doubt at all who was the finest composer for the English church. It was Thomas Cranmer.

6

Church Music and Society in Elizabeth's England, 1558–1603

Reasons set down by th'author, to perswade every one to learne to
sing.

    William Byrd, *Psalms, Sonnets, and Songs of Sadness and Piety*

The Queen's Majesty ... willeth and commandeth ... that first no
alteration be made of such assignments of living, as heretofore have
been appointed to the use of singing or music in the Church, but
that the same so remain. And that there be a modest distinct song,
so used in all parts of the common prayers in the Church, that the
same may be plainly understood, as if it were read without singing,
and yet nevertheless, for the comforting of such as delight in music,
it may be permitted that in the beginning, or in the end of common
prayers, either at morning or evening, there may be sung an Hymn,
or such like song, to the praise of Almighty God, in the best sort of
melody and music that may be conveniently devised, having respect
that the sentence of the Hymn may be understood and perceived.[1]

THE ROYAL INJUNCTIONS of 1559 show Elizabeth I seeking a
'middle way' for church music from the very beginning. It's as if she is
writing with good and evil angels balanced on either shoulder, one urging
her to indulge her love of what she calls 'the laudable science of music',
the other reining in her enthusiasm with an appeal to reason and restraint.

When one gets a 'modest distinct song', the other gets a 'delight in music'; one gets 'the best sort of music', the other gets the words 'plainly understood'; a 'heretofore' gets a 'nevertheless'; an 'it may be permitted' a 'having respect that'. Elizabeth loved, valued, tolerated, promoted and supported church music and musicians. Crucially, her patronage was personal and ad hominem, just as it was of writers and playwrights. When she talks about 'such as delight in music', there's little doubt who she means.

Elizabeth's leading composers received inestimable benefits at her hand. Under her protectorate, English church music produced a body of work which has been of fundamental importance to everything that came after, and still is. The nurturing power of this relatively long period of relative stability becomes even more apparent when compared with the periods of impermanent leadership and religious turmoil which preceded and followed her reign, both of which could entirely plausibly have ended the tradition of English church music altogether. By finding the political and religious 'middle way', Elizabeth saved church music. Perhaps she did so partly in order to save church music. During her reign, the music of the centre – 'art' music – developed an ever-greater maturity and sophistication, and produced some of its greatest glories, to rival any age. It laid the technical and liturgical groundwork for top-end musical composition over the next two centuries, and put in place the basic choral repertoire of the new services which has been its bedrock ever since.

At the same time, church music in the country suffered. Parish church music-making withered under doctrinal pressures, lack of much decent music appropriate to its means, and problems with money. But, as so often, out of the ashes grew something new, distinctive and important: psalm-singing. Devotional music-making in the home became more established too. As the corporate musical life of the parish church dwindled, so psalms, sonnets and songs were increasingly sung around the household hearth, with lutes, viols and virginals, by musicians of many and various types. Composers started to write specifically for this kind of informal act of musical worship, sometimes writing the same piece in two versions, one for church, the other for the home. This kind of music-making has particular significance in the life of the English catholic.

From the start, Elizabeth set her course between the extremes espoused by her two half-siblings. For the reformers, the 1559 Act of Uniformity formally abolished the Use of Sarum and adopted the 1552 Book of Common Prayer: for 'such as delight in music', the wilder Calvinist elements of the 1552 prayer book were removed, and a year later Latin primers were allowed once again. A concrete, practical example of this policy approach was slipped in, almost unnoticed, to the Injunction quoted above: in Edward's reign, music was simplified, therefore choirs were told to pay off most of their trained musicians. Elizabeth also wanted simple, straightforward music, but allowed all the musicians employed in Mary's time to remain in post. The invitation was clear: you should make music for the reformed liturgy, but you could have all the resources you needed to do something original and distinctive. Elizabeth's musicians responded with the now-familiar English genius for compromise and adaptation.

There was, naturally, further dismantling of the Catholic superstructure. Rood-lofts were taken down, and 'wrytynges' put up in their place (the stern 'black-letter' Commandments and Lord's Prayer which can still be seen lecturing their congregations in remote parishes).[2] In a rerun of ten years earlier, the closing-down sale of the old Catholic liturgy involved getting rid of a lot of stuff, and the ever-pragmatic Tudor musician had an eye for a bargain: a choirman from Cambridge bought the face of the Virgin which had been unpicked from the altar cloth 'bi commaundment of the archdeacon'.[3]

Politically, Elizabeth had to manage a good deal of opposition and argy-bargy in getting her way in Parliament and Convocation, including in matters like 'curious singing' and 'the use of organs' in church. But one vote was enough and, once through, the new policy was shown off first at the heart of the establishment. The coronation, which of necessity preceded the passing of any new laws, was sung in Latin, with 'Salve festa dyes'. Soon after, on 'the xij day of May [1559] be-gane the Englys [service] in the quen chapell.'[4] By St George's Day 1562 these English services were draped about with all the trappings of popery, at least according to one typically partisan contemporary opinion: 'the Queen's grace went from her Chapel ... with twenty of her Chapel in copes of cloth of gold ... singing the English procession ...'

As usual with the Tudors – and especially with Elizabeth – politics was never far away. Two years later, Matthew Parker, Archbishop of Canterbury, reaffirmed the main purpose of English church music, showing off to the French: 'they thought we had neither ... persons of our profession in any regard or estimation, or of any ability amongst us ... I did beat that plainly out of their heads. And so they seemed to be glad ... that we did not expel music out of our quires, telling them that our music drowned not the principal regard of our prayer ...'[5] Parker used the phrase 'reverent mediocrity' for this measured approach to music in the liturgy. It's a pity the word 'mediocrity' has since come to connote low standards and poor quality. In Parker's usage, indicating a balance and moderation, his little phrase is a perfect description of the Elizabethan ideal.

The Elizabethan Settlement sounds more planned and deliberate than it was. In many ways, it was a fudge, a compromise between opposing forces which had the happy side effect of liberating a new creativity in church music, at the same time as the corpses on which Edward and Mary had tried out their musical experiments were being laid quietly to rest. By the time Elizabeth had out-reigned both her half-siblings, her settlement was safely launched, 'unless, which God forbid', as one nervous visitor wrote home in late 1559, 'there is another change next week'.[6]

The diarist Henry Machyn charted the spread of the new musical order through London and beyond. In June 1559, at a burial at St Bartholomew's, London, 'the clarkes song Te Deum laudamus in Englys'. A service at Cornhill in April 1561 saw 'xxx chylderyn syngyng the Pater-noster in Englys'. St George's Day that year was celebrated at Windsor, 'the clarkes and prestes ... syngyng the Englys prossessyon'. A year later, Machyn noted polyphonic music, too: 'The xxv day of May was bered master Godderyke sqwyer, the wyche he d[i]ed at ys place with-in Whyt-freres, and cared unto sant Andrew's in Holborne to be bered; and ther was the compene of the Clarkes syngyng pryke-song ...'[7] (Perhaps the chant-like harmonised version of the English burial service in the Wanley Part Books, or something similar.) Machyn is a prime example of an eyewitness filtering his account through his own interests: his business was the supply of mourning liveries, and he records the details of his regular funeral-going with relish.

Another writer to let his own enthusiasms show was Bishop John Jewel in 1560:

> Religion is somewhat more established now than it was. The people are everywhere exceedingly inclined to the better part. Church music for the people has very much conduced to this. For as soon as they had once commenced singing publicly in only one little church in London, immediately not only the churches in the neighbourhood, but also distant towns, began to vie with one another in the same practice. You may now see sometimes at Paul's Cross, after the service, six thousand persons, old and young, of both sexes, all singing together and praising God.[8]

Jewel reflects a vivid light on the sheer excitement uncorked by allowing the people to take part, and also how the practice spread outwards from the centre to 'distant towns'. But his account must be treated with care: no commentator at the time is impartial and Jewel, an enthusiast for reform, clearly wanted to talk up the success of the new ways. Can 6,000 people really sing 'together', outside, without instruments? Is he perhaps talking up the success of this psalm-singing flash-mob in order to make a point? He slightly gives the game away by ending his review of this performance: 'this sadly [i.e. very much] annoys the mass priests and the devil'. But, whatever the detail, Jewel's account clearly indicates that there was a real popular appetite for a new, entirely inclusive form of musical worship: psalm-singing.

The early printed versions of English psalms for singing chart their rapid progress into the public consciousness. It's a tale of two cities: English reformers, translators and printers like Robert Crowley, Thomas Sternhold and John Hopkins working alongside Protestant exiles from Europe in London; William Wittingham working alongside Protestant exiles from England in Geneva. Their appeal was their inclusivity – 'first a psalm sung by the whole congregation'. By 1562, the many early experiments in translation, metre and allocation of melodies had coalesced into something approaching a permanent, accepted, published form.

The Whole Book of Psalms Collected into English Metre has become known as 'Sternhold and Hopkins', after the two Edwardian versifiers who began the task of creating and assembling its contents. In some respects the name is a little misleading: for one thing, the two men didn't actually work together on the translation as Hopkins only got involved after Sternhold's death; for another, other authors, including Wittingham, feature generously (neatly identified by their initials in the text), as the title page freely acknowledges; there is also a lot more Hopkins than Sternhold.

Nonetheless their book tapped into something profoundly populist. Helped on its way by the convinced Protestant, skilled musician and genius publisher (if not always scrupulous proofreader) John Day, *The Whole Booke of Psalms Collected into English Metre* was reprinted 200 times between 1550 and 1640. It remained easily the dominant version until the turn of the eighteenth century, if not always critically acclaimed (a later Poet Laureate called the verse translations 'contemptible', 'an absolute travesty', and 'entirely destitute of elegance'[9]). These were 'metrical' renderings, versified into a regular metre and rhyme scheme. As such they were not part of the liturgy, and were not permitted during services.

But people liked them. This is why Elizabeth allowed 'an hymn' (meaning a metrical psalm) to be sung before and after the common prayer, to 'the best sort of music'. The service itself preserves its verbal virginity, sandwiched between these two musical bookends.

It's a brilliant little compromise: the people get their psalm, but the liturgy remains intact. It's the kind of neat footwork, drawing the sting of potential grievance from both sides, which Elizabeth the politician used so skilfully and which served her so well, and it remained the standard 'legal' position concerning congregational singing and the liturgy for centuries to come.

'Metrical' versions grew out of folk tradition, the old liturgy and the aristocratic pursuit of poetry. Sir Philip Sidney, for example, had all the attributes of the ideal courtier: handsome, brave, clever, good in tights, and dead in battle at the age of thirty-one. He also, of course, wrote poems. Like musicians (and indeed clerics like John Donne), the Tudor poet thought nothing of hymning his mistress and his maker with equal fervour: religion and daily life were not different, and he encountered both his God and his mistress every day. This is Sidney's opening to Psalm 23:

> The Lord, the Lord, my Shepherd is,
> And so can never I
> Taste misery:
> He rests me in green pastures His:
> By waters still and sweet,
> He guides my feet.[10]

This is the same passage from Sternhold and Hopkins (in this case, written by Hopkins):

> My shepheard is the livyng Lord,
> Nothing therefore I neede,
> In pastures fayre with waters calme,
> He set me for to feede.

And this is the 'prose' version, based on the Bible and earlier primers and prayer books by Myles Coverdale and Thomas Cranmer:

> The Lord is my shepherd: therefore can I lack nothing.
> He shall feed me in a green pasture: and lead me forth beside the waters of comfort.

Of course, the point of putting psalms into a regular metre is to sing them. Almost all psalms in Sternhold and Hopkins are in either short or common metre ('Master Sternhold's metre'), and thus any common metre tune could be used for any common metre psalm. A neat application of this principle is the 'bi-fold' psalter, bound at the spine but with the pages cut horizontally halfway up, so that the words on the top half can be opened independently of the music at the bottom, allowing any psalm to be read simultaneously with any tune in the same metre.

Tunes came from a variety of sources. Coverdale, as far back as 1530, adapted Lutheran chorales like 'Ein feste Burg' and old Catholic plainsong tunes like 'Christe, qui lux es et dies', very much in the reformer's spirit of practicality. Many of the next generation of metrical psalters didn't specify tunes at all. Robert Crowley (1549) printed one four-part tune for the entire psalter, leaving the singer to work out how the words fitted (badly, mostly). Later, some gave the name of the tune but no music, like a ballad-sheet, assuming the singer would know it (and, perhaps, that he or she might not be able to read it anyway). Henry Machyn notes the thrilling freedom of this style of singing in 21 September 1559, perhaps the very first record of congregational singing: 'the new morning prayer ... after Geneva fashion – begin to ring at 5 in the morning; men and women all do sing, and boys'; and at a later date, 'The xvij day of Marche [1560] ... after the sermon done they songe all, old and yong, a salme in myter, a the tune of Genevay ways'; 'all the pepull dyd syng the tune of Geneway, and with the base of the organs'.[11]

As new editions appeared, tunes were increasingly printed along with the words, usually with just a single line of music which could be sung in unison or perhaps with simple harmony, 'faburden'-style, or played on a keyboard or lute. By 1563, Day was including four-part tunes throughout his Sternhold and Hopkins, with tune in the tenor, Lutheran-style. Each singer had his own part book with all the words, but mostly only his own voice-part printed, with just a few printed in score (for example Louis Bourgeois's tune to 'The Old Hundredth', which is still sung today). Often a tune was printed alongside one psalm, then singers were referred back to that tune when they reached a later psalm in the same metre: 'Psalme. Cxxxix. Sing this as the 137. psalme.'

Archbishop Parker aimed slightly more self-consciously at the 'art'-music end of the spectrum with his psalter of around 1567 (his book is privately printed, not for general sale). Parker included eight tunes specially composed by Tallis to match the mood of each psalm: 'you ought to conjoin a sad tune or song with a sad Psalm, and a joyful tune and song with a joyful Psalm', he says, adding a personal review of Tallis's efforts: 'the first is meek, devout to see, The second, sad, in majesty ...'[12]

In popular editions like Sternhold and Hopkins, psalms were sung mostly to the 'official' tunes based on musical practice imported from Geneva or, increasingly, newly composed melodies in a similar style, often with different harmonisations of the same tune in a single book. Some people disapproved, of course: the nickname 'Geneva jigs' was used for the tunes by at least one Puritan-inclined nobleman, and allegedly by the Queen herself (though Elizabeth surely would have enjoyed a good tune). Hints could still be heard of a mischievous tendency to break the rules and have some fun by bolting the words onto an old favourite, which didn't always work: 'they do no more adhere and keep place together than the Hundredth Psalm to the tune of Greensleeves',[13] quipped Mistress Ford in Shakespeare's *The Merry Wives of Windsor* in 1602. It sounds as if she, or her creator, had heard someone try.

The keyword now was practicality. Sternhold and Hopkins was music for use by everyone. There's a psalm here rewritten to be sung by a woman. There's a picture of a slightly grim-looking father leading psalm-singing with his wife and children. Boys at the new grammar schools were taught to 'sing together one of these psalms hereafter instituted, such as the schoolmaster shall appoint',[14] skills they could then pass on to their own families and parishes. Parishes would buy one copy so that the clerk could lead the congregation and fill the church with nice, cheap music. Day subtly adjusted the contents of each edition to steer a course between Anglican and Puritan and maximise sales. This was church music 'to be song of all the people together, in all churches ... and moreover in private houses'.[15]

Mistress Ford's throwaway remark shows just how far psalm-singing had become a part of daily life by the turn of the seventeenth century. She taps into an important theme of this story: whatever else may be going on in their lives, the English just love to sing. The church music scholar Nicholas Temperley sums it up with characteristic elegance: 'they sang not because they were Puritans, but because they were singers'.[16]

Psalm-singing was part of a quiet, rather private, revolution. The Reformation had posed two questions: Who sings? Where? Sternhold and Hopkins provided the answers: We all do, wherever we like.

WILLIAM BYRD SPENT THE years from 1563 to 1572 working, rather reluctantly, as Organist of Lincoln Cathedral. Some of his shorter English service music may date from this period of his career: beautiful, practical stuff, deservedly in regular use ever since, but perhaps not revealing the depths of his musical soul.

The leading Protestant composers were likewise at work creating a repertoire for the new liturgy, among them Thomas Caustun, Robert Parsons and the indefatigable Richard Farrant. The 'short' service style, used for the canticles set for matins and evensong, is one step up from the simple, harmonised-chant style and allows some inner-part movement away from strictly syllabic word-setting and some demure imitation. Composers also wrote music for other parts of the liturgy, some of which have remained within its musical framework (such as the sung Preces and Responses), but others not, or to a lesser extent (Responses to the Commandments, Litany, Lord's Prayer, 'sentences' for offertory or communion, choral Venite and defunct liturgical items like the Quicunque Vult). The English communion, naturally, had vastly less opportunity for music than the old Latin Mass. It was even reduced in musical scope compared to Edward's reign: the setting by John Heath in the Edwardian Wanley Part Books has music for all five sections of the Office, while Elizabethan sources of the same piece include only three: Gloria, Credo and Sanctus.

The Elizabethan composer embarked on the task of recreating English church music almost from scratch. One of his new resources was the anthem. Once again, the printer John Day was a crucial figure. Every generation of musicians needs its businessmen and entrepreneurs, and Day was one of the best. (As well as his psalters, he published John Foxe's *Book of Martyrs*, a lurid hagiography of Protestant immolations which wouldn't stop selling: Charles Dickens has David Copperfield's nurse Peggotty owning a 'large quarto' copy three hundred years later, of which David does not recollect 'one word'.[17]) In 1560 Day put together his first version of *Certaine notes* 'set forth in foure and three parts to be song at the morning communion and evening praier'.

Once again, it is impossible to be certain whether all the music dates from Edward's reign and the project was put on hold during Mary's Counter-Reformation, or whether some items were composed in the very early years of Elizabeth. In either case, the book is the main source of English anthems and service music in the early reformed style and a priceless repository of some very fine music indeed: Thomas Tallis's *If Ye Love Me* is simply the best-known (and best) pearl in Day's oyster.

English church music really became just that – English – at the moment when composers started setting their own language. The new style took on some distinctively English musical signatures too. The reformed style is plain, direct and, at its best, has a simplicity and elegance which Latin Catholic music never achieved. A distinctive musical trick carried over from pre-Reformation music was the use of the raised and lowered third degree of a scale or chord in close proximity, known as a 'false relation'. Tallis, for example, uses both kinds of chord on both the first and fifth degree of the mode (what later music would call tonic and dominant major and minor chords) in the first few bars of *O Lord, Give thy Holy Spirit*, written probably in the late 1560s. The 'clash' is allowed to arise naturally from the flow of the lines, one going up, the other down, and the effect can be plangent and expressive, so much so that composers took to writing both spellings of the third simultaneously (for example in Tallis's little *O nata lux*, where it sounds like the many similar appearances in the music of John Sheppard).

English composers particularly enjoyed using a version of this little rhetorical gesture at cadences, where the seventh degree of the scale is lowered in a part moving down, raised in another part moving up. This bit of local colour was already present as far back as the music of Taverner, but it became so much a part of the late sixteenth-century composer's library that it became known as the 'English cadence'. Other countries used it too, of course, but with nothing like the same relish as Tallis, Byrd, Thomas Morley, Thomas Weelkes, Edmund Hooper, Nathaniel Giles, Orlando Gibbons, Thomas Tomkins, William Child, John Blow, Pelham Humfrey and everyone in between. Henry Purcell treated its possibilities as his own personal sweetshop. The day he first heard an English cadence, peering over the music desk as a junior

The composer as professional: Tallis turning his hand to the reformed style in O Lord, Give thy Holy Spirit, *giving (very nearly) 'to every syllable a note' as Cranmer asked.*

choirboy at the Chapel Royal, singing some ancient bit of Tallis or Gibbons, perhaps from the composer's own handwritten copy, he must have thought Christmas had come early. If the voice of the turtle is ever heard in our land, it will certainly be singing an English cadence.

As well as William Byrd, beavering away on his hilltop overlooking the flatlands of Lincolnshire, the principal composers for the new order were, naturally, men who learnt their trade under the old dispensation. All were members of the Chapel Royal. Thomas Caustun and Robert Parsons contributed small-scale service music, as required. Parsons would later put a lot more into the new style, and get a lot more out. Richard Farrant has left us a tiny number of tiny English anthems, perfect within their limits, and shared the running of the Chapel Royal theatre company with William Hunnis (of the alchemy conspiracy) and Richard Edwardes. Tye had given up active membership of the Chapel Royal for his parish in the Fens. Of the leading Catholics, Tallis wrote a fairly small quantity of English service music with his customary genius for adapting to whatever was asked of him. Mundy, like Parsons and Byrd, and Sheppard before him, would make something very grand out of the new English service, and add to the repertoire of works in Latin, as Elizabeth permitted.

Latin church music had to find a new way, just as English music did. Composers could still write a certain amount of sacred music to Latin texts, but the old services had gone, and with them the principal musical forms of the old order – the mass, Latin Magnificat and votive anthem to Virgin or saint. Now, Latin pieces could only be performed during the liturgy as anthems, or in the home, which in both cases meant non-liturgical, usually biblical, texts. Alongside this shift of textual emphasis, and indeed because of it, composers moved away from the compositional techniques which underpinned the old style, such as the use of plainsong and basing sacred music on another piece, and cultivated an interest in counterpoint for its own sake, developing it in new ways, technically and expressively. (As always, of course, there is nothing hard and fast about this: Robert White used the old technique of alternating plainsong with choral polyphony in his settings of a compline hymn, and there was much borrowing between sacred choral music and instrumental composition.)

Comparing the post-1558 work-lists of the leading English composers of works in Latin (Tallis, Byrd, Robert White) with those of their continental contemporaries (Lassus and Palestrina, who between them wrote many hundreds of Masses and Magnificats) shows just how far Latin composition in England, as well as its vernacular sibling, had developed a genuinely English accent.

Most of the composers mentioned here worked in the same place: the Chapel Royal. This body of clergy and musicians could hardly be more important to the development of English high-art sacred music. No single organisation has ever done more to foster composition, creativity, performance and the passing-on of skills, at any time in music history.

The Chapel Royal was, and still is, part of the monarch's household. From medieval to Restoration times, the Master of the Chapel Royal had the power to travel the country, 'impressing' the best singing boys for the royal service. This sounds illiberal to us, but the chosen children received a good standard of care and a unique musical education, and may well have escaped a provincial life with little to offer, musically or otherwise (like Thomas Tusser, who was only too glad to escape from

St Nicholas's chapel at Wallingford Castle). Many leading composers began life as choirboys at the Chapel Royal, and the best had found a place of employment for life: Byrd and Purcell both joined as children (although in Byrd's case this is an inference, not a documented fact), and were adult members until their deaths. They worked on a daily basis with the best adult musicians in the country, trying out new compositions together, receiving a daily immersion in practical musical skills as well as Latin, grammar, Christian morals, Aesop's fables and music theory (and the occasional thrashing) in the schoolroom, helped perhaps by an older boy whose 'brest hath changed', reading from the musical stave painted up on the wall.

The Chapel Royal travelled a good deal in the Tudor and Elizabethan periods, making 'progress' around the country with Henry VIII or Elizabeth I, to escape the plague and intimidate the locals. The choir (slightly reduced in numbers) came along too, travelling in carts and billeted on local householders, allowing suitably splendid royal devotions in whatever noble house the monarch fancied staying in that night. Both men and boys of the Chapel Royal were also intimately involved in the wider musical and cultural life of London: in the period before women were allowed to appear on stage, the boys functioned as a fully fledged theatrical troupe (as did their colleagues at St Paul's, Windsor and elsewhere), and were immensely accomplished and hugely popular – the genuine celebrities of their day. Ben Jonson wrote a touching elegy of one such child-star, Salomon Pavy, a child of Elizabeth's chapel who died in his theatrical prime in 1602:

> Yeares he numbered scarce thirteene
> When fates turned cruel!
> Yet three fill'd Zodiackes had he beene
> The stage's jewell;
> And did act (what now we mone)
> Old men so duely;
> As, sooth, the Parcae thought him one,
> He plai'd so truely ...
> But, being so much too good for earth,
> Heaven vows to keep him.[18]

The men, too, were much in demand to add their skills to the music at other churches on special occasions. In Mary's reign, Henry Machyn noted a service at Guildhall where 'The mass was sung by divers of the queen's chapel and children'[19] (the name 'Chapel Royal' did not come into regular use for another hundred years), and his many references to large bodies of 'clerks' and 'children' singing at other London parishes through into Elizabeth's reign may well also be to the Chapel Royal choir 'moonlighting' in this way. Tallis and Mundy both had strong links with St Mary-at-Hill both before and after becoming Gentlemen of the Chapel Royal.

The Chapel Royal offered the perfect medium for the growth of the best in church music: the best-paid and most secure employment; the personal patronage of the monarch, allowing freedoms and protection not available elsewhere, including, crucially, to Catholics; the daily company of like-minded musicians (and their daughters – many Chapel Royal men married into each other's families); and plenty of perks. At the same time, those other institutions that used to offer opportunities to musicians (monasteries and cathedrals, for example), had either closed or been significantly degraded. Now, every talented, ambitious musician headed for London and the Chapel Royal. Once there, they could work on the new styles together. Their musical neologisms were absorbed, sponge-like, by the bright-eyed little boy in the front row, who might have been the son or nephew of one of them, or a promising lad recently brought in from Newark or Norwich by the Master of the Children, who just might turn out to be the Chapel Royal's next genius. The musical DNA was passed down from generation to generation and, as in biological families, it was easy to spot: Tallis begat Byrd, begat Gibbons (senior), begat Gibbons (junior), begat Purcell (Henry, minor). Not a bad list.

Out in the country, away from the geniuses, the proponents of church music treated the opening of the new reign with the usual mixture of stubbornness, pragmatism and muddle. The vicar of Much Wenlock in Shropshire recalled telling his flock, 'Friends, ye shall pray for the prosperous estate of our most noble Queen Elizabeth', but then 'we in the choir sang the canticle Te Deum laudamus, pater noster, ave maria ... then went I to the altar and said out the Mass of St Catherine',[20] with processions, Latin litanies, Collects specifically addressed to a Catholic monarch, bonfires, bread, cheese and beer. It is traditional, thoroughly Catholic stuff (the priest, as ever, singing with his clerk and others to make up the choir).

Eamon Duffy has a movingly elegiac phrase for what these people were doing: 'and so, with impeccably Catholic ceremonial, all over the country parishes celebrated what were to be in fact the funeral rites of Catholic England'.[21] As usual, Visitations conducted by government officials told people what to do, and, as usual, people didn't do it. Parishes were made to list everything they had got, including 'processionals, hymnals, manuals'. The vicar of Morebath, in Devon, was ordered to surrender his mass book and chasuble. Instead, he gave them to trusted parishioners for safe-keeping: 'Thomas Borrage hath our masse boke ... Edward Rumbelow hath the chesapyll.'[22] This record of the whereabouts of the hidden mass book was repeated annually for three years. Then it stopped.

As usual, the more distant corners of the kingdom were harder to reach. Resistance spilled over into open rebellion in Durham in 1569, with large crowds flocking to hear mass in the cathedral. Exeter Cathedral received a letter from Lord Mountjoye in December 1559 reminding them that 'whereas ... order was taken, that the vicars of your church ... at every such meeting [are] to sing a psalm ... which order, taken by the visitors, you promised by your corporal oath to see observed. We have now of late heard say, that contrary to the said order, and your own oath, certain of your vicars have scoffed and jested openly at the godly doings of the people ...'[23] The clergy, of course, blamed the congregation, and Matthew Parker, Archbishop of Canterbury, had to tell them again to 'quietly permit and suffer such congregation of people ... to sing or say the godly prayers in the morning, and at other times'.[24] Bishop John Jewel saw things the other way around: the ordinary people of his native Devon were surprisingly receptive, while resistance came from the clergy, especially those who used to be 'on our side'.[25] As Jewel had already noted in London, the reformed church had a strong appeal for the ordinary worshipper through congregational singing. Perhaps this was why reactionary clergy feared it.

As at other times of change, ceremonies of the dead and their music proved hardest to dislodge. Visitations in 1560 and 1561 asked if any clerks were singing at funerals 'any other thing otherwise than it is appointed by the common order of the service-book, or no?'[26] The state was forced to carry on sniffing out this sort of deeply ingrained superstition throughout Elizabeth's reign, and indeed well into the seventeenth century.

Cathedral music felt the chill blast of Puritan disapproval too: 'we do not assert that the chanting in churches, together with organs, is to be retained, but we do disapprove of it as we ought to do',[27] wrote the Bishops of London and Winchester in 1567. Four years later, Winchester Cathedral was told that 'in the choir no more shall be used in song that shall drown any word or syllable, or draw out in length or shorten any word or syllable … and … repeating of notes with words or sentences, whereby the sense may be hindered in the hearer shall not be used'[28] – a pretty conventional restatement of Cranmer's ideal of three decades before. But the Puritans did not succeed in closing down cathedral music. Despite getting caught up in doctrinal controversy and, no less importantly, severe financial pressures, cathedral music, like church music generally, found its own way through the dark vales of Elizabethan politics. Once again, English church music proved itself to be the great survivor.

Music in the parish church suffered in Elizabeth's reign. There is precious little evidence for what was actually sung in her early years, but it is likely that those parishes which managed to preserve something of their pre-Reformation choral infrastructure used a mixture of simple, chant-like service music and anthems like those in the collections from Edward's reign; single-lined music like that by John Marbeck, perhaps with some harmony in the old 'faburden' manner; and metrical psalms. Organs, at least in places which had hung onto theirs during the depredations of the Reformation, probably began to play with the voices, rather than separately, from around the 1570s. Choirs may have been on the way down as well, but congregational singing was new, and popular. It is significant that of John Day's two publications of the early Elizabethan period, Sternhold and Hopkins, for congregational and domestic use, got reprinted over and over again, while *Certaine notes* …, aimed at parish choirs, did not achieve a single reprinting after 1565.

The only trained (and paid) parish musician to survive the Reformation was one of English church music's great characters: the parish clerk. Chaucer has 'a parissh clerk, The which that was ycleped Absolon'.[29] He has good clothes, nice legs, a picture of a St Paul's cathedral window on his shoes, doubles up professionally as barber, blood-letter and legal clerk, likes dancing, and can play the 'rubible' (fiddle) and 'giterne' (guitar), to which 'he song som tyme a loud quynyble', or high treble, skills he was probably meant to use more often in church than in the pub, where he liked to impress the 'gaylard tappestere' (pretty barmaid). More than a century later, a parish in Devon discovered only too clearly how central its clerk was to the smooth running of the parish, music included. In the 1530s a dispute over pay led to the temporary absence of a clerk. A villager's wife had given birth to twins, but both had died. The vicar arrived at church to sing a Requiem, but needed the clerk to open and prepare the church as well as to sing the responses and add his voice to the sung liturgy. The door was locked and the bereaved father had to go round the village in search of 'the churche dore key' and enlist the help of a former clerk 'be fore he coud have any mas sayd for hys child: and all was for lacke of a clerke'.[30]

Early in Elizabeth's reign, rules for 'clerks and their duty' specifically forbade this kind of music: they were asked 'whether they use to sing any number of psalms, dirige-like, at the burial of the dead'.[31] The clerk was now a layman, not in minor orders as he would have been before the Reformation. A new coat of arms awarded to the Confraternity, Fellowship and Company of Parish Clerks of the City of London on 30 March 1582 reflected the clerk's changed duties and status: the holy water sprinklers used in the coat of arms a century earlier were replaced by two 'pricksong' books, clearly identifiable as books of psalm tunes rather than choir music. The clerk's traditional role as part of the parish's musical establishment now meant singing the English litany and responses and leading congregational singing. The clerk, in the full finery of his parish livery, is a familiar figure in engravings of parish music-making by William Hogarth and others in the eighteenth century, and in the rich cast of English eccentrics in the works of William Thackeray, George Eliot, Dickens and Thomas Hardy into the nineteenth. He is, perhaps unfairly, often a figure of fun. The descendant of the Elizabethan parish clerk is Mr Bumble in *Oliver Twist*, superbly conscious of his status, his position, his blue coat, his cocked hat and his teaspoons. Today, the parish clerk is an official of local government and the church. Music is not part of the duties.

Sometimes, on his way to the choir stalls, the English church musician found himself having to negotiate his way past the clerk's first cousin, the verger, or his ancestor, the pew-opener, arranging his (or her) congregation 'like a drill sergeant', according to Charles Dickens, who asked himself 'why pew-openers must always be the most disagreeable females procurable, and whether there is any religious dread of a disastrous infection of good-humour which renders it indispensable to set those vessels of vinegar upon the road to Heaven.'[32]

Clerks were also closely involved in another parish activity involving music which withered in the brave, new, anti-traditional world – religious plays. Their association with saints and superstitions was too much for the Puritans. The boy Shakespeare was part of the last generation to see these plays, and he referred back to their themes, as well as to the musical element of rhetorical speech, in Hamlet's fascinating acting lesson to the First Player: 'Speak the speech, I pray you, as I pronounced it to you, trippingly on the tongue' (i.e. like singing); don't 'tear a passion to tatters ... it out Herods Herod' (a reference to a famous scene in the old mystery cycles). His strictures sound curiously like the Puritans' objections to the effects of too much music: 'use all gently: for in the very torrent, tempest, and – as I may say – whirlwind of passion, you must acquire and beget a temperance that may give it smoothness'.[33] His counterpointing of the words 'passion' and 'temperance' is just one of an unknowable number of instances where his audience (or at least the 'judicious' part of it) would have recognised an allusion to contemporary discourse which is lost on us. The link between church music and acting flowered in a new way as boys' choirs started appearing in the wildly popular new type of secular, moralising, tragical-comical-historical (and, later, dangerously political) plays by Ben Jonson, John Lyly and others.

Perhaps the best example of the 'Elizabethan settlement' manifesting itself as the easeful coincidence of old and new is the way the celebration of a much-loved old saint became a celebration of the Queen herself. St Hugh was from Lincoln, and the medieval church had always honoured him once a year with masses and bells all across the vast diocese. After the Northern rising in the late 1560s, such Catholic practices were discouraged even more persuasively in yet another attempt to extend official writ into the wet, reactionary parts of the country. But a happy compromise was at hand. St Hugh's day, 17 November, was also the anniversary of Elizabeth's accession and a new church service was authorised. Bell-ringing and holiday-making carried on, and the people's much-loved traditions merged into the new political order.

Naturally church music was required to play its part. When the Accession service appeared in print in 1578 there were three hymns, the metre designed to fit with melodies from Sternhold and Hopkins (a sure sign that every parish could now be assumed to own and know it): 'A song of rejoicing for the prosperous reign of our most gracious sovereign lady Queen Elizabeth. Made to the tune of the 25. psalm.' The initial letters of the sixteen lines of the text of this piece form an acrostic down the left-hand side of the page: 'GOD SAVE THE QUEENE'. This was part of an already long-established tradition of church music honouring the monarch by name. Gilbert Banester contributed such a piece to the Eton Choirbook, *O Maria et Elizabetha*, where the actual name of the monarch is omitted, presumably supplied by the singers in performance to fit the monarch of the day. The text of Robert Fayrfax's *Eterne laudis lilium*, has an acrostic in praise of Elizabeth of York, the wife of Henry VII: 'ELISABETH REGINA ANGLIE'. The anonymous *O Lord Christ Jesu* in the Lumley Part Books prays for 'thy noble servant our sovereign lord King Edward'. William Byrd, still in Lincoln, wrote a piece, probably for the Accession: *O Lord, Make thy Servant Elizabeth our Queen to Rejoice in thy Strength*. It was all good politics.

Sacred music in the home was largely an Elizabethan invention. It persisted vigorously thereafter, well into the welcoming and rackety home life of Samuel Pepys in the 1660s. It arose from a variety of causes: lack of music elsewhere; Puritan emphasis on study and music for moral edification; the availability of printed music and teaching manuals; and, in wealthier families, the presence of a new kind of professional musician, the household tutor. Catholics were, once again, a special case: with no access to church buildings, the great halls and chambers of the old Catholic families became quite literally their sanctuaries, with watchmen posted on suitable turrets and gatehouses to mark the advent of Lord Burghley or his men so that the priest could hastily be shovelled back into his hole.

John Day's collection *Certaine notes* ... of 1560 was for use in 'the Church of Christe'. His second printing, in 1565, was 'to be song in churches, both for men and children'.[34] The 1565 printing adds that the music is 'also to be played upon the instruments'. The four musical lines can be realised by any available combination of voices, viols, 'broken' consort of plucked and bowed strings, keyboards or lutes. In other words, it could be used for music performed in the home. Many part books of the period have a similar, eminently practical, stipulation. Day emphasises this aspect by including a touching little picture of a family singing together (father holding the book), and by a slightly odd instruction in one of the part books: 'this Base part is for children'. Children were always an integral part of the household ensemble, partly for their education and partly because they could sing the parts other members of the family couldn't reach. But they clearly couldn't sing bass. Perhaps Day provided a simplified instrumental bass part for children to practise keyboard harmony or reading the bass clef (but not playing the bass viol, which was bigger than they were).

IN 1572 THE COMPOSER ROBERT Parsons fell out of a boat on the river Trent in Newark and drowned. The principal beneficiary from his death was William Byrd, who took over his place at the Chapel Royal (and who was, by an amazing coincidence, working just down the road from Newark at the time of Parsons's accident).

By 1572 Elizabeth had reigned for longer than Edward and Mary combined. A generation of musicians that had received its entire musical training under her dispensation was coming of age. John Sheppard and Christopher Tye, emblems of the religious divide among composers who had lived through the white heat of the Reformation years, were both dead. Byrd rejoined his soulmate Thomas Tallis at the heart of English music-making, and together they turned their attention to the next chapter.

The Chapel Royal was where composers worked together. A pleasing by-product is that its leading composers often come in pairs: Orlando Gibbons and Edmund Hooper, Henry Purcell and John Blow, William Croft and Maurice Greene; perhaps William Cornysh and Robert Fayrfax in the earlier period (and there are other examples). It's almost as if the life's work of a great genius is more than can be managed by one man on his own (and it is notable, too, how many of these men were surrounded from infancy by a professionally musical family). Tallis and Byrd worked there together as adults only for about thirteen years, and Tallis was 'very aged'[35] (as he described himself in one of their regular bits of conventional droolery to the Queen). But it is perhaps the most important and productive working relationship in the history of English church music. In January 1572 the two men were granted a twenty-one-year monopoly on the printing of 'songes in partes', music paper, and the import and sale of printed music from abroad. It was a comprehensive and practical acknowledgement of the place the two 'Gent. of our Chappell' occupied on the Elizabethan power list.

Three years later they ventured into print with the six part books of the *Cantiones, quae ab argumento sacrae vocantur*. Their French Huguenot printer, Vautrollier, went to lavish and costly lengths with fancy title pages and flowery epistles, something they soon learnt they could not really afford. The dedication, of course, was to the 'Illustrissima Princeps', the Queen. There are seventeen pieces by each man. Scholars who have noticed that this was the seventeenth year of the reign (dates in official documents are given as the year since the beginning of the reign, so the fact was clearly visible), and that the Accession day itself was the 17 November, are surely onto something.

The texts were in Latin. A few had associations with the old Sarum and Roman rites, and a smaller number use plainsong *cantus firmus* technique, another neat musical example of how the new settlement could absorb elements of the old. But this is not, of course, liturgical music as the Latin liturgy no longer existed. This was music for singing at home or, possibly, as anthems in chapels where the listeners could be expected to understand the words, such as Byrd and Tallis's own congregation at the Chapel Royal and in the college chapels of Oxford, Cambridge, Eton and Winchester. The slightly uncomfortable ambiguity in the status of Latin sacred music is perhaps reflected in the rather cagey Latin title of the set, which translated is 'Songs which by their argument may be called sacred'.

A number of the pieces show the touching habit of composers of emulating each other in their choice of text and musical approach. Byrd pays 'hommage' in this way to Tallis, Parsons and the influential Italian resident in London, Alfonso Ferrabosco. (Thomas Morley later called the practice 'virtuous contention', though in his hands it spilled over in at least one instance into straightforward dishonest plagiarism.) There is a residual medieval fascination with canons, which appear backwards and forwards, elongated and diminished, 'recta et recto'. One of the pieces, Byrd's *Laudate pueri Dominum*, is based on an instrumental fantasy, a good example of the composer's hands-on practical job of making something useful, and fashioning a good bit of counterpoint into whatever is needed. (The piece popped up again later in yet another incarnation, as an English anthem.)

This book was born out of a mixture of high art, deep religious conviction, worldly ambition, political positioning and hard-nosed business. This is what life at the top of Tudor society was like, and these men were very good at it. And at writing music. The collection is rich and varied, from impressive large-scale motets like Byrd's *Tribue, Domine* to polished little hymn settings. Tallis's *O nata lux* has the miniaturised perfection of the Edwardian style, translated into Latin. Unfortunately, the book did not sell well. Printed music was still a novelty in England (lagging well behind its European counterparts), and the market was not yet well enough established for an ambitious venture like this. It would be well over a decade before Byrd the businessman was ready to venture into print again. He did rather better at his second attempt.

Christopher Tye died around 1572, after he had retired from active professional musical life to his parish in the Fens. The early 1570s saw the deaths of some other notable church musicians too. Robert Parsons was another fine composer. Like John Sheppard, he wrote rich-textured Latin motets and carried this sound-world into a large-scale setting of the English canticles in the 'great' service style. Like William Mundy, he gave this impressive work the rather obscure title *In medio chori* ('In the middle of the choir'), which probably meant that a group of singers stood between the two sets of choir stalls in the Chapel Royal to give an extra antiphonal effect. He also wrote a splendid ten-part setting of the Latin canticles, which he called his 'Excellent' service. Like Byrd, resourceful scholars have found coded references to English Catholicism in his choice of texts: his celebrated, rich, rather old-fashioned *Ave Maria* is posited as a reference to Mary, Queen of Scots, already a troublesome presence to the north. Parsons was also a Gentleman of the Chapel Royal, and collaborated with both Richard Farrant and Edwardes on songs with a theatrical flavour, so he may well have been involved with the Chapel boys' plays. As was the case with Mundy and Farrant, there were other composers with the same surname – in Parsons's case, at least four, all apparently unrelated. The service sung today as 'Parsons Short' is by a later Robert Parsons.

Another excellent composer who met his end in tragic circumstances around the same time was Robert White. Born in London around 1538, he studied in Cambridge before becoming Organist of Ely Cathedral (marrying the daughter of a previous organist, Christopher Tye), then Chester Cathedral where he was involved with the very last cycles of the famous mystery plays. He became Organist of Westminster Abbey in 1569 or 1570, but never made the logical next step to the Chapel Royal. He died, along with his entire family, in an outbreak of plague in 1574.

White is another example of Elizabeth getting the best out of her composers by allowing them to do what they did best, and the best sacred choral music written in the early years of her reformed church was music which that church couldn't use: Latin music. White's settings of the compline hymn 'Christe, qui lux es et dies', firmly rooted in the pre-Reformation plainsong-based style, are deservedly still sung today. He seemed to be one of those Elizabethans who responded best to the melancholy: his five-voice *Miserere* is grandly gloomy, and his *Lamentations of Jeremiah* are among the finest settings of that totemic favourite of the self-appointed exile, crying in the waste and wilderness of Westminster.

The old war of words between Protestant and Catholic about the place of music had been replaced by a new war between two species of Protestant – Anglican and Puritan – though the new war sounded remarkably like the old one. Few Puritans went as far as Oliver Cromwell would later do and condemned music in church altogether. 'I saye', wrote John Northbrooke in 1577, 'that godly and religious songs may be retained in church. And yet … this ought to be considered, that if we shall perceive that Christian people doe runne unto the churche as to a stage playe, where they may be delighted with pyping and singing (and doe thereby absent themselves from hearing the worde of God preached), in this case we must rather abstaine from a thing not necessarie, than to suffer their pleasures to be cockered with the destruction of their soules.'[36]

This is conventional Puritan stuff. An anonymous Oxford writer put the opposing, Anglican case in a book printed in 1586. He took an elegant dislike (as only an Oxford man can) to extremes on either side: 'rotten rhymes of popery' are 'more fit for grocers' shops and fishmongers' stalls than for God's congregation'; others 'would wholly banish all music out of divine service', whereas 'I detest both the one and the other'. He carefully filleted the arguments for and against choral music advanced by all the leading thinkers, with much reference to classical and biblical authority, and with good, solid attention to practical matters like having different types of music to suit the relative musical ability of congregation and choir, and making sure words could be understood. He concluded: 'music is rather to be used in church than not, because it is the excellent invention and gift of God himself'.[37] His book is a perfect little summary of the intellectual currents surrounding church music in the 1570s and 80s, and a pretty good example of how to construct an argument and sum it up in a pithy title: *The Praise of Music*.

Essentially, as the reign approached its middle, parishes took up the Puritan position; while cathedrals and some larger urban churches adopted the Anglican. Parishes which had managed to hang onto their organs now mostly lost them. One man who still played the organ in church in the 1570s was told off for playing too much (by his own admission 'four times at the morning prayer and four times at the evening prayer'[38]), but claimed that 'the preacher hath always two hours at the least to make his sermon in'. Such organ pieces, where used, were florid little fantasias on an existing tune (like Tallis's *Felix namque* or *In nomine* pieces by various composers), played during an offertory or while a reader moved to a lectern.

Parishes lost their choirs too. Their music was now the metrical psalm, the litany, canticles, suffrages and various other hymns printed in the new edition of Sternhold and Hopkins's *Whole Book of Psalms*. Everybody sang. There were psalms before and after morning and evening prayer, and before and after the sermon. One striking development was a congregational hymn during communion. Called 'A Thanksgiving', it is set to a melody called 'Martyr's tune', in a minor mode and triple time, and has 124 lines of text. A large congregation with lots of communicants could entertain itself at length by contemplating its own sins:

Nought else but sin and wretchedness
Doth rest within our hearts:
And stubbornely against the Lord
We daily play our parts,[39]

all sung to a true 'Geneva jig'. 'Thus,' noted one parishioner, 'do we spend the Sabbath day.'

In the 1580s, church music began to get its hands dirty. 'There are more than two hundred men of all ages,' wrote Elizabeth I to the French ambassador in 1583, 'who, at the instigation of the Jesuits, conspire to kill me.' Pope Pius V had excommunicated her in 1570, thus tacitly making it the duty of faithful Catholics to overthrow her, by force if necessary. Many tried.

In 1581 Edmund Campion, a Roman Catholic Jesuit priest, was convicted of high treason for printing and disseminating his arguments against the validity of the English church. As always, crowds flocked to the spectacle (he was hanged, drawn and quartered), but this time it was for more than just entertainment. People pressed forward to dip their coats and handkerchiefs in the blood of the Catholic martyr. One witness, probably Henry Walpole, another Jesuit, wrote a poem about the execution, 'Why do I Use my Paper, Ink and Pen?' and William Byrd set it to music. He published his setting twice, the second time in 1588, in an act of sheer brazen defiance, tempered only slightly by Byrd not identifying the author in print, and by the omission of the most obviously treasonable stanza of Walpole's lyric. But his public knew exactly where Byrd was positioning himself by making sweet music for fathers to put these words into the mouths of their wives, servants and children, gathered round the hearth to sing and pray: 'I speak of saints whose names cannot decay.'

In the same decade, Byrd published *Quomodo cantabimus*, a setting of verses from Psalm 137, beginning 'How shall we sing the Lord's song in a strange land?' Many of Byrd's Latin texts of this period deal with the 'Babylonish captivity', the exile of the people of Israel. The comparison with the plight of English Catholicism, in internal exile under a hostile ruler, is clear enough. Of necessity, the reference is encoded in the choice of text and the mood of the music, but the code is not hard to read, even now. In this instance, the music is made to carry even greater political and symbolic weight. Thirty years earlier, when Byrd probably sang as a choirboy at the mass to celebrate the union of the Catholic monarchs of England and Spain, present among the foreign visitors was the Flemish composer Philippe de Monte. Later, de Monte set the first three verses of Psalm 137 (136 in the Vulgate numbering) to music: *Super flumina Babylonis*, 'by the waters of Babylon we sat down and wept'. Apparently, de Monte sent his setting to Byrd in England. Byrd's motet *Quomodo cantabimus* sets a different selection of verses from the same psalm as de Monte, as if continuing the thought. The scoring, for eight voices, is the same. The two composers are lamenting the fate of the English Catholic musician, forced to hang his harp upon the barren trees of Elizabeth's strange land. It is a remarkable gesture of Catholic solidarity, a musical handshake across the water.

During the late 1580s, Byrd wrote songs praising his employer, and others honouring her enemies. In 1586 one of his songs marked the twenty-eighth year of Elizabeth's reign: 'we of England, whom the Lord hath blest these many years, through his handmaid Elizabeth, in peace from foreign fears.' The same year he composed an elegy for Sir Philip Sidney, courtier and poet. In 1587 Elizabeth finally decided to take arms against her sea of troubles and authorise the execution of her cousin, Mary, Queen of Scots. Byrd's elegy for Sidney now reappeared with a different text, lamenting 'a noble Queen ... of divers heinous crimes to be indict, by false suspect'. It is not clear whether Byrd himself made the change, or if not, whether he knew about it. And who sang it? Did they associate the composer with the sentiments his music now so movingly expressed? The source for the second version is the private papers of those notable chroniclers and Byrd fans, the Paston family. Music was thus inextricably intertwined with the twisting tendrils of part-private, part-public posturing and propaganda that is the dangerous stuff of Elizabethan life. Another, undated song by Byrd praised the memory of Mary I, 'a Queen whom Fates refuses a sacred tomb to give of fame immortal', a grammatically rather tangled lament that Catholic England died with the 'noble Queen, of Britain crowned'. Yet another song, 'While Phoebus Used to Dwell', reappears in the Paston manuscript with new words in honour of 'The noble famous Queen, who lost her head of late', that is, Mary, Queen of Scots.

There is a fine, stylised, symbolic painting of Elizabeth awaiting news of the fate of the invasion force unleashed against England by her enemy and ex-half-brother-in-law, Philip of Spain. She sits not in the cloud-capped towers of Greenwich or on the battlements of Dover, but in her own private chapel inside St James's Palace, the spiritual seat of the authority given her by God. When news of the defeat of the Armada reached London in 1588, Elizabeth wrote a poem giving full credit for the victory to herself: 'Look and bow down thine ear, O Lord, from thy bright sphere behold and see thy handmaid and thy handiwork.'[40] Her leading Chapel Royal composer, William Byrd, set it to music for a triumphalist celebration at St Paul's Cathedral. He must have done so with mixed feelings. The elegies for the two Catholic

Marys and for Edmund Campion suggest that he may secretly have wished for the return of the old faith; but no composer had a more supportive patron, and he knew it. In any event, if Queen Elizabeth instructs you to set her words to music, you don't say no, even if you are William Byrd.

In 1589 Catholic England was mourned again by Byrd in the texts of the *Cantiones sacrae*, *Deus venerunt gentes* and *Civitas sancti tui*: 'O Lord God, the heathen are come into thine inheritance'; 'the city of thy holy ones is made desolate, Jerusalem an heap of stones'.

The year 1585 saw the deaths of two composers whose three-score years and ten (and more) fell right across the era of the Reformation: one of them was a genius.

Osbert Parsley sang in the cathedral of England's second city, Norwich, for most of his long life. He composed a long Latin anthem before the Reformation, a 'short' service or two after it, and a set of Lamentations, the standard compositional curriculum vitae. A touching memorial to his good character and 'Golden Fame' is still up on the cathedral wall, an indication that, here at least, cathedral music maintained a good deal of its vitality even through these difficult years.

Thomas Tallis is easily the best composer in this story so far, and one of the two or three best of all. He served four monarchs, adapting uncomplainingly as they kept tearing up the rule book of his trade, garnering Lordships of manors, money and status as he went. He was a Catholic and an artisan, making music for worship, education and pleasure. He was a teacher and a scholar, buying a copy of a composition treatise by Leonel Power when Waltham Abbey binned all the ancient splendours it didn't want any more, and taking his place in the succession of masters and pupils at the Chapel Royal, most notably as mentor to William Byrd, thirty years his junior. He was our last medieval and first Renaissance composer: both a 'servant of society' before 'composers began to blow up their own egos',[41] as Benjamin Britten put it, and among the first to print and publish his own music. He is the first English composer whose music has never fallen out of use; like Shakespeare, each generation has reinvented him for its own purposes, some more respectfully than others.

And then there is the music. Few composers have changed style so radically (perhaps Beethoven and Stravinsky bear comparison), none in response to external conditions. The astonishing thing about Tallis is not that he wrote music for so many and such totally different sets of requirements, but that he did all of them so well. His early *Alleluia* is frankly medieval in character, with florid lines knotted like coloured ribbons to the plainsong. English service music like the Responses and Litany are so simple they sound almost like the chords are being added 'ex improviso' by the singers: then the composer adds a little twist of harmony at a cadence which gives the music its distinctive character, the sort of thing which so captivated Vaughan Williams. There is no more solemn or graceful antiphon for Mary than *Videte miraculum*. *O nata lux* has an old man's prayerful repose. *Spem in alium* is an inexplicable prodigy, a motet in forty real, independent voice-parts, written (according to a later account) in response to a challenge from the Duke of Norfolk to prove that an English composer could match the rumoured achievement of a presumptuous Italian: 'Tallice beinge very skilfull was felt to try whether he would undertake ye matter, wch he did and made one of 40 partes wch was songe in the longe gallery at Arundell house, wch so farre surpassed ye other that the Duke, hearing yt songe, tooke his chayne of Gold from his necke & putt yt about Tallice his necke and gave yt him'.[42] (Who wouldn't? This wasn't the average bit of Sternhold and Hopkins being sung around his fireplace.)

Above all, this music is so singable. The vocal lines in pre-Reformation music can be mightily difficult. William Byrd, the younger composer, was in some ways more old-fashioned in his vocal writing, which could be angular, awkward and rhythmically tricky. But the vocal lines of Tallis's mature style, *O sacrum convivium* or the canonic setting of *Salvator mundi* are real singers' music, their highest notes perfectly placed on the right vowels and at the right place in the phrase for the breath, approached via graceful step-wise scale movement which demands a beautiful *legato* line and well-supported tone. Music which is better to sing sounds better. Tallis was the first composer to really get this. In 1585 Byrd turned to the consort song once again:

Ye sacred Muses, race of Jove,
Come down from crystal heav'ns above
In mourning weeds, with tears in eyes:
Tallis is dead, and music dies.

'The better the voyce is, the meeter it is to honour and serve God there-wit'.[43] The turn of the 1590s was a creative period for William Byrd. The expensively sumptuous publishing venture of 1575 had suffered from a lack of 'vendibility', and by the late 1580s Byrd may also have needed to make up ground with influential circles at court as a result of troubles over his Catholicism and recusancy. He ventured into print as sole author four times between 1588 and 1591, with a much more careful eye on his costs and his market. The results were highly satisfactory.

All four collections were for domestic use. Two are in English (*Psalmes, Sonnets and Songs* of 1588 and *Songs of Sundrie natures* of 1589), freely mixing devotional texts like *A Carowle for Christmas Day* with love songs, elegies, pastorals and madrigals, including one in Italian and one with a Latin refrain, like a fifteenth-century macaronic carol. Scoring is practical. Some are consort songs for solo voice with viols, some are for vocal groups of various sizes with or without accompaniment, some are both, some a mixture. This was music to be used. Two are in Latin (*Cantiones sacrae* of 1589 and 1591). Byrd himself regarded the Latin pieces as being 'things of more depth and skill' than the English, and his choice of texts shows what he meant. A small number of joyful, madrigalian pieces are thoroughly outnumbered by a great wail of contrapuntal lamenting, and there are some strikingly blatant Catholic gestures such as that old torch-song *Salve regina* and a piece with a long-note plainsong in the tenor, just like in the old days.

The professional musician was still, very largely, a church musician. Other career opportunities were opening up, however: some worked as household musicians and tutors to wealthy families, composing songs and madrigals alongside instruction manuals and teaching pieces. At the centre of society, employment in church music meant the Chapel Royal. In the provinces, many cathedral singers worked at other trades during the day, as musicians have always done, or had to give up singing in the choir because they could no longer afford to live on the meagre pay (like Thomas Lawes, father of the celebrated brothers). There was also probably some overlap with other kinds of musicians. Will Kemp, the clown famous for dancing from London to Norwich in 1599, praised the singing of the town waits there, saying 'their voices be admirable, every one of them able to serve in any Cathedral Church in Christendom for choristers'.[44] No doubt these men were drafted into the cathedral choir when necessary. Musical skills have always been highly transferable.

Records of cathedral singing-men at this period comprise mostly descriptions of bad pay and bad behaviour. They are regularly and roundly told off for lateness, inattention, drunkenness and worse. Government injunctions routinely use up far more ink ordering singing-men to avoid 'going to the ale-houses and playing at cards, tables, and dice, and suspect company of women'[45] than on telling them what to sing. Of course, we only hear about this sort of thing when someone complains about it. As every historian has noted, a machine which is running smoothly leaves no smear of oil on the ground behind it.

The professional composer was just beginning to step out from behind his other identities as church musician and middle-grade household lackey. Byrd and Tallis were the first to publish anything like a collected edition of their own works, something their continental counterparts had thought of some time ago. This was an era of flowery encomiums and eulogies, and those who sought the bubble reputation through music may, like Mundy, find themselves being likened to the moon compared to Byrd's sun (all in an elegant Latin pun, naturally).[46] There were musical memorials, too. Byrd's elegy for Tallis is part of a touching trend. In the developing professionalism of the composer, William Byrd is a key figure, as in everything else.

The church musician's educational experience had evolved too. Many top composers, including Thomas Morley, had a Bachelor's degree in music. Several aimed one step higher and got a doctorate: at opposite ends of the century Robert Fayrfax and Orlando Gibbons both wrote highly technical contrapuntal works as their submission exercises. Music, however, was always something of a Cinderella subject in the universities: there was a distinction between the 'academic' composer, who writes 'musica speculativa', a branch of mathematics, and the mere practitioner (and there still is, and it's not always a good thing). For children (meaning boys), pre-Reformation musical education was part of a general training in the practice of the liturgy and was delivered by monasteries and chantries. This ended in the 1530s and 1540s. The many new grammar schools founded under Edward VI did not, usually, have music on the curriculum (though there are exceptions).

By Elizabeth's reign, the best route into a musical education was to become a choirboy. It was a genuinely meritocratic system. Statutes at choral foundations specifically mention 'poor' boys, and the Chapel Royal Master could 'impress' talented boys from parishes and cathedrals into the monarch's service. Most leading composers began their training in this way. Many were from provincial or middling sorts of backgrounds: almost all had music in the family; William Byrd's family were merchants, and both his elder brothers sang as choristers.

In 1593 Elizabeth passed an Act restricting the activities of 'popish recusants'. It is important to be clear exactly what was illegal. 'Recusancy' is not going to church (meaning, of course, lawful, Anglican worship). If you didn't go, you were put under a kind of house arrest, and fines might have followed. Byrd, his wife, and other members of their household all made appearances on recusancy lists. What you did in the privacy of your own house was not mentioned, unless you went too far and harboured 'a Jesuit, seminary or massing priest'. It is vintage Elizabeth: fierce against rebellion and the causes of rebellion, she yet had no wish 'to make a window into mens soules'.

Against this background Byrd wrote, published and sang his three great settings of the Latin Mass between 1592 and 1595, reprinting two of them later the same decade. Now in his fifties, Byrd increasingly withdrew from active musical life at court into the orbit of a series of leading Catholic families, the Pastons, Pagets and Petres. Catholic worship had become a hugger-mugger thing, with secret meetings in country houses, sometimes with dangerous guests like Henry Garnet, Jesuit and future Gunpowder plotter. Byrd was there too: 'Vigilate', his friends and co-religionists sang – 'watch out'.

The Masses are the best of Byrd: concise, intense, passionate,

A 'contrafactum'. Byrd set the Latin words; the English was appended later.

pushing at compositional technique to wring new expressivity out of the old words, like the working out of two melodies at the same time in imitation at the opening of the five-part Sanctus, Palestrina-style. Thomas East, Byrd's publisher and close associate, published the Masses without a title page, without mentioning his own name, and in books of just one page each, easy to conceal and smuggle around the country. The Paston family, Byrd's Norfolk friends, held their masses in the woods.

An intriguing by-product of this divide between Protestant and Catholic musical liturgies is that some pieces ended up serving both. One liturgy required Latin words, the other English, so a decent bit of polyphony can be made to work harder, and reach more people, simply by changing the words. These pieces are known as 'contrafacta', and there are several by both Tallis and Byrd. The Latin came first. The English words are not a translation, but a completely different text. Often, unsurprisingly, the English doesn't fit very well, either the mood of the music or the verbal rhythm of the vocal line. Tallis's first setting of *Salvator mundi*, where the graceful rise and fall of the opening melody matches the stress of the words, comes out as *With All our Hearts* where it doesn't. It is all about the idea of music as something to use: Tallis's communion motet *O sacrum convivium* turns up at the coronation of James I as *I Call and Cry*, and indeed started life as an instrumental fantasia. These composers had no more difficulty with the idea of reusing a workmanlike bit of music than Handel did (though there's no suggestion they made the changes themselves: in Tallis's case the sources of the English 'contrafacta' largely date from after his death). Byrd's *Laudate pueri Dominum* also began life as instrumental music: when you sing it, it sometimes seems there are too many syllables for the available notes. Even the mighty *Spem in alium* got pressed into service as *Sing and Glorify* for the investiture of Henry, Prince of Wales, in 1610, though by the end of the piece the English wordsmith seems to have given up pretending that his text makes sense, in an increasingly tortured effort to cram in enough syllables:

> Live Henry princely and mighty,
> Harry live in thy creation happy.

William Mundy died in 1591. Born between Tallis and Byrd, he was eighteen when Henry VIII died. Like Tallis, his music charts the times he lived in. He was among the pioneers of the very early verse anthem: simple, strophic arrangements of the metrical psalm style for solo voice and instruments with a devout little chorus added to the end of each verse, a strikingly original and highly unusual concept at the time. His English church music shows him feeling his way, producing an oddly square kind of polyphony, light years away from the bold lines of his Latin music, principally his masterpiece, *Vox patris caelestis*. He wrote a fine, large-scale English service. Like White, his Elizabethan Latin music is characterised by penitential texts: *Miserere mei, Domine*. Like Byrd, he composed a setting for a poem by Girolamo Savonarola, a monk who a hundred years earlier had encouraged the overthrow of the civil government of Florence and set up a religious republic. This poem brought together several of the themes dear to the hearts of the English Catholic musician. It is a meditation on their beloved penitential psalms, in this case Psalm 51, 'Have mercy on me, O God'. It was written in prison, where they also believed themselves to be, figuratively speaking. It links them to the career of a violent religious revolutionary of the sort Elizabeth saw around every corner (with some justification), though, crucially, the association is not made explicit but implied through their choice of this text and its familiar coded cry: 'Where shall I go? Whither shall I turn myself? To whom shall I fly? Who will take pity on me?'

This was incendiary stuff, in more ways than one. Byrd published a setting of the same poem in his 1591 collection. It is the perfect example of how a piece of stubborn political and sectarian positioning can become encrypted in music. Like a modern spin doctor, Byrd well knew how these associations can stick.

In 1601 two fanatical Jesuits were executed in London. As they went to their deaths, they sang 'Haec dies quam fecit Dominus': 'This is the day the Lord hath made; let us rejoice and be glad in it'. A man who went to watch them burn later wrote that they were singing the music of William Byrd.[47] They almost certainly were not: Byrd's setting is not exactly suitable for a performance of that kind, and there is another setting which is a much more likely candidate for the music he heard that day. But, like the myriad stories which surround Elizabeth I, whether or not the anecdote is true is absolutely not the point. The point is that people believed it to be true, or at least repeated it as if it was true. By his reaction to the currents swirling around church music in the 1590s, Byrd had firmly fixed his name to this kind of under-the-radar intellectual insurgency, and it stuck. People see references to Catholic solidarity and sedition in his music even when they're not there.

As the century ticked towards its close, the style of discourse was shifting. Papists were still vilified for their excooooo (including, incidentally, in music), but so too, now, were those neo-Papists, the high-church Anglicans. Puritan voices, meanwhile, became ever more stern and extreme. The pamphlet joined the broadside and the printed book as the polemical vehicle of choice.

It is possible to think that Thomas Cranmer and his contemporaries invented the campaign for clarity in church music. Not so. His famous letter of 1544 plugged into a running commentary that was already many centuries old, and had many more to run. The imagery of this dialectic remains remarkably consistent: the pros want to hear the words, not the music for its own sake, and think elaborate music is effeminate, theatrical and bawdy; the antis think that beauty in worship and skill in art are things of God.

As far back as the eleventh century, when the powerhouse monasteries of Northern France set off the explosion of elaboration in their style of singing, the monk Heribert called liturgical chant 'a vanity invented to please men'.[48] A twelfth-century Cistercian thought the monks of Cluny might find better ways of spending their money than on liquorice cordials to help them sing the high notes.[49] And Aelred of Rievaulx demanded: 'Why that swelling and swooping of the voice?... Sometimes you see a man with his mouth open ... Now he imitates the agonies of the dying or the swooning of persons in pain ... his whole body is violently agitated by histrionic gesticulations – contorted lips, rolling eyes, hunching shoulders – and drumming fingers keep time with every single note. And this ridiculous dissipation is called religious observance ... Meanwhile ordinary folk stand there awestruck, stupefied, marvelling at ... the saucy gestures of the singers ... jeering and snickering, until you would think they had come, not into an oratory, but to a theatre.'[50] The Pope had a pop in 1320, as mentioned above, quoting exactly the same passage from St Augustine as

Aelred and everybody else: 'when the singing delights me more than the words ... I would prefer not to listen.' The fourteenth-century Englishman John Anglicus wondered if his brother Cistercians really ought to be sucking lozenges during divine office. Two centuries later, an anonymous Puritan pamphleteer was suitably horrified by the choirboys in Elizabeth's Chapel Royal: 'these pretty, upstart youths profane the Lord's Day by the lascivious writhing of their tender limbs, and gorgeous decking of their apparel.'[51] Later still, William Prynne, the extremist's extremist, made all the same points in his *Histriomatix* of 1633: 'choristers bellow the tenor, as it were oxen; bark a counterpart, as it were a kennel of dogs; roar out a treble, as it were a sort of bulls; and grunt out a base, as it were a number of hogs',[52] none of which, of course, is what Aelred would have called 'manly', but 'shrill ... like women, or, in common parlance, falsetto'.

(Slightly ironically, in the light of his views on 'manliness' in music, Aelred's enthusiasm for certain other aspects of monastic life has led to him being adopted as a colourful patron by a number of modern-day gay organisations. He also had another musical connection: he once cured a man who had swallowed a frog by a combination of earnest prayer and sticking his fingers down the man's throat, causing the frog to jump out, which may be the origin of the phrase 'a frog in the throat' – or it may not.)

Cathedrals became the nursery and sanctuary of musical Anglicanism. This is where the services we know today, including 'choral evensong' were first heard, although still only in their bare bones: there were no hymns; the psalms were metrical not the prayer book versions; there were no organ voluntaries and there was no Latin; anthems were short and sermons long. The main problem was not theology but money. An early seventeenth-century writer dated 'the decay of music in cathedral churches' to 'about the ninth year of Queen Elizabeth', noting that 'unnecessary piping and minstrelsy' gave way to 'sermons and lectures [i.e. readings]', not least because 'stipends for singing' were 'wholly suppressed', so that 'all endeavour for teaching of music or the forming of voices by good teachers was altogether neglected, as well in men as in children, which neglect and little better reputation continueth to this day'.[53] The writer is not entirely right: he says that Elizabeth did away with paid employment for cathedral musicians at the beginning of her reign, whereas in fact she was scrupulous in doing the exact opposite. Under clear leadership, individual cathedrals could function as islands of musical ambition (like Dean Wittingham's Durham).

But the writer identified a general trend. The household musician and tutor Thomas Whythorne wrote in 1575, 'Ye do and shall see it [music] so slenderly maintained in the cathedral churches and colleges, that when the old store of the musicians be worn out which were bred when the music of the church was maintained (which is like to be in a short time), ye shall have few or none remaining.'[54] The tireless Thomas Morley (like S. S. Wesley two and a half centuries later) mounted a one-man campaign against what he saw as lax standards and lack of support: 'though a song be never so well made ... yet shall you hardly find singers to express it as it ought to be ... to draw the hearer, as it were, in chains of gold by the ears to the consideration of holy things.'[55]

There is some uncertainty around the details of the musical liturgy in cathedrals at this time: psalms, for example, are sometimes listed only by number, so it is not clear which versions were used or who sang them. But ceremony survived and prospered in England's cathedrals into the seventeenth century and the age of William Laud, Archbishop of Canterbury, and with it the kind of music which Richard Hooker, writing in the 1590s, memorably called 'a thing for all occasions ... as seasonable in grief as in joy ... a thing which all Christian churches of the world have received ... a thing which always heretofore the best men and wisest governors of God's people did think they never could command enough'.[56]

There is little uncertainty about parish music, however: it was Sternhold and Hopkins, maybe a little Marbeck, and not much else. Almost all parishes had lost their choirs and organs by the turn of the seventeenth century, if they ever had them, so *The Whole Book of Psalms* became their meat day and night. But there are some exceptions. As always, conservatism and resistance to change is most apparent in the further corners of the kingdom, and there are occasional mentions of choirboys, vicars-choral, and bills for organ repair right through to the 1640s in the distant wilds of Devon and Durham, Yorkshire and Somerset.

Parish music in Elizabeth's reign lost its past but invented its future. Parish choirs would not reclaim their pre-Reformation status until the late nineteenth century. On the other hand, congregations only began to participate at all from 1559. This was a direct consequence of developments pioneered at home during Edward's reign and abroad during Mary's, and the radical point is that it was not led by choir or priest – everyone took part. It was inclusive, but musically limited. In 1592 Thomas East took the logical step of assuming John Day's profitable mantle and reprinting *The Whole Book of Psalms*. As usual, a new edition presented canny opportunities for expanding those features that had proved popular, and East included a number of new tunes, mostly in the well-known, eminently practical 'common' and 'short' metres. East started his list of contents with four tunes, two by Edmund Hooper, one each by John Dowland and an otherwise unfamiliar composer he names as Blancks, and tells his reader that 'the Psalmes are song to these 4 tunes in most churches of this Realme'.[57] This must be an oversimplification – using just four tunes would get dull quickly enough – but he reveals for us how this style of church music was used by congregations who probably didn't have enough copies to go round, couldn't read them if they had, and had anyway known these tunes since before they didn't learn to read. Then as now, when it comes to a good tune people know what they like, and like what they know.

Some of East's tunes have survived in use (often identified in modern hymnbooks as coming from 'Este's psalter', using one of the many variants of an apparently unassuming surname which ought to be proof against the vagaries of choirboy spelling). East also added names to his tunes: 'Kentish tune', 'Oxford', 'Glassenbury'. He certainly didn't invent the practice, but he was the first to note it in print. From this moment dates the peculiarly English habit of editors, compilers, composers, arrangers and collectors naming a hymn tune after a place or a person or some whimsical association of their own, as if it were a pet dog.

Like folk-song, many of the psalm tunes have elements of melody and harmony in common, as well as drawing on a common library of metres and modes. Some groups of tunes sound like variants of each other. Sometimes, it turns out, two tunes can be sung simultaneously, so that one acts as a kind of extra upper part or descant to the other. A rare Latin psalm book of the period adds optional upper 'choosing' notes above the main notes of the tune. The practice might be seen as a descendant of the old 'learned' tradition of improvising an upper part to a plainsong, still mentioned approvingly by Thomas Morley in 1597 as part of the complete musical education. But it doesn't always work. Musically, the psalm tunes are both too alike and not alike enough. Note values are the same, so there is no rhythmic variety. At the same time, they go up and down at different places and this only makes musical sense by accident, if at all. Word emphasis doesn't match and harmony gets fudged. Morley would not have approved. This is the distant origin of the modern habit of adding descants to hymns, and the practice sometimes raises the same issues. You don't necessarily improve a well-contoured melody by plonking a different melody on top of it.

Devotional music in the home was well established by the 1590s. East's was just one of several psalm books which could be used around the hearth as well as in church. Richard Allison's *Psalmes of David in Metre* of 1599 makes this explicit in putting the tune in the treble part, like a song, with the harmony arranged for lute, or voices, or both. William Hunnis called his version of the penitential psalms (a tried and trusted editorial selection) *Seven Sobbes of a Sorrowful Soule for Sinne*, adding, like Allison, single-lined tunes in a devotional style and including secular songs under the titles 'A Hiveful of Honey' and 'A Handful of Honisuckles'. Educated householders owned collections of music for their own and their families' entertainment and edification, freely mixing instrumental pieces, rounds, canons, counting songs and teaching rhymes with moralising and devotional pieces. Thomas Lant, a pillar of the establishment which he first joined as a Chapel Royal choirboy, owned such a collection in the 1580s. The ever-popular lute-song can, occasionally, do God too.

One notable sideline of later Elizabethan church music was to add splendour and solemnity to the Queen's regular 'progresses' around the country. Norwich found itself treated to such visits more than once. Osbert Parsley's Te Deum was sung for Elizabeth in 1597, and 'an excellent boy', no doubt a cathedral chorister, 'gallantly decked, in a long white robe of taffata, a crimson scarff wrought with gold, folded in the Turkish fashion about his brows, and a gay garland of white flowers on his head' sang 'musick, which was marvellous sweet and good, albeit the rudeness of some ringers of bells did somewhat hinder the noise of the harmony'.[58]

Noble houses of the sort which Elizabeth graced with the honour (and expense) of her presence on these trips no longer had their own chapel choirs, as the grandest had done before the Reformation. The 'music of the house',[59] as Shakespeare called them, was now a band of secular musicians, who provided tuition for the family as well as background music for dinners and other entertainments. A middle-ranking Shakespearean worthy, Justice Shallow's cousin Master Slender, puts devotional music into its domestic context. Invited to dinner by the Pages, he remarks, 'I had rather than forty shillings I had my Book of Songs and Sonnets here'.[60] A little music, it seems, will ameliorate the social perils of an evening spent in the company of Master Page's hot venison pasty and equally hot daughter.

Is it coincidence that Slender is almost quoting the title of William Byrd's collection *Psalmes, Sonnets and Songes*, published about a decade before this play was written (apparently at the express request of the Queen, who wanted more of her favourite fat man, Sir John Falstaff)? Byrd's book sold well, so there's every reason to suppose that local worthies like Slender and Shallow, and prosperous householders like the Fords and the Pages, would have owned and used a copy, and that Shakespeare's audience would have got the reference.

IN THE PERSON OF THE ageing Elizabeth, the Tudor era hobbled into the seventeenth century for a couple of nervous years. The Earl of Essex made the last mad, romantic attempt at rebellion in 1601. Unsurprisingly, a consort song of William Byrd's appeared at the Paston family home, mocking the foolish Essex:

How comes it then on good evil should attend
And that a silly woman works thine end?

Byrd's music was standard repertoire by this time: in 1601 the Earl of Worcester, reviewing current musical fashions at court, remarked 'in winter lullaby, an owld song of Mr Birde, wylbee more in request as I thinke'.[61] But Byrd himself had largely withdrawn from active musical life at court, and only joined in with the Chapel Royal (and used his lodgings in town) at a prestigious and lucrative event like the new king's coronation. This was not a man to do what mere princes of the earth told him.

Thomas Morley died in 1602. His life fits almost exactly into the years of the reign of Queen Elizabeth. Like Hunnis and Farrant before him, and Giles after, Morley did everything. He was Organist of St Paul's Cathedral, Gentleman of the Chapel Royal, publisher, composer and academic. His body of music for the English church, though not huge, is one of the cornerstones of the developing Elizabethan style, linking the first efforts of the Edwardians and early Elizabethans directly to the mature, confident new language of his fellow pupils of Byrd in the next generation – Orlando Gibbons, Thomas Weelkes and Thomas Tomkins.

His music was deemed practical and beautiful when it was written, qualities which have proved to be enduring. He was the principal vessel for the osmosis of the popular madrigal-flavoured Italian accent into vernacular composition, especially the example of Alfonso Ferrabosco, an important, though, as it turned out, fairly short lived trend. He reached back into his musical inheritance in setting a macaronic sacred madrigal, *Nolo mortem peccatoris*, alternating homophony with plain, expressive imitation and plangent false relations. Almost most importantly of all, in 1597 he wrote a lengthy and detailed treatise on musical education, *A Plaine and Easie Introduction to Practicall Musicke*. This is a fascinating book. Set as an engaging master–pupil dialogue in the Socratic manner (sometimes on an agreeable country stroll), the book is revealing about the musical skills required of the Tudor chorister and composer and how he acquired them. Dedicated fulsomely to Byrd, it also takes some good-humoured swipes at the methods of the teacher, identified mysteriously as 'Master Bold': Morley was perhaps not the first young man to hungrily absorb the guidance of an older mentor and at the same time consider himself wiser than his teachers. Remarkably, in an intellectually forward-looking age, his treatise identifies the music of the past that Morley considered it necessary to study, as far back as Dunstaple (though as an example of what not to do). Perhaps most interestingly, this is a book students can still use. It is a thorough, clear and comprehensive textbook of the late Renaissance style. 'Practicall' is right; 'easie', not always. We can, with Morley, take a harmony and counterpoint lesson with William Byrd.

Morley's reputation was deservedly high, though he was not above a bit of chicanery to achieve it. He published a substantial setting of the Latin penitential text *Laboravi in gemitu meo*, the sort of large-scale contrapuntal showpiece designed to show off a composer's skill to his peers. It succeeded. *Laboravi* is an expressive, accomplished, assured work of art. Unfortunately, he didn't write it. Somehow he had got hold of a copy of the setting by the Franco-Flemish composer Philippe Rogier, and with a couple of minor adjustments he simply passed it off as his own work.[62] He pulled a similar trick with a piece by his contemporary Peter Philips.[63] Only in the late twentieth century, thanks to the patient investigations of another Peter Phillips, the scholar and conductor, was his deception uncovered.

When he died, taking this rather nifty bit of compositional dissimulation with him, his colleague Thomas Weelkes followed the example of their teacher William Byrd by memorialising him in music: 'Death hath deprived me of my dearest friend.'

AS THE QUEEN'S LIFE drew to its end, church music bore the imprint of the forces at work during her reign. Not least among these was her personal enthusiasm. This came from a number of sources: good politics, by using her own court as an exemplar of proper religious observance; her own religious tastes and 'delight in music'; and by enhancing the glamour and prestige of the court to impress foreign visitors and restive natives. Elizabeth's reign is studded with deft bits of legislation and management which had the welcome side effect of allowing the best of English church music to survive and prosper. Her childlessness, too, fed directly into the nurturing of music. Her singing-boys, in chapel, at court and on stage, were the closest she came to having a family, surrounded as she usually was by the threatening sycophancy of court. She cherished them. A visiting duke in the very last months of her reign heard one of her choirboys sing 'so charmingly to the accompaniment of a bass viol that, with the possible exception of the Nuns at Milan, we heard nothing to equal him anywhere.'[64] History does not record what the boy thought of being compared to a nun.

A number of writers looked back from this period on what the Reformation had meant for the church musician: the mass 'wholly suppressed'; psalms 'turned into English'; cathedral music 'decayed'; and a new haircut – the Injunctions of 1547, among others, state: 'Item, the choristers to have from henceforth the crown shaven no more; their heads nevertheless to be kept short.'[65]

'Religion,' wrote the Venetian ambassador to the court of Edward VI, 'is, as it were, the heart of man ... especially in Monarchies it is a wonderful power for good ... This is not so in England, however, where men change their beliefs from day to day.'[66] Fifty years later, the inky pages rolling off the hand-presses of Thomas East show us where this had left the musician: one week, lots of copies of the English psalter for the lucrative, legal English liturgy and large domestic market; the next week, the Masses of William Byrd, just a couple of copies, deliberately aimed just below Lord Burghley's line of sight.

The interface between government and people in the sixteenth century was as much about practical politics and economics as it was about doctrine and music. The 'very aged' could remember that Elizabeth's father began the process of dismantling the old superstructure of superstitious and superfluous saints' days by banning those that fell during the harvest, so the crop would be got in more quickly. A ban on Rogationtide processions turned out to be bad politics, especially in years of poor weather and low yields. Religious food laws were introduced to focus people's minds on the state of their souls – but people focused instead on the resulting run on the price of eggs. One man looked back with nostalgia from 1590 to the comforting certainties of pre-Reformation times, and gave his reasons: 'it was a good world, when the old religion was, because all things were cheap'. So much for doctrinal purity.

The same writer signed off with a comment which could be taken as the motto of the English church musician so far, heeded by some more than others: 'it is safer to doe in religion as most doe.'[67] It is a principle the musician would do well to remember as Elizabeth's 'cousin of Scotland' packed his bags and prepared to head south.

7
Plots, Scots, Politics and the Beauty of Holiness, 1603–1645

Ah! Sinful nation

Isaiah 1: 4

ONE OF THE PROBLEMS with religious disputes is that everyone thinks they're right. The optimism with which diverse and incompatible religious groupings approached the new reign was bound to lead to disappointment, and worse, in the absence of the sort of deft, decisive political management of which Elizabeth had so often proved herself the master. This was the kind of situation to which she was temperamentally perfectly suited and politically perfectly attuned (perhaps more so than any other British political leader in history). Her Stuart successors were not.

Church music chronicled events as they unfolded. It welcomed James from Scotland. It recorded the rumbling undercurrents of discontent as he was asked to reconcile conflicting demands, and failed. It banged the drum loud and clear when his enemies rose up against him and were confounded. It hymned to his rest the last, best hope of peace – Henry, Prince of Wales. It marked the spreading and deepening of an old tradition, psalm-singing. It charted the ascendancy of a new one, Anglicanism. It established one of its key texts, the King James Bible. It took psalms to America. It exported the divine right back to Scotland, in the form of coronation anthems and psalters, crucial steps on the road to war. It was there when music died.

THE SIZE AND SHAPE of the choir hadn't changed much since before the Reformation, maybe because it still had to sing squeezed into the same old set of seats in its churches and chapels. Some features of English church music derive from the architecture. Choirs, for example, are usually divided between the north and south sides of the chancel; composers often write alternately for each half of the choir so the music moves from one to the other, like a game of musical tennis. The early seventeenth-century choir looked much like its modern men-and-boys counterpart, though there are some differences. Unlike today, there were more men than boys: the Chapel Royal had ten boys and a whopping thirty-two men, of whom half would sing the regular weekday services (still comfortably outnumbering the boys).

The division of voices was slightly different too. Counter-tenors (altos) were often given two parts, first and second, with singers of each part on both sides of the choir. The convention of treating the choir as a four-part group came later: the Renaissance composer thought just as naturally in five parts, or three, or six. Another distinction we have lost is between two distinct types of boys' voices: the high 'treble' and the lower, more common 'mean'. Typically, the 'mean' has a range from middle C up a tenth to E, the treble a fourth or so higher, taking in a written top A. Boys' voices are not all the same, any more than men's voices are. The Tudor and early Stuart church musician knew this (and it may partly explain why choirboys often kept going through to the age of fifteen or sixteen, unlike today). Sacred music was written in what appears to us to be surprisingly low keys. Modern scholarship thinks this is because pitch standards, insofar as they existed at all, were different, so that the note written on the page as an F sounded like what we would call an A flat. It is a cogent and well-supported theory, and explains why most modern editions of this music have key signatures of three or four flats (the originals mostly had one flat or none at all). But there is much beauty to be had from experimenting with pitch and combinations of voice type. At lower pitch, 'alto' parts sit perfectly for bright, high tenors, rather than badly for struggling falsettists. The chesty sound of the 'mean' is revealed and low basses gurgle away at the bottom like the noise of the water pipes.

This was the composer's palette of colour and sound. His canvas was the choral parts of the English services. Principally, this meant canticles for morning (usually Te Deum and Benedictus), and evening (Magnificat and Nunc Dimittis); chanted responses; a very limited number of severely curtailed settings of the English communion (Kyrie and Creed and responses to the commandments); and anthems. The 'full' style used the whole choir all together, without an independent accompaniment (though organ or other instruments might double the voice-parts on occasion), as composers had done ever since choirs and composers were first invented. The best composers made music of polished perfection from a subset of 'full' choral music – the 'short' style. One step up from the perfect little ABB anthems of the Reformation, it lavished its full attention on the words by removing musical elaboration altogether. Gibbons and Byrd did it best. The 'great' style – long, many-voiced and impressive – made an occasional appearance.

The main vehicle of musical innovation was the 'verse' style. If the revolutionary sound of the mid-sixteenth century was the choir singing in English, the next big thing was the choir clattering to its feet during service as the organ began to play, and one surpliced chorister, man or boy, starting to sing, all by himself. A 'verse' in this context is a passage of music for one or more solo voices, with an independent accompaniment for organ or instrumental consort. 'Verse' passages alternate with music for the full choir. Its origins lie in the little devotional songs of the early Reformation, strophic pieces to simple tunes with a repeating refrain in harmony between the verses. This was a modest updating of the medieval 'stanza and burden' form and led to the consort song (like those published by William Byrd in the 1580s and 90s), songs for school and home, and the theatre song: it was more sophisticated, but still basically simple and direct in effect. In church, the style presented opportunities for contrast over long spans, a way of varying the texture by using different combinations of solo voices and, above all, the chance to polish and refine the still new art of setting the English language to music. As in the age of Cranmer and Tyndale, the crafting of the new words and the new music are so inextricably linked that they can almost be considered the same thing. Gibbons wouldn't be Gibbons without the Book of Common Prayer and the King James Bible.

At the level of the parish and home, too, wordsmiths helped the reformed style of worship to expand and deepen its range, though inevitably within narrower musical confines. Psalm-singing continued to grow in popularity, and writers, composers and publishers continued to feed the demand for metrical psalters with tunes, with ever more subtle results. This, for example, is part of the text of Psalm 84 from Thomas Ravenscroft's *Psalter* of 1621, where it is set to his own harmonisation of a tune he calls 'Winchester' (in the tenor, marked by a woodcut of a hand with a finger pointing at the tune, as if he thinks his tenor is too dim to spot it on his own), later better known as the tune to 'While Shepherds Watched':

How pleasant is thy dwelling place
O Lord of hosts to me:
The tabernacles of thy grace,
How pleasant Lord they be.

The Sparrowes finde a roome to rest
And save themselves from wrong:
And eke the Swallow hath a nest
Wherein to keepe her young.

These birds full nigh thine altar may
Have place to sit and sing:
O Lord of hosts thou art (I say)
My God and eke my king.[1]

The words, like the music, were getting better. This was well-crafted poetry, learned yet direct, for the people Ravenscroft addresses as his 'Harmonicall brethren' to sit and sing, like the swallow, around the place they keep their young.

Psalm 84 from Ravenscroft's Psalter *of 1621, the sort of book that sold in the hundreds of thousands from the modest beginnings of Sternhold and Hopkins in the 1550s. This sort of page, practical, cheap to produce and easy to read, would have been familiar to every literate householder and church-goer in the later Tudor and Stuart period. The tune is in the tenor part: it may be familiar.*

IN PUBLIC, CHURCH MUSIC marked the ceremonies associated with the change of dynasty. There is a fine picture of the funeral procession for Queen Elizabeth, including heralds with trumpets, and the children and gentlemen of 'the Chapell', the adults in magnificent new cloaks (which they got to keep as part of their fee for the occasion – at the top end, church music was still a comfortable and prosperous place to be). James's ceremonial entry into London was marked with music, pageants, paeans and poems: art and artifice affirming the divinely appointed order here on earth. The sacred had a walk-on part. The title of Samuel Rowlands's welcome ode sums up the sort of sycophantic mixture of God, King and a dash of classical celebrity which thrilled James to the soles of his pointy silver shoes: *Ave Caesar: God save the King*. No doubt the choristers of London's churches found their way onto balconies and roadsides to hymn their new king into his new kingdom. The music for the coronation seems fairly modest by modern standards: the Litany (probably to Tallis's timeless cadences), Te Deum and 'O be Joyfull' by Nathaniel Giles, Morley's Creed, sung prayers and two psalms by Byrd, and three anthems.[2] Instruments very possibly added richness and splendour to the substantial choir.

One piece sung at Westminster Abbey that day provides a perfect example of how an unassuming little bit of sacred music can show us, if we choose to look, what the English have been up to these last thirty years and more. It is listed as *I Call and Cry* by Tallis. Tallis never set these words. They had been put to the music of his setting of *O sacrum convivium*, made for his joint publication with Byrd of 1575. Back then, it was possible – just – to write and sing Latin pieces for use in private places like the Queen's own chapel, where Tallis and Byrd worked, but this was not the case by 1603, and certainly never in a public space like Westminster Abbey. So the music found itself pressed into service to meet the needs of a new worshipping community and a new political context. There is a third version of this piece, too, for instruments alone, which may pre-date the 1575 Latin composition. This was music for use in changing times. Nearly twenty years after his death, Tallis once again shows himself the complete professional.

A year after his coronation, James I faced the demands of both sides of the religious divide at the Hampton Court conference of 1604. He managed to satisfy neither. Church music continued to carry the coded discontent of the Catholic, in William Byrd's abstruse references to various Jesuitical torch-songs. But for James, the structures and practices of the church were part of his right to rule and his means of doing so and music had its part to play. In 1605 Catholic opposition spilt over into open rebellion. The discovery of the Gunpowder Plot confirmed God's will for his people, and church music was on hand to make sure they knew it:

Find out thy foes and let them feel the power of thy right hand.
And like an oven burn them, Lord, in fiery flame and fume;
Thine anger shall destroy them all, and fire shall them consume.

So much for 'Blessed are the Peacemakers'. This was government propaganda, put out swiftly and firmly to emphasise government control in the wake of a serious and dangerous crisis, promulgated by clerics, choirboys and composers, in hastily written homilies and anthems, in churches and market squares. Musicians became speech-writers, little boys spin doctors. This was where church music got political.

James himself attended a ceremony in the Jerusalem Chamber

overlooking the nave of Westminster Abbey to hear a new anthem by his own senior household church musician Edmund Hooper, one of the two organists of the Chapel Royal. Hooper pulled no punches:

> This day the Lord from foes' blood-thirsty ire
> Hath given us brands new taken from the fire

Other composers joined in the jollity, with Thomas Weelkes requesting the Almighty to

> let thine enemies feel thy force, and those that Thee withstand ...
> ... And thou wilt root out of the earth their fruit that should increase:
> And from the number of thy folk their seed shall end and cease

and Nathaniel Giles evokes '... the bloody teeth of those that sought us to oppress'.

There was nothing incongruous in this. Everything was part of a natural, divinely appointed order: to God, the saints, King, people, crops, weather. Disturb one element and you risk wreaking havoc in another. To Shakespeare, the murder of a king was not an individual act, it was the outward sign of something rotten in the state. Ghosts walk and storms rage. As Oliver Cromwell himself told Parliament: 'as in a quinsy or pleurisy, where the humour fixeth in one part, give it scope, all "disease" will gather to that place, to the hazarding of the whole ... I am sure I can lay it to God's account'.[3] Music, the most ordered of arts, was part of this hierarchy of things.

An immediate and lasting consequence of the Gunpowder Plot for church music was that Parliament made 5 November an annual Thanksgiving, with hymns and other music railing against the 'Popish Treachery', and an instruction to the priest to read out the entire Act of Parliament, which may or may not have been always scrupulously observed. Annual ceremonies with secular origins were catching on: 5 November joined 17 November, Elizabeth's Accession Day, in the church diary. More were to follow. (Later in the century 5 November also became the annual celebration of the arrival of William of Orange, so that the church ended up marking the failure of a Catholic coup to overthrow the Protestant James I, and the success of a Protestant coup to overthrow the Catholic James II, both at the same time, which is a neat irony.)

IN 1605 AND 1607 WILLIAM BYRD published two collections of music which he called *Gradualia*. These complement and supplement his mass settings of a decade earlier. The texts of the ordinary of the mass (Kyrie, Gloria, Credo, Sanctus, Benedictus, Agnus Dei) are always the same. The texts of the 'propers' (including the Introit, Gradual, Alleluia or Tract, Offertory and Communion) change according to the day of the year and the saint or festival being marked. The Catholic musician could thus create a musical liturgy for any occasion by 'dropping' the relevant sections from the *Gradualia* into one of the settings of the mass. He would need to be on the ball. Modern liturgical and musico-logical scholars have devoted much effort to decoding Byrd's choice of texts and variety of settings and working out how they fit together. He laid a complex trail for them to sniff out.

Many of the texts reappear from one feast day to another. Typically, Byrd avoids setting them multiple times, but sometimes the text will be shortened in one liturgy compared with another: Byrd provides a 'close', or cadence, in the middle, so that the piece can end at that point or continue, as the liturgy demands, without loss of musical argument. By contrast, the composer relishes the challenge of setting the word 'Alleluia' in many ways, creating a brilliant phantasmagoria of vocal variety from those five little syllables (sometimes four: English com-posers have always found 'Alleluia' a usefully adaptable word, not least because they have allowed themselves to stress whichever syllable they choose: compare the first and last words of Handel's 'Hallelujah' chorus from *Messiah*).

Musically, the collection is terse and concentrated, far removed from the expansive vocal polyphony of the *Cantiones sacrae*. There are beautiful settings of the antiphons to the beloved Virgin Mary; the gem-like *Ave verum corpus*, bringing the virtues of the Reformation anthem and its characteristic ABB structure to Latin words; and some perhaps slightly unexpected items like music for the crowd scenes in the Passion gospel.

Politically, this music, its origins and its use, show us where the English Catholic found himself in the years around the Gunpowder Treason. Catholicism was to a large extent a country-house dweller, away from London and prying eyes. William Byrd himself lived in one such Catholic household in Essex. The *Gradualia* were paid for, at least partly, by his Catholic patron and host, Sir John Petre. The 1605 set pre-dates the Plot. By 1607, Byrd found it necessary to leave out some of the more politically sensitive religious texts. But he still went ahead. This was a man confident and comfortable in his own internal exile. He dedicated the 1607 set openly to Petre, calling his pieces 'blooms collected in your own garden and rightfully due to you as tithes',[4] thus making their Catholic provenance explicit. A French Jesuit, a terrifying and alien creature, was found to be carrying a copy of the 1605 *Gradualia* when he was arrested in the woods after spies had followed him, skulking in the shadows between the country-house redoubts of the enemy within.

Byrd reissued the two sets in 1610, another mark of his confidence in his own position. They didn't sell but they didn't need to – they weren't meant to. By now, Byrd was writing for himself, his God and his own community. He made one last nod back in the direction of the English, domestic side of the sacred music market the following year. Byrd was probably now into his seventies, and described this collection as his 'last labours' and 'final farewell'.[5] *Psalms, Songs and Sonnets* is a mixed bag, as its title suggests: like the similarly titled collection of two decades before, there are sacred and secular pieces, some new, some resurrected from earlier phases of his career, flexibly scored for voices, viols or both (or either), in from three to six parts. The psalms and other devotional items are typically grave and expansive in character, features of the 'motet' style. It is almost as if his English sacred music was expanding into melancholy ripeness even as his Latin music contracted into contemplative introspection. Byrd was the kind of genius who constantly sought to reinvent himself and his art. As his own introduction to this volume puts it: 'The natural inclination and love to the art of music, wherein I have spent the better part of mine age, have been so powerful in me, that even in my old years which are desirous of rest, I cannot contain myself from taking some pains therein.'[6] There is some sprightly Italian-flavoured writing in cheery, madrigalian pieces like *Sing We Merrily* and *This Day Christ was Born*, but for the most part the tone is restful and valedictory: *Turn Our Captivity, O Lord*; *Lullaby, my Sweet Little Baby*; *Arise, Lord, into thy Rest*. Here, the composer almost seems to be talking to himself:

> Retire my soule, consider thine estate,
> And justly summe thy lavish sinnes account.
> Times deare expence, and costly pleasures rate,
> How follyes grow, how vanities amount.
> Write all these downe, in pale Deathes reckoning tables,
> Thy dayes will seeme but dreames, thy hopes but fables.

There is a sense of a personal Nunc Dimittis hovering around this book. Perhaps there was something in the air: this was the same year that Shakespeare bid farewell to the tempest of theatrical London and the 'cloud-capp'd towers' of his own art. Byrd added some words from Seneca to his dedication: 'the sun's light is sweetest at the very moment of its setting'.[7] Shakespeare would surely have agreed with that.

The year 1611 saw another publication of some significance in this story: the Authorised, or King James version of the Bible. Biblical texts were never as fecund a resource for the composer of liturgical music as the psalms and canticles of the Book of Common Prayer, but there are some notable examples. This Bible really came into its own somewhat later, with the growth of the sacred oratorio, where its Old Testament in particular provided plenty of bloody, good stories. But the words of the King James version roll through English literature and rhetoric, a sacred music in their own right. It is no coincidence that the men who assembled this Bible tried out their phrase-making by reading it aloud.

In November 1612, James's elder son, Henry, Prince of Wales, died of typhoid at the age of eighteen. Top royals were surrounded by sacred music more or less all the time, from psalms at home, through daily attendance at the Chapel Royal, to lavish ceremonies on important

Lullaby, my Sweet Little Baby. *This song could be sung by one voice with the lower parts played on a lute or viols, or sung by a group of singers, or some combination of voices and instruments. The ravishing 'English cadence' at the end would surely have woken the baby up (compare Tallis's* O Lord, Give thy Holy Spirit*).*

occasions such as baptisms, birthdays and the signing of marriage treaties. There are many accounts of these musical spectaculars. At the christening of Princess Mary in 1605, for example, 'At the tyme when the Royall Infant should be brought to the Chappell: the gentn of that place … went out of the Chappell two and two in ther surplesses unto the Nurcerie doore: … then began an Antheme …'[8] Henry seems to have occasioned more music than most and was widely celebrated in his lifetime for his love of the arts. He was serenaded at dinner at the Temple in 1605 by John Bull on keyboards and the singing of Nathaniel Giles and the choirboys. His investiture as Prince of Wales was accompanied by Tallis's mighty *Spem in alium*, sung to terrible English words. The treaty marrying him off to the Spanish Infanta was signed in the King's chapel, accompanied by anthems, musicians leaning down from the various galleries, singers on one side, lutes, sackbuts and cornets on the other. These Spaniards needed to know what kind of court they were marrying into, and music certainly had its part to play in ensuring they got the message.

This was conventional stuff. Elegies for royal deaths were part of the composer's routine too. But the laments for Henry have the flavour of genuine regret and sadness about them. Many leading composers contributed. Byrd's text compares Henry to his namesake and great-great-great-uncle Henry VIII, another accomplished, handsome prince (at least to begin with). Thomas Tomkins had the honour of writing music for the actual funeral, adapting the nation of Israel's lament for its own lost prince, Jonathan, in a lengthy, anguished and heartfelt wail of musical mourning.

This elegy touched something in the Jacobean soul – melancholy suited these men. There was a rash of settings of David's laments for Jonathan and Absalom, some of them very fine indeed, particularly those by Robert Ramsey, Thomas Weelkes and Tomkins. The dash of homoeroticism in the Jonathan text shouldn't be glossed over, either, though it is impossible to be too explicit about this, as with Shakespeare's sonnets. It is part of a particular kind of aesthetic world-view. But this element was certainly present at the courts of James I and his successor, and indeed in the emerging 'high-church' party, both at this time and later, in the nineteenth century and beyond. There are no settings of David's 'greater than woman's love' among the more aggressively macho courtiers of Queen Elizabeth I.

These laments were, for the most part, sacred madrigals, designed to be sung at home, not in church. This is an important distinction. Better-educated families sang not just metrical psalms around the household hearth, but favourite bits of scripture and devotional poems set to proper polyphony by real composers who made money by supplying this market. Some of these songs could be accompanied with the household's set of viols, kept in a chest under the stairs. Surviving sources clearly differentiate between part books copied for use in church or chapel, which are marked with the voice-names used by the church choir ('Contratenor Decani', etc.), and those for use at home, which typically contained entirely secular pieces like viol fantasias and madrigals about sheep and pretty girls. Sometimes an anthem appeared in both kinds of book, occasionally with the accompaniment slightly altered to fit the circumstances: the viol introduction to the 'secular' version of Edmund Hooper's *The Blessed Lamb* is one bar longer than the equivalent organ introduction in the 'sacred' source.[9]

Sacred madrigals are not liturgical pieces. It made no sense to stand up in church and just inform your congregation that David 'went up to his chamber and wept'. Where's the devotional point? You can't sing that in divine service. But no doubt people did – and still do. The argument about whether it is right to do so can still be heard among the liturgically aware.

In 1614 there was another significant contribution to the art of praising God at home. Sir William Leighton was a well-educated nobleman who managed to find himself in prison and in debt. Released from one, he attempted escape from the other by asking a number of leading composers to set his own penitential poems to music. Whatever his financial frailties, he clearly had considerable powers of persuasion: his contributors include Byrd, Bull, Hooper, Dowland, Martin Peerson (Organist of St Paul's) and John Milton (father of the poet and a notable composer). The results, published under the title *Teares or Lamentacions of a Sorrowfull Soule*, were intense, expressive and short. Edmund Hooper in particular wrought some surprising harmony from Leighton's verses. Interestingly, the songs were specifically laid out on the page for a 'broken' consort of lutes and viols as well as voices in four parts, no doubt codifying something which was already common practice. The term 'consort song' appeared in print for the first time. A second volume was planned but never completed.

In 1617 James I took a trip home to Scotland. The Stuarts were monarchs of two separate countries, which meant two coronations, English and Scottish. James, of course, was already King of Scotland, so this trip was ceremonial and diplomatic rather than specifically sacramental. But music was still required. Orlando Gibbons, leading court composer and joint organist of the Chapel Royal with Edmund Hooper, chipped in with *Great King of Gods*, an elegant and beautifully constructed setting of a rather dull bit of prosaic praise of the King. The 'For he's a jolly good fellow' school of verse never did bring out the best in the poets of the age of George Herbert and John Donne.

In 1623 there was a splendidly comical attempt at international relations which left a brief footprint in the musical sands. James's second son, Charles, now heir to the throne, wanted to revive the Spanish marriage idea for himself, so he and his father's chief minister, the Duke of Buckingham, set off in person for Spain. They travelled under the names Thomas and John Smith, covering the 1,000 miles on horseback in just ten days, some of it in false beards. When they got to Madrid, the Spaniards wouldn't let them see the Infanta. In what he probably thought was an impulsively romantic gesture, Charles climbed a wall into her private garden. Horrified and offended, the Spanish authorities kept their visitors hanging around all summer, then sent them home with a bad treaty and a flea in their ear.[10] Their return was greeted with 'the greatest celebration of joy that ever I saw',[11] as William Laud told his diary, and the now obligatory thanksgiving service at St Paul's, with music: 'When Israel came out of Egypt,' sang the choir, 'and the house of Jacob from among the strange people.'

The 1620s saw a number of notable musical careers reach their end. Thomas Weelkes died in 1623. His working life provides a pretty good blueprint of the career path open to the able church musician. Born in provincial Sussex, his probable early training was as a choirboy (though the habit of not listing choirboys by name means that no actual record of this exists). He made his way by successful publications of madrigals and by making friends in musical circles, particularly Thomas Morley. He got a good job (at Winchester College), then a better job (at Chichester Cathedral), then had a tilt at the best job of all (describing himself as Gentleman of the Chapel Royal). His church music proves him to be one of the masters of the 'verse' style, arguably second only to Gibbons. His skill as a madrigalist brings brilliant word-painting to descriptive pieces like *Hosanna to the Son of David* with its pealing cries of the crowds at the entry into Jerusalem. He was, and remains, one of the principal contributors to the newly Anglicanised services of matins and evensong.

He was also one of church music's leading bad boys and caused a scandal in Sussex by marrying the daughter of a local wealthy family, probably because she was already pregnant. He was always in trouble for being drunk, and for coming 'eyther from the Taverne or Ale house into the quire as is muche to be lamented, for in these humoures he will bothe curse & sweare most dreadfully, & so profane the service of God',[12] as the Dean of Chichester put it. Stories abound: he urinated on the head of the Dean from the cathedral organ loft during service; he got into a fight in a pub in Fleet Street, leading to his death at the nearby house of a friend. Some of these anecdotes may even be true. He is certainly not the only person in this book to be a fine musician and a difficult man.

Edmund Hooper followed a similar, though better behaved, career path. He started in rural Devon, serving as a chorister in the nearest cathedral, Exeter, then made a well-timed move to London and Westminster Abbey, where he progressed to become Master of the Choristers and, from 1606, Organist, the first person to hold the title still in use today. In 1604 he added the prize of Gentleman of the Chapel Royal to his CV, hanging onto his other jobs at the same time, as was usual practice. He became one of the two Organists of the Chapel with Orlando Gibbons (leading to an amusing little spat about who was the more senior and thus got to play at the best services, which was judiciously settled by the Sub-Dean). Hooper had a unique musical voice. His verse anthems are the longest of the period, almost Purcellian in their reach. His harmonies and vocal lines are bold and innovative: the full anthem *Behold, it is Christ* ends in a riot of false relations and diminished fourths. The comparison with Purcell stands scrutiny once again. His choice of texts, particularly in the verse anthems, was colourful and original, verging on the bizarre. This strong vein of individualism explains both why his music was so popular in his day (*Behold, it is Christ* exists in more sources than any other anthem, according to the painstaking research of the great Peter le Huray[13]) and, ironically, why it has largely failed to hold its place in the repertoire. This was a genius who needs some thinking about. He deserves it.

In 1628 the news came of the death of John Bull. In the congregation of naughty men, Bull probably outranks even Thomas Weelkes. Scandal, usury, dashing of teeth and getting of children followed him all over Europe. He was a brilliant keyboard virtuoso, and composed a small number of intense, skilful, sacred vocal pieces during the short time the Chapel Royal managed to put up with him, as well as at least one really good verse anthem, the splendid, expansive Epiphany piece *O God, who by the Leading of a Star*, which has one of the best last pages of the entire period. He fled the country on charges of adultery and assault, and ended his life in poverty in Antwerp; he was memorably described in a precautionary letter from the Archbishop of Canterbury to the British envoy at Brussels: 'The man hath more music in him than honesty and is as famous for marring of virginity as he is for fingering of organs and virginals.'[14]

Orlando Gibbons died in the middle of the decade. Again, his career is textbook stuff: an East Anglian, part of a musical family, choirboy at King's College, Cambridge, where his elder brother ran the choir, a junior post at the college when his voice broke, a move to London right at the start of James's reign, Gentleman of the Chapel Royal, then joint organist (with Hooper), then senior organist (to Tomkins), adding Organist of Westminster Abbey to his portfolio on Hooper's death in 1623. Gibbons wrote some heart-stoppingly beautiful music. Unlike Byrd, his musical personality was not one which found it necessary to constantly re-create form and technique. Rather, he was content to inherit an existing style and manner, and polish it until he achieved perfection. Full anthems like the six-voice *O Lord, in thy Wrath* make the words glow with gentle despair in the overlapping rising phrases at the end: 'O, save me'. The musical concentration of *Almighty and*

A truly unique musical voice. Part of Behold, it is Christ *by Edmund Hooper. Hooper's harmonic originality is only hinted at here, with his favourite 'false relations', quirky rhythms and melody prominently featuring the interval of a diminished fourth.*

Everlasting God and the 'short' service music is simply perfect – no other word will do. Verse anthems like the biblical *This is the Record of John* show Gibbons as the first real master of the solo voice, telling the story over a beautifully paced span. The larger verse anthems show more ambitious use of variety of texture, often ending with a soaring, polyphonic 'Amen'. Only very occasionally does Gibbons step outside his home territory of the Book of Common Prayer and the King James Bible for his anthem texts, and he seems less comfortable doing so: the text of *See, See, the Word is Incarnate* , a biblical paraphrase by the Dean of Rochester, Godfrey Goodman, is in the extravagant, theatrical manner of Hooper, a manner which probably suits the older man better.

Gibbons could do academic too: for his Oxford B.Mus. he set the psalm-text *O Clap your Hands* in eight parts, a piece of dazzling compositional virtuosity unsurpassed by any English composer, full of changes of texture and little canons chasing themselves around the choir with exhilarating abandon – thrilling stuff. There are the *The Hymnes and Songs of the Church*, perhaps the first genuine congregational music, giving us a number of tunes which turn up in later hymnals bolted onto all sorts of more and less suitable words (George Wither's originals are patchy but full of character). There is smaller-scale service music for practical use: responses and psalm chants. There are florid organ fantasias in the increasingly elaborate approved style. Within a fairly narrow compass, Gibbons is the most complete composer for the English church.

Gibbons was a young man when he died, just forty-two years old. The other notable shuffler-off of the first half of the 1620s was perhaps nearly twice that age. It wasn't hard to grow old in the seventeenth century – you just had to be lucky enough to survive birth without dying, cope with the battlefield of childhood, be a man (so you didn't have to go through childbirth all over again), and avoid the plague. Whosoever could manage these things could happily last his three-score years and ten, and more. Many musicians did.

William Byrd died in 1623, probably aged around eighty-three. His is the most complex, all-encompassing musical personality in this story so far, perhaps in the entire history of English church music. He wrote fluently and consistently over a long career, making him one of our most prolific composers. He published regularly, leaving us a kind of musical road map of the fluctuating fortunes of English Catholicism, told by a determined, articulate insider. His introductions to these volumes provide elegantly expressed insights into the conventions of the time and his own thinking. He took on all the principal musical forms of his day and wrought them into new shapes, creating rich veins of contrapuntal invention. Modern scholars have devoted themselves to teasing out his constant references to Catholic, and particularly Jesuit, thought in his choice of Latin texts, decoding the voice of the enemy within like a kind of musicological Bletchley Park. He was a businessman and a courtier, and a rebel who kept his distance. He was an enthusiastic pluralist, a ruthless monopolist and a stubborn litigant, activities in which he doesn't, frankly, always come across as a wholly attractive character. His musical reputation was high in his lifetime and remained so after his death.

But his innovations proved curiously uninfluential. He must have written in the sure and certain hope that his work would form part of a continuum into the life and witness of a restored English Catholic church. But it didn't. By positioning himself outside the main current of the English church, he almost deliberately ensured that his work would have no immediate successors and would lead nowhere. There are no Latin Masses and barely a handful of Latin motets in England for the next two-and-a-half centuries. There are echoes of his solemn contrapuntal dexterity in the music of Purcell and others, but they are distant echoes. Some of his better-behaved English music stayed in the repertoire and, later, some of his Latin music found its way back with English words, as at the Reformation. But even today, church choirs only scratch the surface of his genius. The might of his music has become the preserve of specialist early music ensembles in the concert hall.

This is a shame. Our liturgy can only be enhanced by the inclusion of great slabs of mourning like *Infelix ego*, with its extraordinary knife-twisting harmony at the end, even if, for Byrd, it's the wrong liturgy. English church music has always been inclusive. That's one of its great strengths. The fact that we have been able to embrace men like Byrd, even when he didn't really want us to, is an example of the way English institutions work. We are the richer for it.

JAMES I DIED IN 1625. The wholesale changing of the guard in the 1620s provides a good opportunity to reassess the state of church music. It is a picture of a widening divide. Psalm-singing at home had lost none of its popularity. Sternhold and Hopkins still sold well, and was joined by several other entrants to the market, including psalters by Thomas East (1592), Richard Allison (1599), Thomas Ravenscroft (1621), and others. Some of their better tunes, or bits of them, have survived in use to this day, usually (though not always) to different words. More musical households, or those which could run to a couple of trained musicians on

'Have mercy upon me O God, according to thy great mercy.' The words of Girolamo Savonarola, composed days before his execution for heresy, set to music by William Byrd.

the staff or ex-choirboys in the kitchen, could ornament their domestic devotions with lutes, citharas, viols, sacred madrigals and consort songs.

In the parish church, psalm-singing had a different character. Congregations preferred their own tunes – short, folksy, easy to memorise and easy to sing, needing just melody and bass with perhaps a dash of improvised harmony – to the 'official' tunes from Geneva and the fancy, expensive psalters. Puritanism ruled in the parish. Musically, the results were sounding increasingly weary. Choirs had largely vanished. The long decline of parish music, begun at the Reformation and hastened in Elizabeth's reign by money as much as dogma, continued its inevitable progress.

In cathedrals, rather the opposite was happening. Here, ceremonial was in the ascendant.

The key figure in this movement was the short, peevish, ambitious son of a cloth merchant from Reading, William Laud. Laud rose through the ecclesiastical ranks with the usual combination of piety and politics. He was consecrated bishop in 1621 (by six episcopal colleagues because the Archbishop of Canterbury had just inadvertently killed a keeper with a crossbow while out hunting), later becoming Dean of the Chapel Royal (1626), Bishop of London (1628) and Archbishop of Canterbury (1633). In every church he worked in, he recorded his liturgical innovations in his laconic but revealing diary (along with his erotic dreams about the Duke of Buckingham: 'That night in my sleep it seemed to me that the Duke of Buckingham came into bed to me; where he behaved himself with great kindness towards me'; a rather coy translation of the more explicit original Latin: '… ubi multo erga me amore se gessit.'[15] 'Amore' does not really mean 'kindness').

Once again, changes in church music were the consequence of changes in religious practice, not a factor in bringing those changes about. There is much talk in Laud's writings of where the altar should go, which way round it should be, whether window glass should be coloured or plain and what should hang on the walls. There is almost nothing about provision for music. His love of heightened ceremony provided the context in which increasingly elaborate church music could flourish.

Other records give us a good idea of how this elaboration was achieved. For example, there is lots of evidence, from first-hand accounts, records of payments and pictorial representations that a mixed band of instruments, including wind instruments, played in services at the Chapel Royal from the end of Elizabeth's reign through into the 1630s.

Not every day, certainly, but as a matter of course at important events. Sometimes the accounts are quite clear that instruments played with the choir, as at the baptism of Princess Mary in 1605: 'then began an Antheme ... (the Chorus whereof was filled with the help of Musicall Instrumentes) ... the Chappell and the Musitions Joyned together, makinge excellent Harmony wth full Anthemes'.[16] The Chapel Royal was Laud's canvas. As in earlier periods of change, the liturgical innovations adopted there, and their music, were specifically intended as the model for worship elsewhere, and were taken up by Laud's patrons and supporters in bishoprics and deaneries around the country – men like Neile of Winchester and Cosin of Durham. Battle lines were drawn.

To the puritan, 'high-church' types were all secret Papists and Arminians, with cringing Jesuits crouching behind every crucifix (which was sometimes perfectly true), making fancy music which encouraged immorality (an impression the louche crowd around Buckingham and the King did nothing to dispel). To Laudians, and others keen to guard their own interests, 'puritan' quickly became a convenient shorthand for anyone you didn't like. Sir Toby Belch calls Malvolio 'a puritan'[17] for trying to stop him waking up the entire house with his boozy partying in *Twelfth Night*. Coal merchants in Newcastle called their London rivals 'puritans' for opposing their monopoly.[18]

So, if we look at a verse anthem by Gibbons or Hooper and see an unassuming piece for choir and organ, conventional and undemanding, we see only a little part of what those modest marks on the page can tell us. It's like looking at a Van Dyck in black and white. Imagine this piece sung in the King's chapel at Whitehall, by a large group of men and boys in rich gowns and surplices, the court instrumentalists leaning over the galleries to sound the 'trumpets, hoboys, flutes and shawms', name-checked in the text alongside the object of all this adulation, 'our Sovereign Lord, King Charles'. Then picture the man in the street outside, heading off to hear a sermon at Paul's Cross, clutching a penny to buy a ballad-sheet copy of a simple psalm to sing with his friends, and wondering what all this exclusive magnificence spilling out from the Palace has got to do with him. Such a street in Whitehall would see the results of these tensions soon enough.

The rule of Charles I increased divisions in society, which subsequently showed up in the arts. Metaphysical poets began to relish abstraction and complexity, while quieter thinkers like George Herbert retired to the country, producing some of the most musical of all religious poetry. The divide which historians used to call 'court and country' could be seen on the page, in music as well as in words. Charles was crowned at Candelmas 1626, with plenty of grand music sung by 'the Quier of westminster, then the Chappell, who went singinge through the Pallace yard, & round about the church through the great Sanctuarie till they came to the west dore'.[19] The music was mostly newly written by Thomas Tomkins, including the first setting for a coronation of that familiar favourite 'Sadock the Priest'.

A notable subtext of the new reign was the inception of a separate, Catholic chapel, with music, for the new Queen. Despite his false beard and his efforts at shinning up walls in Madrid, Charles ended up marrying not the Spanish Infanta but Henrietta Maria of France. There were of course no publicly active Catholic church musicians in England, so she brought her own, men with fancy foreign names, and 'three little singing boys' under the direction of M. Louis Richard, making costly, elaborate and dangerously fascinating music in the chapel at Somerset House.

John Dowland, only begetter of miniaturised melancholy, died in 1626. The lute-song was the perfect vehicle for Dowland's species of self-regarding sadness. There's little room for religion in this world-view, but there is just one lute-song with a sacred flavour, 'Thou Mighty God', where the composer compares his own sorrows to those of Job (naturally), a few chants and harmonisations suitable for domestic use, and a couple of flexibly scored devotional part-songs. Dowland's great peer among the lutenist composers, Thomas Campion, showed a little more interest in his God rather than just himself: 'O come quickly, glorious Lord, and raise my sprite to thee'. The anonymous *Miserere, my Maker* is full of gorgeous, anguished chromaticism: 'Miserere, I am dying'. These are songs for a soloist singing to himself (probably a boy, and certainly not a man singing falsetto). Suitably transcribed, they make perfect little anthems.

Dowland was a Catholic who managed to survive and prosper at the

English court. The years 1628 and 1630 brought news of the deaths of two English composers whose overt Catholicism had driven them abroad. Peter Philips was trained as a choirboy at St Paul's Cathedral, and left England for good as a young man, settling in the Low Countries around Antwerp and Brussels. An attempt to return foundered when he was accused of being involved in one of the many plots (real and imagined) on the life of Elizabeth I, and in the first decade of the seventeenth century he became a Catholic priest. Philips was a prolific composer, and his work shows some strikingly modern touches, including motets for double choir in the manner being pioneered by Gabrieli in Venice.

Richard Dering also worked mostly in the Spanish Netherlands, having travelled widely in Italy as a young man. Another Catholic convert, he made it back to England for a while as part of the music staff at Henrietta Maria's private chapel. Dering's musical innovations include a 'continuo' bass (a separate part for an instrument like a bass viol or cello) in some of his madrigals, very much a feature of the nascent Baroque style. A few cheerful pieces by both men have found their way back into the repertoire of English choirs, for example Dering's *Factum est silentium* for St Michael, one of the few anthems to mention a dragon. Both have left us considerable riches to explore.

The vogue for Italian fashion and style was not limited to Catholic exiles like Dering and Philips. Walter Porter apparently studied with Monteverdi in Venice, and brought the fruits of his studies home to England, with bizarre results. One of his anthems begins with a rather dull chorus, like bad Gibbons, then erupts into Italian opera in the middle in a treble and tenor duet black with semiquavers, before relapsing exhausted back into the musical vernacular at the end – all very odd. The composer John Cooper went so far as to change his name to Giovanni Coperario. Principally, though, the Italian influence shows up in bouncy pieces like *This Day Christ was Born* by Byrd and *Gloria in excelsis Deo* by Weelkes, and in mournful pieces like the Absalon laments. It added character to English church music, but proved to be a briefly brilliant fad.

Nathaniel Giles had been Master of the Children at the Chapel Royal for thirty-six years when he died in 1634. That wasn't all he did. The professional musician was a busy man in Jacobean London. Giles had already served as Organist of both Worcester Cathedral and St George's Chapel, Windsor, by the time of his promotion to the Chapel Royal, and appears to have hung onto his Windsor job after he took up the new post. In addition, he ran both sets of choirboys – Windsor and the Chapel Royal – as theatre companies, working closely with the fashionable playwrights John Lyly, who put the classical 'University' style onto the popular stage, and Ben Jonson. In 1600 Giles took over the theatre built into the remnant of some old monastic buildings on the north bank of the Thames, known as the Blackfriars. A hundred years before, these walls and cloisters had echoed to the footsteps of choirboys offering a very different kind of entertainment. The theatre companies did not have long left to live: the annual warrant permitting Giles to 'take up'(i.e. abduct) singing-boys from wherever he could find them specifically mentioned acting as well as singing up to 1604: by 1606 the theatrical qualification had been quietly dropped. (Incidentally, in a nice aside, Blackfriars is the district of London where the modern-day Chapel Royal choirboys go to school. That's how London works.)

Giles, of course, was also a composer. It's good for us to look at the work of composers who weren't geniuses. The musical vernacular comes through more clearly in the work of the musical moles, burrowing away at the approved style of the day. Apart from one vertiginous experiment with chromaticism (exhilarating but a bit weird), Giles's verse anthems and services are short, easy, straightforward, competent and practical. Plenty of worse music has held a better place in the repertoire. The solo sections in Giles's verse music tend to be short, concise, and often for just one or two voices, like the music of the earlier (and rather more interesting) Thomas Weelkes, and the later (and a bit more interesting) Thomas Tomkins. A more discursive approach to the verse anthem can be traced in a line running from some pieces by Gibbons, through the anthems of Hooper and Bull, and into the later work of John Amner.

Amner is something of an exception among leading composers of the time in that he never worked at the Chapel Royal or anywhere else in London. His family roots were in East Anglia, and he had a life-long connection with Ely Cathedral, serving as *Informator Choristarum* there from 1610 until his death in 1641. His Cesar's service was written for Dean Cesar, and his verse anthems show a real flair for large-scale form and imaginative vocal textures. *O Ye Little Flock* takes an almost childlike delight in its depiction of the Nativity story. A reasonable amount of his music has survived and much of it has been edited and recorded relatively recently, a welcome restoration to a deserved place in the repertoire.

Archbishop Laud set out to impose his vision of ceremonial worship on his church in 1634. His weapon was the 'Visitation', a detailed questionnaire about liturgy and practice delivered to deans and archdeacons across the land. Music got about the same amount of attention as it did in earlier attempts at this method; that is, not much. How you do music is a bit more important than how you kept drunks out of the churchyard and a bit less important than what hood you wore to evensong. For example, Exeter Cathedral was sent a list of eighteen questions. Number four asked 'whether the number of those that serve the quire ... be kept full and the quire sufficiently furnished with a skilfull organist and able singers and dayly service there song'; number nine, 'whether the choristers be well ordered'; and number 17, 'what is the yearly allowance of your schoolemaster and usher of your free schoole (if you have any)'. As far as music goes, that was it. The replies weren't always very helpful either. Two prebendaries of Salisbury told Laud that 'to the 19th [article], they know not the number of the choristers, but conceive them to be under the charge and tuition of Mr Gyles Tomkins, their master ... to the rest, they have nothing to say.'[20] Bishop Wren of Norwich found that 'the Divine Service in ye forenoones is neither performed wth that solemnity of time, manner, and ordr, wch of right it ought', and personally celebrated prayer-book communion in Ipswich, that hotbed of reactionary Puritanism. Laud told the King that Wren had done as much as could be expected 'in such a diocese, in the midst of the humourousness of this age'.[21] Music, as usual, was tugged along in the wake of these forces.

The mid-1630s saw Charles turn his attention to Scotland, with his usual mixture of arrogance and a complete inability to judge popular feeling. In 1633 he went north to be crowned and the English Chapel Royal went with him (by sea, on a ship called the *Dreadnought*), joining with its rather less grand Scottish counterpart when it got there. Four years later, in 1637, he attempted to impose a new Book of Common Prayer (popularly known as 'Laud's Liturgy'), which led to riots. Psalm-singing was a familiar field of battle. The Scots had long had their own psalters, based closely on Sternhold and Hopkins and drawing on the long association of Scotsmen like John Knox with continental Calvinism, but with a flavour all their own. Here are the tunes we sing today as 'O for a Closer Walk with God' and 'God Moves in a Mysterious Way', with their distinctive long note at the beginning of each line. Laud and the King had the psalms bound into their new prayer book. Interestingly, these sometimes included the 'prose' versions of the psalms alongside the 'metrical' ones. 'Metrical' psalms are in a regular metre and rhyme-scheme to aid singing, while the 'prose' versions are in irregular verse, as in the Bible and the Book of Common Prayer. One copy sent north in 1636 states that its text is 'pointed as they (the Psalms) shall be said or sung'.[22] It's not. No 'pointing' (that is, indications of how a psalm verse fits its music) is given. In any event, 'prose' psalms don't lend themselves to singing to regular tunes. That's why they were put into metrical form in the first place. Chanting the 'prose' psalms is an odd hybrid which eventually took hold in the proto-Laudian innovations of late nine-teenth-century high-church Anglicanism. Its proponents claimed they were restoring an ancient tradition. They weren't. But perhaps there is a hint of an early attempt in this direction in that curious rubric of 1636.

Once again, the contrast between the musical splendours stashed away on board the *Dreadnought* by Thomas Tomkins and the beautiful, simple lines of the Scottish psalters allows us to see what Charles I so fatally failed to comprehend: the divide between what he wanted for his Scottish subjects and what they wanted for themselves. It was a bad mistake.

And, as always, music paid the price. John Barnard, a minor Canon of St Paul's Cathedral, issued a substantial collection of choral pieces in 1641 under the title *First Book of Selected Church Music*. It was either very bad timing or very bad luck. Within about a year the Civil War had broken out, blowing church music away in its all-consuming fury. Barnard's book was as obsolete as a Missal at the Reformation.

But his unwise venture has provided us with a precious record of the music being sung by choirs like St Paul's, right at the moment that an important chapter in the history of English church music closed. We have before us, in the handsome survivors from among the original ten part books, the 'choycest Master-peeces, left us in Hymnes, Anthems, and Services' by 'Divers Approved Authors', including Tallis, Mundy, Byrd, Morley, Gibbons, Giles and others, whose work was otherwise in 'danger of perishing, or corrupting in erroneous and manuscript obscurity'. Printing obviates such errors: 'such bookes as heretofore were with much difficulty transcribed for the use of the Quire, are now to the saving of much labour and expence publisht for the general good of all such as shall desire them', and, he might have added, for the preservation of much fine music. Barnard ends his flowery preface with a friendly greeting to his singers: 'So wishing to all those that shall use these books, cleere voices, true measure, and chiefly affections ray'sd to the devout height of these ditties, I take leave.'[23] By the time he died in 1649, the same year as the dedicatee of the *First Book*, Charles I, nobody had been able to take him up on his cheerful invitation. We do now.

THE NAME TOMKINS ECHOES around seventeenth-century church music. This is partly because there were lots of them. Several families regarded church music as a sort of family business: the Gibbonses, Purcells and Lawes all supplied notable names from one generation to another.

Thomas Tomkins had three younger half-brothers, all of whom had successful musical careers, at the Chapel Royal and elsewhere, and his father and son were both respected musicians. But Thomas remains the headline act. His career is familiar stuff – choirboy in his local cathedral (probably St David's, then Gloucester, where his father worked), very possibly 'impressed' into the Chapel Royal while still a boy, selected for some high-level training by the current top composer (Byrd), further study at Oxford; cathedral organist (Worcester), close working relationship with a like-minded contemporary (Morley), establishing a reputation through publication, and finally, Gentleman, then Organist, of the Chapel Royal.

The lives of these musicians were closely intertwined. Morley,

Hooper, Weelkes, Tomkins, Gibbons, Giles and (to a lesser extent) Byrd saw each other more or less every day. They taught each other and each other's children, sang each other's music, ate, worked and prayed together, and married into each other's families. The result was that they all, very broadly, have the same musical style. They wrote in the same forms in response to the same requirements from market and monarch. It was an intensely practical, hands-on way of learning how to do music – starting, crucially, in early childhood. They are, to use an old-fashioned but revealing term, a compositional 'school'. Something similar can be seen in other periods of English church music.

Tomkins's problem was that he lived too long. Born a decade or so before Orlando Gibbons, he outlived the younger composer by thirty years, and thus found himself rather stranded in later life, first in the Chapel Royal of the 1630s with only his brothers for company, then, to a far greater extent, in the land without music of the 1640s and 1650s, eking out his old age in the Worcestershire countryside, *sans* friends, *sans* choir, *sans* job, *sans* everything. He lived to see the magnificent organ he had installed in Worcester Cathedral torn down. Enemies tricked him. His livelihood and his delight – music for the worship of God – was gone.

But he used his vale of misery for a well. He continued to compose some fine instrumental music. He appears to have been close to his extended family who cared for him in his declining years. Most importantly for church music, he collected his work into a series of publications which he called *Musica Deo sacra*, completed by his son after his death, including a wealth of melancholy, expressive verse anthems on texts like *Out of the Deep have I Called unto thee, O Lord*. He specialised in writing for a solo bass, perhaps for some admired friend lately in the Worcester cathedral choir, much as Purcell was to do later in the century.

Tomkins was the last of the 'Golden Age' composers. He died in 1656. Just a couple of years later Oliver Cromwell was also dead. A year after that, a little boy called Henry Purcell was born, full of the grace and talent that would carry church music into fresh woods and pastures new. And one year on, church music was back. It's sad to think how near Tomkins got to seeing these things. He lived in difficult times and his music shows us what it was like in that dawn to be alive.

8

Interregnum, 1644–1660

The rest is silence

William Shakespeare, *Hamlet*

FOR CHOIRS AND COMPOSERS, the story of music in church during the Interregnum years is simply told: there was none. This doesn't mean there was no sacred music; still less does it mean there was no music at all. Even Puritans could enjoy themselves sometimes (just a little) and Oliver Cromwell himself liked music. By a striking irony, it's said that he was particularly fond of some psalm-settings by Richard Dering, a Catholic and an ex-exile. But he didn't like it in church.

In 1645 Parliament abolished the Book of Common Prayer. At the same time, Cromwell's soldiers smashed up churches and tore down organs. Today's 'ruin-bibber, randy for antique',[1] as Philip Larkin put it, often finds himself standing in some vandalised chancel, having to guess if it was Henry VIII or Cromwell who knocked the head off the sad-looking saint staring eyeless at him from his plinth. Sometimes it was both. Sacred music therefore became an indoor thing. There are simple psalm-settings by Thomas Ravenscroft, John Playford, William Child and Henry and William Lawes, often in three parts, sometimes in rounds and canons not far removed from the style of another Raven-scroft composition, 'Three Blind Mice'.[2]

As so often in religiously inspired political conflicts, the forces of Puritanism split into a bewildering variety of offshoots and splinter groups, some highly exotic, others difficult to pin down. Some of the more bizarre sects may even be entirely fictional, set up by their enemies and then entering the popular consciousness as bogeymen. By their very nature, these varieties of Protestant, including the Seekers, the Muggletonians and the Quakers, had neither the desire nor the resources for music, though if you found yourself striding at dawn over the crest of a hill in Weybridge, Cobham or Wellingborough, in the year or so after the execution of Charles I, you might perhaps have come across a tiny group of proto-communists, known as Diggers, tilling their common land, and breaking into a ragged hymn as they worked, just in case today did turn out to be the Day of Judgement after all.

The statement that there was no music in church needs a little qualifying too. Some colleges in Oxford claim to have kept their music going throughout the Commonwealth period: private chapels were always something of a special case in relation to public policy and law. In the parish, psalms were still used 'before and after' the service (and the sermon), in the dosage set out in the Ordinances of 1559. And, way out in the country, were there some stubborn remnants of the colourful, seductive old papist practices, in 'the distant skirts of the North', as one MP told Parliament, 'where the prayers of the common people are more like spells and charms than devotions',[3] still resistant to the blandishments of 'lecturers' and Acts for the Propagation of the Gospel? Probably.

Composers began to turn their attention outside the choir stall. Other forms of music, like the masque and the solo song, became increasingly popular. The mannerisms of the new Baroque style were ready to step in. For the first time, the church was no longer the principal, unchallenged patron of music – a position it would never regain. Alongside what to write was the question of what to do. Some members of the Chapel Royal accompanied the court to Oxford, though there doesn't appear to have been anything for them to do there apart from admire the architecture and dodge the cannonballs coming down upon St Giles from the north. Others found work in private families. Some professional musicians joined the army. Henry Cooke was a Chapel Royal singer before the Civil War and a Royalist captain during it. When he was given the job of re-founding the choir at the Restoration, he was known ever after, in court records and Pepys's diary alike, as 'Captain Cooke'. The Lawes brothers joined up too. Henry survived and rejoined Cooke at the Chapel Royal in 1660; William was killed at the battle of Rowton Heath in 1645.

In January of 1645 Parliament deprived composers of the familiar stage direction which had been their comfort and their cue for a hundred years – 'in quires and places where they sing here followeth the anthem'– by abolishing the Book of Common Prayer. In response, William Child composed a five-part elegy on the psalm verse *O Lord God, the heathen are Come into thine Inheritance*, marking his score 'for the abolition of the Book of Common Prayer 1645'. His style harks back to the world of Thomas Tallis and John Sheppard a century before, as if the notes themselves were a melancholy musical memorial of what had been lost.

Parliament's replacement for the Book of Common Prayer was the *Directory for the Public Worship of God* (also known as the 'Westminster Covenant' or 'Westminster Directory'). Like the prayer book it replaced, the *Directory* was a rich and sonorous piece of prose in its own right:

> … to bewail our blindness of mind, hardness of heart, unbelief, impenitency, security, lukewarmness, barrenness; our not endeavouring after mortification and newness of life, nor after the exercise of godliness … to profess that it is the desire of our souls to have fellowship with God, in the reverend and conscionable use of his holy ordinances …[4]

Composers could do a lot worse than set some of the liturgical rule books to music as much as the liturgies themselves. Thinkers and opinion-formers of the seventeenth century believed that public policy required good writing just as much as literature and argument from

New College, Oxford, in the 1480s. Then, as now, the choir of robed men and boys was an important and prominent feature of the College's foundation and daily life.

Thomas Tallis, our first composer whose work has genuinely held its place in the repertoire, and deservedly so: a wonderful, resourceful, imaginative and hugely professional writer for the liturgy, for the human voice, and for four royal patrons of wildly differing ecclesiastical tastes..

Perhaps the widest-reaching musical mind of all: William Byrd, Catholic, courtier, composer.

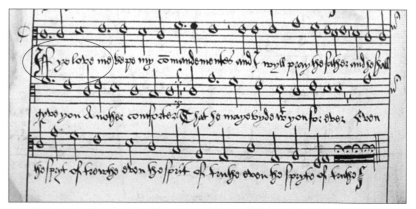

Tudor musical handwriting. The top part of Thomas Tallis's perfect little anthem in the approved 'ABB' form, If ye love me, *from the Wanley partbooks, mid-sixteenth century*

A typical small medieval monastery – Bermondsey Abbey, which stood in what is now Southwark, on the south bank of the Thames in London, from probably before the Norman Conquest to the Dissolution in the 1540s. Its chapel would have heard much plainsong and no doubt plenty of polyphony too.

John Taverner, composer of sumptuous, learned Latin polyphony for the pre-Reformation Catholic liturgy. He lost his job in Henry VIII's land-grab on the English church, and was close to people who lost a lot more than that.

John Day, publisher, 1562. Little more than fifty years after the beginning of printing, this woodcut shows how sophisticated the art had become.

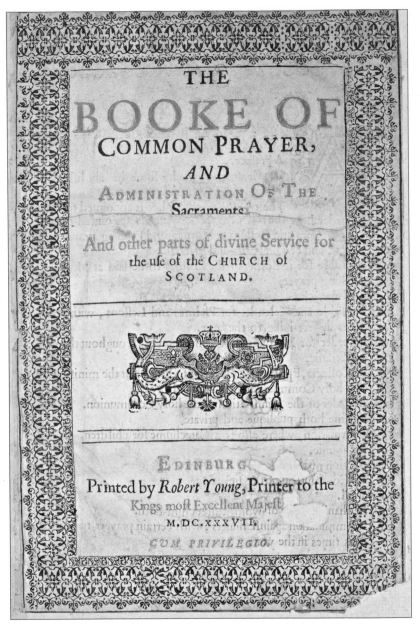

THE
BOOKE OF
COMMON PRAYER,
AND
ADMINISTRATION OF THE
Sacraments.

And other parts of divine Service for
the use of the CHURCH of
SCOTLAND.

EDINBURGH
Printed by *Robert Young*, Printer to the
Kings most Excellent Majestie.
M.DC.XXXVII.
CUM PRIVILEGIO.

*The Scottish Prayer Book of 1637. This tatty title page gives little hint of the forces
it unleashed: Jenny Geddes threw a stool at an Archbishop in the middle of a
sermon. The Scots have always done their churchmanship differently.*

The coronation of James II and Queen Mary, 1685, probably the most musically spectacular of all such events. This is one of the sumptuous illustrations from Francis Sandford's History. John Blow and Henry Purcell were both there, and are possibly to be found among the musicians in the galleries.

An eighteenth-century Gallery choir rehearsing Handel, as seen by Hogarth.

Samuel Sebastian Wesley, scion of a famous family with fingers in all sorts of devotional pies. He had a unique ability both for writing tunes and for annoying the clergy.

Although Hubert Parry's music has earned him a place as flag-waver in chief at national occasions, he was far from a conventional believer or establishment insider. The moustache says English country gent, the eyes (and the music) say something quite different (and much more interesting).

Ralph Vaughan Williams, whose musical sympathies encompassed every aspect of music for the church, from Tudor polyphony to the English Hymnal.

Composers for the church in the twentieth century (above): Benjamin Britten.

And the twenty-first (left):
Peter Maxwell Davies.

In Wales, hymn-singing turns up at sporting occasions and sometimes vice versa: choristers at Llandaff Cathedral.

first principle, because they were basically the same thing. Maybe we will come to believe that again.

The *Directory* is full of familiar stuff about avoiding superstition, reading the Bible, going to church and not getting caught in 'private whisperings, conferences, salutations … gazing, sleeping, and other indecent behaviour' during service. It also mentions music quite a lot, but only one kind of music: psalm-singing. Psalms run through its recipe for godly living, a source of edification and a way to renew a right spirit, in church and at home. Used reverently, discreetly, advisedly, soberly, and in the fear of God, music maketh man. It is, therefore, worth quoting in full what the Directory has to say on the subject:

> Of Singing of Psalms.
>
> IT is the duty of Christians to praise God publickly, by singing of psalms together in the congregation, and also privately in the family.
>
> In singing of psalms, the voice is to be tunably and gravely ordered; but the chief care must be to sing with understanding, and with grace in the heart, making melody unto the Lord.
>
> That the whole congregation may join herein, every one that can read is to have a psalm book; and all others, not disabled by age or otherwise, are to be exhorted to learn to read. But for the present, where many in the congregation cannot read, it is convenient that the minister, or some other fit person appointed by him and the other ruling officers, do read the psalm, line by line, before the singing thereof.

This elegant prescription summed up what psalm-singing was all about. It was done together, both in church and privately. The emphasis was on understanding and order. It was for the whole congregation (including women) – for everyone who could read. And there was provision there, too, for those who couldn't read. Nothing could better illustrate the inclusivity of psalm-singing than this specific attempt to reach the parts of society least able to help themselves. Nothing could be further from the deliberately exclusive glories of Catholic ceremonial and its successor, the liturgical innovations of Archbishop Laud.

The practice of an 'officer' or clerk reading or singing each line of a psalm, which is then sung back at him by the congregation, began to catch on. It's one of the most basic forms of corporate music-making: call and response. Think of squaddies jogging 'at the double', repeating some cheerful nonsense barked at them by their sergeant major to keep their spirits up. This kind of psalm-singing became known as 'lining out', and it became popular and widespread and therefore, of course, controversial and suspect to those who didn't like it. The key to its appeal was its practicality. Congregations could sing to tunes they already knew; you didn't need many books, or indeed any at all apart from the clerk's own copy. You could join in even if you were 'disabled by age'; you didn't even have to be able to read. This really was music for 'young men and maidens, old men and children'.[5] It also allowed the congregation to look up, rather than each member of a congregation becoming 'an islande intire of itself',[6] peering downwards into his own book and his own soul. Modern evangelicals are doing the same thing when they display the words of their worship songs on a screen. The arguments of the Reformation aren't over yet.

Nathaniel Holmes produced an elegant and articulate defence of this kind of psalm-singing in his *Gospel Musick. Or, The Singing of Davids Psalms, &c. in the publick congregations, or private families asserted, and vindicated*,[7] printed in 1644. His six chapter headings (or 'generals', as he calls them) summed up where, for the Puritan, psalm-singing came from, and where it had got to: 'The warrantableness of it ... the unquestionableness of it ... the ancientness of the use of it ... the necessariness of it ... the usefulness of it ... the unjustness of men's exceptions against it ...' His authority, as always, was St Paul: 'This Apostle having cut the Ephesians short of all vain mirth, not allowing them much jesting which the wisest moral men counted virtue, yet enjoins them this heavenly music of singing Psalms.' St Paul, it turns out, was a Puritan all along. There's a surprise.

Holmes wanted his psalms sung 'with grace'. There was probably precious little 'grace' in the way this music actually sounded out of the mouths of ordinary parishioners. How do you know which tune to sing, once the clerk has read you the first line? You guess. What do you do if the person standing next to you knows a different tune to this psalm? You carry on and see if they fit together. How do you get your pitch, in the absence of an organ or other instrument? You wait for someone else to sing it. How do you know when to change chord? You swoop and slide between pitches until the next chord emerges. How do you spice things up a bit once the psalm has set off on its lugubrious way? You add little scales, runs and ornaments between the notes of the tune.

This music would sound very strange and remote to us now: muddled, indeterminate and, above all, slow. Samuel Pepys, a slightly later but extremely reliable musical commentator, heard the clerk and people of his parish taking a whole hour to get through fewer than forty verses. The resistance to central control and the dogged devotion to habit meant that in practice the singing of psalms probably often had little to do with anything written on the page, which only increased its remoteness. Governments tried to issue new psalters. People preferred that hardy perennial Sternhold and Hopkins, now known, appropriately, as the 'Old Version'. Publishers and church authorities tried to tell people which tunes to sing, while people sang what they already knew. It had become, in effect, an oral tradition, resistant to classification, both at the time and since, as such traditions always are.

The modern scholar Nicholas Temperley, the pre-eminent modern chronicler of these matters, has pointed out that this kind of approach to singing psalms, based on a printed version but with a thick layer of unwritten folk tradition added in, resurfaced in various traditions in America, including, fascinatingly, among the Amish communities of Pennsylvania.[8] Perhaps we can hear a hint of the kind of manner of performance, if not of musical style, in the music of some parts of Africa, too, where a bus queue will burst spontaneously into song, one leading, everyone else answering in a species of harmony, part learned, part improvised, embellished according to local custom.

This is a distant corner of our church music history. As Temperley says, 'No period of parish church music is today more remote than this one'.[9] But it was certainly tenacious. It would be the turn of the eighteenth century before a new psalter was successfully adopted to inject a bit of vigour into the psalm-singer's palsied bones. Meanwhile, psalms carried the message and the music of 'moral men' out into all lands. The Scottish psalter and prayer book made its ill-fated way north in the 1630s. *The Bay Psalm Book* became the first book to be printed in North America when it was issued in Massachusetts in 1640. The words already have a discernible New World twang. The voice of the English Puritan entered American thought and discourse, where it emphatically remains to this day. A copy of the *Bay* psalter became the most expensive book ever when it was sold at auction in 2013 for £8.8 million.

In England, the 1640s brought the contrast between the Puritan parish and the Laudian cathedral to a head. Nathaniel Holmes described the differences:

> David's psalms sung in our English metre differ much from cathedral singing which is so abominable, in which is sung almost everything, unlawful litanies and creeds and other prose not framed in metre fit for singing. Besides they do not let all the congregation neither sing nor understand what is sung; battologizing and quavering over the same words vainly. Yea nor do they all sing together, but first one sings an anthem, then half the choir then the other tossing the word of God like a tennis-ball. Then all yelling together with confused noise. This we utterly dislike as most unlawful.[10]

These were familiar complaints. We can hear Erasmus cry 'Amen' from beyond the grave.

Was Holmes right? Does a piece like, for example, the 'Great' service of Byrd involve 'battologizing and quavering over the same words vainly' and 'yelling together with confused noise'? In some respects, it does. For Holmes, psalm-singing was the only way to 'bring religion home to many who would otherwise be deaf to it', including women and the native Indian tribes around the new settlements in America. But, interestingly, he has no time for the singing of 'prose not framed in metre' which he heard in 'Pauls and Westminster &c'. Again, early attempts at chanting the prose psalms were clearly linked in the Puritan mind to the iniquities of Laud and his like.

On 10 January 1645, in the middle of the Civil War and after a trial lasting four years, Laud became the fifth and (so far) last Archbishop of Canterbury to be executed. His faction found itself decapitated too. For the kind of elaborate church music he sought to champion, the party was over. The rest of the Interregnum was barren ground, music-ally. Services at the Chapel Royal petered out around 1642 and music in cathedrals ceased. Organs were destroyed. Every large church and chapel has its own tale of being used as a barracks, a stable or a store-house for ammunition. At Westminster Abbey soldiers pawned the organ pipes for beer and played hare and hounds up and down the nave dressed in the choirmen's robes.

Church music could have gone a number of ways in the mid-seventeenth century. At a popular level, it is possible to see the Civil War and Interregnum as one of the points at which church music was revealed as the music of the people[11] – troops on both sides sang psalms as they marched into battle (especially Parliamentarians but Royalists too)[12] – not just because many of the soldiers were pious Protestants, though they were, but because the metrical versions were popular texts: church music as folk-song.

On the other hand, the tradition of 'art' music in church could easily have trickled to a halt. Composers could have diverted their atten-tions to secular forms, more or less entirely. That was one of the effects of violent revolution elsewhere in Europe. In rural Wales, Thomas Tomkins composed a piece he called *Pavan for these Sad, Distracted Times*. Something dramatic was needed.

9

Restoration, 1660—1714

More suited to the playhouse, or a Tavern, than the church.

John Evelyn

DRAMA WAS NOT IN short supply when the Stuarts returned to power. The whole of the court became a kind of theatre. There was everything to play for in 1660, when the uncertainty occasioned by the unexpected death of Oliver Cromwell in 1658, and the botched attempt to replace him with his ill-equipped son Richard, was finally resolved with the triumphant return of Charles II from his continental exile, and the restoration of the Stuart monarchy and everything that went with it. Music had its part to play and seized the opportunity with all the relish of the stage-struck adolescent.

There were parallels with earlier periods, too. The later seventeenth century, like the sixteenth, showed church music emerging stronger for having been driven underground, until it collapsed like a whore's make-up in candlelight under the withering assault of mismanagement and lack of money, foes far more formidable than war or doctrine. And, like the earlier seventeenth century, there was a 'school' of composers centred around the Chapel Royal, exploring the same musical neologisms through daily contact with each other and each other's music.

The period of interregnum was, for obvious reasons, something of a radical discontinuity in the history of English church music. Its end in 1660 therefore provides a good opportunity to look at how musical style works. The basic question is the extent to which style changes in an ordered progression, with each development leading inevitably to the next in an unfolding sequence whose logic becomes apparent over time; or, conversely, the degree to which changes come about as the result of isolated one-off events such as the birth of a genius, the death of a monarch, a financial crisis or a war, events whose consequences are by definition unpredicted and unpredictable and thus follow no logical pattern.

Did Henry Purcell junior change musical style, all by himself, all at one go, by the sheer force of his revolutionary musical personality? Or did he simply sum up musical changes which were going on all around him and would have happened anyway? Geniuses make the musical weather. There's no doubt about how far Purcell pushed the boundaries of what music could do compared to what he inherited, nor about the lasting influence of his innovations. In his hands, the development of musical style was fast-moving and far-reaching, compared to periods of slower progress either side of his short career. This interpretation tends to support the 'genius-as-natural-phenomenon' view, where brilliant individuals change everything just because they can, and everybody else follows along humbly in their wake, doing their best to imitate the master.

On the other hand, genius needs context. To achieve so much, and especially to do it so young, a voracious and fecund musical personality like Purcell needed to be presented with a complete musical language which he could learn, complete with rules, grammar, techniques, principles and good manners. Only once he has mastered the vernacular can a composer demonstrate that he has the musical personality to add something new. Some can, some can't.

This is Darwinian evolution played out among the warbling flutes rather than the fluttering finches. Like a species, a group of composers can work together to do what it does as well as it can. Then, by luck or talent, a far-sighted individual comes up with an innovation. Such mutations get absorbed into the gene pool if they contribute something which works practically and is useful aesthetically. The natural tendency to reject and kick over the style of the previous generation helps composers create a style which reflects their own. It's the kind of evolution which biologists call 'punctuated equilibrium': periods of stylistic stability interrupted by bursts of creative experimentation, usually with the current top genius taking the lead, a free spirit with an innate understanding of the character of his times and a sufficiently thorough grasp of his inheritance to know instinctively what to hang onto and what to reject.

Henry Purcell was born into a musical world which was changing fast. Some features of church music were resurrected from pre-Civil War days: uniformed choirs of men and boys, organs, the prayer book with all its musical possibilities. But striking new features were soon added, most notably the use of a small band of stringed instruments in services at the Chapel Royal.

Technically, the new weapons in the composer's stylistic armoury included the separate, instrumental bass part, known as a 'continuo', played on a cello or bass viol, with harmonies supplied by a keyboard player or lutenist reading from numbers, or 'figures'. This allowed composers to think in terms of the harmony supporting a single musical line, rather than of equal voice-parts in a many-voiced texture. Colourful new harmonies burst forth. Music for the solo voice exploded in its technical and expressive reach. The band of strings required genuine, idiomatic writing for what were effectively modern violins, violas and cellos, rather than a piece of well-worked counterpoint which could be freely applied across the Renaissance sound-world of viols, voices, 'broken' consort, or whatever was available. The anthem was split into sections and movements, constantly changing tempo, manner and instrumentation, alternating string 'symphonies' with solos, duets and trios, grave choral polyphony and a cheery outburst for the whole ensemble at the end, all supported by a 'continuo' bass and bursting with fancy new harmonies and show-off passages for the composer's favourite singers. There was also a strong whiff of fashionable foreign styles, particularly French.

All this took about twenty years to develop and reach maturity. The new manner would have sounded unutterably bizarre and foreign even to Thomas Tomkins, who died just a few years before it began to take shape and during whose long life the fundamentals of musical style had not really changed at all.

'CAPTAIN' HENRY COOKE ASSEMBLED a starry constellation of composers when he re-founded the Chapel Royal choir in 1660. Many of the adult musicians had, like him, worked there before the Civil War. Henry Lawes had been born as far back as the late sixteenth century but managed to survive long enough to compose an anthem for the coronation of the restored king, Charles II, in 1660, and to sing it in the massed ranks of the coronation choir – who were all no doubt rather surprised to find themselves contributing to this ancient cere- mony once again. All of Lawes's published music dates from the 1650s, though none of it is church music. He is probably the first significant composer for whom music for domestic use completely eclipsed music for the liturgy. This rather boring fact shows us where church music found itself after a difficult war and a difficult peace: like the British Empire in 1945, it was still there, but its status and relevance had shifted fundamentally, and would never come back.

William Child had also witnessed a lot of change in his ninety years. By the time he died in 1697 he had lived through pretty much the entire seventeenth century. He was a choirboy in Bristol, and in 1630 began an association with St George's Chapel, Windsor, which would last for the rest of his life. In 1660 he added membership of the Chapel Royal to his CV and, in a sign of the times, a domestic musical position at court. Once again, sacred music was no longer the only game in town. Child wrote a great deal of church music and was an efficient snapper-up of the various phases of musical style through which he lived. He set the prayer-book canticles many times, music which could probably be pressed into service more often today. One of his services featured the charming and unusual scoring of a quartet of solo boys' voices (or 'four meanes' as he called them), presumably for a particularly strong treble year at Windsor or Whitehall (or for four stroppy teenagers who got cross when one of the others got all the solos, leading their exasperated master to come up with something where they all got a go. It wouldn't be the only piece in the repertoire written in answer to such requirements).

As a boy, Child could have been one of the very last to watch the companies of choirboy actors at their antics. He might, just possibly, have met the composer Robert Stone, who was ninety-seven when he died in 1613, and had thus been born in Henry VIII's reign, when Robert Fayrfax and William Cornysh were still alive. Child lived to see church music flourish, die, come back and wither again. He outlived Henry Purcell, who was more than half a century his junior. Like the psalmist, he might have said, 'I have been young and now am old: I myself have seen the ungodly in great power, and flourishing like a green bay-tree.'[1] Or he might have reflected on his great age in the words of Rosencrantz in *Hamlet*, written just a few years before he was born: 'they say an old man is twice a child.'[2]

Christopher Gibbons was born in the same year as Cooke, around 1615, and probably sang alongside him as a boy under the direction of Christopher's father, Orlando. When Gibbons senior died in 1625, Christopher went to live and study with his uncle, Edward Gibbons, at Exeter Cathedral. Christopher in his turn went on to join the music staff at Westminster Abbey and the Chapel Royal, and in 1638 added the job of Organist of Winchester Cathedral to his CV. In a sign of the times, the restored court of Charles II sought to put an end to this pluralistic holding down of several musical jobs in different parts of the country at the same time. Gibbons was told to give up his job in Winchester. In another sign of the times, he didn't.

Church music was important and valued, but badly organised. You might have a good salary on paper, but you might not actually get it all that often. If you ran a leading choir, as Cooke did, you might well end up paying for the choirboys' upkeep out of your own pocket and never getting reimbursed, passing the debt onto the next generation. It was a sad business. More than once, Cooke kept the Chapel Royal choirboys away from service because their clothes were in tatters and he hadn't received any money to replace them. Gibbons did well to try to hang onto every possible source of paid work. He also needed the money to keep up his impressive reputation as a boozer. His musical scores reveal a competent musical mind in a transitional style, with none of the grace and skill of his father. But they are perhaps more interesting for his own handwritten annotations: 'drunk from the Catherine-Wheele.'[3]

Another familiar name takes its bow at this stage. Henry Purcell senior and his brother Thomas also joined Cooke's choir at the Restoration, but Henry died not long after, in 1664. Thomas went on to hold a number of senior administrative and musical positions in the Chapel and at court. Most importantly for the history of English church music, however, he emulated the Gibbons clan by taking on the care and education of Henry's three young sons, Edward, Henry junior and Daniel. He did a good job.

One of the very best of the generation of composers who had already reached adulthood by the time of the Restoration was Matthew Locke. Like Lawes, Locke's reputation rests largely on his secular music. His output of church music was, however, substantial and impressive and, in particular, throws an interesting light on one aspect of the times. Born around 1621, Locke was a pupil of Edward Gibbons at Exeter and later collaborated with his fellow ex-chorister Christopher Gibbons on theatre music. In the early years of the Civil War, Locke was in the Low Countries. He may have become a Catholic at this time. Certainly he played no part as a performer in the music of the restored Church of England after 1660, something for which he was supremely well qualified. Nonetheless he did compose a good deal of music for the Chapel Royal, including small-scale service music to help the new choir find its nervous way back into musical maturity and full-scale verse anthems ('excellent good',[4] according to Samuel Pepys).

He joined the staff at Queen Catherine of Braganza's private, Catholic, chapel and his verse anthems with strings prove him to be one of the real masters of the 'Purcell' style. They are bursting with the fizz, colour, bold harmony and command of structure which characterise this music at its best but, in a number of cases, with one striking difference from his contemporaries: the words are in Latin. This is curious. Despite Locke's day job running instrumental music at court, just across the road, there is no evidence that the celebrated band of string players ever accompanied the music in the Queen's chapel where he played the organ. Locke's Latin anthems appear to have been written for academic occasions in Oxford, not for church services at all, Catholic or Protestant. Sacred music thus takes up one of its other occasional walk-on roles – as a display of learning. So of course it's in Latin – everything is in Oxford.

In any event, it's a fascinating thought that the Protestant and Catholic royal chapels existed alongside each other – close enough for the congregation in one to hear the music from the other wafting across St James's Park on a Sunday morning – but that the personnel never overlapped. Musical style certainly did, though: there's no doubt about the cross-pollination between Locke and Purcell, a debt acknowledged by the younger composer in his touching and carefully titled piece 'On the death of his Worthy Friend, Mr. Matthew Locke, musick composer in ordinary to His Majesty, and Organist of Her Majesties Chappel, who Dyed in August 1677'. In contrast to the positions of Byrd and Tallis a century earlier, there was no place for the Catholic at the musical top table. Once again, church music shows us what was going on outside the choir stalls. These fine anthems, so similar in musical style but divided by language, reveal a faultline in society which would split open into revolution in 1688.

Captain Cooke's principal contribution to the history of English church music was the choir he assembled at the Chapel Royal. Next he had to turn his attention to the youth squad: an entirely new set of boys to sing alongside his old friends in the adult pews. Cooke still possessed the Chapel Royal choirmaster's ancient power of travelling the country and helping himself to the best choirboys. He found a talented lad called John Blow, aged about twelve, in what must have seemed the rather unpromising territory of Newark, Nottinghamshire. Back in London, perhaps nervously aware of his flat Midlands vowels, Blow made his awkward introductions to another boy who must have seemed an exotic creature indeed: a Londoner, a whole year older, equipped with contacts, confidence and a fancy name – Pelham Humfrey. Next along the pew was a bright-eyed nine-year-old from Oxford, William Turner. Next to him were Michael Wise and Thomas

Tudway, both aged ten. Some of these musicians would still be around in the age of Handel. A few years later, the Purcell family did its greatest service to English church music by sending along a couple of its own little nippers, 'creeping like snail unwillingly to school': Henry junior and his little brother Daniel.

THERE WAS A REAL SENSE of excitement about the emergence of the Chapel Royal choir from the silence of the Interregnum years. 'Very good Musique, the first time that I remember ever to have heard the Organs and singing-men in Surplices in my life'; 'a brave Anthem of Capt. Cookes, which he himself sung, and the King was well pleased with it'; 'a most excellent Anthem (with Symphony's between)'; 'Coronacion Day ... Musique of all sorts; but above all, the 24 violins' – so wrote Samuel Pepys,[5] a discerning and educated musical commentator, who punctuated his diaries with his enthusiastic reviews of the music he heard at his regular attendances at choral services. Sometimes he even joined in.

To begin with, the style inevitably had a transitional feel about it. One of its principal features was the 'symphony', a passage of music for instruments alone. In the anthems of Gibbons and Cooke, the 'symphony' was often nothing more than a florid little roulade for the organist to dash off with his right hand on some suitably bright organ stop. It took some years for this to evolve into the elaborate overtures and separate movements for strings of the fully fledged 'Purcell' style. The other area of experimentation was writing for the solo voice, supported by 'continuo' bass and a discreet harmony instrument. Opera and solo song were increasingly occupying the composer's attention, and it's not hard to catch the whiff of the grease-paint and the sputtering of the footlights hovering behind this most theatrical of church music. Once again, the early practitioners started carefully: the solo writing in the anthems of Gibbons and Cooke looks rather plain on paper, though with plenty of opportunity for the sort of vocal embellishment, which Cooke the singer added to his own music, that was much admired by Samuel Pepys.

As usual, practicalities played a part in the development of style. In

1660 the choirboys were all new and largely inexperienced (with the possible exception of Turner who may have got some early training in a college chapel in Oxford). Training boys, then as now, was done largely by older boys passing on their skills to their younger colleagues in a sort of daily musical osmosis in rehearsal room and choir stall. Skip a couple of generations and inevitably this process was interrupted. You have to start again. The new style, with its longer span and emphasis on contrast between sections, allowed composers to concentrate much of the musical argument into writing for a trio of men's voices, one each of alto, tenor and bass. This also reduced the demands placed on the boys. Later, a second trio was added, of two treble voices and an alto. You only had to rely on your two best boys to stay awake before the little chorus at the end. Matthew Locke made this lack of trained boys explicit: 'above a Year after the Opening of His Majesties Chappel, the Orderers of the Musick there, were necessitated to supply the superiour Parts of their Musick with Cornets and Mens feigned Voices, there being not one Lad, for all that time, capable of Singing his Part readily.'[6] This sounds extremely unsatisfactory. Let's hope the talented lads in Cooke's front row soon managed to convince their adult colleagues that they could manage perfectly well on their own. (In passing, we may note that Locke's use of the term 'feigned voices' implies that men singing falsetto was not a regular feature of the choir, and that the alto parts were probably sung by someone we would more readily recognise now as a high tenor, closer to the French 'haute-contre' or even to some kinds of modern pop and folk singers. Listen online to the American folklorist John Jacob Niles. Once again, the unknowable question of pitch standards means that we can never be certain we are hearing this music as its composers intended.)

Another practical consideration built into the music (not for the first time) was architecture. The galleries of the Whitehall chapel and others were fully exploited for spatial effect: both Locke and Blow had groups of solo voices, choruses and instruments marked 'above' and 'below' in the score, answering each other across the echoing wooden vaults. Increasingly, however, music was moving out of the squat, square spaces of the old Tudor chapels and into the bright, high-ceilinged new buildings of Inigo Jones and Christopher Wren, flooded with light from their large, clear windows. Church music gained several notable new venues after the Great Fire of 1666. These included St Bride's, Fleet Street, where Weelkes and his world lie buried, home to the musically influential new festival of St Cecilia; and Wren's gigantic opera house, St Paul's, whose many thousand seats face east and look up at the raised stage of altar and choir, rather than inwards like the Gothic heart of a building like Westminster Abbey, with every detail demanding ceremonial and display. In 1698 the Chapel Royal moved into Jones's Baroque fantasy the Banqueting House, after the old chapel was destroyed in another fire.

The '24 violins' which Pepys mentioned at the coronation of April 1661 (though he didn't hear them very well because of the racket made by the crowd and because he had to nip out for a piss) were based on a similar ensemble at the court of Louis XIV. Charles II had spent much of his exile in France, and some of his musicians went with him. When he got back, he founded his own band to imitate the intoxicating musical fripperies which he had heard in the chapel at Versailles. The '24 violins' weren't all 'violins' in the modern sense either, and there weren't always exactly that number. The name refers to string instruments of all sizes, including the now-obsolete bass violin, a kind of cello. The full strength fluctuated around the twenty-four mark depending on the vagaries of recruitment. When they played in service at the Chapel Royal, there would typically have been between four and six players: basically one player to a part. This is the sound imagined by Purcell and Blow for most of their verse anthems. Special occasions like larger services or secular performances would command the attendance of half the '24', with the full two dozen only on duty at big events with large choirs, like a coronation.

The strings did not displace the old ways of doing things all at once. There is ample evidence that the old-style mixed consort played from the galleries of the Whitehall chapel in the years immediately after the Restoration, leaning over to make the listening walls resound to the echoes of the sprightly oboe and the old-fashioned sounds of sackbuts and cornets (see Locke's description above). Once again, if we imagine that verse anthems from either side of the Civil War can only be accompanied by organ or the rather weedy sound of viols, we are denying ourselves a whole world of musical colour. Henry Lawes's setting of 'Zadok, the priest', written for the coronation, looks pretty thin on the page. But beef up its strong-boned root-position chords with sackbuts and drums, and encourage your cornettists to colour in the cadences with curlicues and flourishes, and you have something amply able to add grandeur to the spaces of the Abbey that spring day in 1661. And alongside the new instruments came new versions of the old. Magnificent new organs with gorgeous carved case-work were installed all over fashionable London and beyond by continental builders like Renatus Harris and Bernhard Schmidt (who became 'Father' Bernard Smith in his Anglicised incarnation).

The new style also began to see church musicians valued for their specific skill as singers.

Up to the Reformation and beyond it was taken as read that the church musician did everything – compose, play, sing and conduct – much like the modern schoolteacher who teaches geography and history, runs the under-11s football team and plays the piano at assembly, just because she can. The sixteenth-century choirmaster was as much a schoolkeeper as a musician, feeding and accommodating the boys and buying them shoes, firewood and lute strings as well as instructing and directing them in the art of music. As the various aspects of the job became more professionalised, so the job titles evolved, and individuals became known for their particular skill. Tallis and Byrd were the first to refer to themselves as 'organists' of the Chapel Royal, a title which became formalised in the next generation, in the early seventeenth century. After the Restoration, John Blow became the first person to hold the formal title of Composer to the Chapel Royal, though similar posts had existed within the domestic royal household for some time. Later, in the eighteenth century, Handel could be appointed 'composer' to the Chapel Royal without taking any active part in the running or day-to-day performance of the choir at all: he became, in effect, the first ever professional composer. An increasing degree of specialisation is reflected both in the evolution of the job titles and, more importantly, in the music: the Restoration is the first period to showcase the vocal talents of individual, named singers.

THE FIRST OF THE YOUNG composers to synthesise the new style into something intensely personal was Pelham Humfrey. Born in 1647, Humfrey was thirteen when he signed up as one of Cooke's 'music boys' at the Restoration. Shortly after, in November 1663, Pepys heard an anthem which attracted his attention: ' … the 51 psalm, made for five voices by one of Captain Cookes boys – a pretty boy, and they say there are four or five them that can do as much …'[7] After his voice broke, Humfrey continued his studies in France, paid for by the King (from secret service funds, leading to the otherwise unsubstantiated inference that Humfrey was a spy, though it was probably more a bit of typically shifty accounting). He came back armed with ambition and a taste for all things French, and mounted a campaign to take over musical London. He married Cooke's daughter, then succeeded his father-in-law as Master of the Children of the Chapel Royal on the latter's death in 1672. Two years later, possibly as a result of nursing a choirboy through smallpox, Humfrey himself fell sick and died. He was twenty-seven years old.

The main features of the new manner can all be checked off in the music of the curly-haired young Francophile: bold harmonies, expressive writing for solo voice, long anthems made up of short sections contrasting the plangency of the violins up in the gallery with the earthier sound of men down below; above all, the possibilities of the independent bass line. Things we know from Purcell turn up here first: the sinuous, chromatic bass part creeping down to the depths and supporting the scrunchiest of harmonies; and the repeating pattern known as a 'ground bass', itself a pleasing kind of folk-echo of the cheery *pes* motets of the twelfth century, music which Humfrey and Purcell could not possibly have known. The anthem heard by Pepys that wintry morning in 1663 does all this beautifully (though its solo passages are for the usual three voices, not five as stated by Pepys). Little Purcell was probably too young to have been there in person that day. But he would hear and sing this music soon enough – and this is where he got

The opening of the symphony and verse from a setting of Psalm 51 by Pelham Humfrey, which may have been the piece heard at the Chapel Royal by Samuel Pepys. Stylistic features familiar from the later music of Humfrey's pupil Henry Purcell are all here: the chromatic, repeating 'ground bass', the expressive harmony, the freedom of the vocal writing for a trio of soloists.

these ideas from. There would have been no 'Dido's lament' without the example of Pelham Humfrey.

Who was English church music's most precocious genius? Henry Purcell composed his astonishing setting of words from the Song of Songs, *My Beloved Spake*, when he was about seventeen, his first and arguably his best big verse anthem. He added a far greater emotional reach to Humfrey's slightly monochrome melancholia. Like all the most successful geniuses, Purcell's trick was to be born at exactly the right moment, combining the appropriate technical skills with a view of the human condition in tune with the spirit of his times. His musical mind was uniquely able to synthesise the structural mastery of Matthew Locke and John Blow with the emotional insights of Pelham Humfrey. Nobody else could have done it. He reached further than Humfrey, partly because he lived longer (though it seems ungenerous to accord the benefits of longevity to a composer who died at the age of thirty-six).

In the end, these things defy explanation. Purcell was better because he was just better. Immersion in top-level music before he could walk or talk was certainly a prerequisite, but not sufficient in itself. Perhaps he gathered more sympathy for the human condition into his music because he was, in some way, more open to it. Perhaps he was just a nicer bloke. Pepys speaks warmly of the older Purcells whom he knew, and is famously scathing about 'Little Pelham Humphreys', who was

> an absolute monsieur as full of form and confidence and vanity, and disparages everybody's skill but his own. The truth is, every body says he is very able, but to hear how he laughs at all the King's musick here, as Blagrave and others, that they cannot keep time nor tune, nor understand anything; and that Grebus, the Frenchman, the King's master of the musick, how he understands nothing, nor can play on any instrument, and so cannot compose: and that he will give him a lift out of his place; and that he and the King are mighty great! and that he hath already spoke to the King of Grebus would make a man piss.[8]

Humfrey joins our list of composers who deserve more attention than we give them today. Until recently, the same could have been said of Henry Purcell. Not now. For many people, he is English church music's best composer of all.

He had a good start. Pepys noted that several of Cooke's choir-boys composed while still singing treble, and Purcell certainly did the same. His voice broke relatively early for the period, when he was probably around thirteen and a half, and he continued his intensely practical immersion in the day-to-day business of music as assistant to his godfather, a court instrument-maker and organ-builder called John Hingston. His schooling continued at Westminster, and when he was eighteen he got a job copying out music for the Abbey, another time-honoured way of getting to know every dot and squiggle of the work of the best composers, past and present. Two years later he took over from his older friend and mentor John Blow as Abbey organist, and in 1682 he became concurrently one of the organists of the Chapel Royal, where he also sang bass in the choir.

All of this happened within a few hundred yards of his front door. He lived in Westminster the whole of his short life, surrounded by poets and musicians, not least in his own family, probably only saunter-ing up into London for a spot of psalm-singing at Matthew Locke's lodgings at the Savoy or at Samuel Pepys's house at the other end of town, or for a rehearsal at St Bride's or in Wren's building site where Old St Paul's used to stand. If English church music has a genius of place, it is the shade of Henry Purcell hovering around the west front of Westminster Abbey where the buses cough to a stop outside Bar-clays Bank.

Purcell wrote a vast amount of sacred music, almost all of it for the Chapel Royal. It can conveniently be considered under various headings.

Purcell's service music and shorter anthems

Some of Purcell's relatively small output of shorter anthems and service music, with organ or with no independent instrumental accompani-ment, was written not for the Chapel Royal but for services at the ancient Charterhouse in the City of London. A piece like *O God, thou art my God* illustrates the virtues of this music well: varied combinations of chorus and groups of solo voices alternate in short, contrasting sections in rapidly changing time signatures and speeds, musical light and shade playing over the surface of the words like quicksilver, the harmonies colliding in surprising and exhilarating pile-ups at the cadences. Purcell's liturgical settings of the prayer book canticles performed a useful function in the repertoire: short, easy and characterful, they do today exactly the job their composer intended for them when he wrote them in imitation of the 'short' and 'verse' services of Gibbons and Byrd which he sang as a boy. For day-to-day purposes, composers lavished far more musical interest and innovation on the anthem than on the regular, repeating parts of the service like choral settings of the morning and evening canticles, so these needed to be nice and straightforward and not take up too much time in either rehearsal or performance (and, yes, we need to be able to hear the words).

'That stupendious bass': Purcell's 'symphony' anthems

By far and away the most substantial portion of Purcell's contribution to church music can be found in his verse (or 'symphony') anthems. These were turned out on a regular basis for Sunday service at the Chapel or other occasions which merited noting in music, and they represent the later Stuart court at its frilliest. This was music to tap your feet to: church-going as party-going. Purcell's witty, graceful manner matched his monarchs' requirements perfectly. His verse anthems are an astonishing kaleidoscope of invention, delivered week in, week out by a musical magician at the top of his game, and a professional doing his job. Charles and James loved it.

Not everybody did, of course. John Evelyn famously said the style was 'better suiting a Tavern or a play-house, than a church',[9] and the continental influences in the music fed into an innate mistrust of foreigners and a bubbling fear of Catholicism. It was expensive too. The Stuart brothers were, as usual, very good at filling their court with gaudy display without thinking about how they were going to pay for it, and various attempts at retrenchment severely curtailed the elaborate music at the Chapel Royal. When James, as King, stopped slipping into services with his various mistresses altogether and instead sidled across the road to hear Catholic mass with, of all people, his own wife (leaving the musicians of the Chapel Royal performing to an empty chair), the writing really was on the wall. The 'symphony' anthem petered out. By the time James II was kicked out of his kingdom in 1688, it had largely ceased altogether.

Its flowering had been brief, but brilliant. The 'symphony' anthem catches the spirit of the times so well that one example will have to stand duty for a whole universe of music, partly because it has a good story attached. In 1679, Henry's uncle Thomas Purcell wrote in his capacity as court musical administrator to John Gostling, a priest and bass singer then employed at Canterbury Cathedral, asking him to come to London to join the Chapel Royal choir. Gostling was evidently already in touch with Henry, as Thomas thanks him for 'the favour of yours of the 4th with the inclosed for my sonne Henry' (causing early readers to think, understandably enough, that Thomas was Henry's father – it is understood now that the phrase 'my sonne' is used in the adoptive rather than the biological sense). The letter also makes intriguing reference to a piece which 'my sonne is composing wherin you will be chiefly concern'd'.[10]

Five or six years later, Gostling found himself making up one of the party when Charles II and his brother, then Duke of York, decided to amuse themselves with a sailing trip down the Thames. They took a new yacht known as *Fubbs* after one of the King's aristocratic mistresses (something to do with the shape of her stern, apparently). A storm blew up. Sir John Hawkins takes up the story:

> The King and the Duke of York were necessitated, in order to preserve the vessel, to hand the sails, and work like common seamen. By good providence, however, they escaped to land: but the distress they were in made an impression on the mind of Mr Gostling which was never effaced. Struck with a just sense of the deliverance, and the horror of the scene which he had but lately viewed, upon hs return to London he selected from the Psalms those passages wich declare the wonders and terrors of the deep and gave them to Purcell to compose as an anthem, which he did, adapting it so peculiarly to the compass of Mr Gostling's voice,

which was a deep bass, that hardly any person but himself was then, or has since, been able to sing it.[11]

For a king who liked his court composers to commemorate his trips to the races at Newmarket in music, this was the perfect opportunity for an anthem. God must be applauded for scripting such a thrilling, in-the-nick-of-time escape for his anointed representatives on earth. He could have found no better combination than Henry Purcell's music, John Gostling's voice and the words of the Book of Common Prayer. *They that Go down to the Sea in Ships* is church music as pure theatre: sparkling 'symphonies' for strings, a brilliant opening solo for Gostling, dancing down the scale from the 'D' above the bass stave to the 'D' below it, full of breezy, dotted rhythms evoking the 'stormy wind' and the 'works of the Lord' and, above all, the sheer irresistible fun of seeing if he could make the choirboys giggle by getting Gostling to chuck out his highest notes at 'they are carried up to heaven', followed almost immediately by his lowest for 'and down again to the deep'. A second solo voice, an alto, chats away to the bass, adding colour and contrast across the canvas. The composer pilots his sailors safely into 'the haven where they would be', relishing the chance to still the raging of the sea and create a magical moment of stillness, something he always seemed particularly to enjoy.

Among the skills on display here is the ability to select and edit a text. This has always been part of the English composer's genius. In his anthem *O Clap your Hands*, Gibbons set the entirety of Psalm 47 except the last half of the last verse (which is wordy, abstruse and not very obviously lyrical). Handel, too, was a master of the art of filleting a source for his own purposes. Later, Samuel Sebastian Wesley went to enormous pains to assemble an anthem text from all over the Bible to build his musical structures. Sometimes these men would collaborate with a clerical 'librettist', in Purcell's case Sub-Dean Holder of the Chapel Royal or, as here, Gostling. He wouldn't scruple to change the odd word here and there if the music demanded it, something remarked on admiringly by the poet John Dryden. In the anthem referred to above, for example, Purcell clearly thought that the second

They that Go down to the Sea in Ships. *The full splendour of Purcell's 'symphony-anthem' style. His singer, John Gostling, had recently survived a close encounter with the 'stormy winds' alongside two notable members of their congregation, the King and the Duke of York.*

half of the first verse ('and occupy their business in great waters') was too wordy, and simply left it out.

The Book of Common Prayer's rather vague indication of the liturgical function of the anthem has allowed composers to interpret it in all sorts of imaginative ways over the centuries, far more so than in some other, more prescriptive Christian denominations. *They that Go down to the Sea in Ships* is real life set to music. No single piece of church music better evokes the character of its times, its patron, its composer and its performers than this one. It is also one of the first where we can hear the distinctive voice of a real, actual, individual singer in the music. Purcell wrote lots of solos for Gostling. They sprang out of his anthems like a favourite comic actor appearing from the wings or an inspirational batsman coming to the crease: everyone else is excellent, but this performer simply has more things he can do, does them better and can seemingly unfurl them at will.

John Gostling is the first person to feature in this story primarily for his talents as a vocalist. His importance to English church music didn't stop there, however. Later in life, after the demise of the 'symphony' anthem and its principal exponents, he devoted much energy to copying out a substantial collection of works by his friends and contemporaries, many of them featuring a bass soloist (guess who). His manuscript is a priceless record of the music that mattered to a man who was there. He was also, in passing, a rare example of a professional church musician who was also a priest, something which just a hundred and fifty short years before had been very much the norm, but which had become, and would remain, almost unheard of.

Money problems and the King's increasingly open Catholicism largely saw off the 'symphony' anthem in the mid to late 1680s. Composers turned their attentions outside the choir stalls. Church music didn't end, though – far from it. The Chapel Royal certainly put on a good show for the coronation of James II in 1685, perhaps the most musically fecund of all such events, 1727 notwithstanding. Thereafter, regular Chapel Royal services continued with the usual mix of music by the old Elizabethan and Jacobean favourites, probably still sung from the same manuscript books which its composers had used, and new pieces. But the new compositions were more modest in ambition and achievement: verse anthems by Jeremiah Clarke and William Croft, with brief organ solos between the vocal sections rather than full orchestral symphonies. The florid anthems of Purcell and others were rewritten for organ alone, often with the passages for strings severely hacked about to make them shorter and more playable. It was a sad echo of former glories. These pieces are still performed like this today, and for the same reasons: getting decent string players, not to mention the arch-lute and the bass violin, is difficult, expensive and time-consuming. But it's worth it. Without them, these anthems are like Cromwell's decapitated saints, mere ghosts of something we have lost, dead from the neck up.

Purcell after 1685: church music for special occasions
In its third phase, Purcell's church music became something for special occasions. As the seventeenth century tripped towards the eighteenth,

composers were called upon to celebrate royal birthdays, recoveries from illness, victories in battle and returns from overseas with music for specially convened thanksgivings at the Chapel Royal or, for bigger occasions, in whichever bit of Christopher Wren's new St Paul's the builders had got around to finishing. Day to day, they no longer occupied their business in church music. In the last decade of the century, an annual celebration was held just down Ludgate Hill from Wren's dusty building site, in St Bride's church, to mark the feast day of St Cecilia, patron saint of music. Purcell contributed several times, including, in 1694, a setting of the Te Deum and Jubilate in D major. These are the prayer-book canticles for morning service, but this was not functional music like his settings in B flat. Instead they were long, concerted, sectional works, with a big orchestra: liturgy as one-off performance.

All of Purcell's painstakingly acquired skill and lavish natural genius were on display here. There was the theatrical grandeur of the opening, unmatched by anyone except Handel. There was rapt, intimate writing for solo voice at 'Vouchsafe, O Lord' and elsewhere. There was the almost comically good-humoured word-painting of an alto and tenor floating up to heaven followed by a bass – Gostling, perhaps – coming back down to earth with a bottom A bump. There was the effortless charm of a pair of boys' voices depicting cherubim and seraphim in close canon and simple harmony. There was a diminished seventh for the 'sharpness of death' and some of the best counterpoint before Bach. For range, innovation, technical skill and the emotional depth of his response to the words of the prayer book and Bible, perhaps only Tallis, Byrd and Handel deserve to be spoken of in the same breath as Henry Purcell.

Purcell's music intrigued and baffled later generations, nonetheless. Handel learnt it thoroughly, often from people who had sung with Purcell himself, as the evidence of his own music clearly shows. Charles Burney, in the late eighteenth century, admired Purcell greatly, except when he tried 'experiments in harmony ... which, I hope, in spite of my reverence for Purcell, the organists of our cathedrals scruple not to change for better harmony'[12] – which, of course, they did. The nineteenth century continued to perform the bits of him they could amputate from anthems and fit into their rag-bag concert programmes. W. H. Cummings wrote one of the first biographies of him as early as 1881, unearthing much of the tiny amount of primary source material about his life. Elgar 'corrected' Purcell's harmonies when he turned one of his anthems into a bit of Victorian stodge for the Three Choirs Festival,[13] thinking that he'd broken the rules (which of course he had: so does Bach.) Vaughan Williams commented perceptively 'we all pay lip-service to Henry Purcell, but what do we really know of him?',[14] and asked for his own ashes to be interred next to Purcell's in West-minster Abbey. Michael Tippett said, 'we were not taught Purcell in the conservatoire: we discovered him independently for ourselves',[15] and both he and Britten made piano arrangements of Purcell's songs, turning them, like Elgar, into music for their own age. It was the early music movement of the later twentieth century which began to scrub off these layers of accretion, particularly singers like Alfred Deller and James Bowman who sought an authentic, musical way to recreate Pur-cell's unique sensitivity to text. The next stage for Purcell's church music was to put as much of it as possible back where it belonged – in church.

Preachers at the annual St Cecilia events after the 'Glorious Revo-lution' of 1688 took the opportunity to trot out the familiar defence of the place of music in worship: old arguments for a new age. But it was an increasingly enlightened age. God, and his music, would have to justify their place alongside all of mankind's other interests: politics, science, philosophy, economics, the arts, the essay, the coffee shop, and, above all, man himself. The sacred no longer elbowed its way into every corner of life as of right.

It still found a happy place providing entertainment and solace to the educated householder, however. The diaries of Samuel Pepys are full of references to psalm-singing at home in the evenings with a couple of chums, a bottle or two and a theorbo. These were clearly convivial, cultivated, collegiate occasions. Pepys congratulated himself warmly on being able to afford to add a clerk to his domestic establish-ment, and one of the qualities he looked for in the lad was the ability to read music: the successful applicant was a bright-eyed little rascal called Tom Edwards, a recent ex-choirboy of Cooke's from the Chapel

Royal. Like Thomas Tusser a century earlier, an early training in church music was young Tom's passport into the comfortable middle ranks of society. Sacred music at home featured again in a letter owned by the nineteenth-century musical antiquarian Dr Rimbault, which he believed was addressed to Henry Purcell:

> Dear Harry, Some of the gentlemen of His majesties musick will honor my poor lodgings with their company this evening, and I would have you come and join them: bring with thee, Harry, thy last anthem, and also the canon we tried over at our last meeting. This in all kindness, M. Locke. Savoy. March 16.[16]

If the invitee was Harry Purcell, then the canon could well have been one of Purcell's cheerful bits of word-painting on a suitable psalm verse, like *Let God arise* (less likely was one of his less sacred counterpoint exercises, like the one which begins 'a health to the Nut-brown Lass with the Hazle Hyes, She that has good Eyes has also good Thighs').

Entrepreneurial composers and publishers continued to feed this domestic market: John Playford's *The Whole Booke of Psalms* of 1677 is, above all else, music for use. His editorial decisions were all based on practicalities: making the 'largeness of the Volume' such that it might be 'useful to carry to Church'; putting the 'Church Tune' in the 'Treble Part'; arranging the music so that 'All Three Parts may as properly be sung by Men as by Boys or Women'.[17] Playford invented an ingenious way of achieving this laudably egalitarian objective. The three voice-parts are laid out one above the other on the page, as usual, but with the innovation that the treble or 'cantus' part is bracketed with the 'bassus' at the top of the page in a two-stave 'short' score. The middle, 'medius', part and the 'bassus' (again) are then printed separately underneath, so that the three parts are laid out on four staves, with the bass appearing twice. The idea was that an organist or lutenist could read from the two-stave short score at the top, perhaps accompanying one singer on treble, or two taking treble and bass, or himself singing the treble part, probably adding a few notes to fill out the two-part harmony at the cadences. Any other singers present could have joined in by reading from the single voice-parts printed underneath. The 'cantus' part is printed in a 'G', or

Cantus & Bassus.   *Psalm 40.*   *Westminster Tune.*

I Waited long and sought the Lord, and patiently did bear:

At length to me he did accord, my voice and cry to hear.

I waited

Psalm XL.   79

Psalm 40.   *Medius.*   *A. 3. Voc.*

I Waited long and sought the Lord, and patiently did bear:

At length to me he did accord, my voice and cry to hear.

Psalm 40.   *Bassus.*   *A. 3. Voc.*

I Waited long and sought the Lord, and patiently did bear:

At length to me he did accord, my voice and cry to hear.

2 He pluckt me from the lake so deep,
out of the mire and clay:
And on a Rock he set my feet,
and he did guide my way.

3 To me he taught a Psalm of praise,
which I must shew abroad:
And sing new songs of thanks al-
unto the Lord our God. (ways,
4 When all the folk these things shall
as people much afraid: (see,
Then they unto the Lord will flee,
and trust upon his aid.

5 O blest is he whose hope and heart,
doth in the Lord remain:
That with the proud doth take no
nor such as lye and fain. (part,
6 For Lord, my God, thy wondrous
in greatness far do pass: (deeds
Thy favour towards us exceeds
all things that ever was.

7 When I intend and do devise,
thy works abroad to shew:
To such a reck'ning they do rise,
thereof no end I know.

8 Burnt offerings thou delight'st not
I know thy whole desire: (in,
With sacrifice to purge his sin
thou do'st no man require.

9 Meat offerings and sacrifice,
thou would'st not have at all:
But thou (O Lord) hast open made
mine ears to hear withall.
10 But then, said I, behold and look,
I come a mean to be:
For in the volume of thy book,
thus is it said of me: (mind,

11 That I (O Lord) should do thy
which thing doth like me well:
For in my heart thy Law I find,
fast placed there to dwell.
12 Thy justice and thy righteousness,
in great resorts I tell:
Behold my tongue no time doth cease
O Lord, thou know'st full well.
The second part.

13 I have not hid within my breast
thy goodness as by health:
But I declare and have exprest
thy truth and saving health.

14 I

Psalm 40 from Playford's edition of the Whole Booke of Psalms, *1677. The words are Sternhold and Hopkins's 'old' version. The tune is by Gibbons (though Playford appears either not to have known this, or not thought it appropriate to mention it). Note the intensely practical layout of the music. As later publishers have also discovered, flexibility is the key to making the musical resources of the average parish church sound good (and, therefore, to selling lots of copies of your book).*

'treble' clef, the 'medius' also in a 'G' clef which can be read an octave down, like a modern tenor part, and the bass in an 'F', or 'bass' clef. It is a recognisably modern way to lay out a score. It's easy to read, and the upper parts can, as Playford pointed out, be taken at the higher or the lower octave depending on who's around to sing them. You can, if you like, sing them at both octaves at once. It makes a great sound.

This distinctive sonority, rich, inclusive and easy to do, survived in the congregational singing of some Nonconformist and American traditions. It's probably not that far away from the sound of the old, improvised pre-Reformation 'faburden' technique, at least when it was done well. Oddly, it sounds today a bit more like the chanting of Eastern, orthodox music, which would certainly have surprised Playford. It would be well worth bringing this technique back into use.

Playford was himself clerk to a leading London church, a capable musician, skilled businessman and, apparently, a thoroughly nice man. He knew what he was doing. Collections like his might take a while to catch on (the 'Old Version' of Sternhold and Hopkins was still going strong a whole century and more after they first wrote it) but, if they were well designed, they could sell in astonishing quantities. Some estimates put sales of Playford's book at over 400,000. This was church music as popular music.

The Chapel Royal style of Purcell and others, for all its brilliance and lasting fame, reached only a tiny elite around the right circles at court. Out in the wider world, not even the better-supported musical foundations like cathedrals and college chapels could run to such magnificence. Their choirs contented themselves with performing the smaller-scale English anthems and service music (and possibly the cut-down versions of some of the 'symphony' pieces) of the court composers, carried to Canterbury and Cambridge in the saddle-bag of some musical friend (one of the benefits, incidentally, of the tradition upheld by Christopher Gibbons and others of continuing to hold down jobs at court and in a provincial choir at the same time), alongside whatever of their earlier repertoire they'd managed to save from the degradations of Cromwell's soldiers and a small amount of home-grown new music on a modest scale. No violins for them.

The career of Michael Wise illustrates the point well. He secured the kind of list of musical appointments which an able, well-connected ex-Chapel Royal choirboy had every reason to expect: singer at St George's, Windsor, organist of a leading cathedral (Salisbury), Gentleman of the Chapel Royal (without giving up his Salisbury job, naturally), and ultim- ately, Organist of St Paul's Cathedral. He was clearly a bit of a catch. He was also another in our short but growing list of eminent musicians who wouldn't behave themselves. He was always getting himself sacked or suspended: he wasn't allowed to take part in the coronation of 1685 because of some unnamed offence, and got into a dispute at the end of his life about whether he could hang onto his posts at Salisbury, St Paul's and the Chapel Royal all at the same time. Eventually the problem was solved when he got into a fight with the Salisbury night-watchman 'which broke his skull, of the consequence whereof he died'.[18]

Wise's surviving music was probably written for Salisbury, and demonstrates the very different level of resources available to him there compared to his peers at the Chapel Royal. Verse anthems like *Prepare Ye the Way of the Lord* and *The Ways of Zion do Mourn* were beautiful, certainly, but they showed little or no stylistic advance on the music of Orlando Gibbons or Thomas Weelkes of over half a century before. In some ways they were less adventurous even than these earlier com- posers' pieces. Much of the solo writing was for a treble and a bass (no doubt for some favoured singers in the Salisbury choir), with short, conventional choruses and a simple supporting part for the organ. As liturgical music, it was far more serviceable than the expensive elabor- ations of Purcell and others, but to Charles and James and their painted satellites it probably seemed impossibly dull and old-fashioned.

The 'court' style had even less to do with what was going on at parish level. The divide between professional and parish music, always present, was probably never wider than in the final decades of the seventeenth century. By this point, English church music was getting used to what happened when a change of reign brought a change of approach. To begin with, a new monarch would make a statement offering tolerance and freedom of religious conscience. Then, shortly after acceding, he or she would hold a conference designed to thrash out how to accommodate the various strands of church practice, which would fail. Extremists at both ends would sheer off into isolationism, leaving the mainstream churches to plod on down the middle. The ordinary people in the pew, meanwhile, would carry on doing what they had always done: they sang psalms. This was the decorous little dance observed, with some changes of detail in the steps, in 1558, 1603, 1660, 1688 and 1714.

Popular psalm-singing proved largely immune to attempts at central control. You couldn't teach people how to do it because they didn't learn it from a teacher: they absorbed it from each other. Your parish clerk couldn't educate his congregation because, unlike the old days, there was nowhere for him to get a musical education himself. He was probably a poor man appointed to the post because he was going to be a draw on parish funds anyway, so he might as well be put to work and save the parish the expense of recruiting someone who might actually know how to do the job. He would 'line out' the psalm from his copy of Ravenscroft or Sternhold and Hopkins – new versions like Playford would catch on at glacial speed, over decades or even centuries, if at all. With no organ to regulate the singing, his congregation would sing the words back at him to the usual mish-mash of melodies and harmonies, so slowly you had to take a breath virtually every note. Extra notes would be added by a kind of collective compositional process: not because anyone decided to, but rather because nobody decided not to. (Think of 'O Come, All Ye Faithful': why do congregations add a passing-note at 'now in flesh ap-pea-ear-ring'? Can they be stopped? Should we try? It's the same process.)

Samuel Pepys was highly tickled when his parish sang a psalm tune he didn't know: 'I was amused at the tune set to the psalm by the clerk of the parish, and thought at first he was out, but I find him to be a good songster, and the parish could sing it very well, and was a good tune. But I wonder that there should be a tune in the psalms that I never heard of.'[19] The point here was that a literate, musical churchgoer born in 1633 believed it was a given which tune went with which psalm. It was just the way things were. It also came as a surprise to Pepys (a pleasant one, we hope) that the clerk was 'a good songster'. Clearly this was not the usual state of affairs.

John Playford, another highly articulate, interested commentator, was quite clear where responsibility for these deficiencies lay. Writing in 1677, he said, 'It would be much to the Advancement of this Divine Service of singing Psalms if the Clergy would generally more addict themselves to the Study of Musick, and give themselves some little trouble in assisting their several Congregations with their Skill. And also if they would make choice of such persons for their Clerks, as have either some skill in song, or at least a Tunable Voice and good Ear to learn'. This was an early sally in the English church musician's favourite game of Blame-the-Clergy. Later colleagues became very good at it.

All was not lost, however. Playford was at generous pains to point out where things were beginning to get better: 'And here I cannot but commend the Parish Clerks in London, who for the Improvement of Musick have set up an Organ in their Common-Hall, where they meet once a fortnight, and have an Organist to attend them, to practice the singing of Psalms; which Custom (if not neglected) will much augment their Skill, to their Reputation and the better performing the Service of the Church.'[20]

THE NEXT IMPORTANT STEP forward in parish psalm-singing came right at the end of the seventeenth century, with the publication of a new psalter by the poet laureate (and Purcell collaborator) Nahum Tate and a zealous Irish divine and Glorious Revolution enthusiast called Nicholas Brady. Their *New Version of the Psalms of David in Metre* was licensed for use in church in 1696. This was an important distinction. Privately printed versions like Ravenscroft's and Playford's were not meant to be used in church, though they obviously were, as Playford's introduction makes clear. Psalm-singing in church, still restricted to before the liturgy and after the sermon, as noted by Pepys, was meant to be limited to the officially sanctioned versions (though even here the legal status of such an injunction was not entirely straightforward). Despite various attempts at reform and renewal in the intervening century and a half, it fell to Tate and Brady to finally begin to see off the venerable and remarkably tenacious Sternhold and Hopkins. The 'New Version' gradually replaced the 'Old Version'.

The content of these books deserves a little attention too. Playford's book was entitled *The Whole Booke of Psalms, with the usual hymns and spiritual songs*, meaning canticles such as Te Deum and Magnificat, the Lord's Prayer, Creed, and hymns with a liturgical function such as 'Come, Holy Ghost'. Tate and Brady added one – just one – Christmas text which they called 'The Song of the Angels at the Nativity', beginning

> Whilst shepherds watched their flocks by night
> All seated on the ground.[21]

Thus it became the only Christmas 'carol' which could legally be sung in church for most of the eighteenth century.

The psalms and the rest of 'the usual' are in metrical versions, for singing. This raised the problem that the translator had, of necessity, interposed his own poetic voice between the reader and Holy Writ. Some earlier reformers addressed this issue by printing the text of 'prose' psalms in the margins, alongside their metrical versions, so that the reader could compare the two and remind himself what King David, Thomas Cranmer and the Holy Ghost actually wrote. These are known as Mecklenburg editions. All versions have lengthy prefaces justifying their editorial choices and calling down the support of any number of Old Testament types and early church fathers.

Psalm-singing evolved and adapted. Other countries lost their traditions of sacred music altogether when popular revolution hit doctrinal inflexibility. Not in England. This was in no small part because the English just loved singing. Times changed, and so, in its slow, hesitant and deeply idiosyncratic way, did psalm-singing. Tate wasn't the first to encounter the frustrations of such an ill-ordered way of making progress: 'dear experience had taught me, the impediments and oppositions that such a work must meet withal … what is lively and graceful, shall be called light and airy: and barbarity and botching have the venerable appellation of grave and solid!' But his version had something which appealed to the parishioner. Looking back in 1710, he was able to claim that 'Psalmody may clap her wings, and have no occasion to look out any farther'.[22] In time, he was proved right. In the 150 years after

1700, Tate and Brady slowly came to reign supreme in the parish, just as Sternhold and Hopkins had done in the 150 years before.

The adult members of the Chapel Royal class of 1660 mostly reached the ends of their lives in the 1670s and 1680s. The boys of the same generation, the wise children who sang and composed alongside them, took a few more decades to blow away into posterity. Both Humfrey and Purcell died young. Purcell's funeral music, composed for his admired patroness Queen Mary in mid-1695, was sung at his own funeral in the same Abbey church just a few months later. Westminster Abbey rightly venerates its young Orpheus, buried beneath its flagstones (even though Henry Purcell probably didn't write a single note of music for the musicians of Westminster Abbey).

Of the other boys recruited at the Restoration, several survived well into the eighteenth century. William Turner was another of our musical Methuselahs, living to almost ninety and becoming well known as a composer and singer. It is significant that all of his considerable output of church music, mostly verse anthems, dates from the first half of his career, the seventeenth-century bit. After that, both he and the tradition rather ran out of steam. Thomas Tudway got various jobs in Cambridge and spent the rest of his long life in the traditional academic pursuit of whining about contemporaries who he felt were more successful or famous than he was (all of them). Several boys who learnt their trade under Henry Purcell passed these skills on in their turn, like Bernard Gates, who grew up to serve as Master of the Children and a notable soloist in the Chapel Royal's next burst of creative glory.

The most important survivor was John Blow. If posterity has eventually been kind to Henry Purcell, it has yet to catch up with John Blow. Charles Burney was even ruder about him than he was about Purcell. He has become one of that select and unenviable band of composers who tend to be remembered as the teacher of a more famous pupil rather than for their own work. This is unfair. There have been some notable recent attempts to reintroduce Blow's work to modern audiences through recordings and concert performances, but very little of his music holds its place in the repertoire of church choirs.

The music that does turn up on cathedral and college music lists is good stuff. His modest, timidly ambitious setting of the evening canticles, 'Blow in the Dorian mode' (and universally known today, in one of those jokes which each generation of choirboys fondly thinks it has invented, as 'Blow in a boring mood'), proved too adventurous for Burney, but not adventurous enough for the jaded modern chorister. In fact it is another example of a professional composer filling a necessary place in the repertoire with something straightforward but interesting: Thursday evening music. *Salvator mundi* is strikingly modern, discords piling up on top of each other at the opening with a genuinely Italianate, Baroque accent, like the famous *Crucifixus* by Antonio Lotti, still some decades in the musical future. (This is a curiosity among Blow's work: none of his places of employment could have used a Latin motet, of course, so why did he write it? There is a similar anomaly in the work-list of Henry Purcell, the magnificent *Jehovah, quam multi sunt hostes mei*. Was this some sort of private challenge between the two friends? There are plenty of instances of the two men creatively sparking off each other, and some where authorship is disputed between the two of them, like the strange hybrid five-part *I was Glad*, which may actually be by both of them.) Occasionally one of Blow's verse anthems gets an outing with organ, for example the splendidly apocalyptic *I Beheld, and Lo, a Great Multitude*.

But limiting ourselves to some of his deliberately less ambitious works, and to one or two verse anthems performed, as it were, in black and white, without orchestra, only perpetuates the impression that Blow was a bit of a plodder. His main problem, of course, was that he lived at the same time as Henry Purcell. Comparisons inevitably put him in the younger man's shadow. But a big anthem like *God Spake Sometimes in Visions*, to take just one example, shows what he can do. Written for the 1685 coronation of James II, it matches Purcell's contribution to the same occasion for spacious grandeur and vocal variety. He may, perhaps, not match Purcell for sheer tunefulness or grateful felicity of word-setting, but this is a fine piece. There are plenty of others.

Like the work of so many other musicians in this story, Blow's output reveals to us the changes and opportunities of the times he lived in. This was another obstacle to his reputation. He lived long enough to see church music shrink, in some cases quite literally. One of his contributions to the coronation of 1685 was his five-voice setting of *Behold, O God our defender*. By the time of the next coronation, in 1689, music had a much-reduced part to play: there was less of it, it was less grand; there were fewer musicians, less display and less expense. Blow rewrote *Behold, O God* in four parts instead of five. Church music was becoming smaller and less important before our eyes.

The last two Stuarts, Queens Mary and Anne, had increasingly less appetite for elaborate church music. Blow continued to provide tub-thumpers for thanksgiving services at St Paul's, as did Clarke and Croft, but the results were often about as interesting as the sentiments of the occasions they were written for. This hinted at another obstacle in the way of Blow's achievement: he certainly did too much. Partly this was a result of living a long time: he kept trying to give up some of his employments in favour of younger men, including Henry Purcell at Westminster Abbey and Jeremiah Clarke at St Paul's, but they tended to die before him, leaving him to pick up the reins again (Clarke shot himself in the churchyard in 1707, apparently as a result of a hopeless love affair, poor man). At one point John Blow was Organist of the Chapel Royal, Westminster Abbey and St Paul's Cathedral all at the same time, as well as holding positions at court and at St Margaret's church, Westminster, and keeping up with a regular schedule of composing, publishing, teaching and sucking up to the King. No wonder some bits of his large output were a bit workmanlike. He didn't share Purcell's ability to keep the musical juices fizzing and flowing over an entire career. Maybe, in some ways, Purcell was lucky not to have seen so much or lived so long.

Blow died in 1708, honoured, respected and rich. If we think of him today mainly as Purcell's teacher and slightly dull contemporary, we do not do him justice. That certainly wasn't how he was viewed at the time, or for a long time afterwards. On the other hand, being Purcell's teacher was not a bad thing to be able to claim. He was obviously good at it. This was one of the closest and most productive working and personal relationships in the entire history of English church music,

Let my Prayer Come up *by John Blow. This exquisite piece shows all the subtlety of the less flamboyant side of Restoration church music.*

perhaps matched only by that of Tallis and Byrd. Blow earned his honours. He deserves to enjoy them again.

Because we know what came next, there's a sense of waiting for something to happen in the music of the decades around the turn of the eighteenth century. At a professional level, there was some good music, with some forward-looking elements. The best anthems of Jeremiah Clarke effectively evoked the fashionable new sounds of Italian composer Arcangelo Corelli in their elegant instrumental interludes for two violins, and hint at noticeably Baroque harmonic procedures (like the cycle of fifths in the hymn tune 'Bishopthorpe'). William Croft kept the home fires burning without ever really setting the imagination on fire – worthy music, well written but undemanding. At a parish level, Tate and Brady set a new standard. While at an intellectual level, the swirl of ideas known as the Enlightenment gathered force among the clouds of coffee smoke and wig powder and would impact on church music both by reducing the relevance of traditional religious observance and by increasing the demand for a musical voice of a much more personal kind: hymns.

The next great composer of English church music didn't write much church music and wasn't English. When he wrote the names of his soloists into his scores, he got them wrong: 'Elford' became 'Eilfurt'. English music was about to pass into the hands of a German – George Frideric Handel.

10

The Enlightenment, 1712–1760

In reason's ear they all rejoice,
And utter forth a glorious voice,
Forever singing as they shine,
'The hand that made us is divine.'

Joseph Addison in *The Spectator*

IN 1695 JOHN LOCKE published a treatise called *The Reasonableness of Christianity*.[1] There hadn't always been much 'reasonableness' evident in the way Puritans and Laudians discussed religion in the early seventeenth century, still less Protestants and Catholics in the mid-sixteenth century. The new way was to seek proof through reason, not demand obedience to revealed truths. A hymn-writer like Isaac Watts could claim that even parts of the beloved psalms were 'almost opposite to the spirit of the Gospel'[2] because they pre-dated Christ, and therefore needed to be rewritten in the more modern, forward-looking, enlightened spirit of the times. Even an Archbishop of Canterbury like John Tillotson felt perfectly able to do without most of religious orthodoxy – except prayer, the 'two sacraments' and 'what natural light prompts men to'. 'The laws of God are reasonable,' Archbishop Tillotson gently informed his church, politely counselling them not to be 'righteous overmuch' or too 'enthusiastic'.[3] How very English. The Church was well on its way to resembling a 'club for claret',[4] as Locke wanted.

Others went further. The Cambridge divine Samuel Clarke sought, in the Boyle lectures of 1704, to explain religious belief through logic, like a maths problem in Euclid. 'Superstitious ceremonys' and 'fashions of worship',[5] as philosopher John Toland called them, were out. But no one ever set Euclid to music. To a certain extent, music needs the 'ceremonys' and 'fashions' – that's the bit music can 'colour in'. If love could be reduced to a proof in Euclidean geometry, there would be no Schubert, no Lennon and McCartney. The same is true of sacred music. The new ways in which you were allowed to believe, or indeed not believe, left no space for music. 'I believe in God' has a sturdy, declamatory idea behind it which can be realised in sound. 'I believe in rational thought and the evidence of the senses' doesn't have quite the same ring. Deism, still less atheism, produced no music.

The ordinary man in the parish pew probably read little Locke and less Euclid. He probably neither knew nor cared who the Archbishop of Canterbury was. But the manners of an age filter through in the way people think about and interact with each other. This was an age of greater tolerance (though decidedly relative by modern standards) and therefore, by extension, of greater scepticism. You were allowed to question things. Just as the king in his palace and the God in your Bible were no longer the automatic source of authority at a national and a cosmic level, so the parson was no longer necessarily right about everything at a local level. Jesus, as Locke pointed out, wasn't a priest.

This had implications for music. For the first time, the music of the parish church and its practitioners began to develop independently of, and in some cases in opposition to, the parish priest. Increasingly, what went on in church on a Sunday became divided into 'your bit' and 'my bit'. This is a distinction, or at least a perception, which has not gone away.

In many ways the history of English church music is more interesting at parish level in the eighteenth century than at the professional level. Before the Reformation there was no separate tradition of parish music. Into the era of Anglicanism, parishes developed an entirely new music of their own: congregational psalm-singing. In the eighteenth century, a third phase opened up and a brand-new musical voice emerged, with its own repertoire and place in the liturgy: the parish choir. This required new kinds of musical leadership, new composers, new poets, new instruments, a different layout inside the church for both people and furniture, rehearsals, and a new relationship with the law, the liturgy, the priest, the clerk, and with the secular and commercial life of the parish. The results were colourful, uncultured, inspired, incompetent, weird and wonderful.

At a professional level, by contrast, there was little sense of a corporate, collegiate approach to the development of musical style and form. Music of all kinds was led and directed by perhaps the most dominant personality English music has ever known, a German recently blown in from Italy a couple of years ahead of his former employer from Hanover.

A LOOK AT THE WORK-LISTS of four great composers (perhaps our four greatest) over a working span of not quite 250 years gives some idea of the place of church music in the wider musical universe. By title, very roughly 90 per cent of Thomas Tallis's works are sacred vocal pieces. In the case of William Byrd, the figure is about 70 per cent. Music for worship accounts for about 25 per cent of the output of Henry Purcell, and for George Frideric Handel, around 18 per cent. This is a rough and unscientific method for all sorts of reasons, but it does give some idea of the direction of travel. A comparison by minutes of music, rather than just by title, would reveal an even steeper decline in the importance of church music to a working professional composer.

This has something to do with what these men did for a living. Handel was the first great composer of church music in England who was not directly employed by the church, or by a royal or aristocratic patron to run their church music for them. Tallis, Byrd and Purcell had to sing, play and conduct their sacred works as well as write them. Handel did not. His employment at court was in the form of a 'pension' as 'Composer' to the Chapel Royal. Unlike earlier (and later) holders of that title, he did not combine it with the day-to-day activities of a

'Gentleman' or 'Organist' of the Chapel. In practice, this meant that he wrote sacred music only when a suitable occasion arose, or when he wanted to. Choir practice and shoelaces he left to others.

Handel's church music can conveniently be considered in three categories. First, there was the series of concerted anthems composed during his stay at Cannons, the Middlesex estate of James Brydges, Earl of Carnarvon and later Duke of Chandos, in 1718–19. They have all the flair and swagger of the flamboyant, Baroque decoration which Brydges daubed all over the unsuspecting interiors of his blameless medieval parish church, all *trompe l'oeil* and white marble whipped up like meringue. Handel's choral writing is as full of contrasts and surprises as the Middlesex weather. His mastery of the solo voice is here, too, though there's less showing off than in the Latin sacred music of his youthful Italian period, partly because of the fairly modest ensemble at his disposal at Cannons (using, curiously, neither alto voices nor violas). The Earl loved it.

Second, there were the big, public pieces, written for suitable one-off occasions. These include Handel's best-known sacred works. There were settings of Te Deum to mark diplomatic and military success in Europe from both ends of his career, one of which was repeated in Oxford when Handel was given an honorary degree in 1733 (alongside a lecture on flatulence, in Latin, naturally). His royal music included *The Ways of Zion do Mourn*, an extraordinary, intense anthem for the funeral of Queen Caroline in 1737, with its amazing, soloistic writing for chorus and its spare, minimalist, almost futuristic approach to the flow of the long, carefully structured text. There was an anthem for a concert raising funds for Thomas Coram's new Foundling Hospital, a good example both of Handel's skilful reworking of existing material – it ends with the 'Hallelujah' chorus from *Messiah* – and of church music as philanthropy (we might wish we could find more examples of church music doing this).

Most famous of all the occasional pieces are the four coronation anthems of 1727 for George II. Almost as well known as the music was the story of its first performance: 'The Anthems in Confusion: All irregular in the Music',[6] noted the Archbishop in his order of service. One piece listed, by Purcell, was not sung at all, and it appears that at another point the singers in the various galleries got hopelessly out of sync with each other, possibly even singing different pieces at the same time. Westminster Abbey is not an easy place to coordinate large forces: directors of music at similar events have been at great pains ever since to get this aspect right. The results have usually been better than in 1727. Whatever the failings of the performers at the premiere of these works, the sheer skill and character of this music ensured it achieved immediate and lasting popularity.

Handel brilliantly avoided the pitfalls of too much tub-thumpery, carefully rationing out his trumpets and drums, and including an almost painfully elegiac minor tinge in the second movement of the second anthem, *Let Justice and Judgement*. There is some exhilarating hocketing in the chopped-up 'Alleluia' at the end of number three; there are graceful minuets, concise counterpoint, and perhaps the most famous moment in all of English music, the glorious D major sunrise at the beginning of *Zadok, the Priest*. Never was so much art contained in so much splendour: heaven and earth in little space.

The third type of Handelian sacred music is the least well known. This is a shame, as it contains some of his best, and certainly his most liturgically useful music: pieces for smaller scale, private events in the Chapel Royal.[7] The Te Deum in A and the 'Caroline' Te Deum are the shortest of his several settings of this notoriously challenging text, eminently suitable for choirs and places where they sing matins. Some of Handel's Chapel Royal anthems were partial reworkings of earlier pieces. Some use texts also set by his predecessor Henry Purcell, maybe partly in homage. There are some musical coincidences hinting in this direction. Some of his singers had known Purcell. The links between the two men, especially those carved into the woodwork of the Chapel Royal, are intriguing.

Almost all of Handel's sacred music required an orchestra. This added colour, certainly, but also length and expense, aspects which by no means went unremarked in his day. Among the Chapel Royal music is a setting of the psalm-text *As Pants the Hart*, which avoids these problems by casting the accompaniment for organ alone, with a cello doubling the bass, an arrangement known as a 'continuo' anthem. The

Part of one of Handel's several settings of As Pants the Hart. *The words are from Tate and Brady's 'new' version of the psalter, the music, unusually for Handel, is for voices and 'continuo' alone, without orchestra. The 'ground bass' is another unusual feature: a tribute to his predecessor at the Chapel Royal, Henry Purcell, perhaps? A delicious touch of theatricality intrudes in the interjections of the chorus, as if from behind a pillar: 'where is now thy God?'*

scholar Donald Burrows has forensically filleted Handel's settings of this text and identified no fewer than five separate versions (though even something as apparently straightforward as counting them is complicated by Handel's habit of borrowing and reworking music from one to another, making it difficult sometimes to say where a 'version' of an existing piece turns into a discrete new work). But, whatever its parentage, the Chapel Royal setting works beautifully. Intriguingly, Handel combines parts of Tate and Brady's metrical rendering of this psalm from their *New Version of the Psalms of David*, still something of a novelty, with the 'prose' text from the Book of Common Prayer, allowing the measured elegance of enlightenment verse to flow seamlessly into something more impassioned and earthy, just as the music moves from suspension-laden chorus to solo and duet and back again. The piece is in several short sections (not really 'movements'), including a charming little accompanied recitative for treble solo, with a written-out right-hand part for the organ, like a mini-symphony. It's a delightful piece. When modern church choirs perform Handel's music, organists often find themselves wrestling with the problem of how to adapt an orchestral conception for voices and organ. Here, Handel set out to solve that problem himself – and succeeded.

We have noted before that the presence of a great genius tends to make everyone else look a bit like also-rans. In the age of Purcell this may have been unfair on everyone else. In the age of Handel it probably wasn't. England's own Georgian composers were a bit like their Hanoverian masters: competent, admirable, and generally a bit dull.

In the first quarter of the eighteenth century William Croft continued to preside as the best Handelian who wasn't Handel. He wrote much of the music for the coronation of George I in 1715, which indicates what a forgettable occasion it was, at least as far as the music was concerned. Croft's most enduring music is his *Funeral Sentences*, written to provide a complete prayer-book burial service when sung alongside the single movement left by Henry Purcell, and the hymn tune 'St Anne', sung to the psalm-paraphrase 'O God, our Help in Ages Past' by his near-contemporary Isaac Watts. Several later composers, including Handel and Vaughan Williams, successfully incorporated this tune into their own anthems, finding its slightly bumpy outline entirely apposite for the addition of counter-melodies.

Thomas Tudway continued in his chosen career of falling out with people and writing boring music. Like his near-contemporary John Gostling, he did church music a substantial favour by copying out a substantial collection of Anglican choral music, the 3,000-page Harleian manuscript.

The middle of the century saw one of those close, symbiotic musical partnerships which are such a notable and agreeable feature of this story. Maurice Greene and William Boyce were both choirboys at St Paul's Cathedral, though fifteen years apart, Boyce becoming apprentice to Greene when his voice broke. Later they engaged in the traditional pursuit of divvying up the top jobs in London between them as the generation of their teachers left the scene. Boyce set the usual texts for the coronation, with the exception of *Zadok, the Priest* – it seems to have been accepted by both king and composer that the version by the recently deceased Handel could not be bettered, setting a precedent which has been followed ever since.

Perhaps Greene and Boyce's most important contribution to church music was the three-volume collection which they published under the title *Cathedral Music*. This monumental undertaking was begun by Greene and continued after his death by Boyce as increasing deafness curtailed his active music-making. It was the first significant attempt to use the developing publishing industry to bring some sort of standardisation and classification to the music of the country's cathedrals as a coherent whole, rather than each relying on the probably rather eccentric mixture of dodgy editions of Purcell and examples of local musical produce in its own library of tired-looking part books and dog-eared manuscripts, fingered and smudged by generations of inky choirboys. *Cathedral Music* is a major achievement. There is music by admired older colleagues like John Weldon and the polymath Henry Aldrich. Perhaps more striking is their desire to rekindle the Elizabethan sense of 'gravity in Church music' before it was displaced by a 'lighter kind of church music'[8] at the Restoration, as Boyce put it in his introduction. They included music by Christopher Tye, Richard Farrant, Thomas Tallis, Orlando Gibbons, lots of 'Bird' and even a piece by Henry VIII. To reach their target audience, of course, they unashamedly turned these pieces into eighteenth-century church music, adding instrumental figured bass lines and changing language, text, liturgical function and underlay as suited their requirements. Modern scholarship wouldn't approve, but the combination of practicality and an awareness of prevailing liturgical and aesthetic needs ensured wide acceptance for their weighty tomes. They provided the bedrock of cathedral music-lists for generations to come.

The manuscript and printed collections of the eighteenth century were part of the tranquil, yeast-like growth of the Anglican 'cathedral-pattern' service. The leading composers did not, in the main, take an active part in the musical life of cathedral towns: as before, they worked mostly with the more prominent choirs at the Chapel Royal, St Paul's, St George's Windsor, and the universities. Their duties included providing music for the ongoing series of Thanksgiving services for victories over the French and the weather in the English Channel. Musically, these were sounding increasingly tired (Handel notwithstanding), with plenty of repetition of old favourites like 'Dr Croft's famous Te Deum',[9] as one newspaper put it (not any more), music by dead people like Purcell and the latest offerings from luminaries like Staggins, Piggott and Clayton.

Provincial cathedrals have rarely been the engines of musical innovation, but this may have been a blessing – the 'cathedral' manner could thus ripen in solitude. In the cathedral, music, and plenty of it, was provided by a rehearsed choir. A skilled organist contributed a chirpy little piece by a composer like John Stanley, published in a book of pieces called 'voluntaries'. Psalms and canticles were chanted directly from the Book of Common Prayer. The old habit of congregations 'covering the gaps' before and between services and at communion with metrical psalms was being superseded. Hymn-singing had not yet arrived to replace it and there was little for the ordinary worshipper to do except absorb the beauty being summoned up around him. The spirit of Laud moved upon the face of the darkened cloister and the surpliced choirboy.

The main compositional forms for this developing musical liturgy were canticles in a shortish manner, and verse anthems. Verse pieces, particularly the sections for solo voice, were getting longer. Texts continued to be assembled from all over the book of psalms. The music had charm and a character of its own, but, stylistically speaking, it wasn't really going anywhere very much. Textural variety was not helped by the accompaniment being mostly for organ alone. Harmony and structure were often rather less interesting than they were in the hands of Purcell and Matthew Locke a century before. When we listen to John Travers telling us to 'tell it out among the heathen that the Lord is King', we find ourselves wishing we were listening to Henry Purcell telling us to instead. It is perhaps significant that anthems of this period tend to be sung today on the more middle-of-the-road type of occasion, using the sort of texts earlier generations would have called 'indifferent' in mood: *Ascribe unto the Lord, Thou Visitest the Earth, O Come Hither*. These are not the men we reach for when we want grand emotions or the great occasions of the church year. It's music for when we can't think of anything else.

This was not entirely their fault. Every eighteenth-century writer who cared about church music, including Thomas Tudway, Sir John Hawkins and Charles Burney, noted and lamented that popular taste had turned elsewhere, in particular towards what Hawkins memorably called the 'tumid extravaganzas'[10] of the theatre. Church music was expected to be 'solemn', which in practice meant dull. Hawkins rightly picked out Greene's expressive *Lord, Let Me Know mine End* for special praise (the key relationships almost pre-echoing Schubert), and used it as an example of where church music found itself:

Concerning this species of vocal harmony, it may be observed that in an age in which the love of music prevails even to affectation, its merits are but little known. The gay and the fashionable flock in crowds to places of public entertainment, to the opera, to the theatres, and to concerts, and pretend to be charmed with what they hear. It was once as fashionable to be alike attracted by the charms of choral music, where the hearers were sure of enjoying all the delight that could result from the united power of sublime poetry, and harmony the most exquisite.

That this is no longer a practice, is owing to certain prejudices, which it may be deemed a kindness to remove; the one is, that the style of the music appropriated to divine offices is suited to melancholy tempers, of which opinion was the late King of Prussia, when he objected to certain compositions that had been shown him, that they smelt of the church ...[11]

This 'prejudice' took a long time to shake off. The idea that church music needed to 'smell of the church', that it somehow 'ought' to be dull, lasted well into the Victorian period, when it produced music that sounds like mud.

At its best, the music of Aldrich, Weldon, Tudway, Croft, Greene, Boyce, Nares, John Travers and their coevals deserves more attention than we give it. The symphony anthems of William Boyce, in particular, scrub up very nicely under the right conditions. These men brought considerable industry, integrity and ability to bear on the challenges facing church music. The fact that they only partly managed to meet those challenges is more a comment on the times they lived in than it is on them personally. Circumstance and fashion were against them. They heaped up what riches they could. We should gather them.

THERE WAS ANOTHER JOB requiring the attention of the professional church composer at this period, and it was a surprising one: supplying music for amateur choirs. In 1701 Henry Playford published *The Divine Companion: Being a Collection of New and Easie Hymns and Anthems* 'to be used in churches or private families'.[12] The idea that the ordinary parishioner could sing in church at all had been accepted 150 years before. Now, proper composers were giving him proper music. The 'parish anthem' was born.

Playford deliberately followed the intensely practical approach of his father, John Playford, to things like numbers of parts, variety of style, level of difficulty and layout on the page. Some of the two-part pieces even have an entirely optional third part which can be sung (or played) or omitted as circumstances permit. His composers, including many of the top names, responded with admirable professionalism. It was an important moment for the development of the professional composer as much as for the amateur singer.

Parish music had become an ungovernable thing, especially the haphazard 'old way' of singing psalms. The eighteenth century began to tidy it up. Its weapons were the choir, the organ, the singing teacher and the rehearsal. This made the music better, of course, but also less inclusive. For the first time since before the Reformation, congregations found themselves listening to the music instead of joining in.

Town parishes were easier to organise than country ones. The spirit of reforming zeal exemplified by the Society for Promoting Christian Knowledge led to the formation of religious societies of young men, many of which would lead the psalm-singing in their local church, especially in London, bringing a welcome degree of decorum and musical discipline to that tremulous art. The other notable musical novelty, in larger rural parishes as well as in town, was the large choirs of well-drilled, well-dressed charity children. This was the quintessential Enlightenment idea. 'Religion in England', wrote the visiting Abbé Prévost in around 1730, 'finds its expression in hospitals for the sick, homes of refuge for the poor and aged of both sexes, schools for the education of the children.'[13] By the 1730s there were charity schools in a number of rural parishes as well as in towns. Locke, Watts and their acolytes wrote voluminously about every aspect of child-rearing. There was to be 'no real difference'[14] in what was taught to boys and girls.

The charity schools, naturally enough, sang psalms as part of their daily prayers. Thus, when they marched off to their local parish church in a blue-coated crocodile on a Sunday morning, the congregation would find itself treated to the novel experience of listening to a pre-rehearsed performance, just like the opera they might have heard the night before. And the practice caught on. Many churches adapted their medieval galleries, or built new ones, to accommodate the children, often with the organ and conductor in the middle. In 1734, for example, St James, Clerkenwell put its organ in 'the old gallery where the charity children sit, enlarged to fix it in ... for the more commodious placing of them on each side.'[15] The annual charity sermon became their end-of-term concert, and a welcome chance to raise funds through the collection plate, especially if several schools joined together for a massed 'festival' service. This was the tradition of fashionable, rather romanticised musical philanthropy which led directly into Handel's active involvement with the Foundling Hospital, whose handsome red-brick buildings still carry the slightly Spartan echo of John Locke's prescription for successful child-rearing (lots of swimming, leaky shoes and 'milk-pottage, water-gruel, flummery, and twenty other things'[16] for breakfast).

Unlike the choirs of young men, who could quite happily sing the existing psalm tunes, the children's choirs required a brand-new repertoire of pieces for treble voices only, part of a move towards a fashionable, airy, tuneful style, as opposed to the gruff, old-fashioned, tune-in-the-tenor way of doing things. Collections of this kind appeared throughout the century, becoming quite 'classical' in manner by its end, the precursors of the slightly saccharine treble writing in the music of William Crotch and Samuel Sebastian Wesley. Occasionally, they joined together, as in William Richardson's 1729 publication of '… hymns for the use of societies and charity-children, likewise anthems for two and three voices, after the cathedral manner'.[17] The 'cathedral manner' was being consciously imitated and absorbed into the music of the more upmarket parish. There would be more of this later in the century and beyond. Richardson's book was entitled *The Pious Recreation*, which is exactly what its demure pages offered these earnest young musicians.

For parishes that could afford it, the most effective instrument of musical discipline was an organ. It could carry the voices along with 'a kind of grateful violence',[18] as one preacher put it in 1696, correcting, or covering up, 'any such indecent discords as might otherwise arise'. A century later, another writer went further: 'an organ decently played, and loud enough to drown the voices of the clerk, charity children, and congregation, is a blessing.'[19] The ideal was for the organ to keep the congregation honest (and, incidentally, thereby render the clerk redundant) by banging out the tune. Some organists, however, saw their new role as an opportunity for a bit of light entertainment: 'for half-an-hour together they divert their auditors by scouring up and down the whole compass of the organ, and skipping from one subject to another', wrote a correspondent (actually the editor, Richard Steele) to the *Grub Street Journal* in February 1731, taking 'especial notice of their tuning the psalm; for in the middle of a word, Mr *Tweadledum* forgets the tune, and entertains us with the scrap of a song, or a masquerade dance, to the confusion of the audience; when the next verse, perhaps of confession or deprecation, shall be introduced by *Lillebolero*, or *Jumping Joan.*' Church-going, and church music, were an extension of the life of gaiety and fashion, a way of cheering yourself up after the 'irksome impressions receiv'd from the pulpit'.[20] No wonder priests got into the habit of absenting themselves during the psalm.

Psalm-singing was experiencing one of its periodic spasms of reform. The pattern is familiar enough: authorities, in the form of governments, clergy and entrepreneurial printers, attempted to impose some kind of norm on the way psalms were sung. Over time, ordinary people turned this into something quite different and much less disciplined, according to their abilities and their needs. So the authorities tried again. In outline, this is what happened in the tussle between the 'official' and the 'popular' tunes at the end of Elizabeth I's reign. Round two began a century later, with the cherished but peculiar 'old' way coming under attack from the forces of reform and its lieutenants, Tate and Brady. The people, of course, took as little notice as they always did.

Some of the most interesting developments in English church music unfolded at the same time, in an intriguing parallel, in America. Some aspects come into focus rather more clearly when viewed through American accounts, perhaps partly because there is less historical baggage getting in the way. The New World was doing all this for the first time. The long campaign to replace the 'old' way with something better, therefore, can effectively be illustrated with examples from both sides of the Atlantic.

There are plenty of descriptions of what was wrong with the 'old' way: 'I have observed in many places, one man is upon this note while another is on the note before him, which produces something so hideous and disorderly as is beyond expression bad. [Tunes] are now miserably tortured, and twisted, and quavered, in some churches, into an horrid Medley of confused and disorderly Noise,'[21] lamented Thomas Walter in 1721. A few years later the anonymous author of *A Brief Discourse* joined in: 'Where there is no Rule, Men's Fancies ... are various; some affect a Quavering Flourish on one Note, and others upon another which (because they are Ignorant of true Musick or Melody) they account a Grace to the Tune; and while some affect a quicker Motion, others affect a slower, and drawl out their Notes beyond all Reason; hence in Congregations ensue Jarrs & Discords, which make the Singing (rather) resemble Howling.'[22] Others observed with a kind of weary resignation that people seemed to like the 'old' way: 'They use many Quavers and Semiquavers, &c. And on this very account it is they are pleased with it, and so very loath to part with it,'[23] moaned the Revd Nathaniel Chauncey in 1728. Musically informed critics like Thomas Symmes made detailed and revealing analysis of the differences: 'Most of the Psalm-Tunes, as Sung in the Usual Way, are more like Song-Tunes ...; because you've more Supernumerary Notes & Turnings of the voice in your way, than in ours. An Ingenious Gentleman, who has prick'd Canterbury, as some of you Sing it, finds no less than 150 Notes, in that Tune, in your way, whereas in our's there are but 30.'[24] What was supposed to be the same tune had five times as many notes in the 'old' way as in the 'new'.

Laudable attempts to bridge the gap between the two approaches through discussion and democracy sometimes only widened the divisions. West Parish in Barnstaple, near Cape Cod, had to call in the civil authorities in 1725 when disturbances broke out. The minister, Revd Russell, tabled a compromise: 'It was concluded that we sing as formerly for the present to give opportunity for persons to inform themselves as to the regular way and some of the brethren did express their willingness (after some time) to sing the tunes as they were placed in the Psalm-book. None objected (or not above one or two).'[25] But it didn't work and Russell had to exercise the judgement of Solomon: 'to sing one half of a year in the old way and the other in the regular'. This, too, was only partially successful: 'During the half year we sang the old way, the singing was very broken and confused, Bro Bodfish singing the Psalm.' Ingrained habits are difficult to break.

Not far away, in Worcester, Massachusetts, the battle was still raging a full half-century later. In August 1779 (when Americans had plenty else to think about),

… it was 'Voted, that the mode of singing in the congregation here be without reading the psalms line by line to be sung.' The Sabbath after the adoption of these votes, after the hymn had been read by the minister, the aged and venerable Deacon Chamberlain, unwilling to desert the custom of his fathers, rose and read the first line, according to the usual practice. The singers, prepared to carry the alteration into effect, proceeded without pausing at the conclusion. The white-haired officer of the church, with the full power of his voice, read on till the louder notes of the collected body overpowered the attempt to resist the progress of improvement, and the deacon, deeply mortified at the triumph of musical Reformation, seized his hat, and retired from the meeting house in tears. His conduct was censured by the church, and he was for a time deprived of its communion for absenting himself from the public services of the Sabbath.[26]

It is sad to think of poor old Deacon Chamberlain being driven from his own church 'in tears' by the forces of 'musical Reformation'. Let's hope he would have been pleased that the 'old' way can still be heard, more than two hundred years later. Some Gaelic-speaking churches of the Western Isles of Scotland, particularly Lewis, and some Old Order Baptists and others in the USA, still sing their psalms like this. There are recordings of their music online. Verses are 'lined out' by a deacon, quavering and declamatory, then picked up by a large congregation who swoop and gather onto the note, just as the would-be reformers described with such loathing and contempt in the early eighteenth century. Of course it's slow: there is absolutely no sense of time of any kind in this music. Time doesn't seem to matter, or even to be happening. It is ecstatic, corporate, incomprehensible and compelling – the voice of Brother Bodfish on YouTube.

Meanwhile, back in England, away from Brother Bodfish, another important strand in the development of psalm-singing was the gradually increasing willingness to experiment with chanting the 'prose' texts from the Book of Common Prayer. Because of the lack of a regular, repeating metre, singing these versions required expertise, training and practice. It was led, therefore, by the cathedrals, which had the resources and the rehearsal time to get it right. Parishes which could imitate this approach, and wanted to, began with those parts of the service which come up most often, and which singers therefore knew best: the passages of scripture prescribed in the prayer book as 'canticles' for daily use, such as Magnificat and Nunc Dimittis at evening prayer, and Te Deum and Jubilate in the morning. One book, typically, provided what it called 'A chanting-tune to the reading psalms',[27] to differentiate the prose texts from the 'singing-psalms' in metre. The impression that chanting the 'prose' texts was an invention of the Oxford movement in the nineteenth century, like the idea that Tate and Brady replaced Sternhold and Hopkins all at once, is to over-simplify a much more gradual and complex (and more interesting) process.

Initially, this was emphatically music for the choir. Congregational chanting, an important development, was still some way off. So the old argument came round again: who sings? The 'cathedral pattern' was gradually producing something cool, disciplined and beautiful. The attendee would listen with rapt disengagement to anthems from Greene and Boyce and psalmody chanted directly from the Book of Common Prayer, sung for them, and at them, by the choir. Laud's vision was coming true. His apostles were the new breed of high-church Tory Anglicans. These 'high and dries' liked their liturgy and their dinner: Parson Woodforde, Mr Elton and Mr Collins presiding vacantly over Jane Austen's Highbury and Rosings, Trollope's 'hunting parsons'; men whose holy orders were more about their place at table than their place in the hierarchy of the elect, more concerned about the beef roasting in their kitchen than the souls of their parishioners roasting in hell. What they feared and mistrusted was 'Enthusiasm', a new buzz-word for an old bogey. It didn't do to think too much.

'Enthusiasts', on the other hand, wanted a more direct involvement and a more emotional expression of the experience of worship. They found their champion in a new approach to text and music which, in time, produced perhaps English church music's finest achievement of all – hymns.

ONE OF THE FIRST, and still one of the very greatest, of the hymn-writers was Isaac Watts.

Watts was a child of his newly tolerant times. Born in 1674, he came from a family of dissenters and found both education and lifelong employment within the Nonconformist tradition. Studiedly ecumenical, he wrote widely about theology, education and logic (much influenced by Locke), as well as producing sermons, memoirs and over 500 hymns. He was one of the first to write hymns specifically for children.

He began, like everybody else, with the psalms. The preface to his *Hymns and Spiritual Songs* of 1707 makes clear what needed reform. 'Of all our Religious Solemnities *Psalmodie* is the most unhappily managed ... 'tis pity that this of all others should be performed the worst upon Earth'. Lining out made things worse: 'the very next Line perhaps which the Clerk parcels out unto us' produces 'the unhappy Mixture of Reading and Singing, which cannot presently be reformed'. So much for the music. The poetry is little better, having 'something in it so extremely *Jewish* and cloudy, that darkens our Sight of God the Saviour'.[28] In response, he aimed at something which would please every kind of taste, avoid sect or party, and above all 'make the Sense plain and obvious'. He was unforgiving of himself for occasionally allowing a flowery metaphor to get in the way of meaning. He wrote in regular metre, 'fitted to the most common Tunes', and was careful to make the punctuation of words and music match.

Watts divided his collection into three sections: scriptural paraphrases, communion hymns and 'Hymns whose Form is of mere humane Composure'. The last of these were freely composed devotional lyrics, designed to be sung by a congregation. Orlando Gibbons, George Wither and George Herbert made early moves in this direction a century before, but this is perhaps the real beginning of the hymn as a discrete entity in its own right, separate from, though intimately linked to, the venerable old habit of singing psalms in metre.

For all his self-editorial claims to have 'thrown out the Lines that were too sonorous', there is a strong dash of the Enthusiast's emotional engagement with his subject in Watts's work. 'When I survey the wondrous cross' has an intense, almost gruesome physicality in its description of 'his head, his hands, his feet', and 'his dying crimson, like a robe'. This leads directly into the work of later writers like Augustus

Toplady, author of the proto-Freudian 'Rock of Ages'. No wonder the 'high and dries' blushingly sipped their port and turned back to the *Racing Post*.

What Watts wanted was to emphasise the 'peculiarly Evangelical'. This is one of those words which echo through the centuries, appropriated by opponents and adherents alike as a badge of honour or a term of abuse in the latest war of words. At least this time it was only words. By the time Watts died in 1748 that war had not really begun, though the forces which unleashed it were gathering. Others would carry the clefts in society and worship to their logical conclusions, with creative results for music, on both sides.

Isaac Watts was part of a long and noble line of English devotional writers who knew that the ideal is seriousness of thought combined with directness of expression. He knew, too, how difficult this was to achieve: 'if the Verse appears so gentle and flowing as to incure the Censure of Feebleness, I may honestly affirm, that sometimes it cost me labour to make it so.'[29] Every generation of English church musicians has discovered that truth to be self-evident.

The first great wave of hymn-writing in the early eighteenth century had little to do with the established Anglican Church and its parishes, where hymns were, in theory at least, still illegal. The idea was that only the direct word of God, as revealed in the Bible, rather than mere 'humane Composures', were adequate to the task. But there were some grey areas. The two hymns written (on the top floor of Longleat House) by Bishop Thomas Ken in the late seventeenth century, 'Awake my soul, and with the sun' and 'Glory to thee, my God, this night', seem to have become particular favourites, perhaps because their texts for morning and evening allowed them to be slotted into the daily round almost as part of the liturgy. In any event, the legal mechanism for enforcing the ban was rarely used, and probably wouldn't have worked. Watts noted that there were 'some Christians who are not yet persuaded that it is lawful to sing any thing in Divine Worship' except 'the Word of God', which implies that there were plenty like him who were already so persuaded and that he thought everybody else would be one day (hence his neat use of the word 'yet'), as indeed they were.

In the meantime, hymns popped up in all sorts of places. 'Rock of Ages', referred to above, was first printed in a magazine.[30] So was the torch-song of Enlightenment Christianity, Joseph Addison's 'The Spacious Firmament on High'.[31] This was church music as essay (which is perhaps the reason it's still a bit wordy for singing). Actual hymnbooks were the province of Nonconformist groups like the Congregationalists. Often, authors would not specify a tune, either because the poem was meant to be read as much as sung, or, like Watts, to allow the singer to choose a tune in a metre he already knew. The idea that the words and music of hymns were fixed in the pairings and versions we know today is wrong. The tradition was far more flexible, creative and interesting than that.

Out in the English countryside, the prevailing musical and intellectual trends of the first part of the century found themselves filtered into local usage through the inclinations, abilities and aspirations of our old friend, the parish musician; and the most important addition to the rural musical landscape was the itinerant music teacher. This appealing character's main objective was making a living. He would tramp between the various villages of his patch of a couple of counties, giving lessons and selling copies of his latest book, a judicious combination of psalter and primer in music theory. He had pretensions to musical sophistication, though his own grasp of the basics was probably pretty patchy (though certainly better than the parish clerk whose job he was appropriating).

Joseph Addison described the pleasures of a 'Country Sunday' in 1711 on a visit to his friend Sir Roger, the local squire (fictional, but probably all the more realistic because of it). Sir Roger attended church regularly 'to see if any of his Tenants are missing', and with all the wisdom of his rank 'will suffer no Body to sleep in it besides himself'. He gave each of his parishioners a hassock and prayer book 'to make them kneel and join in the Responses'. He also 'employed an itinerant Singing-master, who goes about the Country for that Purpose, to instruct them rightly in the Tunes of the Psalms; upon which they now very much value themselves'.[32] The Bishop of London pointed out, entirely fairly, the drawbacks of this approach in 1724: 'I do by no means recommend to you or them the inviting or encouraging those idle instructors, who of late years have gone about the several counties to teach tunes uncommon and out of the way (which very often are as ridiculous as they are new; and the consequence of which is, that the greatest part of the congregation being unaccustomed to them, are silenced).'[33] It's the old argument resurfacing. Sir Roger didn't care: 'sometimes he will be lengthening out a verse in the Singing-Psalms', reports his friend Addison, 'half a Minute after the rest of the Congregation have done with it; sometimes, when he is pleased with the Matter of his Devotion, he pronounces *Amen* three or four times ...'[34] Little doubt which member of this congregation 'values himself' the most. The practice of church music can serve a variety of ends.

A number of books for the country market stand out from a crowded field: *Lyra Davidica* of 1708 and John Chetham's *Book of Psalmody* (1718), widely used in Yorkshire in the first half of the century and much reprinted, are among several to have sent words and music forth into later hymnbooks. But one in particular will have to stand duty here for this whole tradition and the wandering minstrels who made them: *The Royal Melody Compleat* by William Tans'ur.

Tans'ur's father was a labourer called Edward Tanzer, but this obviously wasn't fancy enough for a man of William's self-appointed standing in the high society of St Neots, Cambridgeshire. (He wasn't alone: Anne Boleyn's family name was Bullen, and the father of the Brontë sisters was an Irish curate called Brunty.) Once he'd dyed his name an appropriate shade, Tans'ur touted his expertise around in the course of 'an Itinerant life, through divers Counties',[35] before settling down and opening a bookshop. His publications cover every aspect of his art and a period of around forty years. *The Royal Melody Compleat* first appeared in 1754, and ran to no fewer than eight editions. It is a window into a vanished world. Following a rather idealised woodcut of a handsome young man composing a canon in a library, Tans'ur introduces the three parts of his book. His headings sum up the range and limits of this kind of musico-parochial universe so completely that they are worth quoting in full:

I.   A New and Correct, Introduction to the Grounds of Musick, Rudimental, Practical and Technical.

II. A New, and Compleat Body of Church Musick, adapted to the most select portions of the Book of Psalms, of either versions; with many Fuging Chorus's, and Gloria Patri's to the Whole.

III. A New, and Select, number of Services, Chants, Hymns, Anthems, and Canons, suited to several Occasions; and many of them never before printed; set by the greatest Masters in the World. For Publick, and Private Use.

The music is in from two to eight parts, he tells his reader, written 'according to the nicest rules'. The mixture of practicality and genteel pretension is clear. So is the reach of his musical ambition.

There is a conventional appeal to scriptural authority and a lengthy justification of the benefits of 'our solid good Church musick', which include getting people out of bed and into church on a Sunday morning ('especially Youth') and encouraging people of 'Higher rank' to set an example to the 'lower classes'. He tells us that when we sing psalms, 'we should all STAND up', and that churches should have 'places convenient for their Quires', a sure sign of the changing musical landscape. Next comes a long and detailed treatise on harmony and counterpoint, all 'solid good' stuff.

In Part II, the psalm-settings begin with the usual picture of King David playing the harp (despite, in this case, apparently having only three fingers on his left hand). The music is laid out in four-part score. This looks perfectly normal to us, but it actually represents something of an editorial breakthrough. Compilers before and since experimented endlessly with how to lay out the music on the page, as the 'tune' migrated from the tenors to the trebles, the congregation to the choir, with harmony parts for men, women, children, instruments or all of the above. In earlier times a particular clef meant a particular voice-part. The adoption of a more standardised, more flexible way of writing a tune down was an important step. Croft was the first to print an anthem collection for choir in full score in 1724, followed by Boyce and Greene and everyone else thereafter. At parish level, what the music looks like on the page tells us something important about who thought they were going to get to sing it. Clefs, those funny little squiggles at the beginning of the line, are the key to a code which tells us how musical manners were developing.

The tunes themselves have an appealing simple beauty. Many are in three-time. Harmonies are square and spare, often reducing the texture to three or two parts. This was the tradition of country psalmody that gives us well-known melodies like 'Rockingham', sung today to 'When I Survey the Wondrous Cross', and 'Abridge' ('Be Thou my Guardian and my Guide'); elegant, rugged things, rising and falling like a row of English hills. Words alternate between the fiery 'old' version and the suave 'new': his readers could begin the 'Durham' tune with 'Thou grindest man thro' grief and pain to Dust, or Clay', or 'How just and merciful is God, how gracious is the Lord!' – as the mood took them. Practicalities were never far away: Tans'ur provided parish clerks with a list of starting notes to be played 'by a concert pitch-pipe; where there is no organ'. Not all parishes out in the Fens, it seems, either wanted or could afford the organ-accompanied style which was catching on fast in London.

The third 'volume' introduces us to one of the most characteristic and engaging inventions of eighteenth-century church music, the 'fuging' tune. The example shown gives a pretty good idea of what this strange, enthralling, hybrid creature is all about. Tans'ur begins with the tune, 'Guilford', 'Composed' (i.e. harmonised) by 'W. T.' He lays it out on the page in four-part score, using a treble clef for the top line, alto clef ('C3') for the next line down, treble clef again for the tenor (the tune, to be read an octave down by tenor singers and at pitch by other voices or, possibly, a violin or oboe), bass clef for the bass. The words of the 'old' version are set out neatly below the music. Both, of course, are in the ubiquitous 'common metre', being modern, practical, flexible and easy to use. Harmonies are strong, well-crafted and unfancy, sometimes closing onto bare intervals with no third, just right for the sturdy, modal melody as it clambers up and down its range of a perfect fifth like a shepherd shinning over a drystone wall. The chord at the beginning of the penultimate bar sounds wrong, and probably is: Tans'ur has attempted to step outside his familiar repertoire of tonic, dominant and occasional sub-dominant chords, and frankly made a bit of a hash of it.

On the next page, his invention takes flight. He takes the opening phrase from the tenor tune, a short, downward scale, and turns it into a simple fugue, with tenor, alto and treble getting the stumpy little fragment of melody one after the other. The word-stress is lumpy, to say the least, with a thumping great accent on the first word, 'to'. Most oddly of all, though, Tans'ur has managed to extract from his hymn tune a musical phrase lasting five crotchet beats ('to shew to us'), which he then attempts to notate in 4/4. As a result, the voice-parts all come in on different beats of the bar. Accents and underlay are, for a few bars, all over the place.

Compilers of country song-books like Tans'ur did this sort of thing all the time. Often it's just a case of misreading the number of beats in a bar and printing a tune in the wrong time signature: William Sandys thought 'I saw three ships come sailing in' was in 3/4. Their grasp of the 'nicest rules' comes up against a wish to treat their readers to a few 'whimsicall Flights', and usually comes off worse.

After his brief contrapuntal flirtation, the rest of Tans'ur's 'fuging chorus' gives us some more revealing clues about his musical world. The 'sharp' signs printed over the top of the bass note in a couple of places suggest that an organ, or possibly some other instrument, is filling in and supporting the harmony. In the last couple of bars, the tenor part takes off on a kind of mini-cadenza, ornamenting the melody with the kind of embellishments described so often in accounts of psalm-singing (with varying degrees of amusement, horror and contempt), and showing that, unlike in larger parishes with their charity children and treble-dominated music, out here in the provinces the tenor was still top dog in the tune department (or at least thought he was). The piece ends with a couple of parallel fifths and the words of the 'new' version, *à choix*.

Parish music was now moving away from the congregation and towards the choir. In Tans'ur, the move happens during the course of the piece. The people sing a verse of the hymn, then the choir does a little riff on it before the next verse. The chorus is optional, and can be left out if the tenor or organist has a sore throat, a sore thumb or a hangover. In the long debate between choir and congregation, the idea of doing both in the same piece has probably not been explored to its full potential.

In a way, parish music in the eighteenth century was doing what church music as a whole did in the eleventh century and afterwards. You started with a well-known tune, sung by the most common voice type, the tenor. Parts were added, by simple rules; harmony expanded from two to three and more parts. Then, bits of the tune appeared in other parts in a form of 'imitation'. You could hear the musicians discovering, or inventing, the tools of their trade as they went along. Some of the more primitive harmonisations in the country choir-books of the eighteenth century, with their strings of parallel intervals and two-part textures, sound like the *organum* of seven centuries before.

One other aspect of these books which deserves attention was the attempt to bring high art to the choir stall. The 'fuging' tune was, in its way, a basic stab at a Handelian chorus. More specifically, compilers included pieces by 'leading masters', though these had usually been knocked around quite a bit: not so much 'by' Clarke and Croft as 'after' them, and in some cases quite a long way after. Tans'ur's *I was Glad* sounds suspiciously like a simplified version of the well-known setting by John Blow (though this may just be a case of the sprightly dotted rhythm reappearing as the composer's cliché of choice for this text, like the trumpet calls in earlier psalm-settings by Byrd and Gibbons).

This creative reworking of an authored original occurred with the words too: a hymn-text which began 'Join, Spirits, to adore the Lamb' turns into Watts's 'When I survey the wondrous cross' halfway through, without acknowledgement of either the original author or his improver. Tate's 'While Shepherds Watched' got this kind of treatment quite frequently. In the days before effective copyright law, this adapting and mangling of both words and music between the original text and the country psalm book and Nonconformist hymnal was very much part of the way this tradition worked. John Wesley, for one, got very cross about it. Sometimes a text would disappear into the greenery of the folk tradition and then resurface, filtered through the editorial process of an oral tradition, some time later: Vaughan Williams collected a 'folk-song' in Northumberland in 1906 which was clearly a half-remembered version of Isaac Watts's 'Cradle Song'.[36] The process of cross-pollination of verbal images and musical phrases alike between all these different strands is rich and strange.

The country style had an intriguing late flowering in America, in particular in the hands of a one-eyed snuff addict of untutored genius, William Billings. The two strands of English parish music, distinct but related, appear in Billings's voluminous publications: metrical tunes for congregational use, and 'anthems' for the choir. Often, he set the poetry of Isaac Watts. Sometimes, like others, he adapted an original text to his own use, with striking results. His version of Psalm 137 transfers the action of the Old Testament Babylonish captivity to revolutionary Massachusetts:

> By the Rivers of Watertown we sat down and wept,
> when we remember'd, O Boston.[37]

Billings took every aspect of the eighteenth-century style to a new level: the expressive potential of text, the opportunities for fun, even the mistakes. His parallel fifths and bad fugues sound engagingly fresh and direct. This music was written off as primitive and uncultured for many decades after his death, as indeed it is. But it survived in 'shape-note' hymnals and the 'Sacred Harp' tradition, particularly in the rural South, and has found its way back into the repertoire of many American choirs as part of a welcome resurgence of interest in the tradition. English church music turns up in some surprising places.

The first two thirds of the eighteenth century were 'pudding time' for church music. The music of Handel gave it some of its loveliest moments, and cast its elegant influence over all kinds of composition for the church for the rest of the century and beyond. The words of Watts set a standard for a new kind of church music – hymn-singing. The two strands, Anglican anthems for choirs and Nonconformist hymns for congregations, would diverge to breaking point by the end of the century, before converging again thereafter. As usual, such creative tensions proved fruitful for music at all levels and on every wing of the argument. Intriguingly, and uniquely, one family sent standard-bearers into battle on both sides: the Wesleys.

II

West Galleries and Wesleys, Methodists and Mendelssohn, 1760–1850

If you'd thrive in musical religion, stick to strings, says I.
Thomas Hardy, *Under the Greenwood Tree*

Now mind, neighbours … You two counter-boys, keep your ears open to Michael's fingering, and don't ye go straying into the treble part along o' Dick and his set, as ye did last year; and mind this especially when we be in 'Arise, and hail …' [1]

NOTHING IN THE HISTORY of English church music is more English than the faded, rustic, idiosyncratic image of the West Gallery choirs and the church bands, and the proud, white-smocked groups of eccentrics and mechanicals who sang and played in them. Thomas Hardy knew these musicians well as a child. His grandfather was one of them. Here they are at Christmas:

The gallery of Mellstock Church had a status and sentiment of its own…. Old William sat in the centre of the front row, his violoncello between his knees and two singers on each hand. Behind him, on the left, came the treble singers and Dick; and on the right the tranter and the tenors. Farther back was old Mail with the altos and supernumeraries ... The vicar looked cross.

Hardy's 'story of the Mellstock Quire and its old established west-gallery musicians' in *Under the Greenwood Tree*, is set in around 1830–40. The tradition had another half-century or so to run, but was probably already past its peak of popularity, which ran perhaps from around 1780 to 1830. Its roots lay in the mid-eighteenth century. Choirs had become a regular fixture by this time, very gradually taking over the musical duties from the clerk and people 'lining out' the psalm. Encouraged and supplied by the multitude of country music books, rural choirs wanted to lift their eyes to the performance of anthems and 'fuging' tunes. Most had no organ, so a bass instrument like a bass viol or cello, or sometimes a bassoon, was employed to give instrumental support and add bottom to their ambition. Treble instruments such as violins, flutes and oboes came later, making up the typical band of around six to eight players. At first, instruments would simply double the voice-parts in the choral items, reading from the same score as the singers, not add anything new. Over time, short, simple instrumental 'symphonies' were added between the vocal sections. Treble and alto parts, sung both at pitch and an octave lower by tenors, would be doubled by treble instruments, giving, typically, a rich and colourful five-part texture from three vocal lines.

The fact that any given line might be used by a number of different kinds of singer or player explains the constant experimentation with layout and use of clefs. *Arise and Hail the Sacred Day* was a Christmas piece by Joseph Stephenson, published in his *The Musical Companion* of 1771. It was based on an existing hymn tune, and the words were also adapted from an earlier source, a *Hymn for Christmas-Day* published in the *Gentleman's Magazine* in 1748, where it was attributed to 'Mr Oats of Devonshire'. The process of cross-borrowing and reworking was in full swing. Stephenson's setting was in three parts, striding along joyously in 6/4 time, with brief 'fuging' passages breaking up the texture (competently done, with imitation at the fifth: better than Tans'ur, for sure). The three lines use, respectively, treble, alto and bass clef. It conjures an evocative picture: the rich, rustic sound of this piece being played and sung by Old William, the 'four men and seven boys' who made up his choir, and the 'half a dozen to ten full-grown players' who played along, Grandson Dick on fiddle, Reuben and Michael on tenor and second fiddle, and maybe a bassoon or serpent honking away on the bottom with Old William and the bass singers.

The instrumentation, of course, was very far from fixed – you used whatever you had. Some of these sounds are lost to us now. There is a gravestone in the churchyard at Minstead in Hampshire which has a picture of a serpent, a kind of bass woodwind instrument, carved on it, with the inscription:

> To the memory of Thomas Maynard
> Who departed this life
> July 9th 1817 aged 27 years.
> The Band of Musicians of the
> South Hants Yeomanry (of which He was a Member)
> In testimony of their esteem
> Caused this stone to be erected[2]

Young Maynard remains forever united with his instrument in death, as no doubt he was in life.

Some early types of bass instruments were specifically designed for the use of the unskilled: the 'psalmody' had just one string, the 'psalterer' two, tuned an octave apart, and a system of easy notation loosely based on lute tablature.[3] These particular inventions didn't catch on. Yet many parishes and villages still have their ophicleides, key-bugles, bass fiddles, drums and plenty of pitch pipes. Perhaps the most exotic of all was the vamphorn. This was basically just a big megaphone. Several churches still have theirs. The one at Ashurst, West Sussex, is painted green and has the words 'Praise Him upon ye strings and Pipe, 1770. Palmer fecit' written on it in yellow letters. The example hanging on the vestry wall at East Leake, Nottinghamshire, is 7ft 9in long and has a plaque which reads: 'This trumpet was formerly used in the gallery of this church for one of the singers to sing the bass through … Replaced in this church 1888.'[4] Hardy tells us that 'fiddle-strings, rosin, and music-paper were supplied by a pedlar, who travelled exclusively in such wares from parish to parish', and how once, 'on the occasion of their producing a new Christmas anthem, he did not come to time, owing to being snowed up on the downs, and the straits they were in through having to make shift with whipcord and twine for strings'. If we want to hear the full symphony of English church music, we have to include in our imaginings the sound of a Christmas anthem, sung through a vamphorn, accompanied by instruments strung with whipcord and twine. Hardy was looking back when he wrote his description, as he so often did. But even at the time he describes, the tradition was coming under attack from several quarters.

When the singing of the Mellstock choir failed to elicit a response from the village's new (and pretty) schoolteacher, one of their number whispered, 'Perhaps she's jist come from some musical city, and sneers at our doings?' City music was certainly different. Hardy lamented that 'these compositions which now lie before me, with their repetitions of lines, half-lines, and half-words, their fugues and their intermediate symphonies, ... would hardly be admitted into such hymn-books as are popular in the churches of fashionable society at the present time'. Much of the hinterland of the rustic style lay in the directness of expression of the Evangelical movement. 'Fashionable society', by contrast, wanted the Anglican virtues of a trained choir, well-drilled children, rehearsed chanting of the prose psalms, treble-dominated anthems and, above all, an organ to discipline (or, better still, drown out), the screeching of the unenlightened, still walking in musical darkness. Some London churches even went as far as to employ professional singers from the concert platform or opera stage to form a quartet on Sunday mornings. Out in the country, the point of contact between the two kinds of aspiration was often the vicar.

Hardy's vicar, Mr Maybold, is more tolerant and consensual in his approach than some, but he knows what he wants:

> I myself, I must own, prefer organ-music to any other. I consider it most proper, and feel justified in endeavouring to introduce it; but then, although other music is better, I don't say yours is not good.

This was the new orthodoxy: a small, single-manual organ (no pedals), pumped by some suitably sinewy village lad, or by the player's own feet, played by the vicar's wife or the schoolteacher, a lady who had learned her Haydn and Scarlatti on the Broadwood in her own father's vicarage, the sort of well-meaning person ignored by Jane Austen because she's not rich. She is a bringer of jollity, and a bringer of change.

Her other musical innovation is the choir of Sunday-school children. The style and sound of these ensembles could hardly have been more different from the all-male West Gallery choirs:

> At the third time of singing, these intrusive feminine voices were
> as mighty as those of the regular singers; in fact, the flood of sound
> from this quarter assumed such an individuality, that it had a time,
> a key, almost a tune of its own, surging upwards when the gallery
> plunged downwards, and the reverse.

It's a psalm, and by the third verse the girls are taking over. Like so many of Hardy's later and wiser heroes, the choirmen find their fate taken out of their own hands. They are not happy:

> 'Brazen-faced hussies!' said Bowman.
> ...
> 'What I want to know is,' said the tranter (as if he knew already,
> but that civilization required the form of words), 'what business
> people have to tell maidens to sing like that when they don't sit in a
> gallery, and never have entered one in their lives? That's the question,
> my sonnies.'
> ''Tis the gallery have got to sing, all the world knows,' ...

In time, the Sunday-school movement created its own distinctive repertoire, and among its favourite subjects were obedience and death. This is from a book published in 1800, set to a catchy, trebly tune:

> Let us remember, while at prayer,
> When at the Sabbath-school,
> Our teachers' kindness, and their care,
> Towards our Sabbath-school.

We'll be submissive, good and kind,
And every rule and order mind,
When we're at school, at Sabbath-school,
When we're at Sabbath-school.

Boys. When each at night shall go to prayer
We'll ask our God above
Girls. T'extend o'er teachers his kind care,
And crown them with his love.
Boys and girls. And when on earth our time is sped,
And we are numbered with the dead,
Teachers and scholars. If faithful, we shall meet above,
We all shall meet above.[5]

But the Sunday schools absorbed something of the more liberal tradition of the charity schools too. Joseph Hart delivered a typical fire-
and-brimstone warning in this hymn, from his collection *Hymns
Composed on Various Subjects* of 1759:

Remember, O Christian, with heed,
When sunk under sentence of death,
How first thou from bondage wast freed –
Say, was it by works, or by faith?[6]

By the time this lyric was published in *Lancashire School Songs* almost
a century later, the fire was out and the brimstone safely stowed away.
Only Hart's last stanza (of seven) remains, and even that has been
softened from his 'This God is the God we adore' to

How good is the God we adore
Our faithful unchangeable Friend!
His love is as great as His power,
And knows neither measure nor end!
'Tis Jesus the First and the Last,
Whose Spirit shall Guide us safe home,
We'll praise Him for all that is past,
And trust Him for all that's to come.[7]

The Sunday-school movement is a notable example of church music as education and social improvement. Hannah More, the writer and social reformer, was roundly criticised by local farmers in the Mendips for teaching the poor to read and write. In an ironic riposte, she called her pet cats Passive Obedience and Non-Resistance, after the pet doctrines of Restoration high-churchmen.[8]

Many parishes couldn't initially boast a competent practitioner on what was known as the 'finger organ', so had to make do with a barrel organ. The 'player' simply turned a handle, which caused raised pins on a metal cylinder to open and shut the wind supply to the pipes, and thus play a tune. Change the barrel and you got a different tune. It was a cheap and popular way of bringing the virtues of accompaniment to your congregational singing. Its limitations included the size of the metal drum, which could only accommodate the shorter tunes. Another problem was that, unlike a sentient human accompanist (at least one who's paying attention), the barrel organ could not of course change the 'tempo' as it went along. Psalm-chants, where the length of the 'reciting note' is different in every verse, presented a particular problem. But there were barrels in existence with chants of this kind on them, and musicologist Nicholas Temperley describes some amusing experiments in trying to use them: basically, you had to guess whether to sing each verse very, very fast or extremely slowly.[9] (Perhaps a dextrous and alert performer on the handle could have learnt to 'play' the reciting note at the beginning of the verse, then stop turning and listen attentively until joining in again when the congregation got to the change of chord. The possibilities are intriguing.) Better results could be achieved by replacing the barrel organ with what Thomas Hardy's Mr Mail describes as 'the things next door to 'em that you blow wi' your foot': the harmonium.

This was another step (or mis-step) in the ongoing development of psalm-singing. Many country song-books featured a kind of halfway house between the 'metrical' and the 'prose' psalms: a chant was given for a prose text, with the reciting note varying in length each verse, but sung in a notated, regular rhythm. With a bit of familiarity, this was within the grasp of a reasonably literate choir, or even congregation.

Another fascinating element was the development of the 'chanting tune'. This combined the attractions of an 'air', or song, with the practicalities of singing verses of differing lengths. The tune lasted two verses, with tenors singing the first, altos the second, with bass voices (and probably instruments) joining in throughout, making a two-part texture. The tune was repeated for each pair of verses, and where the text had more syllables a suitable chord, usually a bare fifth on the dominant, was used as a temporary reciting note in written-out rhythm. The full four-part choir sang only in the 'Glory be to the Father' at the end. An early example is the cheery Magnificat printed by Uriah Davenport in *The Psalm-Singer's Pocket Companion* in 1755. (Davenport lived to be ninety-four and taught psalmody in Leek, Staffordshire, for over sixty years, where he led a substantial band of singers and instrumentalists.)

A later example is the Jubilate by an excise officer from Nuneaton called Joseph Key. It is much more elaborate, mostly in three rather than two parts, and has a florid instrumental bass part ornamenting the vocal line. The titles of Key's publications show the range and reach of the music-making in a medium-sized provincial town in the second half of the eighteenth century; for example his *Five Anthems, Four Collects, Twenty Psalm Tunes* of 1785, which has something for everyone. Sometimes, little overtures and 'symphonies' for strings were added to these anthems, sometimes borrowed from other pieces and other composers like Handel (who surely wouldn't have minded as he was always doing the same thing himself). This was completely different from the rural West Gallery style of instrumentally accompanied choral music, and was nothing less than an attempt to ape the fashionable, high-art manner of Handel and Boyce according to the pretensions and abilities of a prosperous market town. The jealous rustle of the crinolines hovers behind Key's showy little soprano solos.

If the West Gallery was the architectural symbol of the musical hierarchy in the country, in larger churches and in the town it was the three-decker pulpit. This splendid edifice would house the clerk on the bottom tier while he led the singing of the psalm; the vicar would sit above him and read the lesson, then ascend in majesty to the very heights to preach to (or, more accurately, down to) his flock below.

a)

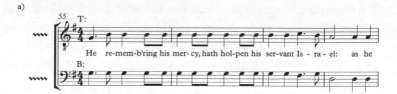

He re-mem-b'ring his mer-cy, hath hol-pen his ser-vant Is - ra - el: as he

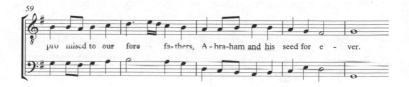

pro - mised to our fore - fa - thers, A - bra-ham and his seed for e - ver.

b)

O__ be__ joy - ful in__the Lord, all_____ ye lands:

O__ be__ joy - ful in__the Lord, all_____ ye lands:

O__ be__ joy - ful in__the Lord, all_____ ye lands:

Instrumental bass (bassoon, cello, serpent):

Eighteenth century parish choir music. Davenport's Magnificat is a 'chanting' tune, using repeated chords to get through the text simply and efficiently. Key's Jubilate is a much more showy affair, for a bigger church with greater musical pretensions. Both pieces vary the texture between men's and women's voices, reserving the full choir for a chordal Gloria Patri at the end.

The principal significance for the development of church music in this arrangement lies in what the vicar would do during the psalm: leave. Typically, he would take advantage of the lengthy musical interlude to retire to the vestry to change into his preaching gown, emerging again when the psalm was finished. This became an ingrained part of the choreography of worship, and contributed to the idea that the sung parts of the service were really none of the vicar's business (and, incidentally, may provide the origin of the phrase 'getting into the habit' for doing something regularly, like the vicar changing his frock).

This separation of powers was never going to help relations out in the country, where the people had their jealously guarded privileges up in the gallery at the back (which may, in its turn, be the origin of the phrase 'face the music'). In the age of revolutions across the water, any stand-off between vicar and choir could be seen as a confrontation between the Establishment and the people. 'Psalm-singing and Republicanism naturally go together,'[10] thundered the *Gentleman's Magazine* nervously in 1781. Church music was getting political again.

But church music survived. In France it didn't. In England, these tensions were played out not in a violent crisis but in a series of amusing little spats between vicars and choirs. England learnt to do its revolutions differently. In its own unassuming, badly harmonised way, church music shows us how it was done. For example, the engagingly leisured Parson James Woodforde told his diary in 1769 how he had ordered the choir of his Somerset parish to say – not sing – the responses, 'but this morning after the first commandment they had the impudence to sing the response, and therefore I spoke to them out of my desk'.[11] The singers reacted to this public dressing-down by not coming to church at all. And in 1833 a country clergyman called Skinner replaced his singers with a group of schoolgirls, whereupon the regular choir 'put on their hats and left the church'. Skinner thought this a great improvement: 'the girls sang both morning and evening, and much more to my satisfaction than the great Bulls of Bashan in the gallery used to do, who, though never in tune or time, were so highly conceited of their own abilities they thought of nothing else the whole time of the service. If they choose to withdraw themselves, we shall do better without them.'

Reverend Skinner eventually proved more wise and patient than some of his profession (before and since), and let the singers back: 'I do not like their mode of performing this part of the service near so well as that of the schoolgirls: but if it induces the people to come to church, I will bear with them patiently.'[12] Quite right.

An interesting footnote to this story is what the adult singers did during their brief exile: they 'determined to sing in future at the meeting house, where the gallery was to be enlarged for their accommodation'. They had decamped en bloc to the Methodists, not out of any religious conviction, but because the music was better. Something important about English church music is revealed by that little detail.

CHARITABLE INSTITUTIONS KNOWN AS 'hospitals' provided care and moral guidance to all sorts of needy types, including chimney-sweeps, prostitutes and sufferers from venereal disease. The motives behind their foundation were rather mixed: a strong dash of paternalistic piety led to plenty of prayer and daily attendance in their handsome and well-endowed chapels, while an equal mixture of fashionable voyeurism made attendance at their services something of a spectator sport. Some of them managed very good music. This, together with the fact that as private chapels they were outside the jurisdiction of the established church, encouraged the participation of both colourful preachers and talented musicians. Handel was actively involved at Thomas Coram's Foundling Hospital. Later, Ann Stainer, sister of Sir John, played the organ in one of the hospital chapels every Sunday for half a century (one of a number of lady organists, or 'organesses'). The Lock Hospital, also in the capital, had as its chaplain Martin Madan, an associate of Charles Wesley and author of a few words of 'Hark, the Herald Angels Sing', who was so horrified by the consequences of venereal disease that he wrote a book advocating polygamy as a remedy for sexual incontinence, which didn't go down very well. Perhaps the most important of these organisations was the Magdalen Hospital for Penitent Prostitutes in Whitechapel. Horace Walpole described a visit:

> The chapel is small and low, but neat, hung with Gothic paper and tablets of benefactions. At the west end were inclosed the sisterhood,

above an hundred and thirty, all in greyish brown stuffs, broad handkerchiefs, and flat straw hats with a ribband pulled quite over their faces. As soon as we entered the chapel, the organ played, and the Magdalens sang a hymn in parts; you cannot imagine how well. The chapel was dressed with orange and myrtle, and there wanted nothing but a little incense, to drive away the devil – or to invite him. Prayers then began, psalms, and a sermon; the latter by a young clergyman, one Dodd; who contributed to the Popish idea one had imbibed by haranging entirely in the French style.[13]

Later on, the congregation was spared the appalling prospect of actually having to look at the fallen women by a green curtain that was hung across their pews at the back. William Dodd, their preacher, contributed further to the 'Popish idea' by providing the words for an anthem, for upper voices in unison with organ accompaniment, written for the Magdalens by Johann Christian Bach, the 'London Bach', who was, perhaps surprisingly given his parentage, a Catholic. Bach wrote a great deal of Catholic sacred music earlier in his career, but this was the only occasion on which he wrote for the English church, despite his long and successful sojourn in musical London. It was published, typically, not in a collection of anthems but in a magazine. Dodd, meanwhile, proved himself one of the more extravagant eccentrics in an age which wasn't short of such characters, and ended up as the last person to be hanged at Tyburn for forgery (despite an eloquent appeal published from prison which turned out to have been written by Dr Johnson, who, when challenged as to whether Dodd could have written it in such circumstances, said, 'Depend upon it Sir, when a man knows he is to be hanged in a fortnight, it concentrates his mind wonderfully'[14]).

Thomas Arne and J. C. Bach were notable examples of that rare, endangered but tenacious species, Catholic musicians in England. Their musical homes were the chapels of the various European embassies in London, the only places in England where Catholic mass could legally be celebrated, and the most important were the Sardinian and Portuguese chapels. Among those who made their music there were the Samuel Webbes, elder and younger, Charles Wesley junior and Vincent Novello. Novello and the elder Webbe both published copiously. Novello introduced the English public to the church music of Haydn and Mozart, and to works by Palestrina, Giacomo Carissimi and other Italian masters, handsomely edited and transcribed from manuscripts in the Fitzwilliam Museum, Cambridge. He published much music for treble voices, including Gregorian chant mass settings (with his own organ accompaniment), under the title *Convent Masses* (1834). All this would later provide an important ingredient in the much-needed revival of high-quality choral music within the Anglican Church. Webbe's publications included *An Essay on the Church Plain Chant* of 1782 and *A Collection of Motetts* ten years later, which was, incidentally, the route by which a hymn by another English Catholic, John Francis Wade, made its way into English popular consciousness as 'O Come, All Ye Faithful'.

Music at these well-heeled chapels attracted the same measure of fascination and fear that Catholic worship always did in England. Novello's daughter, Mary, often heard him play at the Portuguese chapel in South Street:

> His organ-playing attained such renown that it attracted numerous persons, even among the nobility, whose carriages waited for them outside while they lingered to the end of the service, and after; for it was playfully said that his 'voluntaries' – intended to 'play out' the congregation – on the contrary, kept them in, listening to the very last note.[15]

Novello family music-making continued at home, in the company of visitors like Leigh Hunt and John Keats, fuelled by 'true Lutheran beer' in a fine spirit of ecumenism. These Catholic chapels were the successors of the court establishments of the Stuart queens. It's remarkable that they survived. Fires, riots and road-building could have stopped them, but Novello, Webbe and their like didn't let them.

More's the pity, then, that the abilities and enthusiasms of these Catholic composers did not feed into the creation of a genuinely English 'classical' style of church music. It might have been the way to stop Anglican choral music becoming increasingly dull. It certainly needed it.

Away from the choirs, English church music's greatest achievement of the period, perhaps of any period, was the tradition of hymn-singing. Marching at the head of the noble army of its creators were the Wesley brothers, John and Charles. As undergraduates at Christ Church, Oxford, in the late 1720s, the brothers formed a religious society, known as the 'Holy Club', which attracted a number of charismatic devotees including George Whitefield, Martin Madan and Thomas Haweis. Fellow students mocked them for their prim ways, giving them a nickname which, as so often, they adopted as a badge of honour:

By rule they eat, by rule they drink,
By rule do all things but think.
Accuse the priests of loose behaviour.
To get more in the laymen's favour.
Method alone must guide 'em all
When themselves 'Methodists' they call.[16]

Monarchs apart, Isaac Watts and the Wesleys are the most important people in this story who were not themselves musicians. They articulated a desire to express something personal and individualistic about religious faith which was, in turn, part of the progress of Enlightenment ideals from the parleying of the literati in the coffee shops and magazine columns of Edinburgh and London to ordinary people. As the historian Roy Porter has said:

It was public men holding forth on public matters who dominated early Enlightenment debate ... That situation changed, socially, intellectually and culturally, during the course of the century. The focus of intellectual enquiry shifted to enlightenment *within* [his italics].[17]

And church music went with it: 'within' was an important word to the Wesleys.

For both brothers, the change of emphasis was a matter of conversion. In at least one case, music had a part to play. On 24 May 1738,

A page from the Winchester Troper, dating from about 1000, some of the oldest two-part music in existence. The musical symbols appear to be a kind of memory aid, showing the singer where the pitches rise and fall and helping him remember a tune he already knows, rather than a precise scheme of musical notation.

A medieval choir. Tonsured monks and a little boy singing plainsong. Some of them may be adding harmonies to the written melody according to the rules of 'faburden'. This gorgeous picture is from the Ranworth antiphoner, dating from the early to mid fifteenth century.

Polyphonic music of the early fifteenth century: a page from the 'Old Hall' manuscript. Music heard by, and possibly composed by, Henry V.

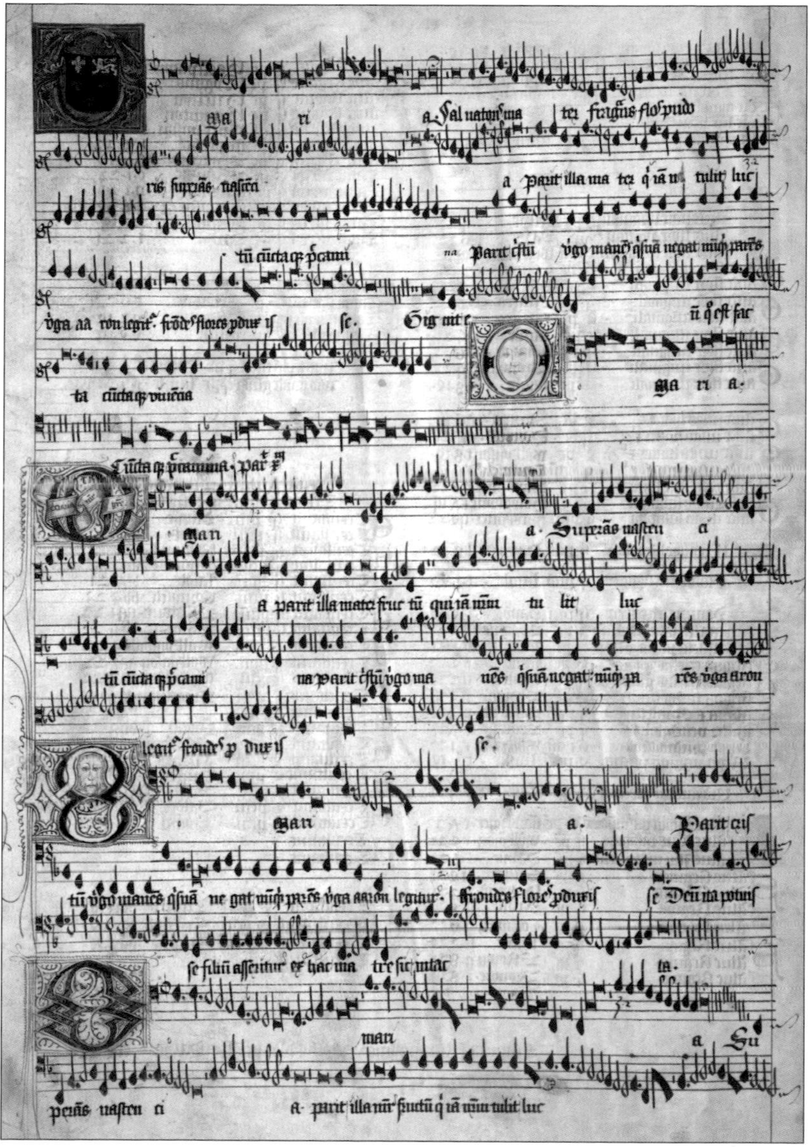

Music as visual art: a page from the Eton choirbook, c. *1520.*

The physical effects of the Reformation. At this church in Linclonshire, as at so many, the medieval wall-paintings were whitewashed over rather than removed, perhaps in the belief that they might one day re-emerge, as many of them have. Something very similar was done with books of music and liturgy. In this case, ironically, the picture re-appeared when a German bomb disturbed the plaster during the Second World War. As well as whitewash, the picture was covered by the lowering of the roof-line, so that only Jesus's pierced feet stick out below the beam.

*The Chapel Royal choir at the funeral of Elizabeth I, 1603. The
sumptuous liveried gowns were part of the fee for taking part.*

*Orlando Gibbons, who probably arrived from East Anglia to take up his poat
at the Chapel Royal just too late to take part in the Queen's funeral.*

Henry Purcell, brightest ornament of a musical family, whose musical manner perfectly matched the tenor of his times and the tastes of his royal patrons.

George Frideric Handel, one of the great masters of setting the words of the Book of Common Prayer *and Tate and Brady's 'new version', even though he was not a native speaker of English.*

An eighteenth or early nineteenth century gallery choir. Note the variety of instruments and mixture of men, women, and children, reading from a psalm-book or collection of "fuging" tunes or anthems.

(above) May morning, Oxford, c. 1880. Choristers singing in (or, in this case, on) a building which was put up in the fifteenth century.

(left) Church music in the twenty-first century: a worship group performing in a building which wasn't.

John Wesley 'was asked to go to St. Paul's. The anthem was "Out of the deep have I called unto thee, O Lord".' Later that same day, at a prayer meeting in Aldersgate Street, 'I felt my heart strangely warmed. I felt I did trust in Christ, Christ alone …'[18] The twentieth-century historian Erik Routley has identified the anthem sung at St Paul's that day as the florid verse setting by William Croft.[19] There is a notable irony that it was the singing of a trained choir which led directly to John Wesley discovering a new style of churchmanship which rejected such elaboration. The ambiguity in the brothers' attitude to Anglicanism is there in their relationship with its music too.

Oddly, given the importance of the tradition, it's a little difficult to pin down exactly what a Wesleyan hymn is, or how many there are. Charles wrote at least 6,000 of them, or perhaps 9,000 if you include devotional poems. These were literary works as much as hymns – to be read or carried around in a pocket, the confident offspring of the Enlightenment concept of an educated, literate readership, able now to put away the childish things of Sternhold and Hopkins, with their short words and nursery imagery.

The brothers themselves were often a bit vague about what was to be sung, and to what. Some publications, like John's *Foundery Collection* of 1742, mentioned tunes. But these were existing melodies taken from elsewhere, not new ones. One of their innovations was the variety of complex metres they used (unlike, for example, Isaac Watts). In part, this was to allow the use of tunes from the Moravian tradition. Later, more sophisticated settings were made for the choirs at the charity hospitals, which, in a limited sense, became the 'choral foundations' of the Evangelical tradition. In the absence of a recommended melody, ordinary singers could, as usual, use any tune which matched the metre of the words. 'Hark, how all the welkin rings' (which we sing today as 'Hark, the Herald Angels Sing') might have been sung by Charles Wesley himself to the tune 'Easter Hymn' from one of the early country song-books (usually sung today to its original words, 'Jesus Christ is risen today'), complete with pealing 'Alleluias'. It works splendidly.

Occasionally, Charles purloined an existing tune by writing words which matched the rhyme and metre of an extant song. Compare, for example, Dryden's lyric for an air from *King Arthur*, one of Purcell's 'semi-operas', with the opening of a well-known hymn:

Fairest isle, all isles excelling,
Seat of pleasure and of love,
Venus here will choose her dwelling,
And forsake her Cyprian grove.

Love divine, all loves excelling
Joy of heaven, to earth come down,
Fix in us thy humble dwelling,
All thy faithful mercies crown.[20]

It is a very skilful bit of imitation. As such, Wesley's words work beautifully with Purcell's rapt, lilting tune. It's hardly suitable for congregational use, but it would still make a gorgeous little anthem for upper voices (*pace* Vincent Novello).

Where the authors did specify a tune, the ones that have stuck are often the strong, unfussy melodies of the country psalmodists ('Helmsley', 'Stockton') or those borrowed from the similarly minded Moravians ('Savannah'). Today, though, the best-loved hymns of Charles Wesley are mainly those sung to tunes added later, such as 'Blaenwern' for 'Love Divine, All Loves Excelling' and 'Aberystwyth' for 'Jesu! Lover of my Soul'. Best of all are those with music by Charles's grandson, Samuel Sebastian Wesley: 'O Love Divine, How Sweet Thou Art!' to the tune 'Cornwall', and 'O Thou who Camest from Above' to 'Hereford'. There is a reason for that (quite apart from a genetic sensitivity to what his grandfather was getting at): the intense 'inwardness' of these texts ('When shall I find my longing heart all taken up by thee? I thirst, I faint and die …') seems to demand more than an eighteenth-century psalm tune can give. It needs more muscle. This was a feature of Evangelical worship as much as of its hymns, and it came from the immersive, all-embracing approach known to its supporters and enemies alike as 'enthusiasm'.

As an artistic creed it had some notable supporters: 'Enthusiasm,' said William Blake, 'is the All in All.'[21] But to begin with, to their opponents at least, enthusiasts were little short of mad. Samuel Johnson's dictionary defined enthusiasm as 'a vain belief of private revelation, a vain confidence of divine favour or communication'.[22] David Hume watched appalled as precious reason was completely rejected, 'and the fanatic madman delivers himself over, blindly, and without reserve ... to inspiration from above'.[23] The Bishop of Exeter, after the deaths of the Wesley brothers, described how 'the mania of Methodism has seized the West of England', calling it 'wild and pernicious enthusiasm'.[24] Take out the insults, though, and surely Johnson and Hume have described exactly the kind of 'belief of private revelation' and 'confidence' of 'inspiration from above' which the Wesleyan hymn-singer was experiencing when he invited his Saviour to 'enter every trembling heart'.

Musically, the rejection of the style of Anglicanism also included rejecting its musical equipment. John Wesley liked music, but only if it suited his purpose. Polyphony and the 'fuging' style did not suit: he was 'greatly disgusted at the manner of singing' at a church in Wales in 1768, where 'according to the shocking custom of modern music, different persons sung different words at one and the same moment; an intolerable insult on common sense, and utterly incompatible with any devotion.'[25] Organs could provide spiritual uplift, as in this account of Easter Day 1751: 'I went to the new church, and found an uncommon blessing, at a time when I least expected it, namely, while the organist was playing a voluntary!'[26] But when he was in full flow, there could only be one leader of the band. This is an account of a visit to Lincolnshire thirty-five years later:

> The organ annoyed him. After the first verse he said 'Let that organ stop, and let the women take their parts'. 'They cannot sing without, sir', replied Mr Robinson. 'Then', he retorted, 'how did they do before they got one?'[27]

It's important to remember that neither Charles nor John Wesley left the Anglican Church (though John precipitated a fundamental breach by ordaining ministers on his own authority to carry on his work in America). Massed crowds at open-air Methodist meetings were exhorted to go to the parish church as well, which must have rather confounded the Woodfordes and the Eltons peering from the vicarage window in their frockcoats and cravats. But they gave the people something the established church was emphatically not giving them – and its musical expression was the hymn.

The Wesleys didn't invent massed congregational singing, far from it. But they built up a popular head of steam behind it which found expression in the multitudinous hymnbooks of the many branches of the Evangelical movement beside their own, such as the Congregationalists, and in the work of lyricists and composers like Philip Doddridge and Thomas Clark. Eventually, the artificial division which attempted to keep this kind of musical worship out of the established church was bound to break down. The old Calvinist idea that only the directly inspired word of God was permissible in service clung on, dug in by stubborn habit. As late as 1814, William Charles Dyer could write in the *Gentleman's Magazine* that 'whatsoever piety may be ascribed to Watts', and 'sweetly pleasing to my ear as almost all sacred music proves, I do not reconcile to the consistency and propriety of our Church duty the unauthorised introduction of the Morning and Evening hymn.' Dyer goes on:

> I shall expose myself to be ridiculed as an old-fashioned fellow, or strongly tinctured with prejudice for the quaint poetry of Sternhold and Hopkins, did I say anything in dispraise of the psalms and hymns and tunes composed for the different chapels in the Metropolis. But thus much, regard for truth, and aversion from the increase of innovation, will compel me to assert that, when the clergyman in the pulpit has mended in his own conceit the Lord's Prayer, and the clerk from his desk has delivered out his psalm, and directed you to turn to page 9 – they deal in smuggled goods. Neither the one nor the other have any sanction for so doing.
>
> The only version of the Psalms, allowed by authority to be sung in all churches, is that of Sternhold and Hopkins, or the new version by Tate and Brady. Consequently, every other hymn and psalm is spurious and illegitimate, and ought not to be used in our churches.[28]

Dyer was right about one thing – he certainly does sound like 'an old-fashioned fellow'. Sternhold and Hopkins was not far off 300 years old by this time. His tone suggests he knew he was fighting a losing battle. In 1819 the Sheffield clergyman Thomas Cotterill published his own *Selection of Psalms and Hymns for Public and Private Use*, with the assistance of his local newspaper editor, the hymn-writer and social reformer James Montgomery. A group of his parishioners brought an action against him in the Consistory Court, which eventually found that hymns had exactly the same status as metrical psalms, and could be sung in church before and after the liturgy. Cotterill's victory was assured when the Archbishop of York allowed his name to be inscribed on a revised version of the new book, widely distributed around the Archdiocese. Dyer had lost – the floodgates were open. The Church of England could follow its Evangelical brethren in the publication of hymnbooks drawing on the best of many different traditions, and did so with voluminous gusto. In one important respect, music brought the divided Methodists and Anglicans closer together again. Anglicanism is certainly the richer for it.

The Evangelical and Methodist approach to hymn-singing found some notable national incarnations. In America, the 'Great Awakening' movement, pioneered by the remarkable and peripatetic George Whitefield, created stirring hymns like 'Lord, I'm Coming Home' by William J. Kirkpatrick (who composed the tune 'Cradle Song', sung in the UK to 'Away in a Manger'), and eventually led to the Gospel style of Ira D. Sankey and the Evangelical movement of the twentieth century. Nonconformism in Wales also bore glorious musical fruit. Its principal poet was William Williams, a near-contemporary of John and Charles Wesley, who, like them, found his calling to the established church challenged by a conversion experience. Like the Wesleys, Williams published many volumes of hymns and led a hugely popular revivalist movement centred on 'fellowship meetings', or 'seiadau'. Like them, his best-known hymns are sung today to tunes written a century and more later, like 'Cwm Rhondda', composed in 1905 by John Hughes for Williams's poem 'Arglwydd, arwain trwy'r anialwch', and sung in England as 'Guide me, O Thou Great Redeemer'. Translation went the other way too, with hymns by Wesley, William Cowper and others being sung in Welsh. The division between 'church' and 'chapel' proved persistent in Wales. The rich sound of Welsh hymn-singing provides the soundtrack to the social and political history of an age just as much as to its churchmanship.

Hughes's tune borrows a noteworthy feature from a particular type of eighteenth-century hymn tune: the repetition of a word or short phrase, often to a rising sequence, usually in the penultimate line. This is distinct from the 'fuging' tune, where the words overlap, and can be an effective way of building towards the end of a verse, though in practice it often has little to do with the original intentions of either composer or author.

In the nineteenth century, the many branches of Nonconformism each brought something distinctive to their shared inheritance of hymn-singing. The hymnbooks of the Baptists, Unitarians, Congregationalists, Universalists, Pentecostalists and others can be read as a sort of giant Venn diagram, with many items shared in common and others unique to a particular book. America proved fruitful ground, giving us, for example, 'Nearer, my God, to Thee' and 'It Came upon the Midnight Clear', both Unitarian. There are some stirring new tunes, as well as much borrowing, as usual. Churches of this kind had no use for choirs.

Eighteenth-century hymn tunes can be classed under a number of headings. There are the tunes from country psalm and hymnbooks, often in three-time, tunes originally in the tenor (for example, 'Rockingham' or 'Oxford New'). There is also the more sophisticated type of tune involving repetition of words near the end of each verse ('Cranbrook', 'Helmsley', 'Adeste, fideles'). A variant of this type allowed the repeated words to be passed from one voice-part to another, like a very brief outburst of the 'fuging' style ('Joy to the World'). Then there are tunes borrowed from other Protestant churches around Europe ('Paderborn', 'Batty'). Another, distinct, type was written in two-part score, the treble line ornamented with grace-notes and trills, the bass figured, almost like a mini-aria. This type was for the treble-led sound of the charity-school hymn ('Invitation', 'Gopsal'). A tune like 'University' appears today with the original ornamental grace-notes incorporated into the melody as passing-note quavers (as, for example, in its very first phrase). As noted above, many eighteenth-century hymns are sung today to tunes added later ('St Ethelwald').

This brief look at the hymns of the period can be ended neatly by uniting two of the great names of eighteenth-century church music, Handel and Wesley (Charles, senior). There are several tunes in use today which bear the name Handel, including two of those listed above. One of them gets it right. 'Gopsal' is by Handel. 'Joy to the World' is not. It was published in 1836 by the American hymn-writer Lowell Mason, who called it 'Antioch' (for no apparent reason) and ascribed it to Handel, though it had already appeared in print more than once earlier in the decade. The Handel link is the suggestion that the tune is derived from the opening phrases of *Lift up your Heads* and *Comfort ye* from *Messiah*. It's a tenuous similarity at best, but if true it was no more than Handel often did himself. Other Handel tunes, most famously 'Maccabeus', are lifted from movements in oratorio or opera.

'Gopsal' is different. It was explicitly composed as a hymn tune, by Handel, to the words to which we sing it today, Charles Wesley's 'Rejoice, the Lord is King'. It is thus a rare instance of words and music staying together as their creators intended, even more precious because of who the creators were. The collaboration was discovered many decades later, in 1826, by Charles Wesley's son Samuel, who was trawling through the archives at the Fitzwilliam Museum in Cambridge. He discovered three tunes, written out in Handel's own hand-writing in the two-stave treble and bass format, and set out to publish 'these combined relics of a real poet and a great musician, hoping that what will probably appear to giddy thinkers, a mere furtuitous [*sic*] coincidence (but which I firmly believe to be the result of a much higher causality) will be ultimately effective of much good, by the union of what delights the ear with that which benefits the soul'.[29] Along with 'Gopsal' (or 'Handel's 148th', as it was also known), one of the other tunes has survived in use under the name 'Cannons'. The other, 'Desiring to Love', has not. The two survivors, of course, have suffered the indignity of being turned into nice, regular, stodgy Victorian hymns in four parts, the spotted dick and custard of the English

verse 1 (Old version) Have Mercy on us, Lord,
And grant to us Thy Grace;
To show to us do Thou accord
The Brightness of Thy Face.`

verse1 (New version) To bless Thy chosen Race,
In Mercy, Lord, incline:
And cause the Brightness of Thy Face
On all Thy Saints to shine``

Two approaches to hymn-singing in the eighteenth-century. William Tans'ur puts
his tune in the tenor, in the usual manner of the country singing teacher, then treats
it as a 'fuging' tune, to be sung between the verses. This version of 'The Spacious
Firmament on High' is from the privately printed hymnbook of one of the hugely
successful Charity Hospitals, 'the choral foundations of the noncomformist movement'.
The treble-dominated style, brief instrumental 'symphonies' and figured bass make this
more of a song than a hymn, miles away from the country style of Tans'ur and from
later ideas of hymns as stodgy Victorian things in four-part harmony.

PSALM XIX

The spa-cious Fir-ma-ment on High and all the blue_ E-the-real_ Sky and

spang-led Heav'ns a shin-ing__ frame their great O - ri - gi -

nal pro-claim

choral repertoire. This is not how they started. They are congregational songs, to be sung in unison, with an instrumental bass supported by a stylish organ realisation of the figures. Their original rhythms are much more interesting than most of the later bowdlerisations allow. 'Gopsal' has a pause at the end of line five: the little organ twiddle is there to pick up the tempo before the last phrase. The organ rounds off the last verse with a well-mannered little play-out as the ladies and gentlemen settle back into their box-pews and the charity children clatter onto their wooden benches in the gallery above. As with all music, we get so much more out of these intriguing 'relics' if we think about how its composers intended and expected them to sound.

Every town in southern England has a place where John Wesley preached. Sometimes it's a plain, elegant, meeting-house. More often it's a tree, or even a gravestone. This is where hymn-singing took root. Alongside the creation of a mass movement, the Wesley brothers created its repertoire. Charles Wesley is still the second most represented lyricist in the *New English Hymnal* (after John Mason Neale, who will become crucially important in the next chapter). Quite apart from their own work, they and their families – both spiritual and biological – set the style and standard for Anglican hymn-writing from that day to this. The few hymn tunes which have successfully gained a place in the repertoire in the last hundred years or so, such as 'Love Unknown', 'Down Ampney', 'Wolvercote', 'Abbot's Leigh' and 'Coe Fen', are, essentially, in the style of S. S. Wesley. A better one has yet to be found.

PROFESSIONAL COMPOSERS, MEANWHILE, CONTINUED to struggle to find a way to renew the music of the church. Jonathan Battishill had the talent, but not the luck. An accomplished singer and organist, he largely turned away from music for the pleasure garden and the pantomime in favour of choral music after about 1764, when he was in his mid-twenties. But personal problems, including alcoholism, depression and the failure of his marriage, prevented his preferment and stopped him getting the job of Organist of St Paul's in 1796. His best music shows a fiery individuality which could certainly have put a bit of grit in the musical oyster. *Call to Remembrance* is a fine, passionate work in seven parts, and *O Lord, Look down from Heaven* contains one of the best moments in late eighteenth-century church music, the anguished cry 'the sounding of Thy bowels' and the extraordinary, hushed, floating chromaticism of the ending: 'are they restrained?' Choir directors should certainly resist the prudish habit of bowdlerising the word 'bowels' in favour of 'heart'. Battishill died in 1801, a reclusive bookworm, beaten and bashed. He wasn't the only one. Puritans who thought that replacing rigid self-discipline with something more permissive and relativist would inevitably lead to unhappiness might have believed they were being proved right.

At least Battishill tried. Other leading composers paid scant attention to the church. Charles Avison wrote a lengthy and elegantly argued account of the state of music in society in 1752, reprinted several times thereafter. A shortish passage about church music was largely negative about its possibilities, and he made familiar complaints about organists 'imitating common songs or airs', and about 'the present method of singing the common psalm-tunes in the parochial service, which are everywhere sung without the least regard to time or measure, by drawling out every note to an unlimited length.' He preferred the European way of doing things, with psalms sung in a nice regular metre and was an enthusiastic Europhile in choral music too. He praised early efforts by men like Dean Aldrich to introduce the music of Palestrina (whom Avison consistently calls 'Palestina'), and believed Purcell could have been quite good if he'd known more Italian music. 'If it should be asked,' continues Avison in full rhetorical flow, 'who are the proper people, to begin a reform of our church-music? It may be answered, the organists of our cathedrals, who are, or ought to be, our *Maestri di Capella*, and by whom, under the influence and protection of their deans, much might be done to the advancement of their choirs.'[30] This is strikingly similar in tone to the complaints of another northern-based church organist, S. S. Wesley, eighty years later.

Like charity, Avison could have begun at home. He was Organist of St Nicholas's, the principal parish church (and now the cathedral) of the elegant Georgian city of Newcastle-upon-Tyne, for thirty-four years until his death in 1770. He wrote just one anthem for the choir there. It's a good piece, certainly, but hardly approaches his own ideal of creating an English version of the church music of Gregorio Allegri and Antonio Lotti. His published works showed a far greater interest in concertos and sonatas for his fashionable concert series in the elegant, white-walled spaces of the Assembly Rooms and Gibside chapel, music designed, as he put it, to 'raise the sociable and happy passions' – and, not incidentally, to make him a great deal of money.

Another working church musician who treated the top jobs in church music very much as the second string to his bow was Samuel Arnold. Arnold was Organist of the Chapel Royal (not inappropriately, as he was probably the illegitimate son of Princess Amelia, George II's second daughter and Handel's pupil), and Westminster Abbey. But he wrote hardly any church music. What he did write is decent enough – his setting of the canticles in A major deserves an outing when there isn't anything more interesting to hand. But it's the smallness of ambition that is striking. These 'short' services are shorter, and much less interesting, than those of Boyce, Purcell, Gibbons, Byrd and even his admired Tallis. Arnold's main contribution was a published collection of choral pieces in score, issued in 1790 under the title *Cathedral Music* and intended as a supplement to Greene and Boyce's earlier collection of the same name. Thomas Attwood Walmisley completed the triptych with another volume, also called *Cathedral Music*, published after his death in 1856 by his father, Thomas Forbes Walmisley, who outlived him by a few months. These are the books which weighed down the choir stalls of our cathedrals in the century after 1750, a mixture of old music pretending it sounded new, and new music trying to sound old.

In many ways, the history of how music is written down runs alongside what the music was like and who it was for: handsome, handwritten medieval part books for rich choirs with their own scribes; Reformation printed music, still in single parts, for devout, well-off householders; psalm books and broadside sheets with nice pictures, for anyone with a penny to spare; printed collections of Anglican church music, still in individual part books and sold from an address in Fleet Street or Paul's Yard, like John Barnard's *First Book of Selected Church Music* in 1641; country psalm books in the eighteenth century, privately printed to be hawked around by their authors; large manuscript collections of cathedral music, assembled by the men who made them, like Thomas Tudway and John Gostling; early publications of choir music in 'foul score', starting with William Croft in the 1720s; big collections, sold by subscription, by Greene, Boyce, Arnold and Walmisley; then, in the nineteenth century, publishing as we know it today, in cheap editions of single pieces, issued by men some of whose names still feature in the trade: Novello, Chappell, Ewer and Clementi.

Arnold put most of his energies into the lucrative musical marketplace of the theatre and the pleasure garden. Church music was a boring and badly paid duty. But he wasn't the worst offender. William Hawes was Organist of the Chapel Royal (where he had himself been a chorister) from 1817. The choirboys were ill-treated and badly educated, getting just three hours instruction each week from a visiting schoolmaster. Their musical skills were far more valuable to Hawes as soloists in the oratorio and concert circuit, where he hawked them around for handsome fees (for himself, naturally).

Music in provincial cathedral towns had an air of stasis about it too: there was plenty going on, but it was not leading anywhere. The Camidge family of York provide a working example. They supplied York Minster with organists for 103 years from 1756 to 1859, as well as organists and choirmasters to other churches in the area. They led the large-scale gatherings of local choirs and bands who would get together to sing oratorios on notable festive occasions. They were composers, but mostly of 'Concertos for the Organ or grand Piano Forte' and 'Useful preludes' for 'Piano-Forte or Harp with an accompaniment for violin or flute' rather than anything new for their own minster choir. Matthew Camidge stated unambiguously that his music was written in direct imitation of the style of Handel and Corelli – he didn't even try to incorporate anything more forward-looking. His published church music is limited to psalm-chants, hymn tunes, some functional service music and books of instruction, of which only a chant or two has survived in use. John Camidge was Organist of the Minster for forty-seven years, his son Matthew for forty-three. Later tradition held that this Matthew only gave up when he became too fat to get up the organ-loft stairs. His son, also John, later suffered a stroke while at the organ bench.

It's open to debate which is the finest period of English sacred choral music. The seventy-five years or so after the death of Handel in 1759 must have a good claim to being the worst. There was a sense of decay, of neglect, in all aspects of cathedral music-making at this time: in the training and treatment of choristers, in the failure to compete with fashionable musical attractions elsewhere, in pay, attendance, uninterested and absentee clergy, and, above all, in the lack of a sense of innovation in musical style. To this point, English church music had always successfully managed to absorb and incorporate musical influences from abroad and from without: for example the Italian madrigal into the full anthems of Gibbons and Weelkes, the French style in the anthems of Purcell and Blow, Italian opera and the manner of Corelli in the church music of Handel. But then it stopped. There was no equivalent of the Viennese church style of Haydn and Mozart in

English music, still less of the brooding, Romantic motets of Bruckner and Brahms; and certainly nothing to sit alongside the great, concerted mass and requiem settings of Beethoven, Berlioz and Verdi. England had none of this.

Church music was always more likely to be killed off by being ignored rather than by being attacked. And yet, somehow, it never quite happened. This absence of activity created a vacuum which, in turn, created a pressure to fill it. The English just liked their singing too much to let it die.

As the eighteenth century minuetted decorously towards the nineteenth, a small number of highly talented and often rather individualistic characters tried, and usually failed, to keep the flag flying. This was an age which liked its geniuses young.

Most, alas, did not achieve the musical maturity hinted at by their youthful promise. Thomas Linley composed just one piece of church music, *Let God Arise* for the Worcester Festival of 1773, before his tragic death at the age of just 22 (in a boating accident, like Robert Parsons two hundred years before).

William Crotch made his first concert tour in 1779 when he was just three years old, an early victim of a pushy mother, the Mrs Worthington of English church music. Where Purcell's infant gifts had found fertile ground in which to grow, Crotch's did not. Church music played a part in his long working life: he was Organist of Christ Church, Oxford, by the time he was sixteen. He made one of the first systematic studies of earlier church music, and published editions of music by Tallis which proved influential in the revival of interest in the period later in the century. But the problem was that this study convinced him that musical style had peaked in about 1650. Church music should belong to the category he called 'sublime', not 'beautiful' or 'ornamental'. Reviewing S. S. Wesley's anthem *The Wilderness* in 1833, Professor Crotch opined that 'the introduction of novelty, variety, contrast, expression, originality, etc, is the very cause of the decay so long apparent in our church music'.[31] As a result, his own church music is charming certainly, but empty. 'And must we, then, have no new church music?' he asked himself rhetorically in a series of *Lectures on*

Music published in 1831, then answered his own question: 'Yes, but no new style.'[32] Crotch deliberately set out not to refresh the streams of living water of his inheritance – and he succeeded. It's sad to think what this most prodigiously gifted of men might have achieved under other circumstances.

Another whose infant gifts rather ran into the sand was a near-contemporary and colleague of Crotch, Samuel Wesley, son of Charles Wesley, senior. The two were once pitted against each other in public, when Wesley was about fourteen and Crotch about five. 'Crotch was not in a good humour,' recorded Daines Barrington, a lawyer and writer, and when the older boy was asked to play to cheer him up, 'Sam constantly declined', saying that 'he thought it would look like wishing to shine at little Crotch's expense.'[33] In adult life the two composers championed the music of Bach. Like Crotch, Wesley's much-admired gifts as a composer never quite found a convincing stylistic manifest-ation. In 1784, rather surprisingly, he became a Catholic (though he later denied it, unconvincingly), to the great dismay of his elderly uncle, John, who wrote him a long and anguished letter: 'O Sammy, you are out of your way! You are out of God's way!'[34] But it wasn't Catholic teaching which attracted him: 'If the Roman doctrines were like the Roman music we should have heaven on earth,'[35] he wrote later.

His Latin church music is his best. *In exitu Israel* is a big-boned exercise in unaccompanied counterpoint, brandishing its plainsong opening like an anti-Anglican flag. *Exultate Deo* borrows the ancient habit of treating this text as a triple-time dance. But perhaps the best of these pieces is the Purcellian *Omnia Vanitas*. All the Latin works show his devotion to Bach, and his inability to ape his idol's mastery of large-scale forms: Samuel Wesley's fugues are too long and get thor-oughly stuck in the home key. His later English music shows rather less engagement. In 1827 he set a text by his father, Charles (a piece later anthologised by his son, Samuel Sebastian). The words are a char-acteristic biblical paraphrase, and make an odd choice for a slightly saccharine treble solo:

Might I in thy sight appear
As the publican distrest;

Stand, not daring to draw near;
Smite on my unworthy breast,
Groan, the sinner's only plea:
'God, be merciful to me'.

Samuel Wesley was an unpredictable character, given to outbursts
of temper and drunkenness. Uncomfortable in his church, his marriage
and his own skin, he never found that equilibrium which is necessary for a creative mind to function properly. There was a lot of this
in the late eighteenth and early nineteenth centuries. Enlightenment
certainly had its downsides.

Samuel's elder brother, Charles junior, was one of the last of the generation to have studied with William Boyce, and another whose surviving church music is modest in reach and range, despite his having played
in public at possibly an even earlier age than young Sammy ('the seeds
of harmony did not spring up in him [Samuel] quite so early as in his
brother; for he was three years old before he aimed at a tune,'[36] wrote their
amused but rather exasperated father, Charles senior, who was frankly
a bit out of his depth trying to educate those two). Although well liked
in musical and royal circles, his attempts to get a job met with repeated
disappointment, partly because of the divisive associations of his family
name: 'we do not want any Wesleys here',[37] commented the authorities
at St Paul's, and Charles felt obliged to withdraw an application for the
post of Organist of the Chapel Royal because of his father's objections
(or at least half-withdraw: he said he would accept it if it were offered
him, which it wasn't).[38] Amiable, indolent, unambitious and unfulfilled,
Charles Wesley junior was another whose great abilities found no sturdy
oak against which to grow in the fractured, feeble, fissiparous musical
and ecclesiastical climate of his times.

Like their friend Crotch, the younger Wesley brothers remained
musically incomplete. Sadly, there is some evidence that they knew
it. In 1837, the seventy-one-year-old Samuel Wesley met the twenty-
eight-year-old Felix Mendelssohn. Mendelssohn courteously compli-
mented the older man on his playing; 'You should have heard me forty
years ago,' replied Wesley.[39]

The youthful talents of the young brothers led to frequent

comparisons with a celebrated near-contemporary, a bright-eyed young visitor from Austria whose feet couldn't reach the pedals. Wolfgang Amadeus Mozart wrote one piece of English church music. It was during his visit to London in 1765, at the age of nine, and intended, rather oddly, for a performance at the British Museum. It's not very good. Leaving aside his tender years, this was his first piece of vocal music, his first and only attempt to set the English language, and was ordered by his father as a harmony and counterpoint exercise. But its relative lack of sophistication reminds us that Mozart achieved so much in teenage years at least in part because he was very well taught, rigidly disciplined, and because he had plenty of opportunities to hear and play new music, including his own. His English contemporaries did not enjoy similar advantages. The fact that both Oxford and Cambridge Universities, for example, appointed teenagers as their professors and chief organists (sometimes the same person, sometimes while still an undergraduate) says as much about the quality of the music going on around them as it does about the individuals concerned, however precocious. Achieving something distinctive in such circumstances required a certain amount of pig-headedness as well as talent. It was left to the last of the musical Wesleys to provide both.

Back in Vienna, Mozart found himself acting as tutor to another Englishman whose name forms part of the slender chain which kept English church music going in the years around the turn of the nineteenth century, Thomas Attwood. Attwood and Mozart appear to have become fond of each other, though the teacher's markings in the pupil's exercises don't always reflect this: 'How can you think of writing this here?': 'Attwood, you are an ass!'[40] These workbooks offer a fascinating insight into what a great genius thought a composer needed to know. It's good, old-fashioned stuff, the sort of thing students have always learned, and still do. Through Attwood's workbooks, lavishly marked and corrected by the master, we can take a lengthy and thorough course in harmony and counterpoint lessons with Mozart.

Like the singers who worked with both Purcell and Handel, Attwood secured his place in music history partly because he shook hands across the ages with two great figures from different eras of musical time: Mozart and Mendelssohn. He knew everybody else too, from his own teacher James Nares, born in 1715, to his pupil John Goss, who died in 1880. If this makes him seem something of a transitional figure, then that may not be entirely unfair.

Attwood was born in 1765. At the age of nine he became a chorister at the Chapel Royal, and in 1796, following his European study tour, he was appointed 'composer' there. In the same year he became Organist of St Paul's Cathedral. He was well connected at court (though his preferment was interrupted by the Hanoverian habit of sons cordially loathing their fathers), and wrote music for the coronation of George IV in 1821 and his brother, William IV in 1831. He was working on a piece for a third, Queen Victoria's, when he died in 1838. Another of his appointments gives us an insight into a vanished remnant of earlier monarchs' penchant for travelling around the country and taking their church music with them: in 1821 he became Organist of the Chapel Royal in Brighton, a plain little building tucked around the corner from the frothy domes and raffish arcades of the Pavilion, marked today with a modest plaque.

Several of Attwood's anthems remain in the repertoire: they are short, simple, tuneful, well crafted, often with a treble solo repeated by the choir in a strophic pattern. The full anthem, *O God, who by the Leading of a Star*, shows a little more ambition, including a nicely paced 'Amen', very much in the Gibbons manner. An organ fugue, dedicated 'to my friend Felix Mendelssohn', clearly relishes the capabilities of new, bigger instruments, and makes a decent enough stab at the Bachian ideal. But it's this very archaism which reveals once again that English church music at this period was pretty small beer, certainly compared with the achievements of some of the people Attwood knew. One of these provides an interesting parallel with music-making a century before. In the second quarter of the eighteenth century, musical life was dominated by a German who lived in England and wrote not very much church music, George Frideric Handel. In the second quarter of the nineteenth century, musical life was dominated by a German who didn't live in England and wrote almost no English church music at all, Felix Mendelssohn. In both cases, their significance is as much about the pervasive influence of their style on everybody else as it is about their own work.

The sharp-eyed will already be reaching for their Blackberrys to query the statement that Mendelssohn wrote no English church music. There is much Mendelssohn in the Anglican repertoire, surely? Of course there is, but the only pieces specifically fashioned for Anglican choral worship, the late settings of the morning and evening canticles, are not often found there and are not his best pieces (perhaps because they were written at the behest of publisher rather than performer). Many of the pieces regularly sung today as anthems are choruses taken from concert works, like *I Waited for the Lord* from the *Hymn of Praise* or *How Lovely are the Messengers* from the oratorio *St Paul*. Mendelssohn wrote a lot of anthems and liturgical music for choirs in his native Germany, some of which have made their way into use in England, either in their original language or in translation (*Judge me, O God*), where the two versions match syllable for syllable (*Richte mich, Gott*. Haydn did something similar in his *The Creation/ Die Schöpfung*).

Mendelssohn's best-known anthem worked the other way around: the English words *Hear my Prayer* came first, and the metrically matching German was added later. This piece deserves its fame. It is beautifully put together, perfectly balanced between the restrained classicism of the final G major paragraph (the celebrated, lilting 'O, for the wings of a dove'), and the outbursts of nascent Romanticism, quickly contained, at 'Lord, hear my cry', and the following 'with horror overwhelmed' (is this a conscious echo of another G minor choral lament, the final chorus *With Drooping Wings* from Purcell's *Dido and Aeneas*? The music is strikingly similar for a bar or two). Significantly, it was written not for a church or cathedral choir but for a concert series at Crosby Hall, 'a renovated Gothic Structure which was once the palace of Richard the Third',[41] according to William Bartholomew, who wrote the words. The most interesting developments were thus taking place outside the choir stalls. Church music and sacred singing would contribute further to this kind of civic gathering, such a notable feature of so many aspects of English nineteenth-century life.

Two other offcuts of Mendelssohn are often heard in church. Neither is his fault. The tune we sing to 'Hark, the Herald Angels Sing' comes from a cantata in honour of the printer Johannes Gutenberg. The March from the incidental music to *A Midsummer Night's Dream* was first played on the organ at an English wedding (in Tiverton) in 1847, and popularised eleven years later at one of the many occasions when one of Queen Victoria's children married the pointy-bearded princeling of Somewhere-in-Germany. *Hear my Prayer* is one of the finest anthems in the choral repertoire. Ironically, it was that very element of tuneful restraint which led to Mendelssohn being regarded as something of a lightweight for many years after his death. This is certainly unfair. Part of the problem was that his immense popularity meant that a great deal of later music by other, lesser composers sounds like a bad imitation. William Knyvett, anyone? The reputation of the whole style – the original as well as copies – becomes tarnished and diluted by association. Mendelssohn was one of those who, like Karl Marx and Jesus Christ, get the blame for what others have done in their name.

Mendelssohn's influence over the progress of church music in England owed as much to his personal example as performer and teacher as to his compositions. He visited many times, often playing the organ at St Paul's as a guest of his good friend 'dear old Attwood'.[42] He virtually invented the music of Bach for the English and pioneered the massed choral festival movement. He befriended and worked with English composers like William Sterndale Bennett and Cipriani Potter, neither of whom paid much attention to church music – and one of his most notable protégés was his compatriot, Prince Albert. Albert set the pattern for those admirable Victorians who thought they could, and should, do everything. He was keenly interested in all sorts of intellectual and artistic ideas, including music. As Chancellor of Cambridge University he personally introduced new subjects like chemistry, causing much fluttering of gowns among the comfortably cloistered classicists and divines. He installed a house organ of his own design in Buckingham Palace, and rescued another from the organ room at Brighton Pavilion, enlarging it for use in the Buckingham Palace ballroom, where it still stands, recently beautifully restored.

Mendelssohn visited Albert and Victoria several times, including an occasion in 1842, recalled in a letter to his mother:

> I begged the Prince to begin playing me something, so that I could boast of it in Germany. He played a chorale by heart, with the pedals – and so charmingly, precisely and accurately that it would have done credit to a professional ... Meanwhile the Queen, who had finished what she was doing, came and joined him, listening with pleasure. Then it was my turn, and I began with the chorus from St. Paul, 'How lovely are the messengers.' Before I had come to the end of the first verse they both began singing the chorus, and Prince Albert managed the stops so cleverly for me ... that I was quite enchanted.[43]

Albert was also a composer. He certainly did not possess a strong enough musical personality to overcome the prevailing tendency to write bad Mendelssohn, but he did it quite well. His Te Deum and Jubilate contain some quite good bad Mendelssohn. In any event, bad Mendelssohn was probably better than bad Spohr, the favoured musical medium of some other English composers of the time. There was no English Mendelssohn. There could have been. There were several well-qualified candidates. But it was a discouraging age.

FOR ENGLISH CHURCH MUSIC, the ninety years or so between the death of Handel and the death of Mendelssohn belong to the Methodists with their hymns, and to the clerks and clarinettists of Hardy's Mellstock and George Eliot's Raveloe in *Silas Marner* with their key-bugles, their 'fuging' tunes, and their choirboys 'rattling up the old wooden stairs of the gallery like a regiment of cavalry'.[44] Writing in 1979, Nicholas Temperley lamented that 'the music of English country parish churches' at this period had yet to be 'thoroughly explored and revived'.[45] That process is now well underway. West Gallery associations and choirs hold singing festivals and make recordings. Thomas Hardy, who was 'inclined to regret the displacement of these ecclesiastical bandsmen by an isolated organist (often at first a barrel-organist) or harmonium player', would surely have been pleased. So would Old

William and his colleagues, sitting in the pub, reminding themselves of the good old days:

> 'Your brass-man is a rafting dog – well and good; your reed-man is a dab at stirring ye – well and good; your drum-man is a rare bowel-shaker – good again. But I don't care who hears me say it, nothing will spak to your heart wi' the sweetness o' the man of strings! ... And harmonions,' William continued in a louder voice, and getting excited by these signs of approval, 'harmonions and barrel-organs' ('Ah!' and groans from Spinks) 'be miserable – what shall I call 'em? – miserable –'
>
> 'Sinners,' suggested Jimmy, who made large strides like the men, and did not lag behind like the other little boys.
>
> 'Miserable dumbledores!'
>
> 'Right, William, and so they be – miserable dumbledores!' said the choir with unanimity.[46]

Fashionable society, meanwhile, looked the other way.

Mendelssohn was once playing Bach at St Paul's Cathedral. Halfway through the piece, the organ wheezed to a stop. The young man pumping the organ bellows wasn't used to music of this length and complexity: bored, baffled and bewildered by Bach, he had given up and gone home.[47] England expected little from its church music at this period. And it got it.

12

Renewal, 1837–1901

The rich man in his castle
The poor man at his gate
God made them high or lowly
And ordered their estate
    Mrs C. F. Alexander, 'All Things Bright and Beautiful'

ON A VISIT TO LONDON in the 1880s, the composer Antonín
Dvořák was taken to St Paul's Cathedral for evensong. The choir began
chanting the psalms. Dvořák listened politely for a few verses, then
turned to his companion and asked 'why do they keep singing that
wretched little tune over and over again?'[1]

To answer that question we need to understand where church music
had got to by that stage, and to get to know a new generation of choristers, composers, clergy, congregations, organists, publishers, politicians
and public, unpicking their often prickly relationships and finding a way
through the complex interweaving of intellectual and social currents of
the period. Paramount among these was the Oxford Movement. It did
not begin the process of musical reform, nor can it claim credit for all of
its manifestations. But it articulated a trend which made those reforms

necessary and created the conditions in which they could be realised, as well, of course, as the inevitable reaction against them.

All of this has some striking echoes of the sixteenth century. People believed passionately in their particular party, and said so. An Oxford college chaplain wrote a book called *The Popery of Oxford confronted, disavowed and repudiated* in 1837: 'I felt an indescribable horror stealing over me, as I carried my eye towards the eastern wall of the building [J. H. Newman's church at Littlemore, just outside the city], and beheld a plain naked cross, either of stone or a good imitation of it, rising up and projecting out of the wall, from the centre of the table of communion.'[2] This was Pope-bashing by pamphlet, seventeenth-century style. In the 1850s, 'Popish' choral services at a church in London led to riots in the streets. The vicar of St Alban's, Holborn, was prosecuted for kneeling, facing east, and using candles and incense during communion. A few clergymen even went to prison. Disagreements about ritualism in the 1850s recalled the Vestarian controversy of the 1560s.

But it would be a mistake to regard opposition to the forces of Catholicism as a sort of illiberal conservative Protestantism. At the time it was really a sort of Protestantism understood to be aligned with English liberty and liberal politics. We can't understand 'papal aggression' in 1850 for example without reference to Cardinal Wiseman's extraordinary pastoral letter announcing his new jurisdiction in England, or the fact that the Pope had recently been restored following the suppression of the Roman republic and backed by the French bayonets of Napoleon III. The Pope was widely seen as a very reactionary figure after 1848 (he would of course go on to proclaim that Catholicism was incompatible with modern thought including 'democracy'). So Catholicism was seen as opposed to British liberalism and British liberties (in a remarkably similar way to how modern secularists regard it), and as a fifth column in the English church trying to draw it back towards the Roman faith, which aroused feelings very similar to those today about entryism by Islamic 'fundamentalists' into British mosques, schools and universities.[3]

Eventually, as in the sixteenth century, opposing musical forces settled down into something approaching a compromise, to meet the needs of a growing population, fed by enterprising publishers keen to exploit a rapidly expanding market, and serving new social and economic conditions which changed beyond recognition during the long reign of an influential and supportive monarch. If the Elizabethans invented sung evensong in the first place, the Victorians introduced evensong as we know it today – a kind of emotionally rich theatrical spectacle.

In the same way, the Victorians gave us our modern idea of hymn-singing. It was at last deemed acceptable by the established church to sing words and music from other Christian traditions, and classically educated hymnologists like John Mason Neale burrowed away in libraries and archives, editing and translating everything they could get their hands on. They came up with the idea of printing words and tunes together, the music on two staves, in 'short' score, equally serviceable for choir, congregation and organist. The market proved to be huge. There was a deluge of new hymnbooks and a torrent of new hymns, on all sorts of subjects and for all sorts of uses, including many of the best and most enduring of all.

Musically, the principal difference with three centuries before was that while the Reformation had rejected the music of the past, chorally inclined Victorian church musicians celebrated and embraced it, almost to the exclusion of all else. This blind infatuation with the past had a rather unfortunate effect on new writing for choirs: composers either didn't do it, or did it in a self-consciously archaic manner. The kindly but deadening spirit of William Crotch, benignly forbidding any kind of innovation or invention from the distant heights of his professorial chair at Oxford, lay across the composer's desk like the wings of a crow. At the same time, if any hint of popular style dared show its face in church, whether from folk-song, opera, the ballroom or the music-hall, it was firmly shown the door. No English composer has ever had a more natural gift for raising the spirits than Arthur Sullivan – but you wouldn't guess it from his church music.

Uniquely, the musical impetus in the Victorian period came from the parish. By its end there were probably more choirs, more organs, and more people singing in the pews than at any time before or since.

The ambitious choir, on the other hand, would have to wait until the end of the era to get any really distinctive new music, and the advent of composers with a musical personality strong enough to force English sacred choral music to look forwards instead of back, and out instead of in, towards Europe and Brahms. Perhaps Thomas Helmore, the most important musical reformer of the century, was right when, at the very end of his life, he mildly admonished himself and his colleagues for 'over-dosing the ancient'.[4]

JOHN HENRY NEWMAN DATED the start of the Oxford Movement to John Keble's Assize sermon in 1833. Its aims were set out in a series of *Tracts for the Times*, giving the wider movement the name 'Tractarians'. Calling it a 'movement' and giving it a local habitation and a name probably makes it sound more cohesive than it appeared at the time. Not all its sympathisers would have described themselves as 'Tractarians', and not all those who did shared all of its aims and beliefs. Mostly these centred on ritual, tradition, 'Catholicity', and a direct connection with the ancient church.

The movement's musical movers and shakers began by identifying the abuses and failings they wanted to change. 'How different', said the hymn-writer C. H. Steggall in 1848, '[are things today] from the soul-stirring meetings of the early Christians at which, St Jerome tells us, the sound of their oft-repeated "Amen" was like a peal of thunder.'[5] Congregations would do better to stand in silence than listen to 'the screaming of a few ill-trained children'. John Hullah wanted parishes to get rid of their 'meretricious music and self-contemplative performers'.[6] Robert Druitt echoed many others in believing that 'the surest method of all, to extinguish anything like singing, is to set up a grinding organ'.[7] At St Paul's Cathedral, 'the choirmen used to straggle in with the procession, and sometimes led their children by the hand' (which is rather sweet, but probably not conducive to high musical standards). On another occasion, 'when the Hallelujah Chorus was to be sung, a message was sent up to Sir John Goss, the organist, that there was only one tenor and one bass. "Do your best", he replied, "and I will do the rest with the organ".'[8] Another cathedral organist 'was induced to stuff his compositions with treble verses', because 'it was too often his fate to take the organ when no vicars were present'.[9]

Cathedral choirs had little or no rehearsal, and there was no way of knowing how many adult singers would turn up until the service began. 'Till I heard the choir at Gloucester,' remarked John Jebb, caustically, 'I imagined that the acme of irreverent and careless chanting was to be found at Lincoln.'[10] Another clergyman, Walter Hook, referred the matter back to doctrine: 'it is of the essence of Protestantism, to refer everything to self; it is of the essence of Catholicism to refer everything to God ... A Protestant may hate Choral Service, though, if he likes music, he may commit the sin of going to church unworthily to hear the anthem; a Catholic, though he knows nothing of music, will go far to attend regularly the choral service, because it accords with his feeling of performing a service. During the last century the mind of England became thoroughly Protestantised, therefore choral service fell into disuse; it is now becoming again Catholicised, and choral service is coming in.'[11]

These protests came from men who made it their business to do something about it.

Hook and Jebb worked together at Leeds parish church and some of the inconsistencies in the progress of musical ideas can be discerned in what they did there. For a start, the robed choir was not their innovation. There had been one at Leeds as far back as 1818, though it was disbanded fifteen years later for financial reasons. When Hook arrived as vicar in Leeds in 1837 he had no intention of starting it up again. He was no Tractarian, nor a musician, and in any case the Tractarian ideal was good congregational, rather than choral, music. Hook found that his new church was too small and in bad repair. His typically Victorian solution was to build a new one. A group of wealthy parishioners thought that the new church, with its chancel and choir-stalls, deserved the daily decoration of choral services sung by a surpliced choir. Hook's innate sense of the dignity of worship led him to agree. He sought liturgical advice from John Jebb, an Irish priest sympathetic to the ritualist approach. To preside over his music he turned first to James Hill, then, from 1841, to Samuel Sebastian Wesley. But, like everything else associated with S. S. Wesley, this project had a touch of the maverick about it. Establishing cathedral-type music in a provincial parish church was certainly not what either the Tractarians or their opponents were about. Attempts to imitate it elsewhere were largely unsuccessful.

Musically, the Oxford Movement was very much a London movement. Its ideals were tried out by like-minded clergy and musicians in the large, often new, churches of fashionable inner London parishes: Benjamin Webb and Joseph Barnby at St Andrew's, Wells Street (where a mass by Gounod was performed with a harp); Frederick Oakeley at Margaret Street chapel, lavishly rebuilt in 1850 as All Saints', Margaret Street; Thomas Helmore and John Hullah at St Mark's, Chelsea; W. J. E. Bennett at St Paul's, Knightsbridge; then by Sir Frederick Arthur Gore Ouseley at St Barnabas's, Pimlico – all big churches set within their own mini-monasteries, complete with cloisters, colleges and choir schools. The most important of these was St Mark's. Here, Thomas Helmore set about reinventing church music. Charles Dickens described his efforts in the magazine *Household Words* in 1850:

> First, St. Mark's College, Chelsea; in which there are always sixty students, who remain there three years *All* learn to sing, and the majority to write in four-part harmony, before they leave. They have a daily choral service, in which they sing (without accompaniment) the services of Tallis, Gibbons, and other (chiefly old) English masters, and the motets and hymns of the old Italian and Flemish schools … Attached to the College is a boys' school, where the boys (upwards of 200) are taught to sing by the students.[12]

The choral diet described by Dickens is the purest 'Oxford'. None of it came easy: it was achieved 'after very extraordinary and long-continued exertions',[13] as the Principal put it. This was very much the point. These young men were being trained to go out into all lands and revitalise parochial choirs in the image of St Mark's, armed with John Hullah's thoroughly practical training in the lost art of sight-singing – and it worked.

At St Barnabas's, Pimlico, in another sorry echo of the Reformation, church music came face to face with mob violence. Musical reform, emerging tentatively from the chrysalis of St Mark's and just learning to spread its wings, could have been squashed flat. The occasion was the week-long dedication festival of the new church in 1850. Many familiar names were there: Bennett as Vicar, Ouseley as curate, Helmore in a visiting capacity as Precentor and musical maître d'. Preachers included Robert Wilberforce, Henry Edward Manning, John Keble, John Mason Neale and Edward Bouverie Pusey. The large choir, augmented by choristers from a number of leading churches, sang plenty of early music, including Lassus and Palestrina in translation, plainsong psalms with organ accompaniments by Helmore, and a tiny sprinkling of new pieces in the approved style, including Ouseley's setting of the canticles in A major. A fascinating and dangerous novelty was the daily choral communion, sung to John Marbeck's setting of 1550. Perhaps most remarkably of all, the congregation sang a plainsong hymn, 'Coelestis Urbs Jerusalem', in English, every day for the entire week until the performance was 'imposing and inspiriting in the highest degree',[14] as the magazine *Parish Choir* put it.

This was the year the Roman Catholic hierarchy was re-established in England. Fear and hatred of Rome, always bubbling away somewhere inside the English consciousness, now sputtered to the surface once more. Lord John Russell, the Prime Minister, caught the mood of public nervousness, almost panic, in an open letter accusing certain clergy of 'leading their flocks, "step by step, to the very edge of the precipice"', and calling the Pope 'a foreign prince of no great power' when 'compared to the danger within the gate from the unworthy sons of the Church of England herself'.[15] The patriotic poor of Pimlico needed no further prompting. A week after Russell's letter was published, an ugly mob began besieging the services at St Barnabas's. On Sunday morning, 8 December, they battered their way in and occupied the church. Russell joined Oliver Cromwell and Henry VIII in the nasty little gang of political leaders who have succeeded in stopping choral worship by force. W. J. E. Bennett was sacked by his bishop. The choir of St Barnabas's was disbanded, its choir school closed. Ouseley, a sensitive, aristocratic aesthete, fled to Europe to recover his nerves.

Not for the first time, a peaceful revolution in church music had met violent resistance. Church music didn't cause the violence, but it was part of the movement that did, and it was there when it happened.

But, also not for the first time, music found a way through. Instead of allowing his carefully (and expensively) trained choirboys to go back to roaming the streets of Pimlico, Ouseley arranged for them to carry on their training at a house in Langley Marish, near Slough, under the direction of a senior boy and a fellow curate, Henry Fyffe. Ouseley, meanwhile, travelled extensively through Europe, playing the best organs, listening to the best choirs (which reduced his opinion of English cathedral choirboys even further), and planning for the future. Back in England, he joined Fyffe and the others at Langley Marish. A temporary chapel was set up in the loft of a nearby stable, offering one of the more arresting images in the history of English church music: choral services, dripping with plainsong, sung by ruffed inner-London choirboys in a barn in Slough, followed nervously up a rickety wooden ladder to the hayloft by a couple of curates in cassocks. Ouseley had found his vocation. 'I will not do without daily service,' he wrote. 'I have no talent for teaching, no powers of preaching, and no health for hard parochial work. But God has given me one talent; and that I am determined to devote to His Service …'[16] His big idea was a college where boys would study and sing daily services to the highest standards, equipping them with skills which they would then carry into the back rows and organ lofts of the country's parishes and cathedrals in adult life and, ideally, into the ranks of the priesthood as well.

Ouseley was an able and principled musical idealist. He was also rich. Eventually, he realised his dream not in a barn in Slough but in splendid, purpose-built premises, complete with imposing chapel in the approved neo-monastic style, in the village of Tenbury Wells, Worcestershire. By the time the College of St Michael opened in 1856, Ouseley had become a priest, Professor of Music at Oxford and Precentor of Hereford Cathedral, jobs which he was, in true Trollopian fashion, apparently able to hold down while living in rural Worcestershire. Give him a cello and Septimus Harding lives and breathes.

The College was dedicated on St Michael's Day, 1856. As at St Barnabas six years earlier, choristers were drafted in for the occasion from all over the place, including the Chapel Royal, among them a promising treble called Arthur Sullivan. Sullivan's choirmaster at the

Chapel Royal was Thomas Helmore. Helmore and Ouseley were thus the first priests to run cathedral-type choirs since the Reformation. Ouseley brought in a couple of young assistants to help him run the choir, an ex-St Paul's choirboy called John Stainer, and one of his own former Pimlico choristers, John Hampton. His training methods were working. Other educational initiatives sprang up to spread the good musical news. John Hullah ran classes whose pupils, as Charles Dickens noted approvingly:

> belong to every class and calling; the highest ranks of the aristocracy, the members of almost every trade and profession, the industrious mechanic and workman; and they all mingle in one pursuit, without regard to station or degree, and with the utmost harmony of feeling. There is a due admixture of the softer sex; and the meetings of the classes are characterised by such uniform propriety and decorum, that the most scrupulous parents allow their children, without hesitation, to attend them. [17]

Similar initiatives followed all round the country, inspired by Hullah's example and using his splendidly practical *Manual*, which was even translated into Welsh. The 'Tonic Sol-Fa' method of sight-singing was widely used. The Society for Promoting Church Music helped local musicians to organise along the new lines, largely through its influential magazine, *The Parish Choir*, founded in 1846 under the editorship of Robert Druitt, and Hullah went around the various local branches of the Society explaining the benefits of the new ways, including daring innovations like letting girls into the choir. Frederick Helmore, brother of the more famous Thomas, became known as the 'musical missionary' for his work travelling the leafy villages of southeast England, taking choir practice, running classes and staging little festivals of choral worship in various picturesque parishes. J. M. Neale recorded one such event in a letter of 1849: '… then procession by moonlight to Chapel singing Benedictus; the effect of alternate moon and deep shade on the surplices very fine: Compline sung in chapel: then Supper in Hall …'[18] If all this sounds as if Neale and Helmore thought they were acting out a scene from some imaginary, romanticised version of the Middle Ages, then that is probably not far from the truth – a Burne-Jones painting brought to life, their own faces peering palely through the *chiaroscuro*.

The College of Organists came into being in 1864, for the purpose of 'elevating and advancing our professional status',[19] in the words of its founder, Richard Limpus, Organist of St Michael's, Cornhill. Organists, suggested *The Parish Choir*, might not then be 'obliged to get their bread by teaching schoolgirls the polka'.[20] The College of Church Music followed in 1872.

Magazines were also important. The snappily titled *The Ecclesiologist* was founded by Neale, Webb and others, who were fellow students at Trinity College, Cambridge, in the 1830s (an interesting inversion, geographical and ecclesiological, of the Methodist Holy Club at Christ Church, Oxford, a century before). *The Ecclesiologist* joined *The Parish Choir* as the public voice of the new musical order, and both published voluminously on all aspects of church music.

One of the principal musical dilemmas enshrined in the Tractarian approach concerned the role of the choir. The clear preference was for everybody to take part in the act of worship. On the other hand, the love of ritual and excellence encouraged the use of music which was not suitable for congregational singing, in particular the beloved plainsong. Solutions to this problem varied according to the tastes and talents of the men on the ground. St Pancras, Euston Road, boasted a low-church vicar, Weldon Champneys (who wore a black Geneva gown to preach as late as 1880), an old-style parish clerk, and the finest accompanist of congregational singing of the age, the nearly blind Henry Smart. The result of this potent mix was lots of good music, sung entirely by a congregation of 2,000, led by the clerk – very reminiscent of the eighteenth century. Everyone joined in the chanting of the canticles, including a group of schoolchildren who were sitting among the congregation rather than separately in either the gallery or the chancel. The whole show was accompanied by Smart with enough variety of harmony and organ registration to stop it all getting dull. Good music, but nothing to annoy the man in black.

St Anne's, Soho, on the other hand, had a huge choir of sixty-four surpliced singers, including thirty-two trebles, under the direction of

Joseph Barnby. The result was that the congregation managed nothing in the way of singing except 'a quiet hum'[21] during the hymns, peering around the pillars to see who was singing a solo, and left after the anthem. 'The canticles', noted J. S. Curwen disapprovingly, 'are merely a musical gratification.'[22]

Wells Street had earlier attempted something of a middle way. Having introduced Helmore's English version of the plainsong psalter, the authorities hurriedly reverted to the less provocative Anglican chants in November 1850, just as the Pimlico riots were getting going. Members of the congregation objected roundly, some out of high-church principle, others because they'd just shelled out for the Helmore book, still others because they'd finally managed to learn how to enjoy joining in with the choir in the Gregorian tones, but didn't know the Anglican ones. War broke out between congregation and organist, publicly prosecuted in the pages of *The Parish Choir*. The organist, John Foster, told the congregation that joining in the psalms was a 'usurped privilege' which properly belonged to the choir. They responded that they didn't want to listen to 'screeching chants'.[23] This little spat clearly revealed the problems that occurred in trying to reconcile the differing aims of choirs and congregations, and different kinds of music, and how difficult they were to resolve.

A similar issue centred on the use of organs. In complete contrast to Smart at St Pancras, the cradle of purity at St Mark's College, Chelsea, had no organ at all in the chapel until 1861. Not so much as a Gibbons verse anthem sullied their vocal virginity.

This was the intellectual, social and educational background against which the Anglican musical revival unfolded. As usual, the notes on the stave give us a musical road map of its progress. But this time the notes, and the staves, were different. Every period of church music history has had to reinvent its system of musical notation and layout, in the process giving us important clues about how it was used. The later nineteenth century was the only period which deliberately reached back to the notation of the past.

And it was a very distant past. Psalms, as always, tell the story. A lively debate centred around two questions: should the psalms and canticles be sung by the choir or by the congregation? And should they be sung to Anglican chant or to Gregorian plainsong? The Bishop of London expressed his view in a letter of 1852:

> Although I am not prepared to assert that the introduction
> of cathedral services into parish churches is contrary to law, I
> think it very inexpedient ... it is hardly possible for an ordinary
> congregation to take part in those portions of the service which
> are chanted, except in the Venite exultemus, the Jubilate, &c.
> when sung to a plain simple chant to which the congregation are
> accustomed.[24]

This was a sensible, moderate position (from the man who had just sacked W. J. E. Bennett precisely for introducing 'cathedral services into parish churches'). Others took a different view: 'Gregorian chants are to be preferred', wrote the educationalist Nathaniel Woodard, 'not on aesthetical, but on religious grounds; not because they are more beautiful but more reverend towards the sacred words, enshrining a treasure which the later composers rather try to embellish.'[25] This was a classic statement of the musico-antiquarian position: Gregorian plainsong has an authenticity which later music has lost.

For others, the matter emphatically was one of aesthetics, leading to exactly the opposite conclusion. 'Some would reject all music but the unisonous chants of a period of absolute barbarism, – which they call Gregorian ... these men would look a Michael Angelo in the face and tell him that Stonehenge was the perfection of architecture,'[26] spluttered Samuel Sebastian Wesley in 1849.

Practicalities were never far away from this debate, particularly in rural parishes. When Woodard became curate of St Mary's, New Shoreham in Sussex, in 1846, his new church organist advised him that 'an ordinary Parochial service' was better for his installation, with an Anglican psalm-chant sung by the whole congregation, unless the choir of Chichester Cathedral could be puffed up the coast on the train to sing a fully choral service. He gently advised Woodard, 'I perceive by the tenor of your letter that you intend to have the ancient Church Music and that the Canticles etc. will be chanted ... I should feel much happiness if no other than unison singing by the whole assembly were used on this solemn occasion',[27] and for the communion he offered Woodard his own, authentically modal harmonisation of John Marbeck's English version (as long as Woodard paid for the copying).

Robert Druitt carried on the debate in the pages of the magazine he co-edited, *The Parish Choir*. The very first issue of February 1846 contained an article headed 'How to begin' and specified that schoolchildren should not act as the 'psalm-singers for the congregation'. No progress could be made until the whole assembly acted as 'a singing, as well as a praying, body'. With care, the ramshackle old parish 'musickers' could 'be made the nucleus of a true congregational choir'.[28] Unlike some others, Druitt recognised early on the necessity of taking people with him: church music has no business to be exclusive. Druitt was another hands-on pragmatist. His magazine gave people not just advice, but music. The second issue included a complete set of Anglican chants, one each for morning and evening for an entire month, thus covering the whole book of psalms as carved up by Cranmer, and others for the canticles. Some readers, of course, objected to Druitt's emphasis on Anglican chants, so the following year he printed Gregorian tones, with harmonies. These were certainly preferable, Druitt conceded, but only where a congregation could make a decent stab at singing them. If the Gregorian tones were used, he cautioned, 'they should be sung in unison, with an organ accompaniment. If sung in harmony, the harmonies should be sung by a few skilled voices only, while the mass of the people should sing the melody.'[29]

At first, no psalm book showed its singers how to fit the words to the new old tunes. E. J. Hopkins at the Temple Church resorted to marking up every copy of the Book of Common Prayer by hand, a time-consuming and probably not very serviceable piece of vandalism. Conditions were clearly propitious for a new generation of psalters. To a large extent, these books were a record of the compilers' own practice as clerics and organists.

The first of the English plainsong psalters was Alexander Reinagle's version of 1838, based on his own usage at St Peter-in-the-East, Oxford. Frederick Oakeley produced *Laudes Diurnae; the Psalter and*

Canticles ... ('Daily Praises') in 1843. His innovation was to print the plainsong tune, on a single line of music, at the top of each psalm. The singer was told how to fit the words to the tune by a system of dots and dashes in the body of the text, known as 'pointing', added by Oakeley's organist at Margaret Street, Richard Redhead, thus 'bringing under the reader's eye the notes of the chant in the same point of view with the words of the Psalm or Canticle which are set to them, so as to enable any one, who can read music, to connect the words with the chant at a glance.' Otherwise, 'persons desirous, and fully capable, of taking part in the psalmody of the Church, often lose half a Psalm, or more, in trying to make out how they are to join in it.'[30] By a happy coincidence, copies of John Marbeck's *The Booke of Common Praier Noted* of 1550 re-emerged at this time. Marbeck, of course, had set himself exactly the same task 300 years earlier, setting the English prayer-book services to the pre-Reformation Gregorian tones, which allowed his spiritual descendants to claim an authentic historical link with the early English church and, to a certain extent, to head off the charge of introducing popish practices. William Dyce simply carried on where Marbeck left off. His *Order of Daily Service* of 1843 rendered Marbeck in modern notation, 'improving' it where he thought his predecessor had not stuck closely enough to the Gregorian tunes, and extending the principle to include the services from the 1662 prayer book.

The completing of this work fell to Thomas Helmore. In 1849 and 1850 he issued successively *The Psalter Noted*, *The Canticles Noted*, and *A Brief Directory of the Plain Song*, which included the litany, communion, and other liturgies from the prayer book. In 1850 these three volumes were combined in one, *A Manual of Plainsong*. Helmore had cracked it. As well as its completeness, his book found a wholly workable synthesis of the old notation and the English words, using four-line staves, his own version of the old plainsong 'neumes', or noteheads, with the text written out underneath the musical stave, à la Marbeck. With a little familiarity, Helmore's notation could produce the smooth flow, respectful of the natural stress and rhythm of the words, which all writers recognised as the ideal but was so hard to do, especially for congregations used to regular tunes and metrical texts. Helmore's *Manual*, thoroughly road-tested on his own choir at St Mark's, remains the basis of plainsong singing today, revised and edited in the twentieth century by H. B. Briggs, W. H. Frere and J. H. Arnold. Gregorians were on the charge. But Anglicans were not far behind ...

Anglican chant is a curious hybrid. Its fundamental contradiction is that it seeks to marry a tune which has a regular, repeating rhythmic pattern with words which don't. That's why the early reformers put the English psalms in regular metre: to make them easier to sing. The later desire to revert to the prayer-book translation of the psalms, which were seen as being closer to the spirit of the original and better poetry (both of which are probably true), produced a problem. The solution was that old favourite of English church music – the fudge. Like all other such compromises, this one emerged rather than being laid down by central authority, through endless experimentation with pointing, layout, underlay, harmony, choirs, congregations, accompaniment and all other aspects of the slippery art, in the pages of the eighteenth-century psalm books and the stalls and galleries of England's churches.

Dvořák had his answer. That's why the choir at St Paul's sang their 'little tune' over and over again. He was present at a particular stage of a very English bit of musical evolution. Whether he was right to call the little tune 'wretched' will for ever have to remain hidden in the myster-ies of anecdote. He may well have been correct. Whenever a new genre of music demands the rapid composition of lots of new examples, not all of them will be any good.

The Anglican brigade pursued the plainsong party into print. Robert Janes, Organist of Ely Cathedral, was in the vanguard with his *Psalter* of 1837, incorporating advice from a Professor of Hebrew, no less. S. S. Wesley's *Psalter with Chants* appeared in 1843. The tireless John Hullah produced his own *Psalter* the same year, and (obviously at a loose end) *Psalms with chants* a year later. John Goss, Edward Rimbault and Thomas Attwood Walmisley all chipped in with books of chants, without words, between 1841 and 1846. William Mercer's *Church Psalter and Hymn Book* of 1854, under the musical supervision of John Goss, was one of the first to achieve widespread use. George J. Elvey, Ouseley and James Turle produced one each in the 1850s and 1860s.

Parish chanting was here to stay. In 1875 the nearest thing to a standard book emerged, the *Cathedral Psalter*, under the musical editorship of three experienced campaigners, John Stainer of St Paul's, James Turle of Westminster Abbey and Joseph Barnby of St Anne's, Soho. The title is instructive. The 'cathedral' pattern of worship was well established and unchallenged. What had not yet coalesced into its present form was the vexed question of verbal rhythm and underlay. The *Cathedral Psalter* left choirs to sing the reciting note as they pleased, which in practice meant gabbling through it without much regard to intelligibility, then provided a lengthened 'gathering-note' just before the bar-line to bring the voices together on a syllable chosen more or less at random, before the closing phrase was sung in strict rhythm. This particular evolutionary pathway had not quite reached its final, finest expression just yet.

THE LOGICAL NEXT STEP was to attempt something similar with hymns. Even after the effective ending in the 1820s of the old ban on anything other than metrical psalms, Anglican ambivalence to hymns remained. Early efforts at a 'house style' were basically in the restrained manner of the eighteenth-century country song-books, with inclusions like Henry Gauntlett's tune 'Irby', written in 1848 for the poem 'Once in Royal David's City'. Reginald Heber mixed in something a bit more sturdy and personal in hymns like 'Holy, Holy, Holy', the tune added a little later by J. B. Dykes. The march towards the muscular sentimentality of the later Victorian hymn tune can be heard advancing over the hill in the steady tread of this stirring song.

Exactly as had been done with psalms, one of the most significant developments was the effort to restore the plainsong repertoire to use. This went to the heart of the Tractarians' ambitions, and at its core was John Mason Neale. Neale's CV could have been written for the Oxford Movement. Born at exactly the right moment, in 1818, he was the son of a clergyman and a descendant of the seventeenth-century Puritan hymn-writer, John Mason (author of 'How shall I sing that majesty'). He was a passionate classicist, top of his year at Cambridge (though rubbish at maths, which prevented him taking his degree), and once under the spell of the Tractarians, he founded their Cambridge outpost, the Ecclesiological Society (initially the Cambridge Camden Society). He was appointed vicar of St John the Baptist in Crawley, Sussex, but was soon forced to resign through a combination of ill-health and his burgeoning high-church sympathies: his own bishop banned him from ministry for eighteen years. He helped found a female order within the Church of England, dedicated to nursing the sick. The papist overtones of all this, in the years immediately following John Henry Newman's secession to Rome, led to mobs threatening to stone him and burn down his house. He was once attacked at the funeral of one of his nuns.

The Tractarian desire to reconnect with the ancient church matched Neale's scholarly interests perfectly. Latin was, to him, the *lingua franca*, the *fons et origo*, the *sine qua non*. 'Why should hymns be less Catholick than prayers and, therefore, why English hymns less Catholick than English prayers?' he wrote. 'We may wish to restore Latin in both, if you like.' But he knew full well that this was a step too far: 'But till we can, surely English Hymns, if good, are better than none.'[31] Neale translated a great many Latin hymns, from Roman Breviaries and post-Tridentine sources, particularly French. He investigated Eastern and Orthodox traditions of hymnody. He raided a rare copy of a sixteenth-century schoolbook from Finland,[32] giving us 'Good Christian Men, Rejoice', 'Unto Us is Born a Son' and the jolly spring song to which he added his own words, beginning 'Good King Wenceslas looked out, on the Feast of Stephen'. The titles of his books give a good idea of the range of his reference and the reach of his ambition: *Hymni Ecclesiae e breviariis: quibusdam et missalibus Gallicanis, Germanis, Hispanis, Lusitanis, desumpti* (1851); *Hymns for Children* (1841; designed 'to free our poor children from the yoke of Dr Watts', and thereby putting them under the yoke of Mrs C. F. Alexander instead); *Medieval Hymns and Sequences* (1862); *Hymns of the Eastern Church* (1870). Many of the plainsong hymns appear in sensible, practical editions in the *Hymnal Noted* of 1851, the successor and companion to the previous year's *Psalter Noted*, both consciously named after Marbeck's great original. In all of this his musical editor and arranger was Thomas Helmore, who in 1852 added some 'Accompanying Harmonies to the Hymnal Noted'.

Neale gave us 'Of the Father's Heart Begotten', 'O Come, O Come, Emmanuel', 'Blessed City, Heavenly Salem', 'The Day of Resurrection' and 'All Glory, Laud and Honour'. Most of his best-known lyrics are translations, but he deserves more than the credit of just a wordsmith. He discovered as well as translated these texts, patiently excavated the many and varied traditions they came from, and shepherded them into English use. He is the most represented author in the *English Hymnal*, outdoing even Charles Wesley. The firm of Helmore and Neale is not well enough remembered today. Their names are familiar, if at all, from the tiny letters in the corner of a tattered page of your hymnbook, the bit you don't read. But their importance in setting a new standard, style and tone for English church music at a period when it desperately needed it, and in giving it much of its music and many of its words, cannot be overstated.

Before leaving Neale's impressively sideburned figure, there is a little story that sums up both his erudition and his central position within the ranks of the Oxford Movement.[33] John Keble was working on some new hymns and asked Neale to visit him in Oxford to give an opinion. Some were translations, and the two men happily pored over old and new, comparing and commenting in contented debate. Then Keble produced a hymn of his own, and went out of the room for a few minutes, leaving Neale to peruse it. When he came back, Neale, to Keble's astonishment, produced from his pocket a Latin poem which matched the new English verses phrase for phrase, almost word for word. Keble spluttered that the English was all his own work, he'd never seen the Latin, but the similarities were too remarkable to be denied. He was about to withdraw his poem as an act of unwitting plagiarism when Neale burst out laughing and let on that, while Keble was out of the room, he had translated his friend's shiny new effort into flawless medieval Latin in a couple of minutes flat.

The movement to bring tunes from old and unfamiliar traditions back into use continued. W. H. Havergal issued *Old Church Psalmody* in 1847, including what he saw as the best of the old-style tunes, squashed into the straitjacket of a regular metre. An important development was the discovery of Graduals from leading centres of Catholic music in Europe, including Mechlin in Belgium, Solesmes in France and Ratisbon (now Regensburg) in Germany, all of which were ransacked for usable tunes.

As with the psalm books, all this activity was tending towards the creation of something approaching a common repertoire. William Mercer took the obvious step of combining hymns and psalms in his book of 1854, mentioned above. In 1861 a new hymnbook appeared under the musical editorship of W. H. Monk, assisted by Ouseley. Like the *Cathedral Psalter* it effectively coalesced the labours of many hands into the nearest thing the church had to an 'official' hymnbook; and, like the psalter, its title says it all: *Hymns Ancient and Modern*.

Three things stand out about this book. First, it printed words and music together throughout, so that the hymnbook was no longer a book of devotional verse to which organist or choir would add music from a separate book or from memory. Second, instead of being made by a particular worshipping community for its own use, this one drew material from many traditions. Third, hymns were grouped by use, according to the time of day, season of the year or liturgical function like a procession, creating something almost approaching a congregational service book. It was a huge hit. Its progenitors 'found themselves almost embarrassed by the success of their undertaking',[34] as the preface to a later edition put it. Various supplements and revisions followed, rebalancing the old and the new and adding the latest good tune by Arthur Sullivan and others in response to public demand, just as the metrical psalters had done in the sixteenth century. The eclectic mix of tunes from all over the musical world and every known period of hymnological history, with words translated, adapted and edited from Genevan psalters, plainsong breviaries, Puritan divines, Watts, Wesley, Williams and everyone else, set the style and standard for every hymnbook thereafter.

In considering nineteenth-century hymns, it is important to note the extent to which English religion had broadened out. The 1851 religious census showed that of all church attendances on 30 March 1851, the Church of England accounted for barely 50 per cent. Of the rest, 2 per cent were Roman Catholic and 48 per cent were Protestant Nonconformists – principally Methodists, Baptists and Congregationalists.[35]

Non-Anglicans thus made up half of all church-goers. Musically, the importance of Nonconformism was its hymns, with each branch contributing its own distinctive voice and repertoire. But it was the Anglican half of the protestant estate which remained on the musical front foot, partly because of its commitment to choirs, organs and ceremonial, and partly because of its ability to absorb the best of other traditions into its hymnody.

Apart from pop music, nothing raises the hackles of writers about English church music quite like Victorian hymns. There's something about the combination of a cast-iron certainty of being right with a certain sentimentality of expression which people not only don't like, but actually seem to find morally offensive. A favourite word, used by Vaughan Williams in 1906, the editors of a hymnbook of 1931, and church music scholar and historian Erik Routley in 1957, is 'debased'.[36] It's a revealing choice of word, implying a falling-off from some sort of prelapsarian ideal. This subject has caused the spilling of so much ink, both in the hymn-writing itself and in commentary on it, that any review here must of necessity barely scratch the surface of the surface. But some sort of objective assessment of this impressive and many-headed creature is required.

Poets and composers clambered over each other to add their own work to the repertoire of the past – to reflect the religious and social preoccupations of their times, to fill gaps in the cosmic overview represented by hymns, and to make money. Production was prodigious. The style encompassed the directness of Mrs C. F. Alexander, aimed at adults and children alike ('Once in Royal David's City', 'All Things Bright and Beautiful'), Hubert Parry and patriotism ('Jerusalem'), the waltz ('The Day Thou Gavest'), the march ('Onward, Christian Soldiers') and prayerful contemplation ('Abide with Me'). Above all, it could do tunes. What other musical tradition has produced melodies which whole Old Traffords-full of fans can, and often do, sing? Lots of hymns get used in this way. Most of them are Victorian.

Victorian hymns succeeded because they filled a hole not just in British religion but in British life. The tunes of John Stainer ('Love Divine'), J. B. Dykes ('Melita'), Parry ('Laudate Dominum'), S. S.

Wesley ('Aurelia'), John Hughes ('Cwm Rhondda') and their peers did for the English what opera did for the Italians. Joseph Barnby wrote 246 tunes, all published in one go. Some really good tunes never get a look-in because there is another really, really good tune to the same words: Charles Villiers Stanford's 'Engelberg', to 'For all the saints' is a cracker, but is never sung because Vaughan Williams came up with 'Sine nomine' for the same words, another winner. A recent Archbishop of Canterbury, no less, made the striking but revealing observation that 'hymns played much the same role in Victorian culture that soap operas do among us today.'[37] So it really doesn't matter if they are not all particularly good. A lot of them are. We may not approve of all of their attitudes, but they're family.

All this new churchmanship led to a range of new arenas for church music. The Victorian period was the greatest era of church-building since medieval times. For music, the significance of this was that it allowed people to think afresh about how the music fitted into the liturgy and, therefore, where in the church it should go. The answer was not in the West Gallery or among the congregation, but in the chancel, medieval-style, in pews facing each other across the aisle. This fed into musical practice: at Margaret Street, Frederick Oakeley and his best choirboy stood on one side, chanting the psalms antiphonally with the rest of the boys on the other. (The head boy in question was C. E. Willing, who went on to become a successful church musician in adult life.) Much debate focused on where to put the new, bigger organ. These echoing spaces provided the perfect stage set for the theatrical confection of the Victorian choral service with its exits and its entrances and its many parts, the fabulous decorations of William Butterfield and Ninian Comper the perfect visual analogue for the music of Barnby and Co.

The mid-nineteenth century saw the opening of a rash of new boarding schools for boys, all with pronounced but varied ecclesiological tendencies. Rugby was the first to have its own hymnbook, in 1824. Much more high-church was Radley, where 'two hours and a half, including the chapel service, were spent in singing daily, and the first class could sing at sight anything put before them, and knew all the services and anthems almost by heart … the staple subject of conversation was not the weather, after the manner of true-born Englishmen, but the service or anthem for the day.'[38] If there is any more meaty congregational singing than a public-school chapel full of muddied oafs from the football field and flannelled fools from the wicket, then surely it is the sound of 'Cwm Rhondda', smartly accompanied by a bright-buttoned brass band, bellowed with tuneless gusto by the Welsh Guards (all of them).

New colleges at the universities had a similar chapel-centric ethos. A much-loved clergyman at Selwyn College, Cambridge (whose chapel looks almost identical to the one at Radley), remembers that the daily evening service was called off once in the 1950s, leading the undergraduates to mob outside the chapel doors in their gowns, chanting 'we want evensong!'[39] Generals, politicians and the rulers of the Queen's Navy built their churchmanship into their professional lives: Prime Minister W. E. Gladstone had a chapel at his Hawarden estate (where Archbishop E. W. Benson died during morning service[40]), and Wellington Barracks has some early, and striking, mosaics in the chancel of its chapel of 1838. These survived the terrible events of Sunday, 18 June 1944, when 'the chapel was packed with Guardsmen, and their families and friends. Just after 11.00 a.m., just after the service started, the congregation heard a distant buzzing. It gradually grew louder and turned into a roar overhead which drowned out the hymn singing. The engine cut out and the V1 glided down and exploded on the roof of the chapel.'[41] One hundred and twenty-one people were killed, many more injured – and yet the candles on the altar remained alight. The chapel was later strikingly rebuilt, incorporating the surviving Victorian chancel.

Progress towards an accepted way of using music at communion was slow. There were plenty of false starts and dead ends, like English bowdlerisations of Masses by Haydn and Mozart, new settings in boring unison, bits of mangled Marbeck and unsatisfactory mixtures of all of the above. The Book of Common Prayer didn't really help: it gave no indication at all about when, and whether, a choir ought to sing. Cathedral choirs would often sing matins, then leave before the celebration of communion began. Even at the end of the Victorian period and beyond, matins and evensong gave composers far more encouragement. The 'complete' services of Stanford and others tended to reuse music from the canticles for the disjointed and unsatisfactory parts of the English communion which were permitted.

The problem for the composers who wanted to write cathedral-type music in the early Victorian period was that the new churchmanship didn't want its new music to sound new. 'There are a certain catalogue of harmonies peculiarly proper for Divine Service,' decreed *The Parish Choir* magazine in 1850. For Nathaniel Woodard, 'Ouseley is the sworn opponent of Church music. I can make every excuse for secular men liking that kind of music. It is effective, and brings credit to the performers. But that is not what we want.'[42] It seems hardly credible to us that music like Ouseley's rather maudlin *O Saviour of the World* was seen as dangerously jolly and subversively modernistic. But Woodard was perfectly explicit: 'If there be a sacred harmony which is the inheritance of the Church, my desire is that our Church should partake in it even though the sons of God should not be able to compete with the advance of civilisation as it is called.' This is exactly the same argument advanced by Crotch a couple of decades earlier. Church music has often struggled to work out how to keep up with 'the advance of civilisation'. Victorian composers weren't even allowed to try.

Some, though, at least made an effort. Magazines like *The Parish Choir* and the *Musical Times* included anthems as supplements, while books with titles like *Parochial Choirbook* got its contributors to write long, practical passages in unison and optional harmony, alongside adaptations of pieces by Handel and others. Novello's *Parish Choir Book* series started in 1866. Its first volume consisted of forty-six settings of the Te Deum.

The organisational aspects of cathedral music-making began to receive the attention they so desperately needed. Maria Hackett made it the business of her long life to improve what she quite rightly called the 'neglected situation'[43] of cathedral choirboys, taking deans and choirmasters roundly to task for letting them wander the streets at all hours of the day and night. S. S. Wesley remembered her giving the Chapel Royal boys buns to help get over the pain and indignity of a thrashing. In 1876, at the age of ninety-one, she visited the new choir school at St Paul's, her principal place of endeavour. Its choir sang at her funeral later that same year. She is commemorated by a modest plaque in the crypt, but, like Christopher Wren, her monument is really to be seen all around her in the vastly better conditions enjoyed by choristers ever since – and their higher musical standards. For an installation service at Barchester in 1857,

> The dean was there ... So also were the chancellor, the treasurer, the precentor, sundry canons and minor canons, and every lay member of the choir, prepared to sing the new bishop in with due melody and harmonious expression of sacred welcome. The service was certainly very well performed. Such was always the case at Barchester, as the musical education of the choir had been good, and the voices had been carefully selected. The psalms were beautifully chanted; the Te Deum was magnificently sung; and the litany was given in a manner, which is still to be found at Barchester, but, if my taste be correct, is to be found nowhere else.[44]

Emblematic of the changing fortunes of cathedral music was the appointment of John Stainer to succeed John Goss as Organist of St Paul's in 1872. Assisted by the reforming Canon (later Dean) Gregory, 'every change was carried out by that admirable musician and devout Churchman with consummate tact, good humour, courage and firmness'; as Archdeacon Sinclair put it in 1913: 'He could do anything he liked with the choir.'[45] It would not be too much to say that in the days of his predecessor things were the other way round: the choir could do anything they liked with him.

As always, Oxford and Cambridge were different. Private chapels made their own rules. At some periods of English church music this was an advantage: under Elizabeth I, for example, their chapels enjoyed some of the same freedoms from official strictures as the Chapel Royal. But this was no longer the case. Music was under the rheumy eye of superannuated dons, unmusical deans and absentee professors. Salaries were feeble and duties were often delegated to ill-qualified deputies. Attempts at change were rebuffed. The ancient choral foundations continued their work, but the mid-nineteenth century was hardly their finest hour: when Thomas Attwood Walmisley arrived as Organist of St John's and Trinity Colleges in 1833, he found that the two colleges shared the same ten choristers and six elderly lay clerks. A few other colleges maintained occasional choral services, but without much enthusiasm or official support. Walmisley became Professor in 1836, though 'at this time the office had become a mere sinecure, the salary being extremely small and the Professor not even being required to reside',[46] as the historian J. S. Bumpus wrote in 1908. Walmisley did his considerable best, but even as late as the last decades of the century Professor Sir Charles Stanford held his classes in the Station Hotel so that he could get back to London and civilisation. When Crotch died in 1847, having long given up his earlier attempts to bring betterment to the musical scene in Oxford, the university elected as his successor Henry Bishop, who had spent his entire working life in the theatre and whose best-known composition is 'Home! Sweet Home!' Bishop thought it perfectly sufficient to turn up in Oxford once a year to play the crumbling old organ in the Sheldonian Theatre, which, since he was paid £12 a year, may be understandable.

Before leaving Cambridge and the Fens, we should note that one of the iconic experiences in English church music – indeed in all music – still worked its magic even in the midst of such great troubles. Bumpus talks of attending a 'wonderful and never-to-be-forgotten evensong in King's College Chapel',[47] and W. E. Dickson pointed out that the woeful standards of the choristers there were largely obscured by 'a resonance which lends a charm to any music performed under its lofty vault, quite independently of the artistic merits or defects of its performance'.[48] He wasn't the only person to notice that. The reputation of plenty of choirs has benefited, or the opposite, from the acoustic properties of their building. A later luminary of King's music said that the chapel's famous fan-vaulting made a burp sound like a seven-fold 'Amen'.

WRITING IN 1968, THE perceptive church music scholar Erik Routley said of English church music that 'most of what we now value in it we owe to the Tractarian movement'.[49] He is still right. The Tractarians rediscovered the music of the past, and put in place the liturgical style and professional standards which have remained the preconditions for all English choral music since. The central debate was an old one: 'there are two theories of church music – the one scriptural, primitive, and protestant, the other opposed to the spirit of scripture, having its origin in a corrupt age of the Church, and peculiarly characteristic of the Church of Rome,'[50] said the low-church schoolmaster Steuart Pears in 1852. In Trollope's Barchester, Mr Slope criticised 'the undue preponderance which, he asserted, music had over meaning … how much of the meaning of the words was lost when they were produced with all the meretricious charms of melody!', while clerical colleagues took the opposite view; intoning the Litany had 'long been the special task to which Mr Harding's skill and voice have been devoted' and the cathedral 'could procure the co-operation of any number of gentlemanlike curates well trained in the mystery of doing so.'[51] And so the Reformation rumbled on.

'High' versus 'low' is, like all such shorthand tags, too simple. Nicholas Temperley, musicologist, has observed 'the striking fact about the two extremes is that they had so much in common, though in the heat of battle they never knew it.'[52] Congregational singing, in particular chanting, was the ideal for both. Good choir music was, in a sense, a by-product of the new emphasis on high standards and the new interest in the music of the past.

This is what the Oxford Movement did for us – and these were the men who did it. They were a distinct breed: determined, idealistic, highly educated, historically and aesthetically aware. They were men of their times and there is a strong sense of *de haut en bas* in the manner in which they did things. But they were not the humourless cliché of popular caricature, any more than their monarch was. Between them, they covered all the skill sets necessary for the advancement of the project: they were writers, teachers, newspaper editors, musical arrangers, scholars and administrators – and almost all of them were priests. What they were not, by and large, were composers.

13

Composers from S. S. Wesley to Elgar, 1830–1934

Onward, Christian soldiers!

Sabine Baring-Gould

SAMUEL SEBASTIAN WESLEY was born in 1810, son of Samuel Wesley and his housekeeper, Sarah Suter. He became a chorister at the Chapel Royal, apparently with a 'sweet and divine'[1] voice, then held a number of teenage appointments as organist of a variety of churches in and around London after his voice broke. From 1832 to 1835 he was Organist of Hereford Cathedral, where he wrote some of his most celebrated works and married the Dean's sister, then Exeter Cathedral until 1842. Relations with authorities appear to have been a little bumpy thus far, and it may have been serendipitous that a combination of a burgeoning reputation as the finest organist in the country, a certain *Wanderlust* and an extremely attractive job offer took him to Leeds in 1842 to head up the elaborate choral forces in W. F. Hook's brand-new parish church. During his seven years there he wrote more of his relatively small output of church music, injured his leg while hurrying home for evensong from a fishing trip out in the North Riding, and issued a celebrated tract on the state of church music as he saw it, *A Few Words on Cathedral Music and the Musical System of the Church.*

In 1849 he moved to Winchester, where the authorities found that they had replaced an organist who neglected his duties for hunting with one who instead neglected them for dabbling in the 'fishful Itchen',[2] as his first biographer calls it. His level of professional commitment may be apparent from a change he made to the organ-loft stairs in 1851, allowing him to arrive late for service without the congregation seeing him, no doubt stashing his rods and catch against some suitably decorated pillar in the aisle before limping up the stairs. He stayed at Winchester longer than any of his other places of employment, directing his compositional activities largely towards the hymn tune in its years in the sun around the time of the appearance of *Hymns Ancient and Modern* in 1861. In 1865 he moved for the last time, to Gloucester, and enjoyed a period of some contentment but little activity apart from a row about the Three Choirs Festival of 1875. In 1872 he issued a long-contemplated collection of hymn tunes under the title *European Psalmist*. He died in 1876.

S. S. Wesley is one of the great originals in this story. His work still divides opinion between those who regard it as little more than 'tolerably good Mendelssohn',[3] as his biographer Erik Routley put it (tongue firmly in cheek), and those who value its sheer skill, range, ambition, tunefulness, sensitivity to text, and, above all, the enormous gulf in quality – much bigger than the beck he didn't jump over that day up on the Yorkshire moors – between this music and anything else being composed at the time. He certainly needs, and deserves, to be considered separately from his contemporaries. This is partly because, working his whole life in provincial centres away from London, he wasn't really involved in the main currents of musical life, which tended to be left to lesser, more politically astute men. (Church music has always had a place for those who are good at sucking up to the clergy and the pen-pusher, and has shown itself concomitantly intolerant of those who find such arts undignified.) His occasional attempts to obtain professorships were met with rejection. But partly, it was to do with his character. He wasn't really interested in what everyone else was doing. There is no evidence, for example, that the debates around churchmanship and the Oxford Movement interested him at all. All he cared about was good musical standards. Most of all, he stood out from the crowd as a composer of real, authentic genius.

There are not many pieces by S. S. Wesley (the family tendency to laziness was certainly there in his complex nature) and his music is certainly patchy, both within and between pieces. But what he did well is so distinctive that it deserves examination in some detail. One of his musical signatures is the verse anthem on a massive, almost symphonic, scale. In this he was the successor not just of the later eighteenth-century style of James Nares and others, but of the cantata-like anthems of Handel and Purcell; he was the first to attempt anything of the kind since their day, and one of very few nineteenth-century composers to do so. He wrote the first real organ accompaniments, in pieces like the service in E major, for Leeds, and *The Wilderness*, for Hereford, with its elaborate bass aria featuring virtuoso work for the organist's feet. He lavished much care on selecting and assembling a text: even the miniature 'Thou Wilt Keep Him in Perfect Peace' uses no fewer than five separate scriptural sources for its journey from darkness to light. His harmonic style is utterly personal and instantly recognisable. It's something to do with his use of the semitone clash: that same little piece spaces out increasingly plangent examples over the course of its first seven bars, and reserves the most expressive of all for the penulti-mate bar – not just lovely harmony, but in exactly the right place. His hymn tune 'Cornwall' makes his favourite move to the mediant minor, then gets back home again through the richest passage of harmony in the repertoire, suspensions sprouting abundantly in every bar and every part. He is a fine contrapuntalist and intelligent builder of struc-tures. The double fugues in *The Wilderness* and *Ascribe unto the Lord* show complete mastery and control, avoiding the prevailing tendency of other composers (including his father) to make a fugue sound like a harmony exercise by little twists of imagination like the splendid change of chord when 'the ransomed of the Lord' finally do 'return and come to Zion' in *The Wilderness*. *Wash me Throughly* is exquisitely put together, the two contrasting opening melodies combined in chro-matic double counterpoint at the end, skill concealed by art with all the assurance of his beloved Bach. Perhaps, above all else, he just wrote such a good tune: the two fugue subjects 'The Lord hath been mindful of us' and 'Ye are the blessed of the Lord', the treble solo 'Love one another with a pure heart fervently', the hymn tune 'Aurelia' and 'Lead me, Lord'. If for no other reason, this music will always return and come to evensong because it's just so good to sing.

And yet, there are boring bits. There is some inert music in the longer anthems. Some of the 'verse' passages are too long. Some of Samuel Sebastian's anthems have held a place in the repertoire, some have not. It's not usually a good idea to chop the good bits out of a long anthem and perform them separately, but with Wesley it works. He is a figure full of contradictions. They show up in his writings too. Although far from the hardest worker described in this book, his commitment to high standards was uncompromising. *A Few Words on Cathedral Music...* of 1849 pulls no punches in its analysis of what is wrong, whose fault it is, and what to do about it: '*no* Cathedral in this country possesses, at this day, a musical force competent to embody and give effect to the evident intentions of the Church with regard to music.'[4] A big problem, as Wesley saw it, was that the choirs didn't have enough men: 'What, for instance, can any one who has visited the Opera Houses, the Theatres, Exeter Hall, or any well conducted musical performances, think of a chorus of *one* to a part? Ask the men working the mills of Yorkshire and Lancashire what they would think of it? And yet, this amount of chorus would be a vast *improvement* on the present state of things at Cathedrals.'[5] Those who are members of the choir often don't turn up: 'the writer, once attending service at Christ Church, Oxford, remarked to the Organist, Dr Marshall, "Why you have only one man in a surplice today, and him I can't hear". The reply was, "No, he is only a beginner." And this was a University town ...'[6] The blame rested squarely with the clergy, who were 'less susceptible of musical impressions than any other class of the community'.[7] They needed to engage enough singers, pay them properly so that they didn't have to keep running off from choir practice to open up the shop or finish their delivery round, and invest in some decent music.

Two things stand out from this splendid rant: Wesley was certainly

The closing bars of 'Thou Wilt Keep Him in Perfect Peace' by Samuel Sebastian Wesley.

right; and this certainly wasn't the way to persuade people to do anything about it. He complained that, when an organist raises these matters with his clerical superiors, he was met with 'evasive politeness at first; then, abrupt rudeness; and ultimately total neglect'.[8] This was exactly how a series of exasperated deans dealt with their musician militant, and you can see why.

S. S. Wesley is a significant figure in this history. He was often his own worst enemy (among a number of candidates). When he brought out his massive collection of hymn tunes in 1872 it failed to make much impact, not least because, a full decade after *Ancient and Modern*, the days of the separate tune-book were over. Wesley, of course, blamed the printer.

His music still divides opinion. This is partly a function of its individuality: listeners respond strongly, for or against. Many see it as sentimental, even kitsch. He has been accused both of wayward modulation and of sticking too much in the same key. Others find the best of England in its naïve charm and idiosyncracies of harmony and form. The modern church musician can sometimes have the unusual experience of welcoming a visitor from continental Europe and trying to explain why the English drooled over these trifles at a time when their culture was bringing us the mighty glories of Wagner and Berlioz. It's like trying to explain cricket to the French. But it's worth it. There is a whole century and more of musical history of which Wesley is the principal ornament. English church music needed Samuel Sebastian Wesley. Though, perhaps to our relief, we will not see his like again.

TRACING A LINE BETWEEN the music of John Goss and that of his pupil John Stainer reveals much about musical style, in the same way as the handing of the baton between the two men at St Paul's does about standards. Goss was a kindly fellow, intensely musical but no disciplinarian, firmly brought up in the bad old days of badly run choirs and neglected choristers. Born in 1800, he was a Child of the Chapel Royal and pupil of Attwood, eventually succeeding him as Organist of St Paul's in 1838. He taught harmony at the Royal Academy of Music for almost half a century, to Arthur Sullivan and Frederick Bridge, among others. His sensitivity made him unsuited to the task of taking on lazy, recalcitrant and pluralistic lay clerks (his own uncle, John Jeremiah Goss, was a member of the Chapel Royal, St Paul's Cathedral and Westminster Abbey, all at the same time). The unsympathetic reaction to his anthem *Blessed is the Man* of 1842 so unnerved him that he wrote nothing else for choir until asked to do so for the funeral of the Duke of Wellington (incidentally, a distant relative of the Wesley family) a decade later, which produced his best-known anthem, *If we Believe that Jesus Died*. Writing in 1890, the perceptive music critic J. A. Fuller Maitland said that Goss's music has 'much grace and sweetness, underlying which is a solid foundation of theoretic and contrapuntal science. It is difficult to resist the assumption that at least some part of this happy combination was inherited, through Attwood, from Mozart.'[9] This is a pretty good description of the whole mid-Victorian church style, though it's probably stretching a point to find much Mozart there.

Stainer was born when Goss and the century were both forty years old. At the age of ten he became a chorister at St Paul's, travelling there daily by steamboat from Southwark. Goss was no doubt relieved at the novelty of finding someone who could actually sing in his choir, and the two came to like and admire each other. Stainer later described the effect produced by his choirmaster's anthem for Wellington's funeral: 'When the last few bars *pianissimo* had died away, there was a profound silence for some time, so deeply had the hearts of all been touched by its truly devotional spirit. Then there gradually arose on all sides the warmest congratulation to the composer, it could hardly be termed *applause*, for it was something much more genuine and respectful.'[10]

Young Stainer struck up a friendship with another choirboy from south London, Arthur Sullivan, and played the organ in various churches before securing gainful employment from Ouseley at Tenbury and, at the age of twenty, as Organist of Magdalen College, Oxford. One of his best anthems, *I saw the Lord* dates from around this time; a striking conception, it is almost operatic in its evocation of the Book of Revelation's hallucinatory imagery, giving way to one of the century's loveliest tunes for the hymn-setting which ends the work, 'O Trinity, O Unity'. Stainer's pioneering work raising standards at Magdalen continued when he succeeded Goss at St Paul's in 1872, bringing the boys, the men and the clergy alike under his charismatically beady eye (all the more so since he only had the use of one, and that sometimes fitfully).

Stainer was a good composer. *The Crucifixion* of 1887 is a completely convincing attempt to give parish choirs a respectful, approachable alternative to the Passion settings of Bach. His interest in folk music also led to one of the most important Christmas carol books of the century. He researched the music of the early fifteenth-century Franco-Flemish composer Guillaume Dufay, a rare foray into the music of the distant past and an extraordinarily bold initiative for his day. It is probably justifiable to suggest that his compositions continued where Goss left off, inheriting the tuneful style and the textbook approach to harmony and form, and moving them on to the point where the next generation could pick them up in its turn. At the same time, there was a continuum: if you listened to *How Lovely are the Messengers* by Mendelssohn, *How Beautiful upon the Mountains* by Stainer and *How Beauteous are their Feet* by Stanford, without knowing them in advance, it would be impossible to tell which composer had written each piece. Melody is central: it may be instructive that among the best-known creations of both Goss and Stainer are hymn tunes, including 'Praise my Soul, the King of Heaven' and 'See, amid the Winter's Snow' by the older man; 'Love Divine', 'All for Jesus' and folk-song arrangements like 'God Rest You Merry, Gentlemen' by the younger.

Another composer whose early orbit was around the Chapel Royal, St Paul's and the Royal Academy was Arthur Sullivan. He seems to have had a rather nicer time as a chorister than Goss or Wesley. During his time at the Chapel Royal, which he joined in 1854 at the advanced age of nearly twelve, the boys lodged with their kindly and dedicated master, Thomas Helmore, at his house in Chelsea. Sullivan's mother corresponded frequently about her son's often delicate health, receiving regular replies about the potential ill-effects of too much riding in omnibuses, and the restorative qualities of a lamb chop. Arthur's own letters were full of parties at Buckingham Palace and the Bishop's, being petted by duchesses after a solo, buying Handel's *Samson* from Novello's after the Bishop gave him half-a-crown for singing 'With verdure clad' ('shan't I be well stocked with Oratorios?'), and the occasional punch-up in the park.

This was better than forty years before, when Goss had his scores of Handel organ concertos confiscated because the boys were there to sing, not play, got three hours of academic tuition per week, and 'as to playing on an instrument and learning thorough bass, what we did we did by and for ourselves!'[11] Boys, of course, however talented, are still boys. Stainer and Sullivan once got a public fit of the giggles when Goss, up in the organ loft, absent-mindedly walked across the pedal-board without putting the stops in, 'before he realised that he was the cause of the alarming thunderings which were frightening the congregation and putting a temporary pause in the sermon.'[12]

Sullivan wrote some pleasing anthems as a boy, frankly Mendelssohnian in manner, as was right and proper. In some ways, his later church music lost its youthful charm without finding anything to replace it with. There are lots of anthems and a few service settings by Sullivan, but not one of them has held a place in the repertoire, even when quite a lot of bad Victorian music has managed to cling on. His work as a whole has been thoroughly put on trial on a charge of lack of seriousness, often the fate of composers whose work people actually like. His church music has the opposite problem: it is too serious. No hint of his melodic felicity penetrates the Stygian gloom. It's as if someone had passed a law forbidding the use of anything but minims. If he had allowed his choirs something of the grace of the 'Madrigal' from *Princess Ida*, or the rum-te-tum of a chorus striding across a stage, as Verdi and Vierne did in their church music, his tunes would still be filling the vaults of cathedrals and the lungs of choristers just as much as they do the stalls and boxes of theatres and village halls all over the world. Even more so than the others, his lasting contribution to church music has turned out to be his hymn tunes, notably 'Onward, Christian Soldiers' and the folk-song he adapted as 'It Came upon the Midnight Clear'.

Away from the glamour of London, neither T. A. Walmisley nor F. A. G. Ouseley made composition their primary activity, though both have had slightly more success than Sullivan at holding a small but secure place in the repertoire. Walmisley was named after his godfather and early teacher, Attwood of St Paul's, whose influence permeated this part of the nineteenth century. (Borrowing middle names from parentally selected role models was a notable Victorian habit: S. S. Wesley got his second 'S' from Johann Sebastian Bach, while the hymnwriter and insurance salesman William Chatterton Dix was named in honour of the Romantic period's favourite forger and suicide, Thomas

Chatterton. Charles Dickens called several of his children after novelist and painter friends of his: Alfred Tennyson Dickens, Walter Landor Dickens, Henry Fielding Dickens.) Walmisley's Evening Service in D minor gets deserved regular performances, though the less often heard setting in D major is probably more interesting and certainly more ambitious and varied. There is plenty of variety in the anthems, too: *Remember, O Lord, What is Come upon Us* is a splendid verse anthem on an almost Wesleyesque scale, beginning with a fine, chromatic quartet for tenors and basses, Handelian in tread, and ending with a really good fugue, stuffed with all the contrapuntal tricks in the book, brilliantly handled. *From All that Dwell below the Skies* brought the charm of the glee to the choir stall, and *Ponder my Words* is for the delicious combination of four-part treble voices and organ. Walmisley shared with Wesley the distinction of writing the first genuine organ music in his accompaniments, as opposed to the older 'continuo' style.

The music of Ouseley showed less willingness to break the mould, though his *O Saviour of the World* drew some plangent dissonances from a text which always seemed to hold a particular resonance for the English composer, in English and Latin, and a fine command of eight-part writing for the two sides of the choir antiphonally, a strikingly early example of a texture used to telling effect by many later composers including Charles Villiers Stanford and William H. Harris. Wesley, Walmisley and Ouseley have much in common besides a second syllable. They advanced musical standards, and provided music to meet them – for choir, organ, and both together. There is more good music to be found in this particular corner of the song-school cupboard.

FREDERICK BRIDGE WAS hardly a major composer. There was a little sacred choral music, including *A Babe ys Borne*, a carol, which is dedicated 'to my grandchild, Flora Helen Stainer' (whose other grandfather was the organist of another big church in London, John Stainer: Christmas must have been fun). Bridge is better remembered today for party pieces like 'The Two Snails' and 'The Lobster's Garden Party', but he represents a type and a period: student of Goss, teacher of Stanford, Organist of Westminster Abbey (leading to the inevitable nickname

'Westminster Bridge'), champion of the music of Purcell, and author of a highly agreeable anecdotal memoir, full of coronations, fishing expeditions, childhood trips to hear West Gallery choirs and barrel organs, cricket matches, sketches of contemporaries like Dickens and Kipling, organ lessons and blind bellows-blowers.

He was responsible for the music at a whole series of royal occasions during the period when some of the most enduring music was composed, including Hubert Parry's *I was Glad*. Bridge relates that, at the first performance, Parry was sitting in the nave next to the actor, Sir Henry Irving. As the anthem ended, Irving turned to his neighbour and remarked, 'Don't think much of the music so far,' not realising he was speaking to the composer. 'I did not enlighten him,' Sir Hubert later told Sir Frederick. Other coronation anecdotes include the effects of the postponement due to the King's illness in 1902, a row with the Queen's Scholars of Westminster School, and the story of the two ladies who 'were standing in the Cloisters talking, when a sound from the Abbey arrested their attention. "Listen," said one, "that's Sir Walter Parratt at the organ". "Oh, no," said her friend, "that's not Sir Walter – he can't play like that – it's Sir Frederick Bridge." Unfortunately it was not the sound of the organ, but the noise made by a vacuum cleaner!'[13]

There's more to Parry than *I was Glad* and there's more to Victorian music than Victoriana. From the outside, Parry looked like the ultimate insider: English baronet, Eton and Oxford, impressive moustache, country house near Gloucester. Even his names roll off the tongue like a beak taking register or a regimental roll call: Charles Hubert Hastings Parry. Not since 1727 had a composer been better matched to an occasion than Parry was to the coronation of Edward VII and Queen Alexandra in 1902 and the confident opening of the Edwardian era. And yet, there is something beneath the surface of this music, something ambiguous which makes it far more interesting than that.

Parry did not compose all that much church music, but his work in the field gave us some of his best-known works, and some of the most famous music of the age: 'Jerusalem', *Blest Pair of Sirens*, the hymn tunes 'Laudate Dominum' and 'Repton', the motet *My Soul, There is a Country*, as well as the curtain-raiser for 1902 and every coronation since, the anthem *I was Glad*. Church music studs his ample work-list throughout his long career. There is some service music and pieces on a smaller scale, including a few Christmas carol-anthems, offshoots of his interest in the part-song. But for such a prolific composer, the number of anthems is small. One of the best, and most characteristic, is *Hear my Words, Ye People*, composed for the massed choirs of the Diocesan Choral Festival at Salisbury in 1894. It begins with an almost symphonic prelude in B flat major, full of fanfares and cycles of fifths, like a dress-rehearsal for *I was Glad*. Soloists alternate with choir across a wide canvas, taking in a variety of texts, ending with a hymn, approached by a pedal note in the bass: 'O praise ye the Lord!' The anthem ends with the 'Amens' chucked with exhilarating abandon between solo quartet and choir. It had a new-found confidence: identifiably Edwardian rather than Victorian. But it was all pretty conventional: harmony, counterpoint, structure, choice of text, the emotion and world-view it evokes. The Diocese must have been pleased as it headed politely off to tea in the cloisters.

I was Glad skilfully synthesised these elements into something more subtle. It starts, not with a look-at-me chord of B flat major, but with the notes of the triad of D minor. Arrival at the tonic is hinted at, delayed, approached almost sideways, just like that other great coronation piece, Handel's *Zadok, the Priest*. When the choir does come crashing in with a chord of B flat, it is off again straight away, sharp-wards, to G major. The 'Vivats' (written with a little help from Sir Frederick Bridge, or so he claimed), lead to a well-paced build-up from the peaceful part-writing of 'O pray for the peace of Jerusalem' to a rousing ending, approached via the flat side, fanfare trumpets gleaming down the nave of the Abbey.

Parry returned to 'Jerusalem' fourteen years later, but this was a very different city. Blake's Jerusalem was not the psalmist's. His Christianity was epic, mythical, personal, ancient, enthusiastic, spiritual and passionately anti-church. Blake excoriated the established church for its emphasis on outward form and its lack of basic social justice, and gloried in the French Revolution. There is something very odd indeed, even disturbing, about putting the words of this man at the very heart of the most self-congratulatory celebrations of church and state. Parry knew this. He was even less of a conventional Christian than Blake. This was the man who didn't even attend his own daughter's christening. His setting of 'Jerusalem' was made not as a hymn but as a rallying song of the 'Fight for the Right' movement at the Queen's Hall in 1916. Parry conducted his own orchestration in 1918 at a concert for the Votes for Women campaign. This Jerusalem was a political one.

Blake didn't call his lyric 'Jerusalem' (which, confusingly, is actually the title of a quite different poem). Instead it formed the preface to his epic *Milton a Poem*, Milton being a favourite writer of both Blake, who was once found reading *Paradise Lost* in the garden with his wife, both of them stark naked, and Parry, whose fine 1887 setting of the ode 'Blest Pair of Sirens' is occasionally sung as an anthem when time permits.

Parry's willingness to embrace the unconventional brings us to one of the most intriguing experiments in this entire book, his set of six 'Ethical cantatas'. These are emphatically not church music, but they represent a fascinating, indeed unique, attempt to use the language and musical structures of the music of the church to reach out in a different direction. The cantatas have titles like *A Song of Darkness and Light* (1898), *War and Peace* (1903) and *A Vision of Life* (1907). The words are by poets like Robert Bridges and A. C. Benson, and by Parry himself. 'Limitless oneness binds us together' sing the dream voices in *A Vision of Life*. We are halfway between eighteenth-century Universalism and the words of a free-thinking musical modern like Michael Tippett, for whom 'The Goddess Joy would make us one'. *War and Peace* ends by borrowing words from the Christian liturgy:

Grant us Thy peace, Lord, that diviner dream,
… that day when all men's hearts shall beat
In sacred unison of life and love!

But this Lord has no special authority to bring these things about, and makes no further appearance. This is not the Lord of mass or Requiem. Why, when the need arises to make a common musical statement of our humanity, do we still reach for the imagery and forms of the Christian church? Parry dared to ask the question.

Part of the last section of the 'ethical cantata' War and Peace *by Hubert Parry.*

The best of Parry is in the *Songs of Farewell*. Written between 1916 and 1918, towards the end of his life and in the middle of the Great War, they reach for the old certainties of the sixteenth and seventeenth centuries: 'Lord, let me know mine end, and the number of my days'; 'Never tired pilgrim's limbs affected slumber more'; 'None can thee secure, but one who never changes'. There is some remarkably bold and forward-looking writing in the many different ways the composer divided up his choir, always with the meaning of the words in mind, for example the eerie, haunting octaves evoking the bleak idea that 'every man therefore is but vanity', the chromatic wail of despair at Donne's 'agues, tyrannies, despair, law, chance' giving way to the stillness of 'Let them sleep, Lord, and me mourn apace', like a pre-echo of Benjamin Britten's *War Requiem*. Beautiful, deep and serious music.

The last word about Parry, at least for now, should go to his daughter, writing in 1956:

> This fantastic legend about my father … that he was conventional, a conservative squire, a sportsman, a churchman … My father was the most naturally unconventional man I have known. He was a Radical, with a very strong bias against Conservatism … He was a free-thinker and did not go to my christening. He … was sensitive, and suffered from bouts of deep depression. The extraordinary misinterpretation of him that exists should not persist. [14]

Perhaps because standards of performance were getting better during the Victorian period, composers got better too – and Charles Villiers Stanford was the best. The lives of Parry and Stanford have a certain amount in common. Near-contemporaries, both were intended by their families for a more conventional career before an obsessive interest in music took over. Neither studied music at university (though that didn't stop Stanford becoming organist of his college, Trinity, Cambridge, while still an undergraduate). Both became influential teachers of the next generation through their work at the Royal College of Music. Both were deeply affected by the Great War, and died at a similar age around the time the war ended. But there were also pronounced differences. Stanford's childhood was happy (born to an affluent and musical family in Dublin); Parry's was lonely and marked by bereavement. The easy charm with which both men made their way through Victorian society could give way to something quite different in each of them: in Parry a depressive nervousness, in Stanford a hot and unforgiving temper which could make him 'nasty and quarrelsome and contradictious',[15] in George Grove's phrase. Parry and Stanford were close friends for much of their lives. Like some other symbiotic partnerships in this book, they worked through questions of style and manner together. Their music has elements in common: tunefulness and a certain formality of structure. But they also fell out badly towards the end of their lives, as rapidly changing conditions began to make their music sound old-fashioned. Only recently has it begun to be reassessed as it deserves.

There is more church music by Stanford than by Parry, and it is performed far more often, perhaps more than that of any other composer. This is partly because it is so good, but partly also because Stanford matched his output so closely to the requirements of the working cathedral choir. It would not be too much to say that he reinvented the art of setting the canticles, for morning as well as evening, and his versions form the backbone of Anglican music-lists all over the world. It is also intensely practical music: most choirs can make Stanford in C sound impressive, and the best choirs can make it subtle as well. The Magnificat in G is a work of imperishable charm, the solo characterising the first-person words of Mary over the sound of her spinning wheel in the organ and the gentle commentary of the choir.

Stanford's efforts in the opera house may be largely forgotten, but he spent much of his life composing and conducting for the theatre. Perhaps those instincts find their expression in this service, as well as providing one of the defining experiences for choirboys' mums (and dads) when their son gets to sing the solo. Stanford did an equal service to choirs who sing matins too (fewer in number now than in his day). His technical mastery allowed him to face the challenge of setting the long, wordy text of the Te Deum bravely. His setting in C major is built on a simple rising and falling motif which recurs throughout the structure, in all sorts of keys, in inversion, augmentation, as a sequence, in voices and organ. Nor is this just aimed at the desiccated analyst squinting at the score in a tutorial: the approach binds the text together in a completely convincing way, leading the listener through his bold but logical key progressions with deceptive ease. This is the direct result of proper study and real understanding of the music of progressive foreigners like Brahms, and brings something entirely new to English church music. A long piece no longer has to alternate chorus, aria and fugue, repeating until no more words are left.

These skills are present in the anthems and motets, too. *Beati quorum via* is in sonata form. The way the first theme returns towards the end, floating up from the tenor part before the upper voices have completed their oblique return to the tonic, is technically assured and musically magical. *O for a Closer Walk with God* is a hymn-anthem, a form Stanford effectively invented for the English, borrowed from the chorale-preludes of Bach: a gentle countermelody hovers around the Scottish psalm tune, playing almost imperceptibly with the underlying rhythm. There are bigger pieces, too. *For Lo, I Raise up* makes theatrical use of a virtuoso organ part and great variety of texture.

Running through all this is Stanford's gift for melody. He wrote a better tune than his friend Parry. Sometimes his best tunes just appear out of nowhere, like 'and his mercy is on them that fear him', in the Magnificat in B flat. But Stanford is perhaps at his best as a miniaturist. While larger works like the *Requiem* perhaps don't quite absorb the shade of Brahms and other emerging European powers into his own sound-world, the *Three Motets* and the best of the services do. Simeon departs in peace in the Nunc Dimittis in G with the same *cantabile* resignation as Drake bidding farewell to the coast of Devon in *Songs of the Sea*.

This authenticity of idea was very much at the heart of both men's teaching methods. Parry and Stanford's influence on the next generation must rate among their most significant contributions to English church music. As Vaughan Williams said:

> The secret of Parry's greatness as a teacher was his broad-minded sympathy … A student's compositions are seldom of any intrinsic merit, and a teacher is apt to judge them on their face-value. But Parry looked further than this; he saw what lay behind the faulty utterance and made it his object to clear the obstacles that prevented

fullness of musical speech. His watchword was 'characteristic' – that was the thing which mattered.[16]

And Gustav Holst told Herbert Howells that Stanford was 'the one man who could get any one of us out of a technical mess'.[17] Both Parry and Stanford insisted that their pupils did not allow through anything which was not convincingly their own. Alongside this was a scrupulous dedication to technique. Inevitably, the next generation of pupils eventually rejected much of this classicism just as Stanford had chafed against the restrictively academic teaching he had received as a young man in Vienna – but they never forgot it.

Among the very first cohort of composition students at the Royal College of Music was Charles Wood. In many ways, Wood, fourteen years his junior, tagged along after Stanford: both left Ireland for London and Cambridge, and later took up teaching posts at their alma mater. Wood succeeded Stanford as Professor of Music at Cambridge in 1924, but held the post for only a short time before his own death in 1926. If this makes Wood sound as if he was rather in the shadow of his older mentor and colleague, this is probably fair. The word often used about his church music is 'fastidious'. He clearly gave a good tutorial. But church music was in his blood: he was born and brought up in the diminutive cathedral precincts of Armagh, and many of his contributions remain in use today on account of their sheer craftsmanship, including approachable service music for full choir and men's voices, and arrangements and harmonisations like 'Ding, Dong, Merrily on High', 'This Joyful Eastertide' and 'King Jesus hath a Garden'. But, unlike some, he refused to push the stylistic boat out. Anthems like *Hail, Gladdening Light, Oculi omnium, Expectans expectavi* and *O Thou, the Central Orb* make the archetypal noise of Anglicanism, but it is a noise borrowed (even diluted) from Parry. In his choice of words, too, he showed little of the adventurousness of some of his contemporaries. The text of *O Thou, the Central Orb* was contrived by H. R. Bramley (Stainer's Christmas carol collaborator) to fit the music of a verse anthem by Orlando Gibbons whose original words were a rather boring ad hominem paean to James I, and thus unusable in regular choral worship. Bramley wanted to bring the music back into use by adding a mainstream devotional text of his own. Unfortunately, as with Tallis's *Spem in alium* four hundred years earlier, the result of trying to add words to pre-existing music was the sacrifice of sense to metre. So when Wood chose to set this curiously parented text, he created the ultimate all-purpose Anglican anthem, equally suitable for every occasion from a wet Thursday to a Diamond jubilee, and every Sunday-after-something in between. It sounds good, and the words don't mean anything at all. Perfect.

As a prep-school boy in Hampshire, Parry received some early instruction and encouragement from S. S. Wesley and there are composers writing for the church today who studied with pupils of Parry. And thus the family tree continues to flourish by the waterside of English church music. With one exception. Our last significant composer of this period was not a member of anybody's composition class, or even of the Church of England. He didn't go to Oxford, and learnt how to orchestrate by conducting the band of a lunatic asylum. He contributed to English church music without ever really touching the sides.

Edward Elgar was a man of deep religious sensibilities, as his oratorios amply show. But, despite living in a cathedral city with a fine tradition and a venerable festival, and having close friendships with a number of organists and choirmasters, including George Robertson Sinclair of Hereford (depicted along with his dog, Dan, in the *Enigma Variations*), he wrote comparatively little church music. The subject matter of the oratorios suggests that he was more attracted to the personal, revelatory religious experience of the Apostles and John Henry Newman's 'The Dream of Gerontius' than to the more abstract aesthetic of canticles and liturgy. His own Catholicism must also be part of it. But this was hardly rooted in family tradition: Elgar's father loathed organised religion, including 'the absurd superstition and playhouse mummery of the Papist; the cold and formal ceremonies of the Church of England; or the bigotry and rank hypocrisy of the Wesleyan'.[18] Nevertheless he took the job of organist of a Roman Catholic church in Worcester purely for the money. Mrs Elgar got into the habit of going with him for the sake of a good walk on a Sunday morning, and eventually found herself converting and bringing up her children as Catholics. The road to religion for many of the musicians in this book has some peculiarly secular twists along the way.

Elgar's church music can be classed into two types. Both suffer somewhat from the fact that, beneath the cassock, each is actually something else in disguise – respectively, parlour music and symphonic music. The symphonic pieces were mostly written for particular occasions, including the Te Deum and Benedictus for the Hereford Music Festival of 1897, *O Hearken Thou* for the coronation of George V in 1911, and *Give unto the Lord* for the Sons of the Clergy Festival at St Paul's in 1914. These are marvellous pieces, amply stuffed with Elgar's abundant melodic gifts and instinct for the big occasion. But, as always with Elgar, there is something less predictable here too, a yearning, expressed in a tune not quite going where it was meant to but taking an unexpected harmonic twist instead, and a seeming inability to settle.

There is some attractive quiet writing, for example the divided trebles at 'that we, being delivered' in the Benedictus. *O Hearken Thou* evokes the intimacy inherent in the coronation rite as effectively as Handel's slow movements. But the basic problem with these pieces is that Elgar was too good at doing something else: writing symphonic orchestral music. Words get pegged to a melody which is there because of its function in the symphonic structure, and they don't quite fit: the two appearances of the fine triple-time melody in *The Spirit of the Lord is upon me*, the opening chorus of *The Apostles*, often sung as an anthem, show this happening.

Elsewhere, the listener who knows the symphonies can hear Elgar treating the vocal line as if it was a fat little inner part for clarinets and violas, a subordinate counterpoint to a main melody in the organ, as at 'when thou hadst overcome the sharpness of death' and 'when thou tookest upon thee to deliver man' in the Te Deum. Clarity of text is not always the winner in this kind of symphonic manipulation of theme and texture.

The smaller-scale pieces have immense charm, for example *Ave verum* and *Ave Maria*. There is some early Latin music too. But the music of *Ave verum* gives not the slightest hint that the words include, among other things, blood, death, wounds and a grieving mother. It's just too nice a tune. Give it to Elgar's friend Billy Reed to play on the violin, and you have a parlour piece to sit alongside *Salut d'amour* and the *Chanson de matin*. Partly, this is because the tune was not originally a setting of these words, but of the Requiem text *Pie Jesu*, though that, if anything, is even more anguished. Choirs will, and must, go on singing it, but there's something missing. Even more so than Parry, Elgar remains English church music's ultimate in-outsider.

VAUGHAN WILLIAMS SAID THAT Stanford was 'in the best sense of the word Victorian'.[19] The best of the Victorians is revealed when we stop thinking of them as Victorians and appreciate just how creative and ambitious they were. They reached back to the past and reinvented the future. The architecture of choral worship today is supported by two great buttresses: the music of the fifty years either side of the turn of the seventeenth century, and Victorian music. One of the side effects of the English musical Renaissance was that sacred choral music came back into the orbit of serious composers and performers, where it has remained, more or less, ever since. English church music effectively slept through the Classical and Romantic periods. Wesley, the Oxford Movement, Parry, Stanford and Elgar collectively proved to be the handsome prince who woke it up again.

14

The Splintering of the
Tradition, 1914–2015

Dancing about architecture.

Elvis Costello (attr.)[1]

'IN THE TWENTIETH CENTURY,' says the American music critic
Alex Ross, '… musical life disintegrated into a teeming mass of cultures
and subcultures.' Classical music became an 'obscure pandemonium on
the outskirts of culture'.[2] As a description of church music, Ross's words
are well chosen. 'Disintegrated' implies a degree of integration prior to
this point. This is right. Despite all the conflicts and disagreements, it
has always been possible so far to find a box within which to categorise a
particular composer: this one's a Catholic, that one's a classicist, the other
is a conservative contrapuntalist. To a large, and increasing, extent, in the
twentieth century everybody made their own box.

This makes it harder to write about them. Simply listing what a
composer did, creating for him 'a pedigree so general in tone, so replete
with Influences and Comparisons, does not lead us to savour whatever
distinctive voice the composer may have had … one might as well study
a train timetable and hope to gain therefrom a clear picture of the land-
scapes that will accompany one's journeys',[3] as Donald Mitchell wisely
and wittily warned us. It brings us back to the basic problem that you
can't describe music in words.

But we have to try. The attempt, then, will be to find a way through the 'teeming mass' and try to work out how church music and its makers fit in, or don't – and will encompass, among much else, individual composers of genius, music for increasingly skilled choirs, music for the parish, church music in wartime, music in society, the assimilation of English folk-song, the effect of the church on other kinds of music and vice versa, nationalism, and hymns. All of these begin with Ralph Vaughan Williams.

Vaughan Williams is a big character. The more you look at him, the bigger he gets. Son of a vicar who died when he was an infant, Vaughan Williams was related to the Darwin and Wedgwood families and was brought up in a literary and musical environment at Leith Hill Place, home of his mother's family, among the rolling Surrey hills. In 1887, when he was fourteen, he went to Charterhouse School, which had just moved from its ancient home in London (where Purcell had worked) to its grand new buildings in Godalming. Music was treated with unusual seriousness at Charterhouse, and his earliest compositions appear in school concert programmes under the name 'Williams' (his name also regularly features in the prefects' discipline lists for unspecified misdemeanours such as 'misbehaviour').[4] He studied history and music at Trinity College, Cambridge, where his circle of acquaintance broadened to include thinkers like Bertrand Russell. Before and after Cambridge he was a student of Stanford and Parry at the Royal College of Music, where many significant friendships took root, most importantly with Gustav Holst.

Vaughan Williams's importance to church music is all-encompassing. His influence includes his work as a hymn-writer and editor, the discovery and assimilation of English folk-song, his love of early music, in particular English music of the sixteenth century, his egalitarian commitment to writing music for amateur musicians, and his own unmistakable compositional voice. His biggest piece of liturgical music, the Mass in G minor of 1922, shows him kicking over the traces of his teachers more comprehensively than any generation of pupils had done, either before or possibly since. Although Parry and Stanford were modernists according to their lights, their harmony was straight out of the same textbook as their predecessors.

The cardinal sin in this textbook was the 'parallel fifth'. Students attempting to recreate the music of Palestrina and Bach have traditionally spent much of their time picking through their exercises and taking out the parallels. In Professor Parry's class you took them out of your own music too. But Vaughan Williams put them back in again. The Sanctus of the Mass floats around the key of G major, voice-parts joining one another in slowly revolving chords. If parallel intervals happen to arise from this movement of the spheres, they are unblushingly left in. So are 'false relations', where a sharp or flat in one voice-part produces a 'clash' with another. The music is written in the ancient church 'modes'. There is no attempt to write a big tune. Centres of tonality are shifted by moving the mode from one place to another, with no pretence at modulation: the Agnus Dei presents its music in E minor, then in G minor, with no attempt to move from one key to the other in any functional sense. This piece was written for the cavernous, incense-filled spaces of the gloomy, half-finished Catholic cathedral in Westminster and its pioneering choirmaster Richard Runciman Terry. It is hard to imagine a better, and more daring, analogue to Terry's revolutionary use of Renaissance polyphony from England and Europe, two sides of the same attempt to recreate the music of the past and its Catholic hinterland.

Michael Kennedy, music critic and biographer, makes the perceptive point that Vaughan Williams's major works are often surrounded by other works of the same period which explore similar preoccupations, like moons around a planet.[5] The disposition of the vocal forces in the mass is distinctive, perhaps owing something to Parry's experiments in the *Songs of Farewell* in his use of two equal choruses and a separate quartet of solo voices. It is the same arrangement used in Vaughan Williams's *Fantasia on a Theme of Thomas Tallis* for strings of 1910: a double string orchestra and string quartet. This is church music *manqué*, dreaming its way through the harmony of Tallis's psalm-chant, first performed, appropriately, in Gloucester Cathedral. Critic J. A. Fuller Maitland was bang on in his thoughtful, moving review of the premiere:

> ... it seems to lift one into some unknown region of musical thought and feeling. Throughout its course one is never quite sure if one is

> listening to something very old or very new ... The voices of the old
> church musicians ... are around one, and yet there is more besides ...[6]

Rethinking choral texture was just one of the ways in which Vaughan Williams simply started again from scratch. Why should a choir be in four equal parts? Who said? Long passages of his most arresting choral music are in two parts. He was one of the great masters of writing in unison. Sometimes, he combined these various antique neologisms. 'Lord, thou hast been our refuge' sets a modal, unison melody against William Croft's hymn tune, 'St Anne', building to a climax where the tune is played by a trumpet with organ accompaniment. In other hands it could have been corny, but Vaughan Williams is somehow so respectful of his tune that it never is, just as he is in his big, brassy arrangement of the 'Old Hundredth' and, equally, in the tiny, intimate scale of the organ prelude on the Welsh tune 'Rhosymedre'. England seems to flow through his musical veins in the music of her past composers, her folk-song and her hymn tunes, so that the boundary between church music and symphonic music, and between old material and new, becomes blurred and bound together by a shared musical inheritance.

And by words. This generation rediscovered, among so much else, the religious poets of the seventeenth century and, through Arthur Quiller-Couch's pioneering *Oxford Book of English Verse* of 1900, the devotional poems and carols of a much earlier period too. These texts resonate through twentieth-century church music. One of Vaughan Williams's most often-performed works is the set of *Five Mystical Songs*, to words by George Herbert, originally composed for baritone, chorus and orchestra and issued in a variety of versions thereafter. It's all here: the freedom of the vocal line, the ancient melody, sung to a wordless hum, the boldness, the exhilarating, modal harmony which ends the work (Vaughan Williams's cadences could generate a chapter on their own), and, above all, the word-setting. 'Rise, heart', indeed, as Herbert commanded. Another important development led by Vaughan Williams was the incorporation of genuine English folk-song into church music. Just one song will have to stand representative for how he did it.

'Our Captain Calls all Hands' was collected and written down by a

Vaughan Williams's hymn tune to Bunyan's verse (adapted by Percy Dearmer), and the tune he based it on — nothing to do with God or goblins.

number of gleaners in the field. Cecil Sharp took down the text from Mrs Ware of Somerset in 1907 and Vaughan Williams got the tune from Mrs Kemp in Essex in 1904. It's a good tune, with a typically quirky change of the underlying rhythm in the last couple of bars, like a peasant tripping over his hobnails. The words are pretty traditional stuff about a young man off to the wars, his girlfriend's fears for his safety (and his fidelity), and his not very convincing replies. Vaughan Williams and the hymn-editor Percy Dearmer put the tune to a verse from Bunyan's *Pilgrim's Progress*, 'He who would Valiant be', which in Bunyan's original has a folksy swagger to its horror-struck evocation of goblin and foul fiend, sadly usually omitted today. Thus a hymn was born. But a fascinating detail emerges from comparing the hymn tune, which they called 'Monk's Gate', with the original folk-song. 'Monk's Gate' repeats its first line, like many hymn tunes. But in the original song it is the second line, not the first, which is repeated – more irregular, but more fun. Vaughan Williams has smoothed it out. He was perfectly unapologetic about this sort of thing: folk-song was a living, oral tradition, and tunes changed between versions, or 'variants', as he called them, from one village to the next. His version is just one more 'variant'. The long note at the beginning of the last line of 'O Little Town of Bethlehem' is his invention: it wasn't there when Mr Garman sang him this tune, to words about a delinquent ploughboy and a dead cow, in Forest Green, Surrey, in 1903. There are lots of examples. The tune 'King's Lynn', set to 'O God of Earth and Altar', started out as a song about a convict being transported to Tasmania.

All the composers of this generation lost admired friends in the war. Alongside those whose music we know are those whose church music we will never hear: George Butterworth, Cecil Coles, and countless others. Church music rang a few passing bells during the Great War, however.

The name of Ivor Gurney is not often mentioned in the context of church music. He wrote many songs, and some of the most sensitive poetry of an age which produced much in the field. He was a native of Gloucester (in passing, it is remarkable how much musical talent that county produced around these years), and received his early musical training as a choirboy and later articled student at Gloucester Cathedral. He shared in the close friendships of the group centred around Stanford's composition class at the Royal College of Music. But his contribution to church music as a composer lay unremarked in the archive until very recently. Robert Bridges's poem 'Since I Believe in God the Father Almighty' is a kind of anti-Creed, setting out what the poet can and cannot know and believe among the 'hours of anguish and darkness'. Gurney set it in 1925, when the 'hours of anguish' were upon him. Bridges was, as well as a fine poet and an important pioneer of hymnody, a believer. Despite the acknowledgement that 'I have seen not, and cannot know Him', he finds a way of 'Confiding always on His excellent greatness'. It is a statement of faith, albeit hard-won. Mental fragility haunted the artists of these post-war years and Gurney in particular suffered cruelly. Perhaps church music afforded him some solace. As a student at the Royal College in 1914, he composed a chant for Psalm 23 and sang it to himself under fire in the trenches at Fauquissart.[7]

Gustav Holst found himself in Salonica during the Great War, running music education initiatives for the troops. He formed a ramshackle choir and orchestra, and the desert broke out with the sounds of Renaissance polyphony: 'I believe my choral music is being unloaded in the docks. Do you know that all this time I've been trying to make people sing without any music? It's been rather a lark ...'[8] Stanford, too old for active service, poured his horror of the war into a setting of a violent Old Testament text: 'that bitter and hasty nation, which march thro' the breadth of the earth, to possess the dwelling places that are not theirs. They are terrible and dreadful ...'[9]

Vaughan Williams served as an ambulance driver in France and the war impacted directly on his church music a little later, when Richard Runciman Terry, preparing the Mass in G minor in 1922, had still not filled the depleted ranks of the men in his celebrated choir at Westminster Cathedral: 'I shall spare no pains to give the work an adequate performance. I shall try to get into touch with all the deputies that the war has scattered ... For this event the attenuated state of my choir will not matter, as I have on hand a number of educated amateurs (first-rate sight-singers) ...'[10] Parry remembered the war in his *Songs of Farewell*, while church music plays its part in remembering still, in the solemn cadences of William Croft's tune to 'O God, our Help in Ages Past', sung at the annual Remembrance Sunday parade in Whitehall from 1919 to this day.

Church music has always reflected changes in society, and the First World War changed society profoundly. Vaughan Williams and Holst had always been passionately keen on the role of music in education and the social and corporate life of ordinary communities; and in 1925 Vaughan Williams provided a simple, flexible setting of the Evening Canticles which he called 'The Village Service'. When he was in Salonica, Holst had dreamed of running 'a kindergarten or the Thaxted choir'[11] in the village in Essex where he and his wife had a house. Its glorious church, 'like a cathedral', demanded to be filled with music, and Holst brought singers from his teaching posts in London to form the nucleus of the Whitsuntide Festival, playing the organ and writing arrangements and original compositions for the school-girls and villagers. As at some other moments in church-music history, there were those who thought that all this music-making among the people was dangerously subversive: there was a strong dash of left-wing politics in artistic circles of the time. The vicar of Thaxted was a famous Independent Labour Party supporter called Conrad Noel, known as the 'Red Vicar', and when Noel demanded greater support from his flock for the Russian Revolution at the festival held in 1918, Holst quietly moved his schoolgirls and his festival back to London. 'Tomorrow shall be my Dancing-Day' can be taken to mean a lot of things.

The war caused changes in the vocal balance within the average parish choir, with an unexpected result. The reduced number of available men led thoughtful hymnbook editors like Vaughan Williams to start reusing the old harmonisations of East and Ravenscroft, with the tune in the tenor. All the available men sang the tune. Upper voices, now more numerous than the men, had a harmony line, pitched above the tune. People liked the sound. Tunes started to appear with a specially com-posed tune added on top: the 'descant' as we know it was born.

As noted above, Gustav Holst is relevant to this story for what his activites as arranger, compiler and conductor tell us about the place of church music in society. Sacred choral music occupied a small but distinctive niche in his work as a composer, too. There is not much music by Holst which can be safely categorised as church music in the accepted sense. His mind was too inquiring and versatile for that. When he borrowed a churchy word like 'Hymns' for the title of one of his pieces, he applied it not to a chocolate-box selection from *Ancient and Modern* but to his own translations of mystical verses from the Sanskrit. *The Hymn of Jesus* sets part of the Apocryphal Acts of St John. This inventive approach to text and subject matter ran throughout Holst's vocal music. The conventional pieties of the Book of Common Prayer were never going to hold much interest for a man of his sympathies.

In a sense this has had a slightly negative impact on his reputation. Certainly, Holst's unwillingness to play to popularity or market has meant fewer performances than he could have had. Perhaps his most important contribution to the repertoire comes in the form of arrangements. There are lots of English Christmas carols, including his original setting of the mysterious text 'Tomorrow shall be my Dancing-day' – one of the first – and his tune to 'In the Bleak Midwinter'. There is a sturdy arrangement of the recently unearthed sixteenth-century song 'Personent hodie'. Its striding bass scales reappear in hymn-anthems like *Turn Back, O Man* – good, useful music, where a strong, muscular tune for the people meets art woven into the accompaniment: William Morris in sound. There are hymn tunes, including 'Thaxted', mined from the 'Jupiter' theme in *The Planets*. The more conventional Christian texts are often set for community groups of various kinds: a *Short Festival Te Deum*, pieces for children's choir, men's or women's voices, sometimes with flexible accompaniment.

Their relative rarity thus makes Holst's genuine church choir pieces all the more precious. *The Evening Watch* is a setting of a 'dialogue between the body and the soul' by Henry Vaughan, the conversation played out between two soloists and the full choir in music full of fifths, marked to be sung with 'no variation from *sempre pp* until near the end': cool, detached, disturbing, unexpected music, like the finale of Vaughan Williams's sixth symphony. Pre-eminent among Holst's sacred choral works is the Latin *Nunc Dimittis*, written in 1915 for R. R. Terry and Westminster Cathedral and then entirely forgotten until the 1970s. It's a wonderful piece, a slowly shimmering chord growing out of an opening bass pedal note, the structure gradually building in speed and vigour to a rousing, high climax. It sounds even more exciting in Holst's original key of B flat major, a semitone higher than modern editions.

Arnold Bax was another whose contribution to church music was a small thing but very much his own. His sacred vocal music is finely wrought and fragrantly harmonised. His Magnificat is a concert piece, not a liturgical work, setting the text as it appears in the King James version of St Luke's Gospel (not the prayer book) for four voices and piano. Early texts interested him, especially Christmas poems associated with the Virgin Mary. *Of a Rose I Sing* is for voices, harp, piano, cello and double bass, a sinuously stringy version of the old 'broken' consort. *I Sing of a Maiden* floats around seemingly unrelated minor tonalities like an Irish mist. Bax's masterpiece in the genre is the ten-minute *Mater ora filium* of 1922. This is a tour de force of unaccompanied eight-part writing, assuming a high degree of technical accomplishment among the singers to keep it in tune and manage the long soprano top 'C' at the end. Bax's thoughtful style was not well suited to the big, public statement, even though he held the official post of Master of the King's Music from 1941 (Vaughan Williams, a much better qualified candidate, had turned it down).[12] When Princess Elizabeth married Philip Mountbatten at Westminster Abbey in 1947, the Abbey organist, William McKie, 'omitted' to ask Bax to write a choral piece, getting him to contribute two fanfares instead. McKie repeated the snub at the coronation in 1953.

Peter Warlock was a musical miniaturist and a prodigious drunk. It was always going to take something far more compelling than the requirements of God or career to get his best work out of him, and he found it in the form of a bar bill. *Bethlehem Down* was written to finance a drinking binge with his friend Bruce Blunt at Christmas 1927. Somehow, they made a thing of rare beauty and intelligence. There are some other choral works, notably carols like the spirited *Benedicamus Domino*, with its frankly medieval swinging refrain, and the hushed *Balulalow*. *Adam Lay Ybounden*, written as a song, is often heard at carol services.

Another enigmatic figure was John Ireland. In some of its details, his story bridges the gap between the confident Edwardians and the complex post-1945 generation. Born in the last quarter of the nineteenth century, Ireland was one of the younger composers to have studied with Stanford. He was a church organist, and taught at the Royal College of Music himself, another link in the long chain of pupil–teacher genealogy. He was also introspective, insecure and almost certainly homosexual at a time when such things found no easy expression. His childhood had been sad and lonely. Is it possible to hear something of this throttled yearning in the choice of texts in his church music: 'many waters cannot quench love'; 'greater love hath no man than this'; 'love to the loveless shown'; 'and yet I want to love thee'; 'O light the flame within my heart'? His pupil Benjamin Britten was present at a performance of *Greater Love Hath no Man* at St Mark's, North Audley Street, on Sunday, 8 March 1931, and wrote in his diary: 'v. fine sermon by Bish. of London, & v. fine anthem "Many Waters" of Ireland v. well sung.'[13] Britten was right: this is 'v. fine', no mere bit of conventional Edwardian church music, despite having been composed as early as 1912. It paces out its carefully selected text through sections for soloists and choir, building to a rousing tune for 'Him who has called you out of darkness'. There is great subtlety and imagination here. So, too, in *Ex ore innocentium*, a setting of William Walsham How's hymn 'It is a Thing Most Wonderful' for treble voices and organ, supple melodies allied to poignant harmony. Britten may have thought Ireland 'a strong personality but a weak character',[14] but something of the ambivalence of these 'innocentes' survives in Britten's own work. Ireland's service music reveals less of his musical personality, but amply takes its place in the little clutch of 'short'-type services which bridge the stylistic gap between Stanford and Howells.

SACRED MUSIC EVOLVED IN other corners of English life too. Performance away from church played its part, as always. Domestic music-making re-emerged in the nineteenth century as the parlour song on a religious text. Stanford's *Six Bible Songs* are a kind of halfway house between church and drawing-room: solo songs, but with organ accompaniment. In the 1920s, a lot of notable sacred music was written for concert ensembles, principally Charles Kennedy Scott's influential Oriana Madrigal Society choir. Scott raised the status of church music in the concert hall, just as R. R. Terry did in the cathedral choir stall. Both brought high standards to new repertoire of past and present. Long, difficult a cappella choral works, aimed at groups with more expertise and more rehearsal time than the average church choir, became a notable sub-genre of sacred composition throughout the twentieth century, thanks in no small measure to Scott.

In the parish church, urban choirs at the beginning of the twentieth century had largely pursued the Victorian mini-cathedral ideal of choral music sung by a robed choir of men and boys, but it was an increasing struggle. Changes in society were reflected in changes in churchmanship. One development with distinctive results was the re-emergence of the high-church party. Among its leaders was Percy Dearmer, a dedicated young priest who was vicar of St Mary's, Primrose Hill, from 1901 to 1915. The liturgical innovations he introduced there shocked many. We are halfway to the world of Barbara Pym, whose tweedy heroines set out from their Pimlico mansion flats to sniff out the local smells and bells: 'I could imagine my mother, her lips pursed, shaking her head and breathing in a frightened whisper, "*Incense*"...' mews Mildred in *Excellent Women*.[15] The music at these 'High' churches would not have been too different from the days of the Pimlico riots a century before: anthems and service music sung by a choir of men and boys in surplices, some plainsong, much congregational singing, a good organist and a separate choirmaster. A small but distinctive band of organist-composers emerged through the incense at the principal Anglo-Catholic parishes in London and their satellites on the south coast. Their work has its own peculiar whiff. George Oldroyd, Percy Whitlock and William Lloyd Webber compressed the sound-world of the Palm Court orchestra and the romantic symphony into well-crafted music for choir and organ, like tinned Gounod.

The generation born in the last third of the nineteenth century produced a number of important composers who were called on to turn their hand to many other things as well. Henry Walford Davies was Organist of the Temple Church (where his assistant was a perhaps surprising scion of English church music, the American conductor Leopold Stokowski) and St George's Chapel, Windsor, where he had been a chorister. His other musical activities give a good indication of the times he lived in. In 1918 he was appointed as the first Director of Music of the Royal Air Force and wrote the rousing *RAF March Past* jointly with his colleague George Dyson. He was also the first musician to seriously exploit the new art of broadcasting, and his long-running radio lecture series and engaging books and articles set an important precedent for musical popularisers ever since. As a choir director, he did much to establish high standards of psalm-chanting, laying down a benchmark for other choirs through his regular broadcasts from the Temple Church. He was a prolific composer, though his most frequently heard works today are, perhaps appropriately, miniatures: a chant to Psalm 121 ('I will Lift up mine Eyes unto the Hills'), and a jewel-like setting of a prayer from a sixteenth-century primer, *God be in my Head*: sixty seconds of peaceful valediction.

Scowling down from the organ loft 200 miles to the north was the blunt Yorkshireman Edward Bairstow. Some of his music sits down under the shadow of Brahms and others, but the best of it is individual to the point of genius. *Let All Mortal Flesh Keep Silence* evokes the modes and movement of medieval monks before exploding into ecstatic 'Hallelujahs' and the best silences of the century. *I Sat down under His Shadow* floats between E major and G major and between 2/4 and 6/8 in a completely original way. Bairstow's most striking conception is *Blessed City*, drawing on the shade of J. M. Neale for his translation of a Latin hymn and its plainsong. The boldness of the harmony puts this grand piece beyond any accusation of parroting Parry, and it ends with a timeless, floating treble solo.

William Henry Harris worked at various times at St George's, Windsor, and at New College and Christ Church, Oxford. There is much church music by Harris, but his most enduring contributions are his two marvellous settings of seventeenth-century devotional texts, *Bring Us, O Lord* and *Faire is the Heaven*, both in D flat major, for unaccompanied choir in eight parts – like thick chocolate.

Harold Darke was Organist of St Michael's Cornhill in the City of London for half a century from 1916, with a break deputising for Boris Ord at King's College, Cambridge, during the Second World War. He initiated a weekly organ recital series at St Michael's which is still going, widely believed to be the longest-running such series in the world. Like other composers in this group, his music hardly pushes at the boundaries of modernism, though his familiar communion setting in F major contains some mildly progressive experiments with speech-rhythm passages, a bit like an eighteenth-century 'chanting tune'. Darke does have one notable compositional feather in his cap: in 2008 his melodious setting of Christina Rossetti's 'In the Bleak Midwinter' came first in a BBC poll to find the nation's favourite Christmas carol.[16]

As at other periods, these composers form an identifiable 'school'. They gave their Edwardian musical inheritance a tuneful twist rather than throwing it out and attempting something new. Their lives crossed and interacted as they moved from choir school to conservatoire, from military service to the organ loft.

Edgar Bainton took English church music to the other side of the world. A native of the north of England, he studied at the Royal College, spent the whole of the First World War in an internment camp after an ill-timed trip to the Bayreuth Festival, and emigrated with his family to Australia in 1934 to head up the New South Wales conservatorium. His masterpiece is *And I Saw a New Heaven*, drifting subtly between D minor and major, a rapt tune arriving to 'wipe away all tears' (except, perhaps, those of the tenors, for whom it lies rather high).

Another whose reputation rests on a single piece is Henry Balfour Gardiner. Balfour Gardiner was an influential supporter of new music between the wars, though his intense self-criticism as a composer led him to destroy much of his own music. His name thus survives on cathedral music-lists through just one early piece, the lush, romantic *Evening Hymn* of 1908.

None of these church composers were musical progressives: Bainton once turned down Arnold Schoenberg for a teaching job because of his 'modernist ideas and dangerous tendencies'.[17] And he wasn't the only one. The English church music of the first half of the twentieth century, for all its glories, can't often be accused of being swayed by the forces of musical modernism.

Also flying the flag for the Northerner was George Dyson. Like Sullivan, he studied abroad on a Mendelssohn Scholarship, and was invalided out of the Great War with shell-shock, later joining the RAF. During his active service he wrote the standard training manual on the safe use of the hand grenade, a fact which always intrigues choirboys. After many years as a public-school music master he became Director of the Royal College of Music, helping to launch many notable careers. Percy Scholes described his music as 'skilful, sometimes deeply felt, but never forward-looking in idiom',[18] which is certainly fair. In church he is represented by his service music, a keystone of the repertoire. The Evening Service in F has a charming treble solo over a rocking organ accompaniment in the Magnificat, a restful bass in the Nunc Dimittis. The service in D is on an altogether grander scale. It is not, perhaps, music of the last degree of subtlety, but its big organ pedal notes build satisfyingly to a big climax, and its generous melodiousness maybe owes something to Dyson's time with the band of the RAF. Its big tune can easily be imagined as the soundtrack to a fly-past of Spitfires – Sunday evensong music, for when the lay-clerks have had a good lunch.[19]

The church music of George Dyson leads directly into consideration of the work of a group of composers, born around the turn of the twentieth century, who were first and foremost cathedral organists and professional church musicians.

Herbert Sumsion became Organist of Gloucester Cathedral in 1928 following the sudden death of Herbert Brewer (thus taking up the reins at that year's Three Choirs Festival, leading Elgar to remark that 'what at the beginning of the week was *assumption* has now become a certainty'[20]). Of his large output of church music, his three settings of the Magnificat and Nunc Dimittis in G major have earned themselves a regular and much-loved place in the repertoire of cathedral choirs.

Sydney Watson laid proud claim to have been one of Stanford's last pupils at the Royal College. In his professional life as choir director and organist, he gave what was probably the first liturgical performance of John Taverner's *Missa corona spinea* for 400 years, in Taverner's own college, Christ Church, Oxford. His own music includes a set of Evening Canticles in E major, which Watson, who had a stammer, referred to as 'm-m-me in E'.[21]

Another familiar setting in E major is the one by Herbert Murrill. Murrill's musical sympathies were broader than some: 'Francophile and mildly middle-Stravinskian', in the words of Ronald Crichton in *The New Grove Dictionary of Music and Musicians*.[22] There is a jazz opera, two fine cello concertos (one for Pablo Casals), and incidental music to a couple of Cocteau-esque plays by W. H. Auden, including *The Dog Beneath the Skin*. Not much of this permeates into the choir stall.

Patrick Hadley was a Cambridge man by birth and employment (and would alarm prospective students at his college, Caius, by sticking drawing pins into his wooden leg through the fabric of his trousers). His music is unblushingly neo-Romantic. His setting of *My Beloved Spake* matches grand climaxes with some effective quieter writing, and the expressive upper-voice carol *I Sing of a Maiden* is often sung. *My Song is Love Unknown* is set as a fine, challenging tenor solo.

These men created a core part of the choral repertoire, especially in their settings of the cathedral choir's daily bread, the Magnificat and Nunc Dimittis. It is music that holds a special place in the heart of choristers of all ages, especially those who learnt it as children. These were composers who knew exactly what their choirs could do, and would enjoy doing. There is more good music to be discovered in their desk drawer.

AN IMPORTANT DEVELOPMENT FOR parish church music during the twentieth century was the changing shape of Sunday mornings, and in particular the replacement of matins with communion as the main musical meal of the day. The cathedral-pattern fully choral setting was not appropriate, or manageable, in most parishes. The congregation could, and should, take part in singing the 'ordinary' of the mass. Marbeck remained the eternal yardstick, usually with organ harmonies in the Thomas Helmore style. Other plainsong adaptations also came into use. More varied and up-to-date music required a new approach.

In his *Anglican Folk Mass* of 1917, Martin Shaw built on the Marbeck model with great skill and carefully concealed artifice. The piece is based on a small number of musical motifs, portioned out throughout the work, allowing the congregation to master the tunes and then recognise them easily each time they return. It was a task well suited to a musician with Shaw's background in hymn-writing and passionate commitment to education and musical inclusivity. Geoffrey Beaumont took the process further in his *Folk Mass* of 1956. The approach here was different. Melodies are sung first by a cantor, then sung back by the congregation, a modern reincarnation of the hoary old practice of 'lining out'. The music is frankly popular in style, with syncopated rhythms and 'show-tune' melodies over a naggingly repeated bass, like an old-fashioned dance band ('remarkably dull and repetitive',[23] according to Erik Routley), accompanied by keyboard, bass and drums. Its 'pop' idiom sounds rather mild to us today, but this was some years before

> Sexual intercourse began
> in nineteen sixty-three …
> Between the end of the *Chatterley* ban
> And the Beatles' first LP…

as Philip Larkin put it.[24] But Beaumont's Mass caused something of a stir at the time, especially when it was televised in 1957. This was new – these were 'show tunes'. A number of writers have noticed that the melody for 'Holy, holy, holy' is similar to Eric Coates's immortal *Dam Busters March*.[25] And why not? Why should the RAF have all the best tunes?

Patrick Appleford continued the process with his *Mass of Five Melodies* of 1961. These composers coalesced around the Twentieth Century Church Light Music Group, one of those informal groupings which from time to time in this story have drawn together a prevailing trend, and often for similar reasons: the drawing-in of the people through the use of familiar music was the main musical impetus for the Reformation psalm and the eighteenth-century hymn. But the introduction of pop music was a new kind of revolution, which is still going on.

Later developments brought the congregational mass setting back towards the traditional verities of organ and antiphony, alternating choir and congregation in a through-composed setting. Many churches use settings of this kind, including Westminster Cathedral for its annual Chrism Mass. Many parish church composers have written their own, which is absolutely in the best tradition of local, home-sourced community music-making. Some of the very best and most serious composers of all, notably James MacMillan, have written settings for choir and congregation, and musicians of all kinds have responded to the challenges and opportunities of new approaches to the communion service, including Series 1, 2 and 3 of the Church of England, and the far-reaching Second Vatican Council in the Roman Catholic Church. The man with a guitar became a familiar sight to congregations of all kinds: a new solution to an old conundrum.

Both Shaw and Beaumont called their pieces *Folk Mass*, but this had nothing to do with indigenous folk-song. Vaughan Williams and others began the process of bringing real folk tunes in from the field and the farmyard, both as hymns with new words attached, and as arrangements of the originals as they found them, mostly for Christmas. Many others followed where they led. Sometimes they set folk texts to original music, like Holst's gorgeous *Lullay my Liking*. Their own music carries the constant stamp of the cadences and inflections of folk music, as well as the atavistic echoes of the medieval and the modal. It was a logical step for a suitably qualified wordsmith to attempt something similar with the words: write something new, which maintained and echoed the style and virtues of folk art.

William Morris and Christina Rossetti began the process by writing poems in a deliberately faux-archaic style, as in 'Masters in this Hall' and 'In the Bleak Midwinter'. The ideal synthesis was achieved much later in the century by Sydney Carter. 'Lord of the Dance' is a real modern folk-song. It uses the structure of burden and refrain. Its imagery has all the vivid immediacy of folk art: 'it's hard to dance with the devil on your back'. The language is simple and unadorned: 'I am the life that will never, never die'. At the same time, there is meaning and an element of mystery. What is this dance?

THE MOST DISTINCTIVE VOICE in the sacred music of mid-century belongs to a composer whose reputation rests almost entirely on church music, Herbert Howells. His CV has much in common with other members of the 'school': a background in the provincial Cotswolds, study with Parry and Stanford at the Royal College of Music, early works for R. R. Terry at Westminster. Unlike others, however, Howells was also a practising church musician, learning the trade under articles to the Organist of Gloucester Cathedral as a young man, and later becoming Assistant Organist at Salisbury Cathedral, though health problems forced him to relinquish this post after just a few months. Perhaps even more important to his development as a composer was the work he found to replace the Salisbury job, acting as Terry's editorial assistant in restoring English church music of the Tudor period to use.

The ebb and flow of Tudor polyphony is there in Howells's choral style, along with its modes. There are clear echoes of Vaughan Williams's ability to synthesise the sound of the old into something not so much new as timeless. Howells was present at the first performance of the *Tallis Fantasia*, and ever after remembered the older composer sitting next to him for the rest of the concert and sharing his score of *The Dream of Gerontius* with his tongue-tied young colleague. But there is so much that is distinctly his own. His melodies have a rhythmic freedom, sometimes almost like plainsong, as in the supple pentatonic opening of the carol *A Spotless Rose*, or the passages for solo voices in the *Requiem*. Melodic signatures include a nagging devotion to the minor third, giving tunes such as *Like as the Hart* an almost jazzy quality, but are utterly assimilated into his own sound-world and wholly convincing. His structures often treat a text as a single unit: in his hands Nunc Dimittis, and sometimes even Magnificat, become a single musical phrase, the vocal lines extended almost infinitely, challenging the power of the human lung as much as the larynx. This gives the perorations of his best pieces an unrivalled power: like Wesley, Vaughan Williams and Gerald Finzi, Howells could do a good last bar. He was the best of all at realising the expressive potential of the organ, as a solo as well as an accompanying instrument.

Unlike Holst and others, Howells found his central inspiration in the core documents of the choral tradition, principally the psalms and canticles of the Book of Common Prayer. Occasionally he would combine these together in original ways, as in the intense, many-faceted *Requiem*, which alternates parts of the Latin Mass for the dead with verses from the English psalms, to unforgettable effect. Devotional poetry interested him too, as in the three *Carol-anthems* of 1918–20. But the best of Howells is in the service music.

It is all the more remarkable, then, that Howells only turned to church music at all as a result of a bet. In 1943, while he was acting Organist of St John's College, Cambridge, during Robin Orr's absence on active service, Howells attended a tea party given by the Dean of King's, Eric Milner-White. Patrick Hadley, Organist of Gonville and Caius, was there too. Milner-White lamented the paucity of good settings of the morning canticles, particularly the Te Deum, and offered a guinea to whichever of his two guests first provided him with a decent setting. Hadley demurred, but Howells produced his *Collegium regale*, 'the only Te Deum to be born of a decanal bet', as he put it. Howells's unique and fecund contribution to church music flowed from that one moment over the Deanery tea-cups. As his pupil and biographer Paul Spicer says, 'that one guinea kickstarted music for the Anglican church into a whole new phase of existence'. Milner-White wrote to Howells soon afterwards 'I personally feel that you have opened a whole new chapter in Service, perhaps in Church, music. Of *spiritual* moment rather than liturgical. It is so much more than music-making; it is experiencing deep things in the only medium that can do it. I cannot help hoping that you will give yourself with renewed hope and vision to composition in a field in which – may I say it? – you can create *masterworks*.'[26]

The Dean was right. Without the contributions of Howells and his teacher Stanford, choral evensong could not have prospered as it has. Howells's evening services for St Paul's, Gloucester and King's College, Cambridge, are among the best-loved liturgical music we have. No composer has been better at writing 'into the building'. The music is always good to sing, but without the slightest hint of facile melodising or compromise – some of it is very difficult.

As so often, enigmas remain. There is some less good Howells. Occasionally the substance does not keep up with the style. Although he wrote a great deal of church music, not much of it dates from before his fiftieth birthday: this is not music full of the optimism of youth or the easy sparkle of a brilliant natural technique. But his style developed. There are angularities, in the man as well as the music. He was often described as vain, and a name-dropper. The composer John Rutter once asked him about the jazz influence in his music, and what he thought of Gershwin. 'Ah,' replied Howells, 'dear George!'[27] He gushed over a not very interesting request to write a piece for Prime Minister Edward Heath for an event at 10 Downing Street. His biographer and pupil Paul Spicer describes him as 'a complex man', and 'a mess, like so many people, underneath'. His own daughter said he was 'ruled by sex', which may or may not show up in the music. The death of his son at the age of nine haunted him 'like a ground bass to his existence',[28] in Spicer's apt phrase. This pillar of English church music was no stained-glass saint. But he deserves his place at the very top table.

No composer is more characteristic of the musical manner of his times than Gerald Finzi. His early teachers included the organists Walter Farrar and Edward Bairstow, as well as the contrapuntal pedagogue R. O. Morris (whose books of exercises are still the best). He wrote slowly and self-critically, and died relatively young, so his reputation rests on a small clutch of carefully crafted works. But his music has a yearning melodiousness and bitter-sweet harmonic sense which gives it an instantly recognisable signature. *God is Gone up* is the best known of a small number of pieces for choir and organ. The triumphant opening of the seventeenth-century poet Edward Taylor's psalm-paraphrase perhaps does not find the composer at his subtle best, but the middle section does: this was a composer who was born to set the word 'enravish'. *Lo, the Full Final Sacrifice* draws its text from a similar source, two poems by the early seventeenth-century metaphysical poet Richard Crashaw. For some church musicians this piece is the best of the mid-century. The music is wrapped around the words with all the poignancy and care this sensitive soul could offer. Pungent dissonances push plangent consonants to the surface of a flexible vocal line, like Purcell. What Finzi does

'A good last bar…' the endings of, respectively, O Taste and See *by Vaughan Williams,* Lo, the Full, Final Sacrifice *by Finzi, and* A Spotless Rose *by Howells.*

not share with Purcell, however, is a complete command of overall form: there are too many short sections in this piece. Observe all the written *rallentandos* and you may never get to the end at all. This would be a mistake: the 'Amen' is the finest since Gibbons – rapt, ambiguous, tender – and one of the defining musical moments of the church-music century.

Perhaps he thought of it while grafting rare varieties of English apple in his Hampshire orchard. It somehow sounds as if he might.

These composers, and their heirs and successors, have noises in common. Partly these come from the mood music of the English church throughout all ages: the sound of a choir in a big, old building, the organ, those words; but there is more to it than that. Modes, polyphony, a touch of imitation at the fifth – it's what Hardy called 'the family face', which lives on:

> … projecting trait and trace
> Through time to times anon.[29]

It still does.

The Reverend Walter Hussey was a clergyman who believed passionately in the place of art in church. As vicar of St Matthew's, Northampton, and then Dean of Chichester, he commissioned Benjamin Britten (*Rejoice in the Lamb*), Finzi (*Lo, the Full, Final Sacrifice*), William Walton, Lennox Berkeley and many other leading names in all fields of artistic endeavour. He called into being a particular kind of large-scale work, often taking a new and oblique look at what sacred choral music could do, which the tradition would otherwise not have. How else would English church choirs find themselves singing the psalms in Hebrew? They do in Leonard Bernstein's jazzy *Chichester Psalms*, half-synagogue, half-*West Side Story*. It is much to English church music's credit that they do, and thanks to Hussey that they can.

HYMNS, IN ALL THEIR incarnations, continue to chart the place of church music in the lives of congregations. It is, as always, a fluid and malleable story, based not on the classified work-list of a particular genius, but on what ordinary people actually do. This makes it hard to pin down – all the more so as technology and the breaking down of cultural barriers allow all sorts of new influences inside the west door. So a few important moments in the story, what evolutionists call 'node points' in the slow emergence of a species, will do duty as exemplars of everything that led up to and away from them.

In 1899 Robert Bridges issued his *Yattendon Hymnal*. The modern era has not had enough people like Bridges: a serious poet and unashamed devotee of high art, willing to use his skills to engage publicly with his Christian faith. He also had strong views about congregational music, and they were emphatically of the good-music-is-good-for-you school of thought. His book set out explicitly to elevate good taste: 'The excellence of a nation in music can have no other basis than the education and practice of the people; and the quality of the music which is most universally sung must largely determine the public taste for good or ill.'[30] The words are Anglo-Catholic in tone, including texts by John Henry Newman and Latin translations by John Mason Neale, and tunes are mostly from ancient sources including Tallis, Bach and plainsong, with a few new offerings in the approved old style. The book looks like a sixteenth-century psalter: the music is in full score, with 'C' clefs, mostly in four parts, sometimes three, with handsome decoration on every page. The inventors of the typeface are credited on the opening flyleaf. This is hymnody as visual art, music as ennobler and enabler: William Morris comes to church.

The problem, of course, was: who decides what is and isn't good? Can a self-appointed guardian like Bridges actually 'determine the public taste'? The attempt was taken much further, and with infinitely greater impact, in *The English Hymnal* of 1906. The editors were Dearmer (words) and Vaughan Williams (it's that man again). Dearmer got straight to the point in his preface: '"The English Hymnal" is a collection of the best hymns in the English language.' Both he and Vaughan Williams told their readers what was wrong with their current tastes and reminded clergy and organists of their responsibility to lead wisely: 'it is indeed a moral rather than a musical issue.'[31] As a result, their book is strongly Anglo-Catholic and rather authoritarian in character. Where a tune or words had been altered by habit, Dearmer and Vaughan Williams altered it back. This is laudable, except for the fact that people won't do it. They also expressed the strong view that hymns were for the congregation, not the choir, and Vaughan Williams issued a plea for the fine old tunes to be sung slower, even going so far as to add metronome marks (how many organ lofts have a metronome?). Dearmer claimed that *The English Hymnal* was 'not a party-book'. It certainly looked like one to many readers, and its theological stance alienated some. One bishop even banned it in his diocese because of its quasi-papist invocation of saints. But its success was assured by two factors: first, its inclusivity; and second, they just did it so well. On the first point, Dearmer was right – these were 'the best hymns in the English language', with fine tunes from all traditions, including the new folk-song melodies and original work like 'Down Ampney', 'Sine nomine' and 'Cranham', among many others. A book that contained so many good tunes was bound to catch on. And on the second point, when Vaughan Williams reached for good harmony he knew what he was talking about. His own harmonies to the folk-song tunes have all the qualities he admired in Tallis and Bach. They remain the standard versions.

The year 1919 saw the appearance of the *Public School Hymn Book*, including the first publication of John Ireland's 'Love Unknown' and W.H. Ferguson's 'Wolvercote'. *Songs of Praise* of 1925 added Martin Shaw to the old firm of Dearmer and Vaughan Williams, and included some remarkably bold new tunes. Most of these books went through revisions and reissues, trying out new hymns and dropping old ones. Vaughan Williams contributed to the revised *Public School Hymn Book* in 1949, and in 1950 the editors of *Ancient and Modern* rolled the best of a number of supplements into an entirely new edition. 'A and M' and the 'EH' continued to pursue notably different paths, as much for copyright as for theological reasons. And in 1951 the *BBC Hymn Book* gave the world 'Abbot's Leigh' by Cyril Taylor.

Outside the Church of England, Nonconformist hymnals gradually absorbed the approach adopted by *The English Hymnal* as far as it suited them. The separateness of each branch of Nonconformism is less apparent in the hymnody of the twentieth century than it was in the nineteenth. One of the most recognisable of all hymn styles, the Salvation Army song, was codified by its founder General Booth in his 1911 book, published without tunes. It lists its contents not under liturgical function or the season of the church year, but under various themes: Hell, War, the Children. Texts draw richly on the Methodist tradition and its American Revivalist cousin, with distinctive use of hymns with a refrain: 'You are drifting to your doom, Yet there's mercy still for you.' The sound of these muscular verses accompanied by a brass band is one of English church music's iconic aural images. This really is music to 'sing so as to make the world hear',[32] as Booth commanded.

'A and M' continued its journey through all the changing scenes of life, with new versions in 1975 and 1993, incorporating the two collections of *Hymns for Today* issued in 1969 and 1980. Here are modern classics like 'Here I am, Lord' and David Evans's 'Be Still, for the Presence of the Lord', alongside spirituals like 'Were you there when they Crucified my Lord' and modern hymns in a more traditional style by Fred Pratt Green and others. *Common Praise* and *Sing Praise* followed in 2000 and 2010. 'EH' begat fewer offspring: *The New English Hymnal* appeared in 1986, maintaining its 'high' tone, under the guidance of that most musical of clergymen, Canon Anthony Caesar (himself a former public-school Director of Music).

Just as in the nineteenth century, psalm-singing responded to changing conditions with a series of evolutionary changes. As noted above, Henry Walford Davies pioneered speech-rhythm chanting at the Temple Church, helped by the new art of broadcasting. Sydney Nicholson's *Parish Psalter with Chants* of 1930 codified this approach in print. The old, unsatisfactory *Cathedral Psalter* manner was superseded, just as the 'old way' of singing died out in the eighteenth century. With it went any real sense that psalm-chanting belonged to the congregation. Today it is a polished art, for many musicians the ultimate test of a church choir's skill and sensitivity to text and the bedrock of all that it does.

The virtues of plainsong, on the other hand, have prospered in a tradition imported from France. Père Gélineau devised a type of flexible melody around his French versions of the Psalms in the 1950s, adaptable to the different shape and stress of each verse. The rhythmic freedom of these tunes allowed them to work in English as well. 'Antiphons' between verses allow the congregation to sing an easily learnt repeating refrain, with the verses sung by a soloist or choir, with or without instruments. The style is often known by the name of the religious community in France where many pilgrims first heard it, Taizé.

Dom Gregory Murray has done much to render the style in English. It is a sensible, sensitive approach to the old question: who sings the psalms? Every generation has asked it. The results, intriguingly, sound not a million miles away from pre-Reformation 'faburden' or the Helmore-Marbeck style of plainsong. To reach for a suitably Gallic *mot juste*: *'plus ça change, plus c'est la même chose.'*

The logical next step was to issue books which combined all this material into one: hymns of all kinds, including the newest 'worship songs', psalms and service music. *The English Hymnal* and *Ancient and Modern* have both done this. The publisher Kevin Mayhew (a former Westminster Cathedral choirboy) has reached a wide market with his *Hymns Old and New*. The Mayhew imprint specialises in music for the parish church, with anthems, arrangements and organ pieces issued in all kinds of versions, for organ with and without pedals and halfway between, and choir music for different combinations, including the intensely practical idea of arranging choir music in three parts (soprano, alto and a sort of all-purpose 'bari-tenor' for all the available men's voices), known as 'S. A. Men'. Many hymnbooks today come with accompaniments on CD or MP3.

Towards the end of his life the editors of one hymnbook described Vaughan Williams as 'the greatest living authority on hymn tunes'.[33] That authority was exercised with wisdom and taste, allowing the tradition to thrive and develop, though he may not have imagined that it would eventually find a way of including as the last item in *Hymns Old and New* a song called 'Zip Bam Boom'.

CATHEDRAL MUSIC EXPERIENCED EVER greater professionalisation during the twentieth century. Education and training were always priorities. The old system of articled study with an established organist produced a notable quintet of two Ivors (Gurney and Novello) and three Herberts (Brewer, Sumsion and Howells) at Gloucester in the second decade of the century. Sir Sydney Nicholson gave up a high-profile career in active church music to devote his time, and much of his personal fortune, to establishing what became the Royal School of Church Music, offering residential courses, accrediting choirs across the country, and providing them with training and resources through visits and publications. A stable of intelligent and resourceful composers has built up around the publishing activities of houses like the RSCM and Kevin Mayhew, many of them leading practitioners. Scholarship in the universities has continued to usher untold wonders of early music into the light. Scholar-practitioners like Terry at Westminster and Edmund Fellowes at Windsor, and scholarly editions like *Musica Britannica* set pioneering standards, and specialist ensembles have achieved world-wide reach for this music in the concert hall. Questions like pitch, pronunciation and voice type continue to be worried over, yielding fresh insights. At the same time, scholar-practitioners like John Harper are putting this music back into the context of its original liturgies, not as historical reconstruction, but as living act of worship.

Meanwhile, down the library steps and across the quad to the chapel, college choirs at Oxford and Cambridge Universities provide the de facto training ground for professional church musicians, as well as demanding and life-enhancing educational opportunities for young choristers. As colleges opened admission to men and women equally, mixed undergraduate choirs emerged, working alongside the old choral foundations with their boys' choir schools. Schools of this kind have had to move with the times too. One former pupil looked back with horror to his choir-school days in the 1960s: a bathroom, echoing and cold, enamel baths all around the edge and one toilet, bang in the middle.[34] Another ex-chorister recalled sneaking out of his choir school and into the cathedral in the middle of the night with a chum and rearranging all the prayer books in the Dean's vestry.[35] Some choir schools have not survived modern economic pressures, including Frederick Ouseley's at Tenbury Wells. Others have adapted by changing from boarding to day, or single-sex to mixed-sex, or some variant of the two. Perhaps the most striking change of all has been the introduction of girl choristers, starting at Edinburgh in the late 1970s. Many cathedrals followed suit. The world did not, as some believed it might, come to an end. The lengthy debate about whether young girls' and young boys' voices sound different has turned out not to be the point: the main differences are educational, not musical. There is room – and a need – for both.

Was Vaughan Williams right? Is the quality of a hymn 'a moral rather than a musical issue'?[36] Yes. A good tune can express meaning better than one which relies on borrowed gestures. But it is emphatically not the case that one style is inherently 'better' than another. Good tunes have the same virtues whatever style they are in: a strong melody, well matched to words which mean something and say it clearly. The best songs are just that – songs. In any event, style is often largely a function of accompaniment. Play 'Here I am, Lord' on guitars and drums, and it's a soft pop song. Play it with a room full of people and a discreet keyboard playing the harmony, and it's just a song. It works the other way too: Paul Simon's 'American Tune' is a moving ballad about the Pilgrim Fathers and the *Mayflower*, sung by a man with a guitar, a modern troubadour. The tune is the 'Passion Chorale', as used by Bach.

The 'worship band' is here to stay. It has proved itself the ideal musical vehicle for Evangelical congregational worship since its introduction in the early 1970s, being approachable and adaptable, with the early preference for acoustic instruments and a folk style mostly giving way to amplified rock. There is an irony here that the strand of ecclesiology which set out to remove the impression of a separate group of musicians giving a 'performance' has ended up with exactly that: a worship leader with a microphone, facing the 'audience', his backing musicians behind him, like any other gig. It's not the only time in this story that a musical idea has in practice 'flipped' from one side of the philosophical fence to the other.

Pop music in church has, it is fair to say, divided opinion. Some find the style and content of 'worship songs' banal. Others think these objections just prove that the clergy are scared of teenagers. Others have attempted an objective analysis (like Erik Routley in 1964, politely discussing the contribution of the artists he calls 'Mr Cliff Richard' and 'Mr Presley from the USA'). But the work of singer-songwriters like Graham Kendrick has established a place for itself on merit and on need, just like all other successful innovations in this story. There is room in our song-book for all of them.

Whoever's right, it's not a new argument. Here are two first-hand reviews of developments in church music:[37]

Instead of the ancient, grave, solemn music … a concert was introduced … better suiting a tavern … than a church.

A thoroughly alien importation and a self-conscious parasite … [which] together with the incidental noise and ironmongery which seems to be a necessary part of its presentation, can be quickly dismissed as an irrelevant and mercifully transient stunt.

One was written in 1970, the other in 1662.

The generation of composers born in the twentieth century started to reinvent not just the music of the church but the whole idea of what church music is. The defining figure was Benjamin Britten. Church music appears throughout Britten's work-list. Some of it is to commission, and some of the commissions seemed to interest him more than others. The Jubilate in C, written at the request of the Duke of Edinburgh in 1961, is a sparkling piece with a joyous, toccata-like organ part. The two much earlier settings of the Te Deum likewise manage the long text with considerable economy, dividing it neatly into three sections at logical breaks in the text, allowing a satisfyingly balanced structure to emerge. But those who find that Britten's natural facility sometimes gets ahead of an emotional engagement may find evidence for their view here. The singer James Bowman has a revealing story. Britten and his companion Peter Pears were always teasing Bowman for his involvement in the fusty, establishment world of church music. On one occasion, in a break from rehearsal, Bowman remarked that he had recently recorded one of Britten's settings of the Te Deum with the choir of New College, Oxford. 'Oh, that,' replied the composer, 'it's like setting the phone-book.'[38]

The best of Britten's commissioned liturgical works is the *Missa brevis*, written for Westminster Cathedral choir and its choirmaster George Malcolm in 1959. This is a truly original approach to sound and function. Treble voices in three parts are surrounded, rather than accompanied, by a brilliantly imagined organ part. Gloria in excelsis subjects the plainsong intonation to thrilling rhythmic manipulation; Sanctus is a twelve-tone row, harmonised triadically; Benedictus is one of the spookiest invocations of childhood innocence which even this composer ever managed; Agnus Dei an apocalyptic build-up of the sins of the world.

Even more expressive is *Rejoice in the Lamb*, a long, cantata-like anthem dating from 1943. The choice of text alone puts this piece in a category all of its own, taken from a long, rambling poem by the eighteenth-century poet Christopher Smart, written while he was incarcerated in a lunatic asylum. It's a remarkable piece, all the more so because of the economy of means: much of it is in unison, melodic as well as rhythmic. Britten used a four-note phrase derived from the musical acronym of the name of his friend Dmitri Shostakovich. (By taking the letters DSCH – from D[mitri] SCH[ostakovich] – and turning them into musical notes using the German system, which gives D, E flat ['s' in German], C, B natural ['h']. Shostakovich himself deployed this trick, borrowed from Bach, who did something very similar with the four letters of his own name. Both composers used this personal musical signature often in their own music). Shostakovich was hounded by the Soviet authorities, and Britten memorably reaches out to his fellow composer by using the DSCH motif for the passionate outburst against injustice and persecution in the middle: 'Silly fellow! Silly fellow!', spits the choir.

Unparalleled in the church music of any period is the *Hymn to St Cecilia*, to a specially written poem by W. H. Auden. Despite the title, this is hardly a conventional appeal to a smiling saint. Its unaccompanied five voices weave magical textures from Auden's musings on music, the role of the artist, and Britten himself. This piece is, occasionally, sung as an anthem by the best church choirs. Singing these words in church sets up some curious ambiguities, almost as if Britten himself has become one of the 'dear white children, casual as birds, playing among the ruined languages'.[39] More conventional in text, though hardly less original in musical form, is *A Ceremony of Carols* for three upper voices and harp, written on the same trip to America with Auden and Peter Pears in the 1940s as the *Hymn to St Cecilia*. Every young chorister should have the chance to sing this. The music is exhilarating and moving, the texture unique and delicious, the selection of texts intelligent and effective. Britten brought a new eye to every kind of music he touched. Church music had nowhere to put pieces like this until Britten wrote them. The sheer originality of the conception forced it to invent a place for them.

Britten was not a conventional believer, in either God or the establishment. So when he was asked to write a set of evening canticles to mark the 450th anniversary of St John's College, Cambridge, in 1962, the college Organist, George Guest, received a polite refusal. The commission passed instead to a slightly older composer, Michael Tippett. Tippett was perhaps the most individual in a generation of composers not short of strong personalities. He wrote an essay challenging the existence of God when he was ten years old. Religion, he later said, 'is all a metaphor'.[40] His most often-performed sacred choral pieces are the brooding, intense arrangements of the spirituals from the oratorio *A Child of our Time*, where they are used as a contemporary equivalent, musical and verbal, of the chorales in Bach's Passions. The imagery is political, not religious. *Plebs Angelica* was written to a commission from Canterbury Cathedral. It is a modern madrigal, wedding the imitative techniques of Tudor polyphony to Tippett's own sound-world. The St John's service is quite unlike anything else. It opens with a fabulous fanfare for the college organ's famous sticky-out 'trompeta real', and a treble solo like something from outer space hovers over a growling cluster of solo men's voices in the Nunc Dimittis. The only slightly inert bit of the piece is the second Gloria. There was a story current at St John's that, when he submitted it, Tippett hadn't realised that he had to set the Gloria at the end of the Nunc Dimittis as well as at the end of the Magnificat, and had to bolt it on afterwards. This is striking, vivid music – but dangerous. Choirs will have to take a deep breath before learning it, and an even deeper one before asking the congregation if they liked it. Whatever the reply, they can't ignore it. Neither should choirs.

William Walton was a chorister at Christ Church, Oxford. His earliest sacred composition is the *Litany*, a setting of a poem by Phineas Fletcher, written when he was about fourteen years old. Originally for upper voices in three parts, it opens with an augmented triad. The challenge to the musical style of his contemporaries is there from the start in this supple piece. His other church music charts his charmed progress through the ranks of high society: *Set Me as a Seal upon thine Heart* for a society wedding in London, the Te Deum for the coronation of Queen Elizabeth II in 1953, a piece full of brilliant, jagged contrasts. *What Cheer?* is one of a small number of carols, bursting with medieval swagger. The *Missa brevis* of 1966 is short, angular and dramatic, one of the few really challenging settings to use the English words (apart from the Kyrie, oddly), reserving the organ for the fabulously bouncy 'Glory be to God on high'). Walton's other liturgical music includes a Jubilate written for his old college, Christ Church, in 1976, and a Magnificat and Nunc Dimittis commissioned by Dean Walter Hussey for Chichester Cathedral. Perhaps the most unusual work saw him turning, like Britten, to a long text by their contemporary W. H. Auden, *The Twelve*. This is a cantata-like piece, scattering solo voices and 5/4 fugue across Auden's meditation on the apostles: it is direct and impressive. Its most haunting moment is the duet for two trebles: 'O Lord my God, though I forsake thee, forsake me not',[41] where music and words grab the gestures of the past and force them to look the modern age straight in the eye.

The lives of these three fine musicians overlapped and interweaved and, as in other periods dominated by a few outstanding composers, there were friendships and rivalries. But it is possible to think of Britten, Tippett and Walton as a 'school'. All three set old texts and new for the church. Each contributed to the liturgy. There is never the remotest hint of any one of them repeating himself: every piece looks at church music as if for the first time. This is music of its time – colourful, demanding and new, like a Chagall window in sound.

Another of Hussey's commissionees was Lennox Berkeley. Berkeley brings a delicately French accent to the choral style of his contemporaries, something of Ravel, or their friend Poulenc in his mellower moods, in the slowly turning organ accompaniment and suave solos of *The Lord is my Shepherd* and *Oh, that I once Past Changing were*. There are two good, short mass settings, and the Evening Canticles for Chichester, which cast a gift for elegant melody within a personal take on traditional tonality. This is not music which hits you between the eyes as Britten can do, but it is compelling, individual and full of charm.

Fundamentals of faith replace shades of churchmanship in considering the composers of this period. Britten and Howells were agnostics at most, Tippett a militant atheist with a background in theosophy and an abiding interest in the work of Carl Jung. Berkeley, by contrast, was born and remained a Catholic. His sons were choristers at Westminster Cathedral, including the composer Michael, who sang in the first performance of his godfather Benjamin Britten's *Missa brevis*.

Edmund Rubbra was brought up in the Congregationalist tradition and converted to Catholicism in middle age. An early memory of church bells, 'whose music seemed suspended in the still air',[42] can be heard in his interest in scale patterns, for example in the Evening Canticles in A flat: as the music builds towards its impressive climax the organist gets to do a welcome bit of scale practice. As a child, Rubbra acted as demonstration pianist for his uncle's piano business, left school at fourteen and worked as a railway clerk and shoemaker while studying harmony and counterpoint in his spare time and writing hymns for the Congregationalist Sunday school. Nothing in this eclectic background hints at his later reception into the Catholic Church, but the move produced a body of powerful, committed music, including three Latin Mass settings and the dramatic *Tenebrae Motets* for Passiontide.

Rubbra was elected a founding lecturer in Oxford University's Faculty of Music in 1947, and a Fellow of Worcester College. Thus began a tradition of this College hosting the university's in-house composer, including some notable contributors to the field of church music.

Kenneth Leighton succeeded Rubbra at Worcester in 1968. His music has an idiosyncratic stylistic signature, with florid vocal lines, plenty of counterpoint, spiky organ parts and a reliance on the interval of the fourth often keeping a definite tonality intriguingly just out of reach. The style embraced the passionate and tender, too, as in his setting of Robert Herrick's *A Christmas Caroll*, the anguished *Crucifixus pro nobis* and the inventive *Coventry Carol*. There is a good deal of service music by Leighton, including one of the most popular modern settings of the choral responses. An innate sense of the practical, learnt as a choirboy at Wakefield Cathedral, is never far away.

Two more composers bring Worcester College up to date. Robert Sherlaw Johnson made some interesting early experiments with free rhythmic notation in his *Missa aedis Christi*. The current incumbent, Robert Saxton, has written some furiously difficult choral music like *Five Motets for Nine Voices*, commissioned for the BBC Proms, which, typically for this composer, sets words from the Latin Bible alongside his own poetry on themes of journeying and the Jewish Old Testament. He has also composed luminous, approachable pieces like *Is it Winter?* and the Epiphany anthem *The Child of Light* for treble voices and organ, which builds from the sombre tread of the magi to a splendid D major revelation at the end. It is to the credit of all these Oxford academics that none of them sounds like one.

Another place which has harboured an in-house genealogy of composers is York Minster. In 1946 Edward Bairstow was succeeded as Organist by his protégé and former choirboy Francis Jackson, composer of much excellent and often-heard church music. His setting of the Evening Canticles in G is a regular fixture, more assured in its approach to variety of texture and ambiguity of harmony than some organ-loft composers. Jackson's successor was Philip Moore, in post from 1983 to 2008. Moore represents the best of the tradition of organist-composers. He is no mere adder to the conventional musical offerings of the church, the sort who can puff up a psalm-chant or an improvisation and call it a piece. He is a craftsman and a thinker about his art. There is a great deal of church music by Moore, including service music for every possible kind of use, within the tradition but never compromising with it. His *Three Prayers of Dietrich Bonhoeffer* has achieved something of the status of a modern classic, setting a challenging text with directness, commitment and skill.

Professional composers who have contributed skilfully crafted pieces in traditional forms include Richard Rodney Bennett and John Gardner, both known for some fun carols. A fecund and resourceful musician whose attempts to bridge the gap between pop and traditional style has not, sadly, kept his name in the public eye was Malcolm Williamson. William Mathias can be taken in the same breath as Kenneth Leighton: witness the sprightly fourth-oriented carol setting

Sir Christèmas. The 'triad-plus' approach yields harsher but effective results in the rhythmic evening service for Jesus College, Cambridge. John Joubert was educated at an Anglican school in his native South Africa, where the high standard of music-making introduced him to the works of 'Parry and Stanford and all the usual blokes',[43] as he put it. A few of his many choral works have become genuine repertoire items, to the extent that a group of carol-singers once came to his front door and treated him to a performance of his own *Torches*, 'without knowing the composer lived inside'.[44]

Some compositional schools did not make it into the choir stall. The Schoenbergian approach, for all the composer's insistence on the fundamentals of traditional harmony and counterpoint, never really succeeded in making anything which a body of English choristers could, or wanted to, just stand up and sing; nor did the forbidding 'new complexity'. Partly, this was a question of fashion. In the brave new world of the 1950s, with William Glock at the BBC and Karlheinz Stockhausen and his acolytes at the Darmstadt Summer School, style became a badge of political correctness, what Michael Tippett criticised as 'the search for the one true way'.[45] Church music didn't stand a chance. To these self-appointed arbiters of taste, it was another country, stuck in the past, the wing-collared world of 'Parry and Stanford and all the usual blokes'. But the simple virtues never lost their appeal. It is notable that composers as different as Alexander Goehr (in his 'white-note' setting of Psalm 4 from 1976) and Michael Finnissy (*Seven Sacred Motets* of 1993) have reached for church music as their medium of choice when wanting to try something simpler.

Sherlaw Johnson's experiments with freely notated rhythm reappear in the church music of Jonathan Harvey. *Come, Holy Ghost* deconstructs the ancient plainchant into little twists of melody, which each individual singer is then invited to sing *ad libitum*, all inside a carefully constructed framework. The piece is thus different every time it's performed. In a big building it sounds like listening to the plainsong from half a mile, or half a millennium, away, echoing and swirling timelessly. *I Love the Lord* sets a penitential psalm-text to increasingly discordant harmony over a constantly repeated G major triad (hence its nickname,

'I love this chord'). These anthems can claim to be among the few genuinely modernist works to have earned and held a place in the repertoire. Among Harvey's other church music is the *Missa brevis*, full of clusters and free rhythms, an exercise in reimagining the liturgy – terse, hard, atmospheric and short.

Even shorter is the *Missa brevissima* by another modernist with lots of church music in the back catalogue, Giles Swayne. This piece combines a kind of modal counterpoint with a fabulously cheeky Benedictus. The whole mass takes about four minutes to sing. Swayne's best-known piece of church music can still knock a new listener sideways: the Latin Magnificat of 1982 opens with a wordless exclamation – a shout, really – taken from African traditional song, swinging irresistibly into an almost minimalist deconstruction of the Latin text to single syllables and overlapping rhythmic patterns. Steve Reich meets fourteenth-century hocketing.

These composers have started to bring influences from all over the musical and philosophical world in through the west door of English church music: Judaism and Broadway (Bernstein), Orientalism (Rubbra), Indian music and mysticism (Harvey), minimalism, Messiaen and African folk-song (Swayne), Orcadian pantheism (Peter Maxwell Davies), orthodox chant (John Tavener), liberation theology (MacMillan), Dietrich Bonhoeffer's 'religionless Christianity' and the more obvious virtues of church traditions (Moore), and how to write a good song (Rutter).

John Tavener began as the lofty high priest of 1960s iconoclasm. A work consisting mostly of whale noises was recorded on the Beatles's record label. *A Celtic Requiem* is a kaleidoscope of children's songs, nursery rhymes and brash modernist music, the sort of thing Ligeti loved to do. Tavener's conversion to Greek Orthodox Christianity in 1977 brought something completely new into his music and that of the English church choir. Hieratic chant, Byzantine-style vocal ornamentation and slow, repeating, strophic structures give his music an unmistakable sound. Its best incarnations are the miniatures: *The Lamb*, *Funeral Ikos* and *Two Hymns to the Mother of God*. Some of the longer works perhaps require more sense of the suspension of time than the average English listener is willing to grant: at the first performance of the *Akhmatova Requiem*, most of the audience left before the end. One of his pieces requires to be performed overnight.

John Rutter was at school with John Tavener, and sang with the Highgate school choir on Benjamin Britten's own recording of the *War Requiem*. He was encouraged to compose by the Director of Music, Edward T. Chapman, for whose memorial service he wrote one of his best-loved works, *The Lord Bless You and Keep You* in 1981. John Rutter is a prolific composer, and many of his choral works have become established favourites. There are several larger-scale works like the *Gloria*, *Magnificat* and *Requiem*, and his many shorter pieces include carols which quickly established themselves as an essential fixture of carol services and Christmas concerts all over the world. The wide reach of his music is aided by his Renaissance-man approach to the business of making music: orchestrator and arranger, often making multiple versions of his own works, conductor, founder and director of his own choir, anthologiser and editor and record producer. The fluency of his gift is always matched to perfectionism of craftsmanship.

And to a particular kind of style. Rutter's stroke of genius was to realise the potential of incorporating the eternal, simple values of the song, be it folk-song or Broadway, into church music: well-shaped melody, equal phrases, clear tonal structure and direct words. The results have sometimes seemed sentimental, even saccharine, to some. Rutter is unapologetic: 'I happen not to believe in erecting needless barriers between composer and listener: given a choice between critical approbation and a chance of touching the hearts of people outside the limited circle of contemporary music *aficionados*, I know which I prefer.'[46]

James MacMillan is a Roman Catholic. This informs every aspect of his art, along with a passionate commitment to social justice and hatred of persecution. Many of his sacred works reflect this theme, for example *Padre Pio's Prayer* of 2008 and the *Cantos Sagrados* of 1989, in which three poems 'concerned with political repression in Latin America … are deliberately coupled with traditional religious texts to emphasise a deeper solidarity with the poor'.[47] The *Strathclyde Motets* are varied in text, approachable and original. There are two responsorial mass settings for choir and congregation, but also some challenging works in a modernist idiom, written for the most versatile specialist ensembles. Always, there is a distinctive voice, recognisable from the long lines, the 'Scotch snap' vocal ornaments, the brilliant organ writing, often rhythmically ad-lib, the rich, low bass line.

Peter Maxwell Davies can hardly be accused of over-deference towards the church. The Priest in his opera *Taverner* is a foul-mouthed, violent hypocrite. But some of Maxwell Davies's earliest musical experiences came in church, at the Sunday afternoon concerts held in the Methodist meeting-house in his native Salford. Iconoclasm and tradition meet in this musician. It is a combination which was always going to make the sparks fly when he dipped his toe into the comfortable waters of English church music. In October 1961 the *Musical Times* printed his *Ave Maria*. Feathers were duly ruffled. Fifty years later, Max can still do it. If some modern music is dangerous, this stuff can bite – hard. But his considerable body of church music has, despite its difficulties for performer and listener alike, demanded attention for its personal voice, its connection with the music of the past, and its respect for text and function. Alongside many settings of early texts are works to poems by his friend and fellow Orcadian George Mackay Brown, taking a holistic, almost pantheistic approach to the natural world: 'we are folded all in a green fable'.[48] Asked to write a choral piece to mark the 400th anniversary of the Gunpowder Plot, Max chose not a bloodthirsty psalm verse, as his brother composers did at the time, but sections from the speeches at the trial of the plotters, almost as much opera as anthem.[49] Christmas pieces span the composer's entire career, from the knotty *O magnum mysterium* sequence of 1961 to the recently completed sequence of carols written for Her Majesty The Queen, full of contrast and invention.

And, alongside a rock-like integrity, there is always practicality. Max knows how to write to the requirements of his performers without ever writing 'down' to them, as his many works for children show. He began his career as a schoolmaster, getting a perfectly ordinary class to sing Palestrina in three parts (like Holst with his squaddies in Salonica).

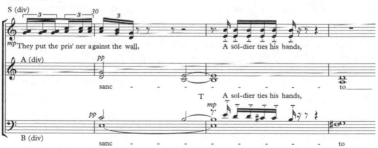

Four aspects of modern church music: the organ fanfare which announces the Magnificat of Michael Tippett's St John's service; African song and a bit of minimalist Latin hocketing in Giles Swayne's setting of the same text; the Orcadian landscape as timeless allegory in Kings and Shepherds *by Peter Maxwell Davies; revolutionary violence meets the Latin Mass in* Cantos sagrados *by James MacMillan.*

Teachers could imitate that (though perhaps not some other aspects of his approach to his duties: on one occasion he took a school party to a concert in London. As they were about to head home, it was noticed that a small boy had gone missing: he turned up wandering about on the roof of the Royal Festival Hall).[50]

This music can 'touch the hearts of people', too. Maxwell Davies's *Kings and Shepherds* is in D flat major. MacMillan's *Christus vincit* makes walls of sound out of just seven words and the seven notes of a D major scale. Just as with hymns, one style is not by definition better than another. The 'touching-the-hearts' style, often imitated, misfires when it sounds as if it is lazily reaching for a borrowed gesture of words or music, Pavlov-style. Borrow the gesture, and you can end up borrowing the thought: touching the heart without going through the brain. But at the same time, nothing sounds as tired as music which is trying to be 'modern'. 'Integrity' is an old-fashioned word, but it still means something.

AND STILL THE 'TEEMING MASS' keeps on teeming. Cathedral choirs today sing more music from more traditions than ever before, including French organ composers, hunks of the Rachmaninov Vespers in Russian, and everything in between. Catholic Mass can be heard sung in all sorts of languages. African gospel churches and American-style evangelicals bring joyous music to halls and cinemas, keeping the local council's Noise Abatement officer busy with complaints from the new Cromwells across the road. The American composer Eric Whitacre has formed a 'virtual choir' to perform his music, together, on opposite sides of the world. In the parish, people turn up to have a good sing, to meet their neighbours, and to enjoy a cup of lukewarm instant coffee, just like always. For their music, some put their trust in Marbeck, and some in drum kits. Some do both.

And church music still turns up in some surprising places. Defenders of the church's declining place in society point out that more people go to church on a Sunday morning than go to professional football on a Saturday afternoon. Church music might reply that you could well find yourself singing 'Cwm Rhondda' at both.

Epilogue

And what remains when disbelief has gone?
… each week
A purpose more obscure.

Philip Larkin, 'Church Going'

SO WHAT HAPPENS NOW? If the music-lover who has wandered through these pages turned up in England today, would he recognise what he saw?

He would find his old friend the cathedral organist in good heart, better trained and more professionally supported than ever (though the stitching in the tweed around his elbow patches needs a little attention). The biggest change in his life is that he is no longer necessarily a he – nor are his choristers or the priest intoning the responses (which, for some, took a little getting used to).

He would recognise some old arguments, like the one about whether to allow instruments in church, currently the cause of much argle-bargle among the 'Wee Frees' in Scotland, some of whom want to hang onto the ancient rough-hewn splendours of 'lining out', without accompaniment, while others point out that singing about praising the Lord with strings and harp without strings and harp is a bit odd.

He would relish the voracious capacity of our hymn tradition to swallow up every kind of music and turn it to account. He would permit himself an affectionate smirk at its capacity for muddle and inconsistencies, like the fact that there are two tunes to 'Love Divine', so that when a bride-to-be rings her local organist to discuss the music for her wedding he has to ask her which one she wants, which usually involves singing them both down the phone, or, in the single greatest advance of modern technology, referring her to YouTube.

As an educated chap, he would be satisfied that the words of Cranmer and the King James Bible are still heard in our land, and alive to their presence in the hinterland of all the best writers of English ('my will is willing, but my won't is weak', sings Cole Porter's hedonistic heroine in 'Don't Look at Me that Way'[1]). And he would point out the best music of the past that we should use more: Old Hall, Worcester, Lumley, and pieces by Browne, Hooper, Humfrey, Locke, Blow and Walmisley, among many others. He would suggest that we stop singing the same old bits of Byrd every year, but have a proper nose around in the complete edition. There are more things in there than are dreamt of on most cathedral music-lists. Much non-copyright music is now available free, online, in perfectly serviceable editions.

He would reflect that, of all the periods of church music he has observed, the most productive have been those which have looked forward as well as back. The worst have been those when its composers have been, in the words of Olivier Messiaen, 'paresseux, les artisans du sous-Fauré … paresseux, les vils flatteurs de l'habitude et de laisser-aller, paresseux'[2] ('Lazy, writing bad Fauré and thinking that'll do, lazy, the vile flatterers of habit and let-it-go, lazy, lazy, lazy'). Children aren't scared of the new. I once asked a group of choirboys to choose their all-time favourite piece for the last service of a choir year, and the winner by a country mile was the *Missa brevissima* by Giles Swayne. They are right. If you think you do enough contemporary music – you don't. Do more.

And what about ideas? Our church music can do Addisonian enlightenment, and Edwardian patriotism. So what are the defining ideas of today? Where are our hymns to equality? Or democracy? Or freedom? Can't these things be rendered unto God too?

And where is faith? Is it possible for a musician to create church music without being a believer? Manifestly, it is. Most leading composers of church music of the last hundred years have not been conventional believers. For them, as for Michael Tippett, 'the music of the angels ... is all a metaphor'.[3] Peter Maxwell Davies said, 'I admire the church as a work of art, but I find it impossible to *believe*.'[4] Today's composer echoes Tennyson:

> Perplext in faith, but pure in deeds,
> At last he beat his music out.
> There lives more faith in honest doubt,
> Believe me, than in half the creeds.[5]

Or Terry Pratchett: 'The presence of those seeking the truth is infinitely to be preferred to the presence of those who think they've found it.'[6]

Music is their way of seeking. Diarmaid MacCulloch sums up the question with characteristic elegance:

> It is one of the curiosities of Western society since the
> Enlightenment that much of its greatest sacred music (though by
> no means all) has been the work of those who have abandoned any
> structured Christian faith ... What do we make of this paradox? ...
> Perhaps music might be one way past the impasse which has been
> the experience of some versions of the Protestant Reformation,
> tangled in the torrent of words which has flowed around the Word
> which dwelt among us, full of grace and truth.[7]

Elizabeth I would surely have answered Amen to that.

Does it matter? Will future generations encounter choral evensong as a 'liturgical reconstruction', an offshoot of 'music in abandoned churches', the soundtrack to a suite of fine but forgotten old buildings? Maybe. Lots of good music has been resurrected this way.

Or maybe we won't find it necessary to think about it too much. After all, 'the Church of England', as Anthony Trollope reminds us, 'is the only Church which interferes neither with your politics nor your religion'.[8]

Or will the church musician of the future be the bored representative of Philip Larkin's church-goer, wandering into an empty building without really knowing why, peering at 'some brass and stuff / Up at the holy end', and, completely by accident, 'surprising / A hunger in himself to be more serious'? Will he stand in the 'tense, musty, unignorable silence' and find that church music and its history becomes, for him, 'A serious house on serious earth … proper to grow wise in, / If only that so many dead lie round'?[9] If there is a message for the future from this rich, muddled, colourful, joyous, sonorous story of the past, it's probably that English church music will find a way of embracing all of these.

Church music still has a lot to offer. As an educator, it can provide an unparalleled training encompassing aural skills, sight-reading and exposure to a whole world of wonderful words and music (though the education may not always hit home immediately: a little choirboy was recently solemnly inducted into the correct form of behaviour at the 'sign of the peace' during communion in his parish church – Go round the congregation, shake them by the hand, and greet them politely and clearly with the words 'Peace be with you'. When the moment came, he scurried obediently around the pews saying 'pleased to meet you').

The skills it teaches are not limited to the purely musical. Nothing better instils the virtues of teamwork and old-fashioned things like concentration and standing still. It is one of the very few activities children can do in mixed age groups. This age-blindness extends to its social function too. It is the only corporate activity that really is open to people aged eight to eighty. It can provide a focus for communities and a way of keeping fine old buildings in regular use.

Church music reaches other parts of society as well. There was a carol service held not long ago in a high-security prison in rural Buckinghamshire. The bishop came. The men of 'D' wing had formed a choir. There were two anthems, 'Silent Night' and 'Bridge over Troubled Water'.

And, whatever the outside world throws at it, the ancient cycle of choral worship keeps turning. A little later on the day of the 'D' wing carols, evensong was sung in a late fifteenth-century chapel in Oxford.

The robed choristers walked slowly in through the pools of flickering candlelight as daylight drained from the stained-glass windows. A blackbird joined in from outside. There was plainsong, sung in English and harmonised in the style of Thomas Helmore, and music by Tallis, Stanford and Leighton. The words of the liturgy, like the building, acted as an ancient shell into which each generation poured its own species of ornamentation. In both cases the main contribution of the modern age was to improve the lighting.

A tradition that can still do that has plenty left to offer. William Byrd was wrong. Tallis is not dead, because people are still using his music and doing what he did, in the places where he did it, and for the same reasons.

Notes

Preface

1 Richard Dawkins (2007), *The God Delusion*, London: Black Swan, p. 402.

1 In the Beginning

1 Matthew 26:30.

2 Diarmaid MacCulloch (2009), *A History of Christianity: The First Three Thousand Years*, London: Allen Lane, pp. 158–9.

3 Ibid., pp. 183–4.

4 Quoted, for example, in John Earle (1901), *The Alfred Jewel: an Historical Essay*, Oxford: Clarendon Press, pp. 153–4.

5 Hugh Cobbe (ed.) (2008), *Letters of Ralph Vaughan Williams 1895–1958*, Oxford: Oxford University Press, p. 217.

6 See Christopher Page (1997), *Discarding Images. Reflections on Music and Culture in Medieval France*, Oxford: Clarendon Press, chapter 1.

7 Bede, *Historia Ecclesiastica Gentis Anglorum: Liber Secundus*. The original Latin reads 'Qui, quoniam cantandi in ecclesia erat peritissimus, recuperata postmodum pace in provincia, et crescente numero fidelium, etiam magister ecclesiasticae cantionis juxta morem Romanorum seu Cantuariorum multis coepit existere …'

8   Bede, *The Abbots of Wearmouth and Jarrow* (2013), edited by C. Grocock and
    I. N. Wood, Oxford: Oxford University Press. See J. F.Webb (trans.) (1983),
    The Age of Bede, London: Penguin, p. 190.

9   *The Anonymous Life of St Ceolfrith, Abbot of Jarrow*, quoted, for example, in
    Henry Wansbrough (2010), *The Use and Abuse of the Bible: A Brief History of
    Biblical Interpretation*, London: T & T Clark, p. 64.

10 Charles Herbermann (1913), 'Councils of Clovesho' in *The Catholic
    Encyclopedia*, New York: Robert Appleton Company.

11 See Edward Cuthbert Butler (2005), *Benedictine Monachism: Studies in
    Benedictine Life and Rule*, Eugene, Oregon: Wipf & Stock Publishers,
    p. 278, n. 3: 'there is no doubt that the entire office was modulated with notes'.

12 The Order of St Benedict, *The Rule of Benedict*, Chapter IX.

13 See Gro Steinsland, Preben Meulengracht Sørensen (1998) *Människor och
    makter i vikingarnas värld* ('Humans and Powers in the Viking World'),
    Stockholm, Sweden: Ordfront.

14 Giraldus Cambrensis [Gerald of Wales] (1194), *Descriptio Cambriae* [The
    Description of Wales]: '...discrimina vocum varia ... consonantiam et
    organicam convenientia melodiam'. Giraldus goes on: 'In their musical
    concerts they do not sing in unison like the inhabitants of other countries,
    but in many different parts ... You will hear as many different parts and
    voices as there are performers who all at length unite with organic melody.'
    See F. D. Wackerbarth (1837), *Music and the Anglo-Saxons, An Account of the
    Anglo-Saxon Orchestra*, London: William Pickering, pp. 36–7, n.

15 Dom Thomas Symons (trans.) (1953), *Regularis Concordia Anglicae Nationis
    Monachorum Sanctimonialiumque ('The Monastic Agreement of the Monks and
    Nuns of the English Nation')*, London: Thomas Nelson and Sons, p. 50. The
    Latin is 'Cum ergo ille residens tres, velut erraneos ac aliquid quaerentes,
    viderit sibi approximare, incipiat mediocri voce dulcisone cantare *Quem
    quaeritis?*... Cuius iussionis voce vertant se illi tres ad chorum, dicentes
    Alleluia.'

16 Henry Mayr-Harting (2011), *Religion, Politics and Society in Britain,
    1066–1272*, Harlow: Pearson Education, p. 38. See also David Hiley (1986),
    'Thurstan of Caen and Plainchant at Glastonbury', *Proceedings of the
    British Academy* 72, pp. 57–90, esp. p. 82; and William of Malmesbury, *Gesta
    Pontificium Anglorum*, edited and translated by M. Winterbottom and R.
    M. Thomson (2007), Oxford: Oxford University Press, vol. I, pp. 308–11.

17 Aelred of Rievaulx, *Speculum caritatis* [*The Mirror of Charity*], quoted, for
    example, in Bruce Holsinger (2001) *Music, Body, and Desire in Medieval
    Culture: Hildegard of Bingen to Chaucer (Figurae: Reading Medieval Culture)*,
    Redwood City, CA: Stanford University Press, p. 160 ('Aliquando, quod

pudet dicere, in equinos hinnitus cogitur, aliquando virile vigore deposito in feminieae vocis').

2 Music for a New Millennium

1 Charles Joseph Hefele (1896), *A History of the Councils of the Church*, London: T & T Clark, p. 385.

2 See Anne Bagnall Yardley (2006), *Performing Piety: Music in Medieval English Nunneries*, New York: Palgrave Macmillan.

3 Cambridge, Corpus Christi College MS 473, in Susan Rankin (ed.) (2007), *The Winchester Troper: Facsimile edition and introduction*, Early English Church Music series, vol. 50, London: Stainer & Bell for the British Academy; *et seq.*

4 I am grateful to Henry Mayr-Harting for this information.

5 Quoted, for example, in Michal Andrzej Kobialka (2003), *This Is My Body: Representational Practices in the Early Middle Ages*, Ann Arbor, MI: University of Michigan Press, p. 183.

6 Quoted, for example, in William Marriott (1838), *A Collection of English Miracle-Plays or Mysteries; Containing Ten Dramas from the Chester, Coventry, and Towneley series, with two of latter date*, Basel: Schweighauser and Co.

7 R. I. Moore (2012), *The War on Heresy: Faith and Power in Medieval Europe*, London: Profile, pp. 180–81.

8 William of Newburgh, *Historia Rerum Anglicarum* (*c.*1198), Preface (Cambridge, Corpus Christi College, MS 262) in R. Howlett (ed.) (1884–9), *Chronicles of the Reigns of Stephen, Henry II and Richard I*, Rolls Series 82, vols 1 and 2, London.

9 Quoted, for example, in Jacob Hammer (ed.) (1951), *Geoffrey of Monmouth, Historia regum Britanniae, Liber Primus*, Medieval Academy Books, no. 57, Cambridge, Mass.: The Medieval Academy of America. Geoffrey's Latin reads: 'Conventus quoque vel concentus multimodorum ordinatorum miris modulationibus praecinebat'.

10 Walter Map, *De Nugis Curialium* in M. R. James (ed.) (1914), *Anecdota Oxoniensia*, Medieval and Modern Series, Oxford: Clarendon Press, p. 6 (Latin text).

11 Quoted, for example, in H. O. Coxe (ed.) (1841), *Rogeri de Wendover Chronica, sive Flores Historiarum,* [with] *Appendix, in qua lectionum varietas additionesque quibus Chronicon istud ampliavit Matthæus Parisiensis*, p. 193.

12 Giraldus Cambrensis [Gerald of Wales] (1194), *Descriptio Cambriae* [The Description of Wales]: '…discrimina vocum varia … consonantiam et organicam convenientia melodiam'. Giraldus goes on: 'In their musical concerts they do not sing in unison like the inhabitants of other countries, but in many different parts … You will hear as many different parts and

voices as there are performers who all at length unite with organic melody.'
See F. D. Wackerbarth (1837), *Music and the Anglo-Saxons, An Account of the Anglo-Saxon Orchestra*, London: William Pickering, pp. 36–7, n.

13 See William Dalglish, 'The Origin of the Hocket', *Journal of the American Musicological Society*, vol. 31, no. 1 (Spring 1978), pp. 3–20.

14 The Latin reads: 'Nonnulli novella scholae discipuli, dum temporibus mensurandis invigilant, novis notis intendunt, fingere suas quam antiquas cantare malunt; in semibreves et minimas ecclesiastica cantantur, notulis percutiuntur. Nam melodias hoquetis intersecant, discantibus lubricant, triplis et motetis vulgaribus nonnumquam inculcant; adeo ut interdum antiphonarii et gradualis fundamenta despiciant, ignorent super quo aedificant; tonos nesciant quos non discernunt, imo confundunt cum ex earum multitudine notarum, ascensiones pudicae descensionesque temperatae plani cantus, quibus toni ipsi cernuntur adinvicem, obfuscentur. Currunt enim et non quiescent, aures inebriant et non medentur, gestis simulant quod depromunt; quibus devotio quaerenda contemnitur, vitanda lascivia propagatur.' It is quoted in, for example, Charles Edmond Henri de Coussemaker (1841), *Mémoire sur Hucbald et sur ses traités de musique, suivi de recherches sur la notation et sur les instruments de musique*, Paris: J. Techener, p. 204.

This passage does not appear in the earliest copies of the Papal Bull, and contemporary comments are strangely silent on it, leading to the inference that the passage about hockets and minims may have been added later. I am indebted to Matthew Thomson for this insight.

15 Bonnie J. Blackburn, 'Fa mi la mi sol la: Music Theory, Erotic Practice', paper given at Indiana University, 2004, referred to in Elizabeth Eva Leach, 'Gendering the Semitone, Sexing the Leading Tone: Fourteenth-Century Music Theory and the Directed Progression', *Music Theory Spectrum*, 28/1 (2006): 1–21.

16 Johannes de Grocheio, *Ars musicae* (*c*.1300), quoted in, for example, Nicolae Sfetcu (2014), *The Music Sound* (self-published e-book).

17 Christopher Page (1997), *Discarding Images: Reflections on Music and Culture in Medieval France*, Oxford: Clarendon Press, pp. 79–80.

18 Bodleian Library, University of Oxford, MS. Lat. liturg. d. 20; *et seq.*

19 See Alan Coates (1999), *Early Medieval Books: the Reading Abbey Collections from Foundation to Dispersal*, Oxford: Clarendon Press, p. 45.

20 Printed in Historical Manuscripts Commission, *Archives of the See of Ossory*, p. 240. See Leighton Greene (ed.) (1974), *The Lyrics of the Red Book of Ossory*, pp. iii–iv. The Latin is: 'Nota: Attende, lector, quod Episcopus Ossoriensis fecit istas cantilenas pro vicariis Ecclesie Cathedralis, sacerdotibus, et clericis suis, ad cantandum in magnis festis et solaciis, ne guttera eorum

et ora Deo sanctificata polluantur cantilenis teatralibus, turpibus et secularibus; et cum sint cantatores, provideant sibi de notis convenientibus secundum quod dictamina requirunt.'

21 See Page (1997), *Discarding Images*, chapter 1.

22 In John Wycliffe, 'On Prelates', chapter xi, quoted in Charles Webb Le Bas (1832), *The Life of Wiclif*, London: printed for J. G. and F. Rivington, p. 346.

23 Richard Rolle, *The Psalter, or psalms of David, and certain canticles*, edited by H. R. Bramley (1884), Oxford: Clarendon Press, p. 3.

24 Ibid.

25 Geoffrey Chaucer, *The Canterbury Tales; The Parliament of Fowls; The Book of the Duchess*. William Langland, *The Vision of Piers Plowman*; *et seq.*

26 There are interesting things about transactions for indulgences and paying for people to pray for you in Alastair Minnis, 'Purchasing Pardon: Material and Spiritual Economies on the Canterbury Pilgrimage', p. 63ff. in Lawrence Besserman (ed.) (2006), *Sacred and Secular in Medieval and Early Modern Cultures: New Essays*, New York: Palgrave Macmillan.

27 Francis James Child (1904), *The English and Scottish Popular Ballads*, Boston, Mass.: Houghton Mifflin, gives the Royalist anthology *Wit Restor'd* (1658), London, as the earliest printed source of this ballad. There are many others.

28 Wycliffe, 'On Prelates', chapter xi, quoted in Le Bas (1832), *The Life of Wiclif*, p. 346.

3 The Fifteenth Century: Possibilities and Promise

1 Andrew Hughes and Margaret Bent (eds) (1969), *The Old Hall Manuscript*, 3 vols, Middleton, WI: The American Institute of Musicology.

2 *Henry V*, Act IV, scene 8.

3 *War and Peace*, Book 14, chapter 7.

4 Letter from Yorkshire East Riding archives, MS reference: Durham, Prior's Kitchen, Dean and Chapter Muniments: Locellus XXV.18.

5 Quoted, for example, in Nicholas Temperley (1979), *The Music of the English Parish Church*, Cambridge: Cambridge University Press, p. 10.

6 The French original reads:
   Car ilz ont nouvelle pratique
   De faire frisque concordance
   En haulte et en basse musique,
   En fainte, en pause, et en muance,
   Et ont pris de la contenance
   Angloise, et ensuivy Dunstable.
   Pourquoi merveilleuse plaisance
   Rend leur chant joyeulx et notable.

It is quoted, for example, in Claude Pierre Goujet (1745), *Bibliotheque françoise Vio: Ou Histoire de la litterature françoise*, p. 218.

7   Tinctoris (1477), quoted, for example, in Douglas Gray (2008), *Later Medieval English Literature*, Oxford: Oxford University Press, p. 110.

8   John Stanbridge (1507), *Vulgaria*, Oxford.

9   'Churchwardens' accounts: 1531–2', in Henry Littlehales (ed.) (1905), *The Medieval Records of a London City Church (St Mary At Hill), AD 1420–1559*, London: K. Paul, Trench Trübner & Co. for the Early English Text Society, pp. 358–60; http://www.british-history.ac.uk/early-eng-text-soc/vo1128/pp358–360 [accessed 30 March 2015].

10 Eton College Library, MS. 178.

11 I am grateful to Peter Phillips for his illuminating insights into the character of the Eton composers, especially John Browne. See his sleeve notes to John Browne, *Music from the Eton Choirbook* (CD), Gimell, CDGIM 036 (2005).

12 Andrew Ashbee, *Records of English Court Music*, vol VII, p. 361 Farnham, Surrey: Ashgate.

13 Trinity College, Cambridge, MS 0.3.58.

14 The Henry VIII manuscript (British Library Add MS 31,922) and the Fayrfax manuscript (British Museum Add MS 5465).

15 Robin Leaver (1987), '*Goostly psalms and spirituall songes' English and Dutch metrical psalms from Coverdale to Utenhove 1535–1566*, Oxford: Clarendon Press, p. 81.

16 There is some uncertainty about the circumstances of this remark. Some commentators believe the meaning of the question, asked during Richard Nixon's historic visit to China in 1972, was lost in translation, and Zhou thought he was being asked about the effects of the recent student riots in Paris, which makes more obvious sense. However, when the error was pointed out to the Chinese, they decided that Zhou had accidentally made rather a good point about the French Revolution, and deliberately omitted to correct it. Other accounts attribute the remark to Lin Baio.

4   Keeping Your Head: The Approach of the Reformation, 1509–1547

1   John Foxe, *Actes and Monuments* [Foxe's *Book of Martyrs*] (1563), Book 3, p. 493.

2   Ibid.

3   John Marbeck (1550), Introduction to *Concordance*, London: printed by Richard Grafton, quoted in Joseph Ames, William Herbert, Thomas Frognall Dibdin et al. (1816), *Typographical Antiquities; Or the History of Printing in England, Scotland and Ireland*, vol. 3, London: printed for William Miller , p. 470.

4   John Foxe (1570 edn), *Actes and Monuments*, Book 8, p. 1213.

5   J. A. Froude (1894), *Life and letters of Erasmus*, quoted in, for example, Peter le Huray (1978), *Music and the Reformation in England, 1549–1660*, Cambridge: Cambridge University Press, p. 11.

6   Thomas Wolsey, Regulations for the Augustinian Order in England, issued on 22 March 1519, quoted in Rob C. Wegman (2005) *The Crisis of Music in Early Modern Europe, 1470–1530*, New York: Routledge. The Latin is: '... in quo non lasciva melodia astantium auribus blanditur, nec favor humanae laudis in divisione notarum appetitur ... cantus fractus vel divisus "Prick-Song" vulgariter et Anglice dictus ... planus cantus et modesta ...'.

7   W. D. Hamilton (ed.), *A Chronicle of England during the reigns of the Tudors, 1485–1559 by Charles Wriothesley, Windsor Herald* (1875 and 1877), 2 vols, London: J. B. Nichols and Son for the Camden Society.

8   Ibid.

9   Letter from Henry VIII to Cranmer of 1544: see John Edmund Cox (ed.) (1846; reprinted 2001), *Miscellaneous Writings and Letters of Thomas Cranmer*, Cambridge: Regent College Publishing, p. 494.

10 Ibid., p. 412

11 W. H. Frere and W. P. M. Kennedy (1910), *Visitation Articles and Injunctions*, London: Longmans Green and Co.

12 Quoted in Eamon Duffy (2005), *The Stripping of the Altars: Traditional Religion in England, c.1400–c.1580*, London and New Haven: Yale University Press, pp. 446.

13 Ibid., p. 408.

14 Ibid., p. 430.

15 Ibid., p. 432.

16 Ibid., 396.

17 Ibid., p. 438.

18 Desiderius Erasmus, 'A Prayer for the Peace of the Church', in the primer of 1545, printed for example in *Three Primers put forth in the time of Henry VIII* (1834), Oxford: published on behalf of the Church of England at the University Press, p. 513.

19 Duffy, *The Stripping of the Altars*, p. 418.

20 See plates 132, 133 and 136 in Duffy, *The Stripping of the Altars*.

21 See http://www.broadsideparishes.org.uk/bspicons/manuscript.htm.

22 Thomas Tusser (1557–80), 'The Epistle to the Lord William Paget deceased' (*c.* 1575) in *Five hundred pointes of good husbandrie*, edited 'from the Unique Copy in the British Museum' of *A Hundred Good Poixtes of Husbandrie* by W. Payne and S. J. Herrtage (1878), London: Trubner and Co., for the English Dialect Society. The lines of verse are quoted in, for example, Walter Scott

(1810), *A Collection of Scarce and Valuable Tracts on the Most Entertaining Subjects*, London: T. Cadell and W. Davies, p. 408.

23 Tusser (1557–80), *Five hundred pointes of good husbandrie.*

24 The Almonry Heritage Centre, Evesham, Worcs.

25 The Henry VIII manuscript, British Library Add. MS 31,922, and the Fayrfax manuscript, British Museum Add. MS 5465.

5 The Children of Henry VIII: Reformation and Counter-Reformation, 1547–1558

1 Paul Ehlers, 'Die Musik und Adolf Hitler', in *Zeitschrift für Musik*, April 1939, p. 361.

2 Widely reported comment on accepting membership of the Communist party, 1963.

3 William Byrd and Thomas Tallis (1575), *Cantiones, quae ab argumento sacrae vocantur*, Introduction.

4 J. Ayre (ed.) (1844), *The Catechism of Thomas Becon, with other pieces written by him in the reign of King Edward the Sixth*, Cambridge: Cambridge University Press, for the Parker Society, p. 429.

5 J. A. Froude (1894), *Life and letters of Erasmus*, quoted in, for example, Le Huray (1978), *Music and the Reformation in England, 1549–1660*, p. 11.

6 R. Potts (ed.) (1851), *The Huntyng and Fyndyng out of the Romish Fox, written by Wyllyam Turner* (1543), London: John W. Parker.

7 Temperley (1979), *The Music of the English Parish Church*, p. 18.

8 Ibid.

9 Ayre (ed.) (1844), *The Catechism of Thomas Becon.*

10 Frere and Kennedy (1910), *Visitation Articles and Injunctions.*

11 Ibid.

12 Hamilton (ed.), *A Chronicle of England during the reigns of the Tudors, 1485–1559 by Charles Wriothesley*, p. 187.

13 H. Robinson (ed.) (1847), *Original Letters Relative to the English Reformation*, Cambridge: Parker Society, vol. 1, p. 72.

14 Quoted, for example, in Peter le Huray (ed.) (1982), *The Treasury of English Church Music 1545–1650*, Cambridge: Cambridge University Press, p. xii.

15 Judith Blezzard (ed.) (1985), *The Tudor Church Music of the Lumley Books*, Middleton, WI: A-R Editions, Inc.

16 Bodleian Library, MSS Mus. Sch. e. 420–22.

17 R. Crowley (1549), *The Psalter of David newely translated into Englysh metre …*, London: R. Crowley.

18 T. Sternhold (*c.*1549), *Certayn psalms chosen out of the psalter of David*, London, dedication.

19 *Injunctions given by the most Excellent Prince, Edward VI*, 1547, printed in, for example, Thomas Cranmer (1833), *Remains*, edited by Henry Jenkyns, Oxford: J. H. Parker for the University, vol. 4, p. 335.

20 Quoted, for example, in Le Huray (1978), *Music and the Reformation in England, 1549–1660*, p. 10.

21 Act 'for the defacing of images and the bringing in of books of old Service in the Church', 1550, quoted in Duffy *The Stripping of Altars*, p. 469.

22 Christopher Tye (1553), *The Actes of the Apostles*, London: Wyllyam Seres, dedication.

23 Quoted in, for example, Duffy, *The Stripping of the Altars*, p. 531.

24 Ibid.

25 John Milsom, 'English Polyphonic Style in Transition: a study of the sacred music of Thomas Tallis', DPhil, University of Oxford, 1983.

26 J. G. Nichols (ed.) (1848), *The Diary of Henry Machyn, Citizen and Merchant-Taylor of London, 1550–1563*, London: J. B. Nichols and Son for the Camden Society.

27 Injunctions, 1556, quoted in Temperley (1979), *The Music of the English Parish Church*, p. 10.

28 Nichols (ed.) (1848), *The Diary of Henry Machyn*.

29 Quoted in Eamon Duffy (2001), *The Voices of Morebath: Reformation and Rebellion in an English Village*, London and New Haven: Yale University Press, p. 153.

30 Duffy, *The Stripping of the Altars*, p. 532.

31 Nichols (ed.) (1848), *The Diary of Henry Machyn*.

32 Eamon Duffy (2012), *Saints, Sacrilege and Sedition: Religion and Conflict in the Tudor Reformations*, London: Bloomsbury, p. 220.

33 Duffy, *The Stripping of the Altars*, pp. 543–5.

34 Ibid.

35 J. Payne Collier (1840), *Early English Poetry, Ballads and Popular Literature of the Middle Ages*, vol. 1, London: C. Richards for the Percy Society (the volume contains many entertaining poems on a similar theme).

36 Temperley (1979), *The Music of the English Parish Church*, p. 29. John Knox used an identical phrase in his version of 1564.

37 Ashbee, *Records of English Court Music*, vol. VII, pp. 422–3.

38 Ibid., vol. VII, p. 115.

39 William Tyndale, 'An Answer unto Sir Thomas More's Dialogue', in Thomas Russell (ed.) (1831), *The Works of the English Reformers: William Tyndale and John Frith*, Paternoster Row, London: for Ebenezer Palmer, p. 64.

40 Duffy, *The Stripping of the Altars*, p. 137.

41 Ibid. p. 426.

42 Duffy (2001), *The Voices of Morebath*, p. 178.

43 Collect at Compline, The Book of Common Prayer (1549).

6   Church Music and Society in Elizabeth's England, 1558–1603

1   The Royal Injunctions, 1559, article 49, quoted for example in Thomas Busby (1819), *A General History of Music, from the earliest times to the present*, London: G. and W. B. Whittaker, vol. 2, p. 3.

2   For example Wenhaston, Suffolk. See Duffy, *The Stripping of the Altars*, plate 55.

3   Duffy, *The Stripping of the Altars*, p. 585.

4   Nichols (ed.) (1848), *The Diary of Henry Machyn*.

5   J. Bruce and T. T. Perowne (eds) (1853), *Correspondence of Matthew Parker, D.D., Archbishop of Canterbury ...* , Cambridge: Parker Society.

6   Spanish Ambassador to the Bishop of Arras, 9 October 1559, in Le Huray (1978), *Music and the Reformation in England, 1549–1660*, pp. 33–4.

7   Nichols (ed.) (1848), *The Diary of Henry Machyn*.

8   Letter to Peter Martyr in Frankfurt, March 1560, quoted in, for example, Beth Quitslund (2009), *The Reformation in Rhyme: Sternhold, Hopkins and the English Metrical Psalter, 1547–1603*, Burlington, VT: Ashgate, p. 153 (translation adapted from Quislund and Temperley).

9   Thomas Warton (1824), *The History of English Poetry*, London, p. 152.

10 Philip Sidney, 'Dominus regit me: The Twenty-Third Psalm'.

11 Nichols (ed.) (1848), *The Diary of Henry Machyn*.

12 Quoted in, for example, Le Huray (1978), *Music and the Reformation in England, 1549–1660*, p. 385.

13 *The Merry Wives of Windsor*, Act II, scene 1.

14 Foster Watson (1908, reprinted 1968), *The English Grammar School to 1660: Their Curriculum and Practice*, Cambridge: Cambridge University Press, p. 42 (and further examples).

15 Sternhold and Hopkins, *The Whole Book of Psalms*, epigraph printed in the Introduction to editions from the 1560s through the entire seventeenth century. See, for example, Amy M. E. Morris (2005), *Popular Measures: Poetry and Church Order in Seventeenth-Century Massachusetts*, Newark, Del.: University of Delaware Press, p. 141.

16 Temperley (1979), *The Music of the English Parish Church*, p. 46.

17 Charles Dickens, *David Copperfield*, chapter 10.

18 Ben Jonson, 'An Epitaph on S. P., A Child of Queen Elizabeth's Chapel'; see George Parfitt (ed.) (1996), *Ben Jonson: The Complete Poems*, London: Penguin.

19 Nichols (ed.) (1848), *The Diary of Henry Machyn*.

20 Much Wenlock Parish Register, quoted in Duffy (2012), *Saints, Sacrilege and Sedition*, p. 213.

21 Duffy (2001), *The Voices of Morebath*, p. 170.

22 Ibid., p. 171.

23 David Wilkins (1737), *Concilia Magnae Britanniae et Hiberniae*, London: R. Gosling, p. 200 (Wilkins's translation).

24 Ibid., p. 201.

25 John Jewel (1888), *The Apology of the Church of England*, edited by Henry Morley, London: Cassell.

26 Questions 'for clerks and their duty', 1560; see Temperley (1979), *The Music of the English Parish Church*, p. 44.

27 Le Huray (1978), *Music and the Reformation in England, 1549–1660*, p. 37.

28 Ibid., p. 38.

29 Geoffrey Chaucer, *The Miller's Tale*, line 300.

30 Duffy (2001), *The Voices of Morebath*, p. 64.

31 Temperley (1979), *The Music of the English Parish Church*, p. 45.

32 *David Copperfield*, chapter 43.

33 *Hamlet*, Act III, scene 2.

34 Temperley (1979), *The Music of the English Parish Church*, p. 53.

35 Petition, 27 June 1577, in Le Huray (1978), *Music and the Reformation in England, 1549–1660*, p. 193.

36 John Northbrooke (*c.*1577; reprinted 1843), *A Treatise against Dicing, Dancing, Plays and Interludes, with Other Idle Pastimes*, London: Shakespeare Society.

37 Ben Byram-Wigfield (ed.) (2002), *The Praise of Music* (by Anon. formerly attributed to John Case; printed in Oxford in 1586 by Joseph Barnes), published online.

38 Temperley (1979), *The Music of the English Parish Church*, p. 45.

39 Temperley (1979), *The Music of the English Parish Church*, p. 44.

40 Quoted in, for example, Anna Whitelock (2013), *Elizabeth's Bedfellows: An Intimate History of the Queen's Court*, London: Bloomsbury Publishing, p. 201. For an account of the first performance, see David Starkey and Katie Greening (2013), *Music and Monarchy*, London: BBC Books (Random House), p. 116.

41 Interview with Benjamin Britten in the *New York Times*, 16 November 1969 (see also Humphrey Carpenter (1992), *Benjamin Britten: a biography*, London: Faber and Faber, p. 441).

42 Letter from Thomas Wateridge, 1611, quoted in, for example, Suzanne Cole (2008), *Thomas Tallis and his Music in Victorian England* (Music in Britain, 1600–1900 series), Martlesham, Suffolk: Boydell Press, p. 97.

43 William Byrd (1588), Introductory poem to *Psalmes, Sonnets and Songs of Sadness and Pietie*, London: Stainer & Bell, 1964 (edited and revised edition).

44 William Kemp or Kempe (1600), *Nine Daies Wonder*.

45 A regular complaint. This particular example is from Archbishop Lee's Injunctions for Ripon, Second Set, Item 3 (1537). Frere and Kennedy (1910), *Visitation Articles and Injunctions*, vol. 2, p. 29.

46 Robert Dow: 'Dies lunae Ut lucem solis sequitur lux proximae lunae Sic tu post Birdum Munde venis': 'Moon-day: As the light of the moon follows close on the sun So you after Byrd, Mundy, next do come'. Quoted in Le Huray (1978), *Music and the Reformation in England, 1549–1660*, p. 217.

47 The reference is to the execution of Mark Bosworth and Roger Filcock at Candlemas 1601.

48 Moore (2012), *The War on Heresy: Faith and Power in Medieval Europe*, p. 58.

49 See Allan Doig (2008), *Liturgy and Architecture: From the Early Church to the Middle Ages*, Farnham, Surrey: Ashgate, p. 166.

50 Aelred, *Speculum caritatis* ('The Mirror of Charity') in A. Hoste and C. Talbot (1971), *Aelred of Rievaulx, Opera Omnia*, vol. 1, Turnhout: Brepols.

51 From a now-lost broadside entitled 'The Children of the Chapel Stript and Whipt'; see Le Huray (1978), *Music and the Reformation in England, 1549–1660*, p. 222.

52 William Prynne (*c.*1631), *Histriomastix: The Player's Scourge or Actor's Tragedy*, London: M. Sparke.

53 British Museum, Royal MS. 18. B. XIX; see Le Huray (1978), *Music and the Reformation in England, 1549–1660*, p. 36.

54 J. M. Osborn (ed.) (1961), *The Autobiography of Thomas Whythorne*, Oxford: Clarendon Press, p. 245; see Le Huray (1978), *Music and the Reformation in England, 1549–1660*, p. 40.

55 Thomas Morley (1597), *A Plaine and Easie Introduction to Practicall Musicke*, London: Peter Short.

56 Richard Hooker (1597), *Of the Laws of Ecclesiastical Polity*, vol. 2, Book 5, section 38; see Temperley (1979), *The Music of the English Parish Church*, p. 50.

57 Thomas East (1592), *The Whole Booke of Psalmes*, London: Thomas Este, Preface.

58 See http://www.british-history.ac.uk/topographical-hist-norfolk/vo13/pp277–360.

59   *The Merchant of Venice*, Act V, scene 1.

60   *The Merry Wives of Windsor*, Act I, scene 1.

61   J. Harley (1999), *William Byrd: Gentleman of the Chapel Royal*, Farnham, Surrey: Ashgate, p. 360.

62   Peter Phillips, 'Laboravi in gemitu meo": Morley or Rogier?', *Music and Letters*, vol. 62, January–April 1982, pp. 85–90.

63   Lionel Pike, '"Gaude Maria Virgo": Morley or Philips?', *Music and Letters*, vol. 50, no. 1, January 1969, pp. 127–35.

64   G. von Bulow, 'The Diary of Philip Julius, Duke of Stettin-Pomerania', *Transactions of the Royal Historical Society*, VI, 1892; see Le Huray (1978), *Music and the Reformation in England, 1549–1660*, p. 220.

65   Frere and Kennedy (1910), *Visitation Articles and Injunctions*.

66   R. Brown (1890), *Calendar of State Papers in the Archives of Venice, VII, 1558–91*; quoted in Le Huray (1978), *Music and the Reformation in England, 1549–1660*, p. 26.

67   William Perkins (*c.*1590), *The Foundation of Christian Religion gathered into six principles* (1627); quoted in Duffy, *The Stripping of the Altars*, p. 591.

7   Plots, Scots, Politics and the Beauty of Holiness, 1603–1645

1   Thomas Ravenscroft (1621), *The Whole Booke of Psalmes*.

2   Ashbee, *Records of English Court Music*, vols 1–9, *1986–1995*, vol. 4.

3   Oliver Cromwell, Speech to Parliament, 23 January 1654/5.

4   William Byrd (1607), *Gradualia*, Dedication. For a modern edition, see Philip Brett (ed.) (1976–2004), *The Byrd Edition*, vols 5–7b, London: Stainer & Bell.

5   William Byrd (1611), *Psalms, Songs and Sonnets*, Introduction.

6   Ibid.

7   Ibid.

8   Ashbee, *Records of English Court Music*, vols 1–9, *1986–1995*, vol. 4.

9   A number of scholars have worked on the many sources of Hooper's surviving works. I am grateful to Mrs Bridget le Huray for permission to consult the unpublished researches of the late Dr Peter le Huray in the University Library, Cambridge, and to Michael Rintamaa of the University of Kentucky, David Allinson and other Hooper enthusiasts.

10   Barry Coward (1980; 4th edn, 2011), *The Stuart Age: England, 1603–1714*, Abingdon, Oxon: Routledge, p. 135.

11   William Laud, *Diary*, 6 October 1623, in James Bliss (ed.) (1852), *The Works of the Most Reverend Father in God, William Laud*, 7 volumes, vol. 3, Oxford: John Henry Parker, p. 143.

12 Quoted in, for example, C. E. Welch (1957), 'Two Cathedral Organists: Thomas Weelkes (1601–1623) and Thomas Kelway (1720–1744)', The Chichester Papers, no. 8, Chichester City Council.

13 See R. T. Daniel and Peter le Huray (1972), *Early English Church Music*, Supplementary volume, vol. I: *The Sources of English Church Music 1549–1660*, Part 1, London: Stainer & Bell for the British Academy.

14 Quoted, for example, in Julie Anne Sadie (ed.) (1998), *Companion to Baroque Music*, Oxford: Clarendon Press, p. 275.

15 Laud, *Diary*, 21 August 1625, in Bliss (ed.) (1852), *The Works of the Most Reverend Father in God, William Laud*, p. 170.

16 Ashbee, *Records of English Court Music*, vols 1–9, *1986–1995*, vol. 4.

17 *Twelfth Night*, Act II, scene 3.

18 See, for example, Coward (1980; 4th edn, 2011), *The Stuart Age: England, 1603–1714*, p. 53 *et seq*. Christopher Hill (1964) called Puritanism 'an admirable refuge from clarity of thought' in *Society and Puritanism in Pre-Revolutionary England*, London: Martin Secker & Warburg, pp. 1–2.

19 E. F. Rimbault (1872), *The Old Cheque-Book or Book of Remembrance, of the Chapel Royal, 1561–1744*, London: The Camden Society, p. 157.

20 Kenneth Fincham (1994), *Visitation Articles and Injunctions of the Early Stuart Church*, vol. 1 *1603–25*, Martlesham, Suffolk: Boydell Press, p. 110 *et seq*.

21 P. King, 'The Reasons for the Abolition of the Book of Common Prayer in 1645', *The Journal of Ecclesiastical History*, vol. 21, Issue 04, October 1970, pp. 327–39.

22 *The Psalter or Psalmes of David* (1636–7), Edinburgh: printed by Robert Young.

23 J. Barnard (1641), *The First Book of Selected Church Music*, London: printed by Edward Griffin, Preface.

8 Interregnum, 1644–1660

1 Philip Larkin (1954), 'Church Going', in *Philip Larkin Collected Poems* (1988), London: Faber and Faber.

2 Thomas Ravenscroft (1609), *Deuteromelia or The Seconde part of Musicks melodie, or melodius Musicke. Of Pleasant Roundalaies*, London: printed for Thomas Adams, 'Rounds or Catches of 3 Voices, no. 13'.

3 S. J. Fleming (2008), 'The Religious Heritage of the British Northwest and the Rise of Mormonism', *Church History*, vol. 77, Issue 01, March 2008, pp. 73–104.

4 *The Directory for the Publick Worship of God*, approved in Edinburgh, 6 February 1645.

5   Psalm 148, verse 12.

6   John Donne (1624), 'XVII Meditation', in *Devotions upon Emergent Occasions*, London: printed for Thomas Iones.

7   N. Holmes (1644), *Gospel Musick, Or The Singing of Davids Psalms*, London; see the edition by C. Matthew McMahon and Therese B. McMahon (eds) (2012), Coconut Creek, FL: Puritan Publications, Preface.

8   Temperley (1979), *The Music of the English Parish Church*, p. 96.

9   Ibid., p. 99.

10 Holmes (1644), *Gospel Musick*, edited by McMahon and McMahon (2012), pp. 45–6.

11 I am grateful to Dr Mark Smith for the idea and indeed the words of this paragraph.

12 Christopher Marsh (2013), *Music and Society in Early Modern England*, Cambridge: Cambridge University Press.

9   Restoration, 1660–1714

1   Psalm 37, verses 25 and 36.

2   *Hamlet*, Act II, scene 2.

3   Christ Church, Oxford, Library MS no. 1142A, quoted in *The New Grove Dictionary of Music and Musicians* (2001), 2nd edn, vol. 9, Oxford: Oxford University Press.

4   Samuel Pepys, *Diary*, 1 September 1667.

5   Pepys, *Diary*, entries for 8 July 1660, 18 May 1662, 8 September 1662 and 23 April 1661.

6   Matthew Locke (1673), *The Present Practice of Music Vindicated*, London.

7   Pepys, *Diary*, 22 November 1663.

8   Pepys, *Diary*, 15 November 1667.

9   John Evelyn, *Diary*, 21 December 1662.

10 Letter dated 8 February 1679, quoted in, for example, Curtis Price (ed.) (1995), *Purcell Studies*, Cambridge: Cambridge University Press, p. 54.

11 John Hawkins (1776), *A General History of the Science and Practice of Music*, vol. 4, London: T. Payne and Son, chapter 9.

12 Charles Burney (1789; reissued 2011), *A General History of Music, From the Earliest Ages to the Present Period*, 4 vols, vol. 3, Cambridge: Cambridge University Press, p. 482.

13 Henry Purcell, *Jehova, quam multi sunt hostes mei* (1628; orch. Elgar, 1929).

14 R. Vaughan Williams (1951), Foreword to Purcell Society concerts for the Festival of Britain, quoted in, for example, Michael Kennedy (1992), *The Works of Ralph Vaughan Williams*, 2nd edn, Oxford: Clarendon Press, p. 375.

15 'Purcell', in Michael Tippett (1980), *Music of the Angels: Essays and Sketchbooks of Michael Tippett*, London: Eulenburg Books, p. 67.

16 Quoted in W. H. Cummings (1881; revised 1937), *Henry Purcell*, London, p. 27.

17 J. Playford (1677), *The Whole Booke of Psalms*, London, Introduction.

18 Widely quoted, though I have been unable to find the original source.

19 Pepys, *Diary*, 9 August 1663.

20 Playford (1677), *The Whole Booke of Psalms*.

21 In the Supplement to Tate and Brady, *New Version of the Psalms of David in Metre* of 1700.

22 N. Tate (1710), *An Essay for Promoting of Psalmody*, London: printed for J. Holland.

10 The Enlightenment, 1712–1760

1 John Locke (1695), *The Reasonableness of Christianity*, in *The Works of John Locke*, vol. 6, London: Rivington.

2 I. Watts (1707), *Preface to Hymns and Spiritual Songs*, London: J. Humphreys, for John Lawrence.

3 J. Tillotson, quoted in Roy Porter (2000), *Enlightenment: Britain and the Creation of the Modern World*, London: Allen Lane, p. 102.

4 John Locke, quoted in Porter (2000), *Enlightenment*, p. 107.

5 J. Toland, quoted in Porter (2000), *Enlightenment*, pp. 117–18.

6 Archbishop Wake, MS note in his copy of the order of service, now at Lip. Cod. Misc. 1079B, p. 5, quoted in, for example, Matthias Range (2012), *Music and Ceremonial at British Coronations: From James I to Elizabeth II*, Cambridge: Cambridge University Press, p. 139.

7 See Donald Burrows (2005), *Handel and the English Chapel Royal*, Oxford: Oxford University Press.

8 W. Boyce (1760), *Cathedral Music*, 4 vols, London, Preface.

9 Newspaper report, *The Weekly Journal or Saturday's Post*, 9 January 1719, see Burrows (2005), *Handel and the English Chapel Royal*, p. 601.

10 John Hawkins (1788), *Memoirs of Dr. William Boyce*, London.

11 Ibid.

12 Henry Playford (1710), *The Divine Companion: Being a Collection of New and Easie Hymns and Anthems*. See Temperley (1979), *The Music of the English Parish Church*, p. 163.

13 A. F. Prévost (1728–32), *Mémoires et aventures d'un homme de qualité*, Paris, p. 136.

14 John Locke (1693), *Some Thoughts Concerning Education*; See James L. Axtell (ed.) (1968), *The Educational Writings of John Locke*, Cambridge: Cambridge University Press, p. 117.

15 Temperley (1979), *The Music of the English Parish Church*, p. 118.

16 Locke (1693), *Some Thoughts Concerning Education*, section 14.

17 Temperley (1979), *The Music of the English Parish Church*, p. 126.

18 Gabriel Towerson, sermon at St Andrew Undershaft, 31 May 1696. See Temperley (1979), *The Music of the English Parish Church*, p. 101.

19 Thomas Busby (1800): see Temperley (1979), *The Music of the English Parish Church*, p. 120.

20 *The Gentleman's Magazine*, no. 57, 4 February 1731.

21 Thomas Walter (1721), *The Grounds and Rules of Music Explained or An Introduction to the Art of Singing by Note*, Boston: J. Franklin for S. Gerrish; quoted in, for example, Michael L. Mark (2008), *A Concise History of American Music Education*, Lanham, Md: Rowman & Littlefield Education, p. 17.

22 See Frédéric Louis Ritter (1884), *Music in America*, New York: Scribner's and Sons, p. 21.

23 George Hood (1846), *A History of Music in New England: with Biographical Sketches of Psalmists and Reformers*, Boston: Wilkins, Carter and Co.

24 Thomas Symmes (1722), *Utile Dulci, or, A Joco-Serious Dialogue concerning Regular Singing*; quoted, for example, in Gilbert Chase (1992), *America's Music: From the Pilgrims to the Present* (Music in American Life series), Champaign, IL: University of Illinois Press, p. 23.

25 See Donald G. Trayser (1939), *Barnstable, Three Centuries of a Cape Cod Town*, Hyannis, Mass.: F. B & F. P. Goss; on the website of the West Parish of Barnstable United Church of Christ; http://www.westparish.org/?page_id=34.

26 William Lincoln (1837), *History of Worcester, Massachusetts: From Its Earliest Settlement to September 1836*, Worcester: Moses D. Philips and Co., p. 179.

27 William Tans'ur (1754), *The Royal Melody Compleat*, London: R. Brown (3rd edn).

28 Watts (1707), *Preface to Hymns and Spiritual Songs*.

29 Ibid.

30 *The Gospel Magazine*, 1775.

31 *The Spectator*, 23 August 1712.

32 *The Spectator*, no. 112, Monday, 9 July 1711.

33 Bishop Edmund Gibson, message to diocese, 1724. See Temperley (1979), *The Music of the English Parish Church*, p. 152.

34 *The Spectator*, 9 July 1711.

35 Tans'ur (1754), *The Royal Melody Compleat*.

36 Collected from Mr Thomson, Northumberland, 1906.

37 William Billings (1778), *Lamentation over Boston*.

11 West Galleries and Wesleys, Methodists and Mendelssohn, 1760–1850

1   Thomas Hardy (1872), *Under the Greenwood Tree: A Rural Painting of the Dutch School*, London: Tinsley Brothers, chapter 4. The quotations in this chapter are from the Preface and chapters 4 and 6.

2   See http://www.westgallerychurches.com/hants/minstead/minstead.html.

3   Temperley (1979), *The Music of the English Parish Church*, p. 148.

4   See http://www.westgallerychurches.com/instruments.html.

5   *Union Hymns* (1835), Philadelphia: American Sunday School Union, no. 542.

6   Joseph Hart (1759), *Hymns Composed on Various Subjects with the Author's Experience*, London.

7   Rev. J. Compston (ed.) (1857), *Lancashire Sunday School Songs*, London.

8   See, for example, J. C. D. Clark (2000), *English Society, 1660–1832: Religion, Ideology, and Politics during the Ancien Régime*, Cambridge: Cambridge University Press, p. 299.

9   See Temperley (1979), *The Music of the English Parish Church*, pp. 237–8.

10 *The Gentleman's Magazine*, August 1781.

11 James Woodforde (1949), *The Diary of a Country Parson*, edited by J. Beresford, Oxford: Oxford University Press, entry for 12 November 1769.

12 J. Skinner, *Journal of a Somerset Rector*, 14 July 1822, quoted in Temperley (1979), *The Music of the English Parish Church*, p. 157.

13 Horace Walpole, letter to George Montagu, 28 January 1760, quoted in John Wright and George Agar-Ellis Dover (eds) (1840), *The Letters of Horace Walpole, Earl of Orford*, London: R. Bentley, p. 21.

14 James Boswell (1824), *The Life of Samuel Johnson*, vol. 4, London: printed for J. Brumby, p. 7.

15 Mary Cowden Clarke (1896), *My Long Life: An Autobiographic Sketch*, London: T. Fisher Unwin, p. 11.

16 Quoted in, for example, L. Tyerman (1871), *The Life and Times of Rev John Wesley M.A.*, London: Hodder and Stoughton, vol. 1.

17 Porter (2000), *Enlightenment*, chapter 12.

18 *The Journal of John Wesley*, 26 volumes, online resource, vol. 1, pp. 472ff., entry for 24 May 1738.

19 Erik Routley (1968), *The Musical Wesleys*, London: Herbert Jenkins, pp. 26–7.

20 Ibid. p. 31.

21 Blake's annotation to the comment 'Mere enthusiasm will carry you but a little way' in Joshua Reynolds's lecture of 1769. See Jon Mee (2003), *Romanticism, Enthusiasm, and Regulation: Poetics and the Policing of Culture in the Romantic Period*, Oxford: Oxford University Press, chapter 6, 'Energy and Enthusiasm in Blake'.

22 Samuel Johnson (1755), *A Dictionary of the English Language*, 2nd edn, London.

23 David Hume (1742), *Essays Moral, Political, and Literary* (1742–54), Edinburgh, Essay X, 'Of Superstition and Enthusiasm'.

24 Bishop Butler, quoted in *The Gentleman's Magazine*, March 1800.

25 *The Journal of John Wesley*, vol. 15, p. 24; 5 April 1751; vol. 7, p. 411, n.

26 Ibid.

27 Ibid.

28 *The Gentleman's Magazine*, December 1814.

29 Routley (1968), *The Musical Wesleys*, Appendix 2, pp. 250–53.

30 Charles Avison (1752), *An Essay on Musical Expression*, London: C. Davis.

31 William Crotch, letter to Maria Hackett on reviewing Wesley's anthem for the Gresham prize, quoted in J. S. Bumpus (1908), *A History of English Cathedral Music, 1549–1889*, 2 vols, London: T. Werner Laurie, vol. 2, p. 370.

32 William Crotch (1831), *Substance of Several Courses of Lectures on Music*, London: Longman, Rees, Orme, Brown and Green, p. 83.

33 Daines Barrington (1781), *Miscellanies*, London: J. Nichols, p. 302.

34 John Wesley to Samuel Wesley, 19 August 1784; see George Eayrs (ed.) (1915), *Letters of John Wesley*, London: Hodder and Stoughton, vol. 7, pp. 230–31.

35 Samuel Wesley to Benjamin Jacob, 5 November, 1809; see Philip Olleson (ed.) (2001), *The Letters of Samuel Wesley: Professional and Social Correspondence, 1797–1837*, Oxford: Oxford University Press, p. xxviii.

36 *Anecdotes of the early life of Samuel Wesley, Esq, by his Father, the late Rev Charles Wesley, M.A.*, reprinted from the *Wesleyan Methodist Magazine* in *The Methodist Magazine and Quarterly Review*, vol. 5, 1834.

37 See, for example, Gareth Lloyd (1998), 'Charles Wesley Junior, Prodigal Child, Unfulfilled Adult' in *Proceedings of the Charles Wesley Society*, vol. 5, p. 30.

38 Methodist Archives, John Rylands Library, University of Manchester, 'finding-list' no. DDWes 4/23.

39 'Professional Memoranda of the late Mr Samuel Wesley's life', in *The Musical World, A Weekly Record of Musical Science, Literature and Intelligence*, no. 84, vol. 7, 20 October 1837.

40 *Mozart – New Edition of the Complete Works*, vol. 30/1 (1965), Theoretical and Compositional studies for Thomas Attwood, K. 506a, Kassel, Germany: Bärenreiter.

41 Letter from William Bartholomew to Felix Mendelssohn, 1843; see R. Larry Todd (ed.) (2006), *Mendelssohn Studies*, Cambridge: Cambridge University Press, p. 100 and note 43.

42 See, for example, S. Hensel (1882), *The Mendelssohn Family: From Letters and Journals*, vol. 1, New York: Harper & Bros, p. 219.

43 Letter from Mendelssohn to his mother, 19 July 1842, quoted in, for example, Hensel (1882), *The Mendelssohn Family*, vol. 2, pp. 207–10.

44 Hardy, *Under the Greenwood Tree*, chapter 6.

45 Temperley (1979), *The Music of the English Parish Church*, p. 203.

46 Hardy, *Under the Greenwood Tree*, Preface and chapter 6.

47 See *The Musical World*, 15 September 1837.

12 Renewal, 1837–1901

1 Much-repeated anecdote: see, for example, Bernarr Rainbow (2010), *Bernarr Rainbow on Music: Memoirs and Selected Writings*, Martlesham, Suffolk: Boydell Press, p. 382.

2 P. Maurice (1837), *The Popery of Oxford Confronted, Disavowed and Repudiated*, London: Francis Baisler, p. 52.

3 I am indebted to Dr Mark Smith for the idea and indeed the words of this paragraph.

4 Thomas Helmore, letter to Frederick Helmore (1890), see F. Helmore, *Memoir of the Revd. Thomas Helmore, M. A.*, London: J. Masters & Co., p. 133.

5 C. H. Steggall and W. J. Hall (1849), *Church Psalmody ...* , London: Charles Coventry, Preface.

6 J. Hullah (1855), *Music in the Parish Church: a lecture ... at a meeting of the Durham and Northumberland Association for the Promotion of Church Music*; see Francis Hullah (ed.) (1886), *Life of John Hullah*, reprinted Cambridge: Cambridge University Press, 2013, p. 66.

7 R. Druitt (1845), *A Popular Tract on Church Music*, London: Francis and John Rivington.

8 Archdeacon W. M. Sinclair (1909), *Memorials of St Paul's Cathedral*, London: Chapman & Hall, p. 328 *et seq.*

9 J. Peace (1839), *An Apology for Cathedral Service*, London: J. Bohn, p. 50.

10 Bernarr Rainbow (1970; revd edn 2001), *The Choral Revival in the Anglican Church, 1839–1872*, Martlesham, Suffolk: Boydell Press, p. 255.

11 Ibid., p. 30.

12 Charles Dickens, 'Music in Humble Life', in *Household Words*, vol. 1, p. 163, 11 May 1850.

13 Rainbow (2001), *The Choral Revival in the Anglican Church*, p. 51.

14 Ibid., p. 156.

15 Lord John Russell, open letter to the Bishop of Durham, 4 November 1840.

16 Letters of 1 and 26 September 1851, from Lucerne and Munich, to Revd J. Wayland Joyce in F. W. Joyce (with G. R. Sinclair) (1896), *The Life of Rev. Sir F. A. G. Ouseley, Bart*, London: Methuen, pp. 73–4.

17 Dickens, 'Music in Humble Life'.

18 Letter from John Mason Neale 'to B.W.', 28 December 1849; see *The Letters of John Mason Neale, Selected and edited by his daughter* (1910), London: Longmans, Green, p. 128.

19 See, for example, Trevor Beeson (2009), *In Tuneful Accord: The Church Musicians*, London: SCM Press, p. 47.

20 *The Parish Choir or Church Music Book*, vol. 1, p. 6.

21 Ibid.

22 John Spencer Curwen (1901), 'St Anne's, Soho', in *Studies in Worship Music*, First Series, London: J. Curwen and Sons, p. 382.

23 *The Parish Choir or Church Music Book*, vol. 3, p. 189.

24 Quoted in, for example, Nigel Yates (1999), *Anglican Ritualism in Victorian Britain, 1830–1910*, Oxford: Oxford University Press, p. 180.

25 Rainbow (2001), *The Choral Revival in the Anglican Church*, p. 239.

26 S. S. Wesley (1849), *A Few Words on Cathedral Music and the Musical System of the Church, with a plan of reform*, London, p. 15.

27 Letter of 8 January 1846, in Rainbow (2001), *The Choral Revival in the Anglican Church*, p. 238.

28 *The Parish Choir or Church Music Book*, vol. 1, p. 6, February 1846.

29 Ibid., p. 87.

30 F. Oakeley and R. Redhead (1843), *Laudes Diurnae*, London: James Toovey, Preface.

31 Letter to Benjamin Webb, 1843, in Helmore (1890), *Memoir of the Revd. Thomas Helmore*, p. 58.

32 Theodoricus Petri (1582) *Piae Cantiones ecclesiasticae et scholasticae*, Greifswald, Germany: Augustin Ferber.

33 This widely cited story originated with the hymn-writer and schoolmaster Gerard Moultrie (1829–85).

34 See *Hymns Ancient and Modern*, Revised Edition (1950).

35 I am grateful to Dr Mark Smith for this information and for pointing out its significance.

36 In the Preface to *The English Hymnal* (1906), London: Oxford University Press; Introduction to P. Dearmer, R. Vaughan Williams and M. Shaw, *Songs of Praise* (1931), London: Oxford University Press; and E. Routley (1957), *The Music of Christian Hymnody*, London: Independent Press, p. 134.

37 Lord Runcie, review in the *Daily Telegraph* of Ian Bradley (1997; new edn 2010), *Abide with Me: The World of Victorian Hymns*, London: Faber and Faber.

38 *The Radleian*, no. 146, February 1884.

39 Revd John Sweet, personal communication.

40 See E. F. Benson (1940), *Final Edition: Informal Autobiography*, London: Longmans, Green and Co.

41 See 'The Guards Chapel Tragedy' online at http://www.flyingbombsandrockets.com/V1_maintxtc.html.

42 Rainbow (2001), *The Choral Revival in the Anglican Church*, p. 241.

43 Letter to the Bishop of London, 12 January 1811, reprinted in Maria Hackett (1827), *A brief account of cathedral and collegiate schools*, London: J. B. Nichols and Son, p. 61.

44 Anthony Trollope (1857), *Barchester Towers*, chapter 6.

45 Sinclair (1909), *Memorials of St Paul's Cathedral*.

46 Bumpus (1908), *A History of English Cathedral Music, 1549–1889*.

47 Ibid.

48 W. E. Dickson (1894), *Fifty Years of Church Music*, Ely: T. A. Hills and Son, p. 19.

49 Routley (1968), *The Musical Wesleys*, p. 109.

50 S. A. Pears (1852), *Remarks on the Protestant theory of Church music*, London: T. Hatchard, p. 2.

51 Trollope (1857), *Barchester Towers*, chapter 6.

52 Temperley (1979), *The Music of the English Parish Church*, p. 275.

13 Composers from S. S. Wesley to Elgar, 1830–1934

1 Routley (1968), *The Musical Wesleys*, p. 102.

2 Ibid., p. 106.

3 Ibid., p. 145.

4 Wesley, *A Few Words on Cathedral Music*, p. 5.

5 Ibid., p. 9

6 Ibid.

7 Ibid., p. 11.

8 Ibid., p. 11.

9   J. A. Fuller Maitland (1890), 'Sir John Goss', *Dictionary of National Biography*, Oxford: Oxford University Press.

10 William Spark (1909), *Musical Memories*, 3rd edn, London: W. Reeves, p. 145.

11 A. Lawrence (ed.) (1907), *Sir Arthur Sullivan: Life Story, Letters and Reminiscences*, New York: Duffield and Co., p. 10.

12 Frederick George Edwards, 'Sir John Goss', *The Musical Times and Singing Class Circular*, vol. 42, no. 698 (April 1901), pp. 225–31.

13 Sir John Frederick Bridge (1918), *A Westminster Pilgrim*, London.

14 Dorothea Ponsonby, 'Hubert Parry', *The Musical Times*, vol. 97, no. 1359, May 1956, p. 263.

15 Paul Rodmell (2002), *Charles Villiers Stanford*, Farnham, Surrey: Ashgate, p. 169.

16 David Manning (ed.) (2007), *Vaughan Williams on Music*, Oxford: Oxford University Press, p. 296.

17 Herbert Howells, 'Charles Villiers Stanford (1852–1924). An Address at His Centenary', *Proceedings of the Royal Musical Association*, vol. 79, 1952–3, pp. 19–31.

18 Jerrold N. Moore (1984), *Edward Elgar: a Creative Life*, Oxford: Oxford University Press, p. 6.

19 In George Dyson, 'Charles Villiers Stanford, by some of his pupils', *Music and Letters*, vol. 5, 1924, p. 195.

14 The Splintering of the Tradition, 1914–2015

1   Interview with Nick Kent, *New Musical Express*, 25 March 1978. Costello appears to have been the first person to use this idea in this form in print, though he probably borrowed it from a live recording of the comedian Martin Mull. In other forms, the idea dates back to at least 1918, where it appears in *New Republic* magazine as 'Strictly considered, writing about music is as illogical as singing about economics'.

2   Alex Ross (2008), *The Rest is Noise: Listening to the Twentieth Century*, London: Fourth Estate, p. xviii.

3   Donald Mitchell (1993), *The Language of Modern Music*, London: Faber and Faber, pp. 164–5.

4   I am grateful to the archivist at Charterhouse, Catherine Smith, and the Headmaster, Richard Pleming, for allowing me access to the records of Vaughan Williams's time at the school.

5   Kennedy (1992), *The Works of Ralph Vaughan Williams*, p. 158.

6   J. A. Fuller Maitland, review of Vaughan Williams's *Fantasia on a theme of Thomas Tallis* in *The Times*, 7 September 1910.

7 See the website of the Ivor Gurney society, www.ivorgurney.org.uk/music.

8 Gustav Holst, letter from Salonica, 15 January 1919, quoted in Imogen Holst (1969; repr. 2008), *Gustav Holst, A Biography*, London: Faber and Faber, chapter 7.

9 The anthem *For Lo, I Raise up*, text from Habakkuk, 1 and 2.

10 Kennedy (1992), *The Works of Ralph Vaughan Williams*, p. 160.

11 Letter, 29 December 1918, in Holst, *Gustav Holst, A Biography*, chapter 7.

12 Alain Frogley and Aidan J. Thomson (eds) (2013), *The Cambridge Companion to Vaughan Williams*, Cambridge: Cambridge University Press, p. 281.

13 Donald Mitchell and Philip Reed (eds) (1991–2012), *Letters from a Life: the Selected Letters and Diaries of Benjamin Britten, 1913–1976*, London: Faber and Faber, letter of 8 March 1931.

14 In conversation with Bruce Phillips: see Lewis Foreman (2011), *The John Ireland companion*, Martlesham, Suffolk: Boydell Press, p. 20.

15 Barbara Pym (1952), *Excellent Women*, London: Jonathan Cape, chapter 1.

16 See BBC News, 17 November 2008.

17 Vincent Plush, 'They Could Have Been Ours,' *ABC Radio 24 Hours* (January 1996), quoted in Peter Biskup, 'Popper in Australasia, 1937–1945', *Quadrant*, vol. 44, no. 6, June 2000, pp. 20–28.

18 Percy A. Scholes (1938), *The Oxford Companion to Music*, London: Oxford University Press.

19 The phrase is James Bowman's.

20 Often quoted: see, for example, Keith John, notes to his recording of Elgar's Organ Sonata, Hyperion records CDA67363.

21 He also told the counter-tenor James Bowman: 'J-J-J-James, you are like a R-R-R-Rolls R-R-R-Royce in an old garage'.

22 R. Crichton, 'Herbert Murrill' (1980), *The New Grove Dictionary of Music and Musicians* (2001), 2nd edn, vol. 17.

23 Erik Routley (1964), *Twentieth-Century Church Music*, London: Herbert Jenkins, p. 164.

24 Larkin, 'Annus Mirabilis', in *Philip Larkin Collected Poems* (1988).

25 Routley (1964), *Twentieth-Century Church Music*, p. 157.

26 Paul Spicer (1999), *Herbert Howells*, Bridgend, Wales: Seren Books, p. 131.

27 I am grateful to John Rutter for recently illuminating a conversation about this incident we had while recording Howells's *Requiem* in the Lady Chapel of Ely Cathedral in 1992, on the coldest day ever recorded.

28 Spicer (1999), *Herbert Howells*. These references are to a conversation with the composer's daughter, Ursula.

29 Thomas Hardy, 'Heredity'; see (1994) *The Works of Thomas Hardy: with an introduction and bibliography* (1994), Ware, Hertfordshire: Wordsworth Editions, p. 407.

30 Robert Bridges, Harry Ellis Wooldridge (eds) (1899), *The Yattendon Hymnal*, privately printed; later issued in 1905 by B. H. Blackwell, Preface.

31 *The English Hymnal with Tunes*, 1st edn, London: Oxford University Press, 1906, Preface.

32 General William Booth (1911), *Salvation Army Songs*, London: Salvation Army Book Department.

33 George Thalben-Ball (ed.) (1950), *The BBC Hymn Book*, Oxford: Oxford University Press, Preface.

34 Personal communications.

35 Ibid.

36 *The English Hymnal with Tunes*.

37 L. Dakers (1970), *Church Music at the Crossroads: A Forward-Looking Guide for Today*, London: Marshall Morgan and Scott; and John Evelyn, *Diary*, 21 December 1662.

38 Personal communication. As well as shedding some light on Britten's attitude to these commissions, this is also a revealing comment from a professional composer: the first part of the Te Deum is indeed just a long list of names, like a phone-book; it is very difficult to set to music.

39 From W. H. Auden's poem 'Song for St. Cecilia's Day', to which he later added the dedication 'For Benjamin Britten'.

40 Tippett (1980), *Music of the Angels: Essays and Sketchbooks of Michael Tippett*, p. 66.

41 Words by W. H. Auden, *The Twelve: An Anthem for the Feast of Any Apostle*.

42 Ralph Scott Grover (1993), *The Music of Edmund Rubbra*, Aldershot, Hampshire, Surrey: Scolar Press, pp. 3–4.

43 Christopher Morley, 'Just the Joubert', interview with John Joubert for the *Birmingham Post*, 1 March 2007.

44 Ibid.

45 Tippett (1980), *Music of the Angels*.

46 From the sleeve notes to the recording of his *Requiem*, Hyperion records, CDA66947.

47 James MacMillan, Composer's Notes to *Cantos Sagrados*, 1989; see Boosey & Hawkes website: http://www.boosey.com.

48 George Mackay Brown (1989), 'Christmas Poem', *The Wreck of the Archangel*, London: John Murray.

49 Peter Maxwell Davies (2005), *Prayer of Thanksgiving in Time of Terror*, for a concert given by the choir of HM Chapel Royal at Waltham Abbey on

the 400th anniversary of the Gunpowder Plot, 5 November 2005, in the presence of the composer.

50   Personal communications.

Epilogue

1   Cole Porter, from the Broadway show *Paris* (1928).

2   Olivier Messiaen, 'Contre la Paresse', *La Page musicale*, 17 March 1939.

3   Tippett (1980), *Music of the Angels*, p. 66.

4   Personal communication.

5   Alfred Lord Tennyson (1849), *In Memoriam A. H. H.*, verse XCVI.

6   Terry Pratchett (2003), *Monstrous Regiment* (a Discworld novel), London: Doubleday.

7   MacCulloch (2009), *A History of Christianity: The First Three Thousand Years*, pp. 1014–15.

8   The attribution to Trollope, though widespread, appears in fact to be apocryphal, perhaps based on a number of his other 'bons mots' on a similar theme. If so, it is a case of 'se non è vero, è ben trovato'.

9   Larkin (1954), 'Church Going', in *Philip Larkin Collected Poems* (1988).

Further Investigations

Reading

The principal source material for this book is a lifetime of working with this music. I have, at some stage, sung, played, conducted, edited, produced and/or taught all the pieces named in the text. This is a necessarily brief list of further reading, concentrating on books which cover a particular aspect or period of church music, or a particular part of an individual composer's work, as well as some primary sources and a few of the best or most historically significant individual biographies. There are, of course, many more.

Contemporary sources

Avison, Charles (1752; reissued 2004), *An Essay on Musical Expression*, edited by Pierre DuBois, London: Ashgate

Bumpus, J. S. (1908), *A History of English Cathedral Music*, London: T. Werner Laurie

Burney, Charles (1776–1789; reissued 2010), *A General History of Music from the Earliest Ages to the Present Time*, 4 volumes, Cambridge: Cambridge University Press

Cummings, William Hayman (1896), *Purcell,* London: Sampson Low, Marston & Co.

Hawkins, John (1776; reissued 2010), *A General History of the Science and Practice of Music*, 3 volumes, Cambridge: Cambridge University Press

Machyn, Henry (1848 reissue), *The Diary of Henry Machyn, Citizen and Merchant-Taylor of London, 1550–1563*, edited by J. G. Nichols, London: Camden Society

Pepys, Samuel (2003), *Diaries, 1660–1670. A selection*, edited by Robert Latham, London: Penguin

Wesley, Samuel Sebastian (1849; reissued 1965), *A Few Words on Cathedral Music and the Musical System of the Church, with a plan of reform*, London: Hinrichsen

More recent sources

Ashbee, Andrew (1986–1995), *Records of English Court Music*, vols 1–9, Farnham, Surrey: Ashgate

Britten, Benjamin (1991), *Letters from a Life: the Selected Letters and Diaries of Benjamin Britten, 1913–1976*, edited by Donald Mitchell and Philip Reed, London: Faber and Faber

Burrows, Donald (2005), *Handel and the English Chapel Royal*, Oxford: Oxford University Press

Carpenter, Humphrey (1992), *Benjamin Britten: a Biography*, London: Faber and Faber

Dibble, Jeremy, C. (1992), *Hubert H. Parry: His Life and Music*, Oxford: Clarendon Press Press

Dibble, Jeremy (2002), *Charles Villiers Stanford: Man and Musician*, Oxford: Oxford University Press

Duffy, Eamon (2001), *The Voices of Morebath: Reformation and Rebellion in an English Village*, 2001. London and New Haven: Yale University Press

Duffy, Eamon (2005), *The Stripping of the Altars: Traditional Religion in England, c.1400–c.1580*, London and New Haven: Yale University Press

Frere, W. H. and W. P. M. Kennedy (1910), *Visitation Articles and Injunctions*, London: Longmans Green and Co.

Gatens, William J. (1986), *Victorian Cathedral Music in Theory and Practice*, Cambridge: Cambridge University Press

Griffiths, Paul (1982), *Peter Maxwell Davies (Contemporary Composers* series), London: Robson Books

Horton, Peter (2004), *Samuel Sebastian Wesley: A Life*, Oxford: Oxford University Press

Keates, Jonathan (1995), *Purcell: A Biography*, London: Chatto & Windus

Keates, Jonathan (2008), *Handel, the Man and his Music*, London: Bodley Head

Kennedy, Michael (1964; 2nd edn 1992), *The Works of Ralph Vaughan Williams*, Oxford: Clarendon Press

Kerman, Joseph (1981), *The Masses and Motets of William Byrd*, Berkeley, California: University of California Press

Le Huray, Peter (1978), *Music and the Reformation in England, 1549–1660*, Cambridge: Cambridge University Press

MacCulloch, Diarmaid (2009), *A History of Christianity: The First Three Thousand Years*, London: Allen Lane

McCarthy, Kerry (2007), *Liturgy and Contemplation in Byrd's Gradualia*, Abingdon: Routledge

Phillips, Peter (1991), *English Sacred Music 1549–1649*, Oxford: Gimell Records

Porter, Roy (2000), *Enlightenment: Britain and the Creation of the Modern World*, London: Allen Lane

Rainbow, Bernarr (1970; revd edn 2001), *The Choral Revival in the Anglican Church, 1839–1872*, Martlesham, Suffolk: Boydell Press

Ross, Alex (2008), *The Rest is Noise: Listening to the Twentieth Century*, London: Fourth Estate

Routley, Erik (1968), *The Musical Wesleys*, London: Herbert Jenkins

Routley, Erik (1957), *The Music of Christian Hymnody*, London: Independent Press

Routley, Erik (1964), *Twentieth Century Church Music*, London: Herbert Jenkins

Spicer, Paul (1999), *Herbert Howells*, Bridgend: Seren Books

Temperley, Nicholas (1979), *The Music of the English Parish Church*, Cambridge: Cambridge University Press

Tippett, Michael (1980), *Music of the Angels: Essays and Sketchbooks of Michael Tippett*, London: Eulenburg Books

Looking

Readers are also strongly recommended to refer to the many beautiful reproductions and facsimiles of original sources which are available online. Imagining these pages in front of you on a carved, four-faced medieval music-desk, on the oak table in front of your Elizabethan household fireplace, held aloft by your parish clerk in the eighteenth-century West gallery of your parish church, or weighing down the choir stalls of your local cathedral will give you far more flavour of how this music was used than any written text. Above all, try to sing it.

The Winchester Troper: http://www.omifacsimiles.com/brochures/winchester.html

The Old Hall manuscript: http://www.diamm.ac.uk/

The Eton Choirbook: http://www.omifacsimiles.com/brochures/eton.html

The Booke of Common Praier Noted: http://justus.anglican.org/resources/bcp/Merbecke/Merbecke.htm

Latin church music *c.* 1580 (The Dow Partbooks): http://www.diamm.ac.uk/the-dow-partbooks/

A Reformation psalter (Thomas Ravenscroft): http://www.pbm.com/~lindahl/ravenscroft/psalter/

An eighteenth-century country songbook: http://imslp.org/wiki/The_Royal_Melody_Compleat_(Tans'ur,_William)

Listening (in roughly chronological order)
Early chant: https://www.youtube.com/watch?v=DCxhHTAZArI

In Praise of St Columba: The Sound World of the Celtic Church. Choir of Gonville and Caius College, Cambridge. Barnaby Brown, triplepipes and lyre. Geoffrey Webber, director (Delphian, DCD34137)

Sarum Chant: Missa in gallicantu. The Tallis Scholars. Peter Phillips, director (Gimell records, CDGIM017)

The Old Hall Manuscript: English Music c. 1410–1415. The Hilliard Ensemble (Virgin Veritas, 7243 5 61393 2 9)

Dunstaple. Orlando Consort (Metronome, MET 1009)

More Sweet to Hear: Organs and Voices of Tudor England. Choir of Gonville and Caius College, Cambridge. Magnus Williams, organ. Geoffrey Webber, director. Part of the Early English Organ Project (OxRecs, OXCD-101)

Music from the Eton Choirbook: Vol. 1: *More Divine Than Human*; Vol. 2: *Choirs of Angels*; Vol. 3: *Courts of Heaven.* Choir of Christ Church Cathedral, Oxford. Stephen Darlington, director (Avie, B002I16I127/E etc.)

John Browne: *Music from the Eton Choirbook.* The Tallis Scholars, Peter Phillips, director (Gimell, CDGIM 036)

John Taverner: *Missa Gloria Tibi Trinitas* and other sacred works. Choir of Christ Church Cathedral, Oxford. Stephen Darlington, director (Avie, AV2123)

The Tallis Scholars Sing Thomas Tallis. Peter Phillips, director (Gimell, CDGIM 203)

Thomas Tallis: *Complete works.* Chapelle du roi. Alistair Dixon, director (Brilliant Classics, 94268 10 CD set)

John Sheppard: *Gaude, Gaude, Gaude Maria.* Choir of St John's College, Cambridge. Andrew Nethsingha, director (Chaconne CHSA, 0401)

Christopher Tye: *Missa Euge bone and Western Wynde Mass.* Choir of Westminster Abbey. James O'Donnell, director (Hyperion, CDA67982)

Christopher Tye: *Latin and English Sacred Choral Works.* Choir of Magdalen College, Oxford. Bill Ives, director (Harmonia Mundi, HMU 907 396)

Mary and Elizabeth at Westminster Abbey. Choir of Westminster Abbey. James O'Donnell, director (Hyperion, CDA67704)

An Emerald in a Work of Gold: Music from the Dow Partbooks. Marian Consort with the Rose Consort of Viols. Rory McCleery, director (Delphian, DCD34115)

Robert White: *Hymns, Psalms and Lamentations.* Gallicantus. Gabriel Crouch, director (Signum, SC15723)

The Tallis Scholars sing William Byrd. Peter Phillips, director (Gimell, CDGIM 208)

William Byrd: *The Great Service.* Choir of King's College, Cambridge. Stephen Cleobury, director (EMI, CDC 747712)

William Byrd: *The Three Masses.* Choir of Westminster Cathedral. Martin Baker, director (Hyperion, B00M2D7KTM)

William Byrd: *Assumpta est Maria and other sacred music*. Music from the first volume of *Gradualia*, 1605. The Cardinal's Musick. Andrew Carwood, director (Hyperion, CDA 67675)

William Byrd: *Consort songs*. Robin Blaze, counter-tenor. Concordia Consort of Viols (Hyperion CDH55429)

Thomas Weelkes: *Anthems*. Choir of Winchester Cathedral. David Hill, director (Hyperion, Helios CDH55259)

Cathedral music by John Amner. Choir of Ely Cathedral. Paul Trepte, director (Hyperion, CDA66768)

With a Merrie Noyse: Anthems and Service Music by Orlando Gibbons. Choir of Magdalen College, Oxford with Fretwork. Bill Ives, director (Harmonia Mundi, HMU907337)

Behold, it is Christ. Sacred Music by Edmund Hooper and his Contemporaries. Choir of Selwyn College, Cambridge. Andrew Gant, director (Lamas records, LAMM096D)

Thomas Tomkins: *When David heard. Sacred choral works*. Choir of St John's College, Cambridge. Andrew Nethsingha, director (Chandos, CHAN0804)

Christopher Gibbons: *Motets, Anthems, Fantasias and Voluntaries*. Academy of Ancient Music. Richard Egarr, director (Harmonia Mundi, HMU 807551)

Music from the Chapel Royal: 'The King's Musick'. Anthems by Henry Cooke, Pelham Humfrey, John Blow and William Turner. The Sixteen. Harry Christophers, director (Coro, COR16041)

Pelham Humfrey: *Verse Anthems*. Choir of Clare College, Cambridge with Romanesca. Nicholas McGegan, director (Harmonia Mundi, HMU 907053)

Matthew Locke: *Anthems, Motets and Ceremonial Music*. Choir of new College, Oxford with the Parley of Instruments. Edward Higginbottom, director (Hyperion, Helios CDH55250)

Henry Purcell: *The Complete Anthems and Services, vols 1–11*. Choir of New College, Oxford with the King's Consort. Edward Higginbottom, director (Hyperion, CDA66585/609/623/644/656/663/677/686/693/707/716)

Henry Purcell: *Choral Works*. Choir of Christ Church Cathedral, Oxford with the English Concert. Simon Preston, director (Archiv, 0289 459 4872 0 2)

Music at the Coronation of James II. Choir of Her Majesty's Chapel Royal with the Musicians Extraordinary. Andrew Gant, director (Signum, SIGCD094)

A Solemn Musick: Funeral Music for Queen Mary. Music by Purcell, Croft, Blow, Humfrey, Greene and Battishill.Choir of Winchester Cathedral with the Baroque Brass of London. Martin Neary, director (EMI CDC 7 47772 2)

John Blow: *Anthems*. Choir of Winchester Cathedral. David Hill, director (Hyperion, Helios CDD22055)

William Croft: *Burial Service and Anthems*. Choir of Sidney Sussex College, Cambridge. David Skinner, director (Obsidian, CD714)

George Frederic Handel: *Music for the Chapel Royal*. Choir of Her Majesty's Chapel Royal with the Musicians Extraordinary. Andrew Gant, director (Naxos, 8.557935)

George Frederic Handel: *'Chandos' Anthems*. The Sixteen. Harry Christophers, director (Chandos, CHAN0554–7)

George Frederic Handel: *Coronation Anthems*. Choir of King's College, Cambridge. Stephen Cleobury, director (EMI/Warner Classics, 4094082)

The Restoration and Georgian Anthem. Music by Purcell, Croft, Greene, Boyce, Battishill, Samuel Wesley, Crotch, Attwood, Walmisley. Choir of New College, Oxford. Edward Higginbottom, director (five CDs. CRD, 3504/3491/3518/3483/3510)

West Gallery music: https://www.youtube.com/watch?v=_xnW69BeBJc

Glad Tidings: A West Gallery Christmas. The Mellstock Band (Serpent Press, SER 008)

While Shepherds Watched: Christmas Music from English Parish Churches, 1740–1830. Psalmody, The Parley of Instruments. Peter Holman, director (Hyperion, CDH55325)

Vital Spark of Heav'nly Flame: Music of Death and Resurrection from English Parish Churches and Chapels, 1760–1830. Psalmody, The Parley of Instruments. Peter Holman, director (Hyperion, CDA 67020)

O for the Wings of a Dove. Music by Mendelssohn and others. Ernest Lough, treble. (Pearl)

S. S. Wesley: *The Church Music of Samuel Sebastian Wesley*. Choir of St Peter's College, Oxford. Roger Allen, director (OxRecs, OX-CD 129)

John Stainer: *Choral Works*. Choir of the Abbey School, Tewkesbury. Benjamin Nicholas, director (Priory, PRCD 833)

That Glorious Song of Old: Choral Music of Arthur Sullivan. Choir of Ely Cathedral. Paul Trepte, director (Cantoris)

Hubert Parry: *Songs of Farewell and Jerusalem*. Choir of St George's Chapel, Windsor. Christopher Robinson, director (Hyperion, CDA66273)

Charles Villiers Stanford: *Choral and Organ Works*. Choir of St John's College, Cambridge. Christopher Robinson, director (Naxos, DDD 8.555794)

Charles Villiers Stanford: *The Complete Morning and Evening services and Music for the Communion*. Choir of Durham Cathedral. James Lancelot, director (Priory, PRCD437)

Edward Elgar: *Sacred Choral Music*. Choir of St John's College, Cambridge. Christopher Robinson, director (Naxos, DDD 8.557288)

The Choral and Organ Music of Charles Wood. Choir of Blackburn Cathedral. David Cooper, director (Priory, PRCD 484)

Ralph Vaughan Williams: *Mass in G minor* and Herbert Howells: *Requiem*. Corydon Singers. Matthew Best, director. (Hyperion, CDH55220)

Gerald Finzi: *Lo, the Full, Final Sacrifice*. Choir of St John's College, Cambridge. Christopher Robinson, director (Naxos: 8.555792)

The Choral Music of Sir Edward Bairstow. Choir of York Minster. Philip Moore, director (Priory, PRCD 365)

Herbert Howells: *Requiem and other Choral works*. Choir of St John's College, Cambridge. Christopher Robinson, director (Naxos, DDD 8.554659)

Herbert Howells: *The St Paul's Service*. Choir of St Paul's Cathedral. Christopher Dearnley, organist; John Scott, director (Hyperion, B000002ZK3)

WilliamWalton: *Sacred Choral Works*. Choir of St John's College, Cambridge. Christopher Robinson, director (Naxos, DDD 8.555793)

Michael Tippett: *Choral Works*. The Finzi Singers. Paul Spicer, director (Chandos, CHAN 9265)

Benjamin Britten: *The Sacred Choral Music*. Choir of New College, Oxford. Edward Higginbottom, director (Novum, NCVR 1386)

Benjamin Britten: *English Choral Music*. Choir of St John's College, Cambridge. Christopher Robinson, director (Naxos, DDD 8.554791)

Britten conducts Britten: includes *The Burning Fiery Furnace*, *A Ceremony of Carols*, etc. English Opera Group (including Peter Pears), London Symphony Orchestra. Benjamin Britten, Norman Del Mar, and George Malcolm, conductors. 10 CDs. (Decca, B000AC5AY4)

The Hussey Legacy. Sacred choral music by Leighton, Howells, Britten, Finzi, Crosse, Judge, Tavener. The Finzi Singers. Paul Spicer, director (Cantus, CAN 301–2)

There is a Spirit. Sacred choral music by Rubbra, Leighton, Sherlaw Johnson, Saxton and others. Choir of Worcester College, Oxford. Tom Primrose, director (Lammas, LAMM 195D)

Francis Jackson: *Sacred Choral Works*. The Exon singers. Matthew Owens, director (Delphian, DCD34035)

The Sound of St John's. Music by Howells, Langlais, Orr, Tippett and Hoddinott. Choir of St John's College, Cambridge. George Guest, director (Nimbus, NI5335)

Jonathan Harvey: *I Love the Lord*: *Sacred Choral Music*. The Joyful Company of Singers. Peter Broadbent, director (ASV, CD DCA 917)

The John Tavener Collection. Sacred choral music by John Tavener. Choir of the Temple Church and The Holst Singers. Stephen Layton, director (Decca, 0289 475 0962 2 CD)

Giles Swayne: *Choral Works*. BBC Singers. Stephen Cleobury, director (Collin, 15312)

James MacMillan: *Choral Music*. Wells Cathedral Choir. Matthew Owens, director (Hyperion: CDA67867)

Peter Maxwell Davies: *Sacred Choral Works*. Choir of St Mary's Cathedral,
Edinburgh. Matthew Owens, director (Delphian: DCD34037)

Philip Moore: *Sacred Works*. Vasari Singers. Jeremy Backhouse, director (Guild:
GMCD 7129)

Roxanna Panufnik: *Westminster Mass*, with music by Tavener, Pärt, Howells,
Rubbra etc. Choir of Westminster Cathedral. James O'Donnell, director
(TelDec: 3984–28069–2)

Bob Chilcott: *Requiem and other Choral Works*. Choir of Wells Cathedral.
Matthew Owens, director (Hyperion: CDA67650)

John Rutter: *Be Thou my Vision*. Church anthems by John Rutter. The
Cambridge Singers. John Rutter, director (Collegium: CSCD514)

Evensong and Vespers at King's. Choir of King's College, Cambridge. Stephen
Cleobury, director (Brilliant Classics 8896)

100 Best Hymns. Various artists (EMI 9483062)

The World of Psalms. Choir of St John's College Cambridge. George Guest,
director. (Universal Classics ASIN: B00000266QX)

Acknowledgements

I am extremely grateful to Peter Phillips, Matthew Thomson, Paul Spicer, James Bowman, Henry Mayr-Harting and Mark Smith, who have read some or all of the text and made many valuable comments, not to mention the many pleasant discussions which have fed into the narrative. This book is much the better for their wisdom and generosity, though any infelicities which remain are my own. Thanks also to Dr John Kitchen, Gareth Miller, Julian Wiltshire, Tim Storey, Dr Tim Blackmore, Rob Rolfe, Christopher Eva and David Bruce. I am grateful to a number of friends and colleagues mentioned by name in the later chapters, in particular John Rutter and the late Sir Peter Maxwell Davies for allowing me to refer to various conversations over the years, and to Mrs Bridget le Huray for permission to consult the unpublished researches of the late Dr Peter le Huray held in the University Library, Cambridge. Like all researchers, I am indebted to the expertise and good humour of library staff all over the academic world, including the Bodleian and other libraries in Oxford, especially the Faculty of Music. I would like to thank all the students with whom I have worked on various aspects of this story: there is a lot of mileage left in the old adage that the best way to learn a subject is to teach it, especially to students who won't let you get away with not knowing what you're talking about. Thanks too to my agent, Ian Drury. The fact that I first met Ian rehearsing the Handel Coronation anthems says it all. Finally, thanks to Andrew Franklin, Penny Daniel and all at Profile Books, and especially to John Davey, who as well as being a sensitive and erudite editor is a genuine connoisseur of English church music. What better place to discuss editorial niceties than after evensong in an Oxford chapel, unless perhaps it's in the pub opposite.

Illustration Credits

Black and white plates

New College, Oxford and its one hundred clerks, *c.* 1453. Photo by Hulton Archive/Getty Images

Composer Thomas Tallis. Found in the collection of the Russian State Library, Moscow. Photo by Fine Art Images/Heritage Images/Getty Images

Composer William Byrd. Found in the collection of the Russian State Library, Moscow. Photo by Fine Art Images/Heritage Images/Getty Images

The Wanley Partbooks'. 16th century, fol. 055v Part setting for the text: 'If ye love me, keep my commandments'. Roll title: MSS. Mus. Sch. e. 420. Reproduced by permission of The Bodleian Library, Oxford

Woodcut of Bermondsey Abbey

A possible likeness of John Taverner in an ornamental capital E from the Forrest-Heyther partbooks, *c.* 1520

Woodcut of John Day (dated 1562) included in the 1563 and subsequent editions of Actes and Monuments

The 1637 Scottish *Book of Common Prayer* © National Museums Scotland

The Coronation of King James II (1633–1701) and his second wife Mary of Modena (1658–1718) 1685 (engraving), English School, (17th century)/Private Collection/The Stapleton Collection/Bridgeman Images

'The Chorus', from *The Works of William Hogarth*, published 1833 (litho), Hogarth, William (1697–1764)/Private Collection/Ken Welsh/Bridgeman Images

Engraving of Samuel Sebastian Wesley

Charles Hubert Hastings Parry, from the Cabinet Portrait Gallery, London, 1890–94 Woodburytype after photography by W & D Downey. © World History Archive/Topfoto

Ralph Vaughan Williams, 1958. © Ullstein Bild/Getty Images

Photograph of Britten with The London Boy Singers, (formerly the Finchley Children's Music Group), at a rehearsal for Britten's Missa Brevis, June 1962. © Hendon & Finchley Times/Britten-Pears Foundation (PH/4/272)

Sir Peter Maxwell-Davies, composer at the Royal Albert Hall, 2000. © Sisi Burn/ArenaPal www.ArenaPal.com

Callum Hughes from Cathedral School, with other choristers at evensong. © Media Wales Ltd

Colour plates

Manuscript Winchester Troper, MS473 137r. Reproduced courtesy of The Master and Fellows of Corpus Christi College, Cambridge

Illuminated C Cantate Domine from the Ranworth antiphon. Reproduced courtesy of Ranworth PCC

Opening of a Gloria, with decorated initial 'G', and musical notation Image taken from Old Hall Manuscript. Add. 57950, f.12v © The British Library Board

Eton Choirbook. Opening of the O Maria Salvatoris mater, MS.178 F.1v by John Browne, *c*.1520 Reproduced by permission of the Provost and Fellows of Eton College

Over-painted Medieval wall-paintings, whitewashed during restoration © Peter Mullins

The Chapel Royal choir at the funeral for Queen Elizabeth I. add.35324 f.31v © The British Library Board

Orlando Gibbons (oil on panel), English School/Faculty of Music Collection, Oxford University/Gift from Dr. Philip Hayes, before 1795/Bridgeman Images

Portrait of Henry Purcell, 1695 (oil on canvas), Closterman, Johann (1660–1711)/ National Portrait Gallery, London, UK/Bridgeman Images

George Frideric HANDEL, 1685–1759 German composer. The Art Archive/ Handel Museum Halle/Gianni Dagli Orti

Village choir, Webster, Thomas (1800–86)/Victoria & Albert Museum, London, UK/The Stapleton Collection/Bridgeman Images

May Morning on Magdalen Tower (oil on canvas) (see also 106479), Hunt, William Holman (1827–1910)/© Lady Lever Art Gallery, National Museums Liverpool/Bridgeman Images

21st century choir group on stage. © David Ball

Index

Figures in *italics* indicate musical examples.

A

ABB anthem 88, 153
'Abbot's Leigh' 272
'Aberystwyth' 264
'Abide with Me' 304
Absalom laments 162, 174
Act for the Advancement of the True Religion (1543) 69
Act of Uniformity (1559) 107
Acts for the Propagation of the Gospel 181
Adam and Eve 19
Addison, Joseph 223, 242, 243
'The Spacious Firmament on High' 242, 270
'Adeste, fideles' 268
Advent 4
Aelred, Abbot of Rievaulx 14, 141, 142
Aesop's Fables 43, 118
African gospel churches 372
African music 185, 368, *371*
Agincourt, battle of (1415) 38, 39
Agnus Dei 66, 83, 158, 334, 361
Aidan, St 3

Albert, Prince Consort 282–3
Te Deum and Jubilate 283
Aldrich, Dean Henry 230, 233, 273
Aleppo, Syria 2
Alexander, Mrs C.F. 301
'All Things Bright and Beautiful' 285, 304
'Once in Royal David's City' 300, 304
Alexandra, Queen 321
Alfred, King 4
Alfred Jewel 4
All Saints' church, Margaret Street, London 290
Allegri, Gregorio 273
Alleluia 12, 17, 26, 48, 158
Allison, Richard 169
Psalmes of David in Metre 145
Alma Redemptoris 31
Alnwick Castle, Northumberland 34
Ambrosian hymn 9
Amelia, Princess 273
America
campaign to replace the 'old way' 236–8
country style 248
'Great Awakening' movement 267
hymns 268